CARICATURE AND SATIRE

ON

NAPOLEON I.

THE EXILE.

A Sketch from Life at Longwood.   April 1820.

ENGLISH
CARICATURE AND SATIRE

ON

NAPOLEON I.

BY

JOHN ASHTON

BENJAMIN BLOM   New York / London

First Published 1888
Reissued 1968
by Benjamin Blom, Inc. Bronx, New York 10452
and 56 Doughty Street London, W.C. 1

Library of Congress Catalog Card Number 68-25953

Printed in the United States of America

PREFACE.

THIS book is not intended to be a History of Napoleon the First, but simply to reproduce the bulk of the Caricatures and Satires published in England on our great enemy, with as much of history as may help to elucidate them.

The majority of the caricatures are humorous ; others are silly, or spiteful—as will occasionally happen nowadays ; and some are too coarse for reproduction—so that a careful selection has had to be made. Gillray and Rowlandson generally signed their names to the work of their hands ; but, wherever a caricature occurs unsigned by the artist, I have attributed it, on the authority of the late Edward Hawkins, Esq., some time Keeper of the Antiquities at the British Museum, to whatever artist he has assigned it. I have personally inspected every engraving herein described, and the description is entirely my own.

Should there, by chance, be an occasional discrepancy as to a date, it has been occasioned by the inconceivable contradictions which occur in different histories and news-papers. To cite an instance : in three different books are given three different dates of Napoleon leaving Elba, and it was only by the knowledge that it occurred on a Sunday, and by consulting an almanac for the year 1815, that I was able absolutely to determine it.

The frontispiece is taken from a very rare print, and gives a novel view of Napoleon to us, who are always accustomed to see him represented in military uniform.

I have ascribed, on the authority of the British Museum Catalogue, the authorship of the metrical *Life of Napoleon*, from which I have quoted, to Wm. Combe. This, however, is a disputed point; and, as it is not one which can be definitely settled, and, really, is of no consequence, I let it stand as written.

That my readers may find some instruction, mingled with the amusement I have provided for them, is the earnest wish of

JOHN ASHTON.

CONTENTS.

CONTENTS.

CONTENTS.

CHAPTER LV.

CHAPTER LVI.

CHAPTER LVII.

CHAPTER LVIII.

CHAPTER LIX.

CHAPTER LX.

CHAPTER LXI.

CHAPTER LXII.

ENGLISH CARICATURE AND SATIRE

ON

NAPOLEON THE FIRST.

CHAPTER I.

BIRTH AND GENEALOGY—HIS OWN ACCOUNT—MAJORCAN OR GREEK
EXTRACTION—ENGLISH BIOGRAPHIES.

CURIOUSLY enough, it has never been practically settled whence the ancestors of Napoleon Bonaparte came. He, himself, cared little for the pride of birth, and when, during his Consulate, they manufactured for him a genealogy descending from a line of kings, he laughed at it, and said that his patent of nobility dated from the battle of Montenotte.

But, still, one would think he ought to know, for family tradition is strong ; and if it can be trusted, this is his own account. 'One day Napoleon questioned Canova about Alfieri, and Canova found an opportunity to render an important service to Florence, &c. " Sire," said he, "authorise the President of the Academy of Florence to take care of the frescoes and pictures. I heartily wish it. That will reflect great honour on your Majesty, who, I am assured, is of a noble Florentine family." At these words the Empress (Maria Louisa) turned towards her husband and said :—" What ! are you not Corsican ? " " Yes,"

B

replied Napoleon, "but of Florentine origin." Canova
then said :—" The President of the Academy of Florence,
the Senator Allessandria, is of one of the most illustrious
houses in the country, which has had one of its ladies
married to a Bonaparte, thus you are Italian, and we boast
of it." " I am, certainly," added Napoleon.'[1]

Prince Napoleon Louis Bonaparte (brother to the Emperor) published in 1830, at Florence, a French translation
of an old book[2] about the sack of Rome, 1527, which gives
an account of the family of the writer. But Majorca also
puts in a claim to the older Bonapartes ; and in 1852, Don
Antonio Furio, a learned man, Member of the Royal Aca-
demies of Belles Lettres of Barcelona and Majorca, &c.,
made a declaration as to 'the rank, dignity, and extinction
of the noble family of Bonapart in the island of Majorca ,'
and quotes from a book kept in the archives of Palma, in
which are preserved the armorial escutcheons of the noble
families of the Island, the arms of Bonapart—which were
Dexter, on a field Azure, six stars, Or, placed two by two,
Sinister, on a field gules, a lion rampant, Or ; and the Chief
Or, bears a scared eagle, sable. He says the family came
from Genoa to Majorca, in which island its members were
considered noblemen, and they filled several distinguished
offices. In a register of burials relating to knights and
gentlemen, written in 1559, the antiquity and nobility of
the Bonaparts are clearly authenticated ; and it would
seem from Don Furio's account (for all of which he
gives chapter and verse) that the learned jurisconsult Don
Hugo Bonapart left Majorca and went to Corsica, where,
in 1411, he was made Regent of the Chancery of that
place ; and, as he settled there, his name was inscribed in
the Golden Book of France.

This seems pretty circumstantial, until another theory
appears—namely, his Greek extraction Sir J. Emerson
Tennent says:[3] 'There is a story relative to the family

---

[1] Chevalier Artand's *Italy*, p. 377 ; 'L'Univers pittoresque, Europe,' tome
2, Paris, 1857, ed. Didot.
[2] 'Ragguaglio Storico di tutto l' occorso, giorno per giorno, nel Sacco di
Roma dell' anno 1527, scritto da Jacopo Bonoparte, gentiluomo Samminiatere '
(from San Miniato, near Florence) ' che vi se trovò presente.'
[3] *Notes and Queries*, 3rd series, vol. xi. p. 307.

name of the Bonapartes, that somewhat excites curiosity as to the amount of truth which it may contain. In 1798, when Napoleon was secretly preparing for his descent upon Egypt, among other expedients for distracting and weakening the Porte, French emissaries were clandestinely employed in exciting the Greeks in Epirus, and the Morea, to revolt. In Maina especially (the ancient Sparta), these agents were received with marked enthusiasm, on the ground that Bonaparte was born in Corsica, where numbers of Greeks from that part of the Morea had found an asylum after the conquest of Candia, in 1669, but they were eventually expelled by the Genoese.

' One of the persons so employed by Napoleon to rouse the Greeks in 1798 was named Stephanopoli ; and one of the arguments which he used was, that Napoleon himself was a Greek in blood, and a Mainote by birth, being descended from one of the exiles who took refuge at Ajaccio in 1673. The name of this family, he said, was Calomeri, Καλόμερις,[1] which the Corsicans accommodated to their own dialect by translating it into *Buonaparte.*'

Another writer, signing himself *Rhodocanakis*, in the same periodical,[2] says : ' I am happy to be able to assert with confidence, and on the authority of General Kallergis, the intimate friend of the present Emperor, of Prince Pitzipios, and others, that the story devised by Nicholas Stepanapoulos, and mentioned by his niece, the Duchesse d'Abrantes, in her *Memoirs*, that Napoleon was a Greek in blood, and a Mainote by birth, being descended from the family of Calomeri, who took refuge at Ajaccio, Corsica, was never authoritatively denied. On the contrary, both the first and third Napoleon appeared pleased at the story, whenever it was alluded to in their presence ; probably because they thought it good policy not to deny what they might in future wish to turn to their advantage. As regards the name of Καλομέρης or Καλόμερος, there are still many families of that name in Greece.'

Now let us hear what Madame Junot, the aforesaid Duchesse d'Abrantes, the intimate friend of Napoleon,

---

[1] From Καλὸς, good, and Μερὶς, part or share—Buona-parte.
[2] *Notes and Queries*, 3rd series, vol. xi. p. 507.

whose families were the closest of neighbours at Ajaccio, says on this subject.[1] 'When Constantine Comnenus landed at Corsica in 1676, at the head of a Greek colony, he had with him several sons, one of whom was named Calomeros. This son he sent to Florence, on a mission to the Grand Duke of Tuscany. Constantine dying before the return of his son, the Grand Duke prevailed on the young Greek to renounce Corsica, and fix his abode in Tuscany. After some interval of time, an individual came from Italy—indeed from Tuscany—and fixed his abode in Corsica, where his descendants formed the family of Buonaparte ; for the name *Calomeros*, literally Italianised, signified *buona parte* or *bella parte*.[2]

' The only question is, whether the Calomeros who left Corsica, and the Calomeros who came there, have a direct filiation. Two facts, however, are certain—namely, the departure of the one, and the arrival of the other. It is a singular thing that the Comneni,[3] in speaking of the Bonaparte family, always designate them by the names *Calomeros*, *Calomeri*, or *Calomeriani*, according as they allude to one individual, or several collectively. Both families were united by the most intimate friendship.

' When the Greeks were obliged to abandon Paomia to escape the persecutions of the insurgent Corsicans, they established themselves temporarily in towns which remained faithful to the Republic of Genoa. When, at a subsequent period, Cargesa was granted to the Greeks for the purpose of forming a new establishment, a few Greek families continued to reside at Ajaccio.'

I have been thus diffuse on his ancestry, because English satirists could not tell the truth on the subject— they were too swayed by the passion of the moment, and had to pander to the cravings of the mob. Take an example, from a broad sheet published in 1803, when our

[1] *Memoirs of Madame Junot, Duchesse d'Abrantes*, Bentley, London, 1883. When quoting from her memoirs I always use this translation.

[2] Napoleon omitted the ' u ' in Buonaparte while general-in-chief in May 1796.

[3] Madame Junot was very proud of her descent from Constantine Comnenus, the tenth Protogeras of Maina, who quitted Greece in 1675, landed at Genoa Jan. 1, 1676, and arrived at Corsica March 14, 1676.

island was in deadly fear of invasion, a ' Histoiy of Buonaparte.' 'Napoleon Buonaparte is the son of a poor lawyer
of Ajaccio, in Corsica, in which city he was born on the
15th of August, 1769. His grandfather, Joseph, originally
a butcher of the same place, was ennobled by Count
Nieuhoff, some time King of Corsica. He was the son of
Carlos Buona, who once kept a liquor shop, or tavern, but
who, being convicted of robbery and murder, was condemned to the Gallies, where he died in 1724. His wife,
La Birba, the mother of Joseph, died in the House of
Correction at Geneva (? Genoa). On the 3rd May, 1736,
when Porto Vecchio was attacked, Joseph Buona brought
to the assistance of King Theodore a band of vagabonds
which, during the civil war, had chosen him for its leader.
In return, Theodore, on the following day, created him a
noble, and added to his name *Buona* the termination
Parté. Joseph Buonaparte's wife *Histria*, was the daughter of a journeyman tanner of Bastia, also in Corsica.'

And yet one more, from another equally veracious
'life.' 'Buonaparte's great-grandfather kept a wine-house
for factors (like our gin shops), and, being convicted of
murder and robbery, he died a galley slave at Genoa, in
1724: his wife was likewise an accomplice, and she died
in the House of Correction at Genoa in 1734. His grandfather was a butcher of Ajaccio, and his grandmother
daughter of a journeyman tanner at Bastia. His father
was a low petty-fogging lawyer, who served and betrayed
his country by turns, during the Civil Wars. After France
conquered Corsica, he was a spy to the French Government, and his mother their trull. What is bred in the
bone will not come out of the flesh.

CHAPTER II.

DESCENT FROM THE MAN IN THE IRON MASK—ANAGRAMS, ETC., ON HIS
NAME—THE BEAST OF THE APOCALYPSE—HIS MOTHER'S ACCOUNT
OF HIS BIRTH.

THE foregoing was the sort of stuff given to our grand-
fathers for history ; nothing could be bad enough for
Boney, *the Corsican Ogre*—nay, they even tortured his

name to suit political purposes. It was hinted that the keeper of 'the Man with the Iron Mask,' who was said to be no other than the twin (and elder) brother of Louis XIV., was named *Bon part* ; that the said keeper had a daughter, with whom the Man in the Mask fell in love, and to whom he was privately married ; that their children received their mother's name, and were secretly conveyed to Corsica, where the name was converted into *Bonaparte*, or *Buonaparte;* and that one of these children was the ancestor of Napoleon Bonaparte, who was thus entitled to be recognised, not only as of French origin, but as the direct descendant of the rightful heir to the throne of France.

They put his name into Greek, and tortured it thus :—
Napoleon, Apoleon, Poleon, Oleon, Leon, Eon, On,
Ναπολεων, Απολεων, Πολεων, Ολεων, Λεων, Εων, Ων,
which sentence will translate, ' Napoleon, being the lion of the nations, went about destroying cities.'

In the ' Journal des Débats,' 8 Avril, 1814, although not an English satire on his name, it is gravely stated that he was baptised by the name of Nicholas, and that he assumed the name of Napoleon as an uncommon one ; but this name, Nicholas, which was applied to him so freely in France, was but a cant term for a stupid blockhead. Whilst on this subject, however, I cannot refrain from quoting a passage from a French book : ' I do not know what fellow has held that *Napolione* was a demon, who in bygone times, amused himself by tormenting a poor imbecile. The fellow can not have read the life of the Saints : he would then have learned that St. Napolione, whose name is given at length in the legend, is as good a patron as any other ; that he performed seven miracles during his life, and twenty-two and a half after his death—for he had not time to finish the twenty-third : it was an unfortunate tiler who, in falling from a roof, broke both his legs. St. Napoleon had already set one, when an unlucky doctor prescribed some medicine to the sick man which carried him off to the other world.' [1]

There is an extremely forcible acrostic in Latin on his name, which deserves reproduction :—

[1] *Buonaparte et sa famille, ou Confidences d'un de leurs anciens amis*, Paris 1816.

N ationibus[1]
A uctoritatem
P rincipibus
O bedientiam
L ibertatem
E cclesiæ
O mni modo
N egans

B ona
U surpavit
O mnium
N eutrorum
A urum
P opulorum
A nimas
R evera
T yrannus
E xecrandus.

But not only was his name thus made a vehicle for political purposes, but the expounders of prophecy got hold of it, and found out, to their great delight, that at last they had got that theological bugbear, *the Apocalyptic beast.* Nothing could be clearer. It could be proved to demonstration, most simply and clearly. Every one had been in error about the Church of Rome ; at last there could be no doubt about it, it was NAPOLEON. Take the following handbill as a sample of one out of many :—

A PROPHECY

(*From the 13th Chapter of Revelations*)

ALLUDING TO

BUONAPARTE.

Verse 1st.

' And a Beast rose out of the Sea, having ten crowns on his head,' &c.

This Beast is supposed to mean Buonaparte, he being born in *Corsica*, which is an island, and having conquered ten kingdoms.

Verse 5th.

' And a mouth was given him speaking blasphemies ; and power given him upon the earth, forty and two months.'

Buonaparte was crowned in December, 1804 ; it is therefore supposed the *extent* of his assumed power upon earth will now be limited, this present month (*June*) 1808, being exactly the forty-second month of his reign.

Verse 16th.

' And he caused all to receive a mark in their hands, and no one could buy or sell, save those that had the mark of the Beast.'

[1] Denying by every means the authority of nations, obedience to princes, or liberty to the Church. He usurped the goods of all, the treasure of neutrals, the souls of nations : in very truth he was an execrable tyrant.

To persons conversant in commercial affairs, these verses need no comment. There are, at present, some of *these marks* to be seen in this country ; they had the Crown of Italy, &c., at top, and are signed ' Buonaparte,' ' Talleyrand ' ; and all of them are numbered.

Verse 18th.

' Let him that hath understanding, count the number of the Beast, for it is the number of a man, and his number is SIX HUNDRED, SIXTY AND SIX.'

This verse is curious, and should be read attentively. The method of using letters for figures at the time the Revelations were written is proved by many monuments of Roman antiquity now extant.

The Ancient Alphabet of Figures		Buonaparte's name with the Figures		Ten Kingdoms conquered
A .	. . 1	N .	. . 40	France
B .	. . 2	A .	. . 1	Prussia
C .	. . 3	P .	. . 60	Austria
D .	. . 4	O .	. . 50	Sardinia
E .	. . 5	L .	. . 20	Naples
F .	. . 6	E .	. . 5	Rome
G .	. . 7	A .	. . 1	Tuscany
H .	. . 8	N .	. . 40	Hungary
I .	. . 9			Portugal
K .	. . 10	B .	. . 2	Spain
L .	. . 20	U .	. . 110	
M .	. . 30	O .	. . 50	
N .	. . 40	N .	. . 40	
O .	. . 50	A .	. . 1	
P .	. . 60	P .	. . 60	
Q .	. . 70	A .	. . 1	
R .	. . 80	R .	. . 80	
S .	. . 90	T .	. . 100	
T .	. . 100	E .	. . 5	
U .	. . 110			
V .	. . 120	The Number		
X .	. . 130	of the Beast . 666		
Y .	. . 140			
Z .	. . 150			
	Napole 6		an Buon 6	aparte 6

The above verses are not the only parts of the chapter which have reference to Buonaparte, but the *most prominent ones* ; the connection throughout has been clearly ascertained.

In a curious little book called *The Corsican's Downfall*, by a Royal Arch Mason, published at Mansfield in 1814, at p. 6, it says, with reference to the numeration, 'The oldest treatise on the theory of arithmetic is comprised in the seventh, eighth, and ninth books of Euclid's *Elements*, about two hundred and eighty years before the Christian era. The first author of any consequence who used the modern way of computing by figures, instead of letters of the alphabet, was Jordanus of Namur, who flourished about 1200 ; and his arithmetic was afterwards published and demonstrated by Johannis Faber Stapulensis, in the fifteenth century. The name, then, and number of the Beast must be discovered (if at all) by the ancient method of computation in use at the time when the prophecies were written.'

But Bonaparte ungratefully refused to fulfil prophecy by being destroyed at the end of forty-two months, *i.e.*, in June, 1808, which must have put the expositors on their mettle. They were, however, fully equal to the occasion, and ingeniously solved the quotation this way.[1] 'Power was given unto him to continue forty-and-two months : now it is well known that he was self created, or crowned Emperor of France, on the 2nd day of December 1804, and that he reigned in full power and authority over the prostrate States upon the Continent until the 2nd day of May 1808, the very day on which the gallant Patriots of Spain made so noble and glorious a struggle to throw off the abominable yoke that he had imposed upon them, which is exactly a period of three years and a half, or forty two months.'

An ingenious lunatic, named L. Mayer, found out another way of fathering the Mark of the Beast upon Napoleon. He took the number of sovereigns who had reigned in Europe until Napoleon's arrival— some he has left out to suit his convenience, but that is a trivial matter—

[1] *The Corsican's Downfall*, p. 9.

the case had to be made out against the unfortunate Emperor.

Sovereigns included in the Number of the Beast.[1]

	Numbers
Roman Emperors	77
Popes	186
Kings of France	40
Kings of Spain	78
Kings of Portugal	26
Emperors of Germany	57
Kings of Bohemia	31
Kings of Hungary	34
Kings of Poland	35
Kings of Denmark	35
Kings of Naples and Sicily	30
Kings of Sardinia	36
Bonaparte	1

Total 666

The Society of Antiquaries have, among their hand-bills, one published in 1808, as follows :—

Mr. Urban,—The following singular coincidences may furnish matter for reflection to the curious. It has been generally admitted that the Roman Empire, after passing under *seven* different forms of government (or *seven* heads), was divided into *ten* kingdoms in Europe (the ten horns of Daniel and John) ; and that, notwithstanding the various changes Europe has undergone, the number of kingdoms was generally about ten.

It is not a little surprising that the *Heads of the Family of Napoleon*, who has effected such a change in the same Empire, *are exactly seven*, viz.:—

1. Napoleon.
2. Joseph, King of Italy.
3. Louis, King of Holland.
4. Jerome.
5. Murat, Duke of Berg and Cleves.
6. Cardinal Fesch.
7. Beauharnais, the adopted son of Napoleon.

[1] *Buonaparte the Emperor of the French considered as the Lucifer and Gog of Isiah and Ezekiel, &c.*, by L. Mayer, Lond. 1806, p. 86.

And also that *the Members of the New Federation are just ten,* viz. :—

1. Bavaria.	6. Ysembourg.
2. Wirtemberg.	7. Hohenzollern.
3. Baden.	8. Aremberg.
4. Darmstadt.	9. Salm.
5. Nassau.	10. Leyen.

It is also remarkable that in the *man's name*, NAPOLEON BUONAPARTE, there are precisely three times six letters :—

Napole	on Buon	aparte	
6	6	6	= 666

And in his name is contained the name given by John to the King of the Locusts, who is called 'Apoleon,' or 'the Destroyer.'

Even the date of his birth was disputed, for some said he was born on February 5, 1768—in his marriage registry it is the same, and he used to tell De Bourrienne, his school-fellow, that he was born on August 15, 1769, and it is so noted in the registry of his entrance into the military school at Brienne in 1779, and the Ecole Militaire in 1784, besides being the date used in all documents necessary to his promotion. But probably his mother knew somewhat about it, and Madame Junot says,[1] speaking of Madame Lætitia Bonaparte, ' I recollect she this day told us that, being at Mass on the day of the fête of Notre Dame of August, she was overtaken by the pains of childbirth, and she had hardly reached home when she was delivered of *Napoleon*, on a wretched rug. .. . . I know not why,' said she, 'it has been reported that Paoli was Napoleon's godfather. It is not true ; Laurent Jiubéga[2] was his godfather. He held him over the baptismal font, along with another of our relations, Celtruda Buonaparte.'[3]

[1] *Memoirs*, p. 269.
[2] His nephew was afterwards prefect in Corsica. He was a relation of Napoleon.
[3] Daughter of Charles Bonaparte, the Emperor's uncle, and wife of Paraviccini, a cousin, also, of Napoleon.

CHAPTER III.

COUNT MARBŒUF, HIS PUTATIVE FATHER—POVERTY OF THE BONAPARTE
FAMILY—EARLY PERSONAL DESCRIPTION OF NAPOLEON—HIS OWN
ACCOUNT OF HIMSELF—SATIRISTS' NARRATION OF HIS SCHOOL-DAYS.

IN after life, when Napoleon was successful, and had made
a position, reports were spread that his real father was
Count Marbœuf, who had been in Corsica, and in after life,
or at all events at his entrance into it, acted as his bene-
factor and patron.   Lætitia Ramolini, afterwards Madame
Lætitia Bonaparte, was very graceful and pretty, indeed
Madame Junot says of her,[1] ' Lætitia was indeed a lovely
woman.   Those who knew her in advanced life thought
her countenance somewhat harsh ; but that expression
instead of being caused by any austerity of disposition,
seemed, on the contrary, to have been produced by
timidity.'   Indeed, no one can look at any portrait of
Madame Mère, and not be struck with her lofty beauty.

This scandal about Count Marbœuf, it must be remembered, is of French origin, and was well known, and
recognised, probably, at its value.   To give one illustration,[2]
' La malignité a fait honneur de sa naissance au Comte de
Marbœuf, gouverneur de l'isle, qui rendait des soins assidus
à Madame Buonaparte, jeune femme, belle et intéressante
alors.'

All our English squibs repeat the tale, and the subjoined
is certainly the cleverest of them.[3]

> About his parentage indeed,
> Biographers have disagreed ;
> Some say his father was a farmer,
> His mother, too, a *Cyprian* charmer :
> That his dad Carlo was quite poor,
> Letitia a French General's —— ;
> If, faithless to her marriage vows,
> She made a cuckold of her spouse,
> Then Nap (some characters are rotten)
> Has been a *merrily begotten.*

[1] *Memoirs*, p. 7.
[2] *Buonapartiana, ou Choix d'Anecdotes curieuses*, Paris, 1814.
[3] *The Life of Napoleon, a Hudibrastic Poem in Fifteen Cantos by Doctor
Syntax* (William Combe). London, 1815.

But other writers, with civility,
Insist he's sprung from *old Nobility*,
And therefore to his father's name
Attach the highest rank and fame :
Nay, furthermore, they add as true,
Nap was Paoli's godson too.
But what to this said great Paoli ?
' I stood for one, but 'pon my soul, I
At present do not rightly know
Whether it was for Nap or Joe.'
It was for Joe, if he'd have said it,
But Joe has done him little credit.
Now let the honest muse despise
All adulation, barefaced lies,
And own the truth—Then Boney's father
Was member of the law, or rather,
A pettifogger, which his friends,
To serve their own politic ends,
Would keep a secret, knowing well
That pettifoggers go to Hell.
When France occasioned some alarms.
And Corsica was up in arms,
This Carlo Bonaparte thought fit,
His parchments for the sword to quit.
He fought, they say, with some applause,
Tho' unsuccessful in the cause :
Meanwhile, with battle's din and fright,
His wife was in a dismal plight ;
From town to town Letitia fled,
To shun the French, *as it is said ;*
Tho' others whisper that the fair
Was under a French Gen'ral's care,
And that to keep secure her charms
She fondly trusted to his *arms.*
Be this however as it might,
After incessant fear and flight,
Letitia ('fore her time, mayhap)
Was brought to bed of Master Nap :
The Cause, we think, of his ambition
And of his restless disposition.

The Bonaparte family was not rich, their sole means of living being from the father's professional exertions, and the family was very large, and many mouths to feed ; in fact, they were in somewhat straitened circumstances, but not in such squalid poverty as Gillray depicts them, in the accompanying illustration, where our hero may be seen,

DEMOCRATIC INNOCENCE.

The young Bonaparte and his wretched Relatives in their native Poverty, while Free Booters in the island of Corsica.

with his brothers and sisters, gnawing the *bony part* of a shin of beef.

Madame Junot [1] says, ' Saveria told me that Napoleon was never a pretty boy, as Joseph had been; his head always appeared too large for his body, a defect common to the Bonaparte family. When Napoleon grew up, the peculiar charm of his countenance lay in his eye, especially in the mild expression it assumed in his moments of kindness. His anger, to be sure, was frightful, and though I am no coward, I never could look at him in his fits of rage without shuddering. Though his smile was captivating, yet the expression of his mouth when disdainful, or angry, could scarcely be seen without terror. But that forehead which seemed formed to bear the crowns of a whole world; those hands, of which the most coquettish woman might have been vain, and whose white skin covered muscles of iron; in short, of all that personal beauty which distinguished Napoleon as a young man, no traces were discernible in the boy.'

Napoleon said of himself: ' I was an obstinate and inquisitive child. I was extremely headstrong; nothing overawed me, nothing disconcerted me. I made myself formidable to the whole family. My brother Joseph was the one with whom I was oftenest embroiled; he was bitten, beaten, abused: I went to complain before he had time to recover his confusion.'

[1] *Memoirs*, vol. i. p. 10.

At ten years of age, through the medium of his patron,
Count Marbœuf, he was sent to the military school at
Brienne, which he entered on April 23, 1779.   Here he was
shy and reserved, and not at all liked by his schoolfellows,
who twitted him with his poverty, the country whence
he came, his name, and made reflections on his mother ;
the last particularly exasperating him.   His veracious
Hudibrastic historian says :—

When he two years at school had been,
He proved more violent and mean :
Unlike his sprightly fellow boys,
Amused with playthings and with toys ;
At shuttlecock he'd never stop,
Nor deign to whip the bounding top.
His garden was his sole delight,
Which ne'er improv'd his mental sight ;
But thus in childhood serv'd to show
He was to all mankind a foe.
His schoolfellows, in keen sedateness
He robb'd to prove his urchin greatness :
Deluded by his wheedling art,
Some cheerfully resign'd a part
Of their possessions, and to these
He added what he chose to seize ;
Then, planting it with num'rous trees
And putting palisades all round,
He strutted monarch of the ground ;

.   .   .   .   .

.   .   .   .   .

'Twas on a welcome festive morn,
For some great saint divinely born.
No matter why, it was a jolly day,
Boys must be merry on a holiday ;
And now behold their bulging pockets,
Enrich'd with pistols, squibs, and rockets—
When some, but humbly begg'd his pardon,
Threw fireworks into Boney's garden ;
'Twas chiefly manag'd by the breeze
Which sent them 'mong his plants and trees :
Bursting, the cracks were oft repeated,
Nap's ears were with the thunder greeted :

Th' explosions discomposed, I wot,
Th' arrangement of the lovely spot.
Nap saw it with corroding spite,
And now began his lips to bite ;
But strove his anger to restrain,
Until revenge he could obtain.
For weeks he plann'd what he should do,
And in about a month or two
Contrived his infamous design,
By having made a kind of mine
Beside the garden ; where, in haste,
Long trains of gunpowder he plac'd ;
Deliberately now, as stated,
He for the little fellows waited ;

NAPOLEON BLOWING UP HIS COMRADES.

And just as they were passing through it,
A lighted bit of stick put to it ;
The boys were suddenly alarm'd,
And some were miserably harm'd,
While all, with fright and consternation,
Were in a state of perturbation.
Th' *heroic* Boney, with a club,
Now came the sufferers to drub ;
But soon the master was in sight,
Which put the Conqueror to flight.

CHAPTER IV.

NAPOLEON AT THE ECOLE MILITAIRE—PERSONAL DESCRIPTION—*PUSS IN BOOTS*—VISIT TO CORSICA—SOLICITS SERVICE IN ENGLAND—REPORTED VISIT TO LONDON—SIEGE OF TOULON.

ON October 14 or 17, 1784, he left Brienne for the Ecole Militaire at Paris.

Gillray, when he drew the picture of the abject, ragged, servile-looking Napoleon, could hardly have realised the fact that Napoleon was then over fifteen years of age, and that, having been already five years at a military school, he must necessarily have carried himself in a more soldierly manner. He stayed at the Ecole Militaire till August 1785, when he obtained his brevet of second lieutenant of Artillery in the regiment of La Fère. Madame Junot[1] tells an amusing anecdote

DEMOCRATIC HUMILITY.

Bonaparte when a boy received thro' the King's bounty into the Ecole Militaire at Paris.

of him at this period, which I must be pardoned introducing here, as it helps us to imagine his personal appearance. ' I well recollect that on the day when he first put on his uniform, he was as vain as young men usually are on such an occasion. There was one part of his dress which had a very droll appearance—that was his boots. They were so high and wide, that his little thin legs seemed buried in their amplitude. Young people are always ready to observe anything ridiculous ; and, as soon as my sister and I saw Napoleon enter the drawing-room, we burst into a loud fit of laughter. At that early age, as well as in after

[1] *Memoirs*, vol. i. p. 33.

C

life, Bonaparte could not relish a joke ; and when he found himself the object of merriment he grew angry.

'My sister, who was some years older than I, told him that since he wore a sword he ought to be gallant to ladies; and, instead of being angry, should be happy that they joked with him. "You are nothing but a child—a little *pensionnaire*," said Napoleon, in a tone of contempt. Cecile, who was twelve or thirteen years of age, was highly indignant at being called a child, and she hastily resented the affront by replying to Bonaparte, "And you are nothing but a *puss in boots*." This excited a general laugh among all present, except Napoleon, whose rage I will not attempt to describe. Though not much accustomed to society, he had too much tact not to perceive that he ought to be silent when personalities were introduced, and his adversary was a woman.

'Though deeply mortified at the unfortunate nickname which my sister had given him, yet he affected to forget it ; and to prove that he cherished no malice on the subject, he got a little toy made, and gave it to me. This toy consisted of a cat in boots, in the character of a footman running before the carriage of the Marquis de Carabas. It was very well made, and must have been rather expensive to him considering his straitened finances. He brought along with it a pretty little edition of the popular tale of *Puss in Boots*, which he presented to my sister, begging her to keep it as a *token of his remembrance.'*

Napoleon afterwards frequently called Junot, *Marquis de Carabas*, and, on one occasion, Madame Junot, in badinage, reminded Napoleon of his present to her, at which he got very angry.

During his sub-lieutenancy he was very poor, yet he managed to go to Corsica for six months, whilst Paoli, who had been living in England, was there. There is a curious idea that, about this time (mentioned in more places than one [1]), he applied for service under the British Government.

> At this time Bonaparte scarce knew
> What for his maintenance to do—

[1] For instance, see *Notes and Queries*, 3rd series, vol. vii. p. 364.

So he sat down, and quickly wrote
A very condescending note,
(Altho' a wretched scrawl when written)
Which to a Chieftain of Great Britain,
He, soon as possible, dispatch'd,
In which he swore he was attach'd
Unto the British Constitution,
And therefore form'd the resolution
Of fighting in that country's cause,
For George the Third, and for his laws,
If that his services were needed,
And to his wishes they acceded.
It seems that Bonaparte could trade well,
He'd fight for any one that paid well ;
But he a disappointment got,
Because his services were not
By Britain's chief Commander tried ;
The rank he sought for was denied.
This was the cause of great displeasure,
It mortified him above measure,
And he gave England now as many a
Curse, as before he e'er gave Genoa.

Nay, more extraordinary than all, it was even pretended
that he lived some time in England. The *Birmingham
Journal* of April 21, 1855, affirms, on the authority of ' Mr.
J. Coleman of the Strand, who is now 104 years of age,
and whose portrait and biographical sketch appeared in
the *Illustrated London News*, Feb. 1850, and who knew perfectly well M. Bonaparte, who, while he lived in London,
which was for five weeks, in 1791 or 1792, lodged in a house
in George Street, Strand, and whose chief occupation appeared to be taking pedestrian exercise in the streets of
London. Hence his marvellous knowledge of the great
metropolis, which used to astonish any Englishmen of
distinction, who were not aware of the visit. I have also
heard Mr. Matthews, the grandfather of the celebrated
comedian, Mr. Thomas Goldsmith of the Strand, Mr.
Graves, Mr. Drury, and my father, all of whom were tradesmen in the Strand, in the immediate vicinity of George
Street, speak of this visit. He occasionally took his cup
of chocolate at the Northumberland, occupying himself in
reading, and preserving a provoking taciturnity to the

gentlemen in the room ; though his manner was stern, his deportment was that of a gentleman.'

Timbs [1] endorses this statement, in identically the same words of a portion of the above, which he fathers on old Mr. Matthews, the bookseller in the Strand, but we must recollect that Mr. Timbs was writing the ' Romance of London.'

A personal description of Napoleon in 1793 may be interesting, especially as it comes from a trustworthy pen. [2] ' At that period of his life Bonaparte was decidedly ugly ; he afterwards underwent a total change. I do not speak of the illusive charm which his glory spread around him, but I mean to say that a gradual physical change took place in him in the space of seven years. His emaciated thinness was converted into a fulness of face, and his complexion, which had been yellow, and apparently unhealthy, became clear and comparatively fresh ; his features, which were angular and sharp, became round and filled out. As to his smile, it was always agreeable. The mode of dressing his hair, which has such a droll appearance as we see it in the prints of the bridge of Arcola, was then comparatively simple, for young men of fashion (the *Muscadins*), whom he used to rail at so loudly at that time, wore their hair very long. But he was very careless of his personal appearance ; and his hair, which was ill-combed and ill-powdered, gave him the look of a sloven. His little hands, too, underwent a great metamorphosis : when I first saw him, they were thin, long, and dark; but he was subsequently vain of the beauty of them, and with good reason.

' In short, when I recollect Napoleon entering the courtyard of the Hotel de la Tranquillité in 1793, with a shabby round hat drawn over his forehead, and his ill-powdered hair hanging over the collar of his great-coat, which afterwards became as celebrated as the white plume of Henry IV., without gloves, because he used to say they were an useless luxury, with boots ill-made and ill-blackened, with his thinness and his sallow complexion ; in

[1] *Romance of London*, vol. iii. p. 172, ed. 1865.
[2] *Memoirs of Madame Junot*, vol. i. p. 73.

fine, when I recollect him at that time, and think what he was afterwards, I do not see the same man in the two pictures.'

He was fortunate in obtaining a higher rank in the army, being promoted to be commandant of artillery, and he joined the army besieging Toulon on September 12, 1793.   He found his chief, General Cartaux, incompetent, and, from representations made to Paris, Cartaux was superseded. There was very hard fighting at Toulon before it was taken, Admiral Hood, and General O'Hara, commanding the British forces. The latter being taken prisoner, much disheartened the English, but, at the final assault, when the town was retaken by the French, the English

NAPOLEON WORKING THE GUNS
AT TOULON.

and Spanish gunners died fighting at their posts.

Our metrical History of Napoleon says,—

> The first shell 'gainst Toulon, 'tis said,
> The hand of Bonaparte had sped.

The vengeance of the French, on entering the town, was terrible ; but many thousands had taken shelter on board the British ships, leaving only a few hundreds to be executed 'according to law.'   Our poem somewhat exaggerates.

> One of the Jacobins, whom Hood
> Had sent to prison for no good—
> A noted character indeed—
> By the republicans was freed.
> As vengeance he on all design'd
> Who to the English had been kind,
> Or in their dreadful situation
> Promoted the Capitulation,

This miscreant selected then
One thousand and four hundred men,
Whom they determin'd to assassinate—
A testimony of surpassing hate ;
And Boney was, with general voice,
For executioner their choice.
Indeed the choice was very good,
For Boney was a man for blood.
In sets, it was these wretches' lot,
To be brought forward to be shot :
Nap gave the order with composure,
The loaded guns were pointed so sure
A dreadful carnage soon ensued—
A carnage—horrible when view'd.
Yet, *gallant* Boney, with delight,
Remain'd spectator of the sight.
Nay, more, himself vers'd in hypocrisy,
He thought he might perhaps some mock'ry see :
So ' Pardon ! pardon ! ' loud he said,
To know if they were really dead ;
Some, who had counterfeited death,
Rose up, and were deprived of breath !
Poor souls ! they knew not when he said it
His word was not deserving credit.
However two there were more wise, ⎫
Who, having put on death's disguise, ⎬
Could not be tempted thus to rise, ⎭
But tarried till the wolves were gone,
And then—a father found his son !

CHAPTER V.

NAPOLEON'S PROMOTION—HIS POVERTY—JUNOT'S KINDNESS—REVOLT OF
THE SECTIONS—NAPOLEON'S SHARE THEREIN—MADE GENERAL OF THE
INTERIOR—INTRODUCTION TO JOSEPHINE—SKETCH OF HER LIFE.

FOR the capture of Toulon, Bonaparte was speedily promoted ; indeed, his superior officer, Dugommier, in his report, said, ' Reward and advance this young man, otherwise he will find means to advance himself.'

He afterwards joined the army at Nice, and was sent on a secret diplomatic mission to Genoa ; on his return from which he was arrested and thrown into prison, where he remained a fortnight before he obtained his release.

He was without any employment during the remainder of 1794, and till the autumn of 1795. He was then in very poor circumstances financially, and Madame Junot gives a graphic picture of his distress at this time.[1] 'Bonaparte's servant informed Mariette that the general was often in want of money;' but, he added, 'he has an aide-de-camp who shares with him all he gets. When he is lucky at play, the largest share of his winnings is always for his general. The aide-de-camp's family sometimes sends him money, and then almost all is given to the general. The general, adds the man, loves this aide-de-camp as dearly as if he were his own brother.' The aide-de-camp was Junot, who got a commission after Toulon.

> The wretched Boney, we are told,
> Reduced, and shivering with the cold,
> To public houses used to rove,
> And warm his hands before a stove ;
> Nay, in Corrozza, it is said,
> A large score still remains unpaid.
> He in an humble garret slept,
> Which never very clean was kept,
> Hence got he a disorder, which
> The vulgar people call the ' itch.'
>   Long might have been poor Nap's dejection,
> But for a pending insurrection ;
> For now was entertained th' intention
> Of overturning the Convention.
> The party by Barras were led,
> He of the rebels was the head ;
> But, neither brave nor skilful reckon'd,
> He wish'd to have an able second.
> This task, by many, as we find,
> Was conscientiously declin'd ;
> For every one of them well knew,
> A dreadful slaughter must ensue.
> Barras said in a thinking mood,
> ' I know a rascal fond of blood—
> A little Corsican blackguard,
> But now to find him may be hard.'
> Then, having mentioned Boney's name,
> They all agreed upon the same ;

---

[1] *Memoirs*, vol. i. p. 80

And Tallien gladly undertook
For the said Corsican to look.
Soon Boney on their honors waited,
Though all in rags as it is stated ;
And, matters being quick concluded,
No ' saucy doubts or fears ' intruded ;
Nap with a horse was soon provided,
And regimentals he beside had.
 This scheme began they to contrive
In seventeen hundred, ninety five.
And of October, we may say,
The fourth was now a fatal day !
For, lo ! the insurgents sallied out,
And desolation spread about ;
All honest opposition fail'd
And blood-stain'd tyranny prevail'd.
Men, women, children, at a bitter rate
The cries of ' Treason,' did reiterate,
But nothing could their fury quell,
For women, men, and children fell !
 Now owing to this revolution,
Was formed another Constitution ;
Nap this assembly went to meet,
And laid his *trophies* at their feet :
These trophies were *eight thousand carcases*,
Among the wounds, too, many a mark was his.
A *second* victory like this,
Was to Barras extatic bliss.
And Nap, for bravery extoll'd,
No longer was a blackguard called ;
But as a hero now regarded,
Was amply by Barras rewarded.
 In this life there is many a change,
As unexpected and as strange :
Then let us hope that this day's sorrow
May be tranquillity to-morrow :
For, mark you how our hero rose,
Who wanted money, shoes, and clothes ;
All those he had—and, what is more,
His garret chang'd for a first floor ;
And such, too, was his happy lot,
That he a place for Lucien got ;
Who, after this notorious slaughter,
Had married an innkeeper's daughter.

This is the satirist's account of the revolt of the Sections, and Bonaparte's part therein. When applied to, he accepted the command, but declared that he must act untrammelled, and not like Menou, who failed through having three representatives of the people to counsel him. This was agreed to, and Barras was chosen chief, with Napoleon under him. The insurgents numbered some 40,000, the troops but 7,000 ; and such was the moderation of the latter, that when the insurrection was quelled, there were but seventy or eighty of the people killed, and between three and four hundred wounded.

He was then made General of the Interior, and consequently Governor of Paris, and this position led him more into society.

It is now that we come to a great epoch in his life, his meeting with Josephine, which came about in a somewhat singular manner. At one of his levées, a boy of twelve years, or so, called upon him. The lad was Eugène de Beauharnais, son of a general of the Republic, who was executed a few days before the death of Robespierre, and his errand was to petition Napoleon that his father's sword might be given to him. To quote Napoleon's own words, ' I was so touched by this affectionate request, that I ordered it to be given to him. On seeing the sword he burst into tears : I felt so affected by his conduct, that I noticed and praised him much. A few days afterwards, his mother came to return me a visit of thanks ; I was struck with her appearance, and still more with her *esprit.*' He was always meeting her in society, especially at Barras's house ; and this intimacy, ripening into affection, brought about their marriage. The following series of eight plates, illustrating her life, were drawn by Woodward.

Josephine (Marie Josephine Rose de la Pagerie) was born at Martinique, according to De Bourrienne, on June 23, 1763, but others say it was the same day of the month, only four years later. She was the daughter of a planter in that island, and was a Creole, *i.e.* one born in a French West Indian settlement. She was fourteen years old when she was brought to France by her father, and being very graceful and pretty, it was not long before she was married, which was to the Vicomte de Beauharnais, on December 13, 1779. The union was not at first a happy one. She went to Martinique, to see her mother, and stayed

A PLANTER'S DAUGHTER.   A FRENCH COUNTESS.   A WIDOW.

there about fifteen months. Her husband was a general in the army of the Rhine, but was singled out by Robespierre as a victim of his tyranny, was imprisoned and

A PRISONER.   A LOOSE FISH.   BARRAS' MISTRESS.

beheaded. Josephine was also imprisoned, and it was at La Force that she met with Madame Tallien—'Nôtre Dame de Thermidor,' as Arsène Houssaye calls her—who was also in prison. Here, uncertain as to their fate, the female prisoners played at mock trials and executions (for the trials always ended in condemnation), and day by day their numbers grew less, as they were taken away to the real tragedy which they had rehearsed. Scandal (French before it became English) says that Barras, smitten by her charms, had her released on condition that she became his mistress. Here is one French account : [1] ' A cette époque, la jeune veuve du malheureux vicomte de Beauharnais, mort sur l'échafaud, languissait aux Magdelonettes, où, depuis longtems, elle était détenue comme suspecte. Intimement liée avec Hoche, elle le pria de parler pour elle à Barras, alors tout-puissant. Celui-ci ne connaissait la vicomtesse que de réputation ; il voulut la voir, et lui rendit visite dans sa prison. . . . Barras, séduit par la conversation et les charmes personnels de la jeune veuve, devint, à la première visite, et son protecteur, et son ami. Deux jours après, elle fut rendue à la liberté.'

That Josephine gave rise to this scandal, is probably owing to her intimacy with Madame Tallien and Barras. Barras, she was bound to be grateful to, for by his means, a part of her husband's property was restored to her ; but it was Tallien who, at his wife's entreaty, obtained the liberty, both of Josephine and Duchesse d'Aiguillon. Madame Tallien's receptions were the most brilliant in Paris, where the prettiest and wittiest women met the men most distinguished in any way, and common gratitude, at least, would have led Josephine to the assemblies of her dear friend, who had shared her imprisonment, and obtained her release.

CHAPTER VI.

JOSEPHINE'S DRESS AND PERSONAL APPEARANCE— HER REPUTED CONNECTION WITH BARRAS—MARRIAGE WITH NAPOLEON—HER TASTES AND DISPOSITION.

LET us for a moment, as an antidote to the caricaturist's pictures, see what was Josephine's dress at this period.[2] 'Here is Madame de Beauharnais, that excellent Josephine, whose heart is not made for coquetry, but who throws a

---

[1] *Amours et Aventures du Vicomte de Barras*, Paris, 1817.
[2] *Notre Dame de Thermidor*, p. 429.

childish joy into her dress. With an air less dramatic and superb than her rivals,[1] the joyous and kindly creole is, perhaps, the most French of the three, Madame Tallien is the most Greek, and Madame Viconti the most Roman. Josephine wears a wavy dress, rose and white from top to bottom, with a train trimmed at the bottom with black bugles, a bodice six fingers deep, and wearing no *fichu* ; short sleeves of black gauze, long gloves covering the elbow of *noisette* colour, which suits this beautiful violet so well ; shoes of yellow morocco ; white stockings with green clocks. If her hair is dressed after the Etruscan manner, ornamented with cherry-coloured ribbons, I am sure it is impossible to approach nearer to the antique. To tempt the fashion is the sole ambition of the pretty Josephine, but it happens that the celebrated Madame de Beauharnais sets it.'

It is impossible to quit this subject without some contemporary quotations, as they help us to realise the truth, or falsehood, of the caricaturist.[2] ' Madame Tallien was kind and obliging, but such is the effect on the multitude of a name that bears a stain, that her cause was never separated from that of her husband. The following is a proof of this. Junot was the bearer of the second flags, which were sent from the army of Italy to the Directory. He was received with all the pomp which attended the reception of Marmont, who was the bearer of the first colours. Madame Bonaparte, who had not yet set out to join Napoleon, wished to witness the ceremony ; and, on the day appointed for the reception of Junot she repaired to the Directory, accompanied by Madame Tallien. They lived at that time in great intimacy ; the latter was a fraction of the Directorial royalty with which Josephine, when Madame Beauharnais, and, indeed, after she became Madame Bonaparte, was in some degree invested. Madame Bonaparte was still a fine woman ; her teeth, it is true, were already frightfully decayed, but when her mouth was closed she looked, especially at a little distance, both young and pretty. As to Madame Tallien, she was then in the full bloom of her beauty.

---

[1] Madame Tallien and Madame Viconti.
[2] *Madame Junot's Memoirs*, vol. i. p 249.

Both were dressed in the antique style, which was then the prevailing fashion, and with as much of richness and ornament as were suitable to morning costume. When the reception was ended, and they were about to leave the Directory, it may be presumed that Junot was not a little proud to offer to escort these two charming women. Junot was then a handsome young man of five and twenty, and he had the military look and style for which, indeed, he was always remarkable. A splendid uniform of a colonel of huzzars set off his fine figure to the utmost advantage. When the ceremony was ended, he offered one arm to Madame Bonaparte, who as his general's wife was entitled to the first honour, especially on that solemn day ; and offering his other arm to Madame Tallien, he conducted them down the staircase of the Luxembourg. The crowd stepped forward to see them as they passed along. "That is the general's wife," said one. "That is his aide-de-camp," said another. "He is very young." "She is very pretty.— *Vive le Général Bonaparte !— Vive la Citoyenne Bonaparte !* She is a good friend to the poor." "Ah !" exclaimed a great fat market woman, "She is *Notre Dame des Victoires !*" "You are right," said another, "and see who is on the other side of the officer ; that is *Notre Dame de Septembre !*" This was severe and it was also unjust.'

We must not trust to the caricaturist's portrait of Josephine. She was good looking and graceful then, but, afterwards, she did become very stout. We must never forget in looking over the folios of caricatures of this period, that the idea of caricaturing then was to exaggerate everything, and make it grotesque ; it is only of modern years that the refinement of a Leech, Tenniel, or Proctor, gives us caricature without vulgarity.

After seeing Josephine as she really was, it will be worth while to compare the satirist's idea of her, and her marriage with Napoleon.

> Nap changed on entering Society,
> Obscurity for notoriety ;
> He to Barras only inferior,
> Commands the army of th' interior.
> As pride in office is essential,
> His manners now were consequential ;

Conducting all affairs of weight,
The little man was very great ;
And by this sudden rise to dignity,
He gave full weight to his malignity.
Barras, now moved by his persuasions,
Consulted him on all occasions ;
A greater compliment, too, paid he,
He got for him, a *cast off* lady :
A widow rich, as they relate,
But how so rich, 'tis hard to state,
Her spouse, for politics reputed,
By Robespierre was executed,
And she was by Barras *protected*,
Till he at length the fair neglected.
However, she procured with great art,
A man of colour for a sweetheart ;
By which no fortune's manifested,
For men of colour are detested ;
They married would have been, moreover,
But that—in stepped another lover ;

.   .   .   .   .

.   .   .   .   .

There are some writers who pretend,
The lady's virtue to defend ;
For, in the character they draw,
She's guilty of but one *faux pas* ;
But others, probably censorious,
Declare her lapses were notorious,
And that, devoid of sense and shame,
She even gloried in the same ;
So reckoning all things, the amount is,
She was a *condescending* countess.
The lady was, as it appears,
Older than Nap by twenty years ;
But, for a man, who scorned to prove
The votary or slave of love—
Whispering soft nonsense, and such stuff—
She certainly was good enough.
Short, like himself, and rather bulky,
But not so insolent and sulky.
As by Barras, too, recommended
(No matter from what stock descended),
It certainly must be allow'd
Of such a wife he should be proud.

So, locked together, soon were seen,
Brave Boney and fair Josephine.

The pictorial caricaturist, Gillray, gives us February 20, 1805, 'Ci-devant occupations, or Madame Tallien, and the Empress Josephine Dancing Naked before Barras, in the Winter of 1797—a fact.'[1]

[1] Gillray, evidently, was not particular as to dates, for Napoleon married Josephine in 1796.

At the foot of this etching, which depicts the sensual *bon viveur*, Barras, looking on at the lascivious dancing of his two mistresses, Madame Tallien and Josephine, it says : ' Barras (then in power), being tired of Josephine, promised Bonaparte a promotion, on condition that he would take her off his hands. Barras had, as usual, drank freely, and placed Bonaparte behind a screen, while he amused himself with these two ladies, who were then his humble dependents. Madame Tallien is a beautiful woman, tall and elegant. Josephine is smaller, and thin, with bad teeth something like cloves. It is needless to add that Bonaparte accepted the promotion, and the lady, now Empress of France ! '

Barre, who notoriously wrote against Napoleon, says :[1] ' And not satisfied by procuring him a splendid appointment, he made him marry his mistress, the Countess de Beauharnais, a rich widow, with several children ; and who, although about twenty years older than Bonaparte, was a very valuable acquisition to a young man without any fortune. The reputation of the Countess de Beauharnais was well established, even before the Revolution : but Buonaparte had not the least right to find fault with a woman presented to him by Barras.'

At all events they were married, and here is G. Cruikshank's idea of the ceremony, and here, also, he depicts the bridesmaids and groomsmen.

[1] *History of the French Consulate under Napoleon Buonaparte, &c.*, by W. Barre, London, 1804.

Their honeymoon was of the shortest, for De Bourrienne says : ' He remained in Paris only ten days after his marriage, which took place on the 9th of March, 1796. Madame Bonaparte possessed personal graces and many good qualities. I am convinced that all who were acquainted with her must have felt bound to speak well of her ; to few, indeed, did she ever give cause for complaint. Benevolence was natural to her, but she was not always prudent in its exercise. Hence her protection was often extended to persons who did not deserve it. Her taste for splendour and expense was excessive. This proneness to luxury became a habit which seemed constantly indulged without any motive. What scenes have I not witnessed when the moment for paying the tradesmen's bills arrived! She always kept back one half of their claims, and the discovery of this exposed her to new reproaches. How many tears did she shed, which might easily have been spared!'

A GENERAL'S LADY.

We here see the caricaturist's idea of Josephine as a French general's wife.

CHAPTER VII.

NAPOLEON MADE COMMANDER-IN-CHIEF OF THE ARMY OF ITALY—HIS SHORT HONEYMOON—HIS FIRST VICTORY—STATE OF THE FRENCH ARMY—THE ITALIAN CAMPAIGN—FRENCH DESCENT ON IRELAND— ITS RESULT—STATE OF ENGLAND.

NAPOLEON now waxed great. Through Barras' influence he was made Commander in Chief of the army of Italy, and bade adieu to his wife after the very brief period of conjugal life, as aforesaid, and, on the way to join the army, he visited his mother and family, at Marseilles, writing frequent and affectionate letters to his newly married bride.

Montenotte was his first victory, the precursor of so many ; and on April 11, 1796, he there defeated the Aus-

D

trian general, Beaulieu, who was compelled to retreat, leaving behind him his colours, and cannon, about two thousand prisoners, and about a thousand killed.

The French army then was in a bad state, according to a serious historian.[1] ' The extreme poverty of the treasury may be understood from the fact that the sum of two thousand louis was all that could be collected to furnish him (Napoleon) with means for so important a command. By an organised system of pillage, says Lanfrey, the Republican coffers were soon replenished to the amount of several millions ! ' Another historian [2] says : ' Scherer, who was at that time commander-in-chief of the army of Italy, had recently urged for money to pay his troops, and for horses to replace those of his cavalry which had perished for want of food ; and declared that, if any delay took place in furnishing the requisite supplies, he should be obliged to evacuate the Genoese territory, and repass the Var. The Directory found it easier to remove the General than to comply with his request.' Our poetic history relates :—

Such was the army's sad condition,
They had no clothes nor ammunition,
Besides, a scarcity of food,
And even that little, was not good.
They had no money—may be said—
And why ?   The men were never paid.
But his intentions wisely Nap hid,
Whose methods were as strange as rapid.
He promis'd, when he was appointed,
To get them everything they wanted ;
And, what is more, too, their protector be,
Without expense to the Directory.

In his deceptions he succeeded,
And now procur'd all that he needed.
His troops which were with hunger nigh dead,
Were with good victuals soon provided ;
They for new clothes exchang'd their rags,
And then with Rhino fill'd their bags ;
While Nap, as you may well believe,
These people laughed at in his sleeve.

[1] R. H. Horne.   [2] G. M. Bussey.

It is not within the province of this work to follow Napoleon in his victorious career in Italy, except the English caricaturist should notice him, and he had not yet attained to that questionable honour ; but a very brief synopsis of his battles in 1796 may be acceptable. Montenotte, April 11 ; Millesino, April 14 ; Dégan, April 15 ; Mondovi, April 21 : Lodi, May 10 ; Lonado, August 3 ; Castiglione, August 5 ; Roveredo, Sept. 4 ; Bassano, Sept. 8 : San Giargo, Sept. 13 ; Arcola, Nov. 15.

Barre says : 'The campaign in Italy was extremely brilliant, and withal revolutionary. Buonaparte attributed all the glory almost exclusively to himself. His secretary, who wrote his despatches, did it so as to flatter the generals and the army, but still as if all the merit belonged to the commander-in-chief. It seems that General Berthier made a bargain with Buonaparte, to whom he sold his talents for the sake of becoming rich without any responsibility. When Buonaparte was raised by the mixed faction, he made Berthier Minister of War ; and in that capacity he has shown himself more rapacious than any of his predecessors. Every contractor is obliged to give him *one hundred thousand livres* as a present (*pot de vin*) without which there is no contract.' He tells a story which bears somewhat on the above. 'It happened once, that whilst he was playing at cards, having General Massena for his partner, that general made a mistake ; when Buonaparte started, all of a sudden, in a violent passion, and exclaimed, *Sacré Dieu ! General, you make me lose.* But General Massena instantly retorted with a happy sarcasm : *Be easy, General, remember that I often make you win.* Buonaparte could never forget nor forgive that *bon mot.*' This story also figures in poetry :—

> In numbers being three to one,
> A Battle at Monte Notte he won ;
> The Austrian General he defeated,
> And therefore with huzzas was greeted.
> But, tho' of this affair Conductor,
> Massena had been his instructor.
> Yet, when (would you believe it, Bards ?)
> Nap's partner at a game of Cards,

He scrupled not his friend t' abuse—
'Zounds ! general, how you make me lose ! '
The general, patient all the while,
Thus answer'd with a gracious smile,
' For such a loss don't care a pin,
Remember, Nap, I've made you *win*.'
Tho' nothing but the truth he spoke,
Nap never could forgive the joke.

It is impossible to pass over in silence an event which happened in 1796, in which, although Napoleon was not personally interested, all England was. This was no less than an attempted invasion of Ireland by the French ; relying on being supported by the Irish, who were disaffected then, as now. The expedition failed, although it was numerous and well-found, having General Hoche and 25,000 men with it. By defective seamanship, many of the ships were damaged, and a 74 gun ship, the *Seduisant*, was totally lost. Only one division, commanded by Admiral Bouvet, reached Ireland, but anchored in Bantry Bay, where they did nothing, but speedily weighed anchor, and returned to France. The following is an official letter on the subject :—

Dublin Castle, December 29, 1796.

My Lord [1]—The last accounts from General Dalrymple are by his aide-de-camp, Captain Gordon, who left Bantry at ten o'clock A.M. on Tuesday, and arrived here this morning. Seventeen sail of French ships were at that time at anchor on the lower part of Bear island, but at such a distance that their force could not be ascertained. A lieutenant of a French frigate was driven on shore in his boat, in attempting to quit his vessel, which was dismasted, to the admiral. He confirms the account of the fleet being French, with hostile views to this country, but does not appear to know whether the whole fleet, which consisted of about 17 sail of the line, 15 frigates, and including transports and luggers, amounted to fifty sail, were all to re-assemble off Bantry. General Hoche was on board, commanding a considerable force. I have the honour to be, my lord,

Your lordship's most obedient servant,
T. PELHAM.

Just let us glance for one moment at the social position

[1] The Lord Mayor of London, Thomas Blackhall.

of England at that time. For the first three months of the year the quartern loaf was 1s. 3d. ; in April it fell to 10d. : in June it rose to 11d. ; in September it fell to 8¼d. ; at which it remained all the year. There was a surplus of revenue over expenditure of over twenty-three millions, which must have gratified the Chancellor of the Exchequer ; the exports exceeded those in 1795 by 1,781,297l., and the London Brewers brewed 142,700 more barrels of porter than the previous year ; 3 per cent. Consols varied from 71 in January (the highest price) to 56⅜ in December (nearly their lowest).

CHAPTER VIII.

NAPOLEON DESPOILS ITALY OF HER WORKS OF ART—THE SIEGE OF MANTUA—WÜRMSER'S SURRENDER—EARLIEST ENGLISH CARICATURE OF NAPOLEON—INVASION OF ENGLAND—LANDING IN PEMBROKESHIRE —NELSON'S RECEIPT TO MAKE AN OLLA PODRIDA—'THE ARMY OF ENGLAND.'

SUCH a subject as the spoliation of Italian works of art was not likely to go a-begging among caricaturists, so George Cruikshank illustrated the poet Combe.

SEIZING THE ITALIAN WORKS OF ART.

As Nap (for his extortions fam'd),
Of livres twenty millions claim'd ;
Which sum, we also understand,
Pope Pius paid upon demand ;

And sixteen million more, they say,
Was bound in two months' time to pay.
With these exactions not content,
To further lengths our hero went ;
A hundred paintings, and the best,
Were, we are told, his next request.
At his desire, the precious heaps came,
(It was indeed a very deep scheme),
Loretta's statues so pleased Boney,
They instantly packed up *Madona* :
These relics then, without delay,
To Paris Boney sent away ;
And there they formed an exhibition
As proof of Papal superstition.

At the siege of Mantua, Würmser sent his aide-de-camp Klenau to Napoleon to treat for terms of peace. G. Cruik-

NAPOLEON AND HIS GUARD.

shank depicts the scene. Klenau is brought in blindfolded, and Bonaparte, surrounded by his guard, strikes a melodramatic attitude, worthy of a pirate captain at a transpontine theatre.

The real facts are thus described by Horn. 'Mantua was now without hope of relief. The hospitals were crowded, the provisions exhausted ; but Würmser still held out. Napoleon informed him of the rout and dispersion of the Austrian army, and summoned him to surrender. The old soldier proudly replied that "he had provisions for a year ;" but a few days afterwards he sent his aide-de-camp, Klenau, to the head-quarters of Serrurier to treat for a surrender.

'At the conference, a French officer sat apart from the two others, wrapped in his cloak, but within hearing of what passed. After the discussion was finished, this officer came forward and wrote marginal answers to the conditions proposed by Würmser ; granting terms far more favourable than those which might have been exacted in the extremity to which the veteran was reduced. " These," said the unknown officer, giving back the paper, " are the terms that I grant, if he opens his gates to-morrow; and if he delays a fortnight, a month, or two months, he shall have the same terms. He may hold out to his last morsel of bread ; to-morrow I pass the Po and march upon Rome." Klenau, recognising Napoleon, and struck with the generosity of the conditions he had granted, owned that only three days' provisions remained in Mantua.'

The earliest English caricature of Napoleon that I have met with, was published on April 14, 1797, all those hither-to given, being of later date. It is not worth reproducing, as the artist had evidently no knowledge of what manner of man Napoleon was. It is called the ' French Bugabo[1] frightening the Royal Commanders.' Bonaparte (a per-fectly fanciful, and horrible sketch) is seated on the back of some impossible Saurian—meant, probably, for the devil—who is vomiting armies and cannon. He calls out, ' Egad, they run well. Courez donc Messieurs les Princes!!!' Of the two royal commanders running away, Frederick Duke of York is calling out to his companion, ' I wish I was at York. Come on, Charles, follow me.' Fox, who acts the part of ' the sweet little cherub that sits up aloft,' says, ' Run, Frederick, run Charles, Mack, Wurmsell, Kell ; well done D'Alvinzi, now Davidovich.' The poor Pope is being trodden under the beast, and cries out, ' Oh Lord ! this rebel son of mine pays me no homage whatever.'

Of all the attempts of the French to invade England, perhaps the most ludicrous was that which took place in February 1797. On the 22nd of that month, a French corvette, and a lugger, made for the coast of Pembrokeshire, and there landed some 1,200 men. Two days after, they surrendered to Lord Cawdor, and were sent to Haverford-west : but, before the arrival of the military, the peasants attacked them with rough weapons, such as pikes and scythes. The ships, which brought this invading army over, were captured on their return to Brest. The follow-

[1] A bogey, a bugbear.

ing is an official letter to the Lord Mayor, respecting the event :—

My Lord,—I have the honour to acquaint your lordship that intelligence has been received that two French Frigates, a Corvette, and a lugger, appeared off the East of Pembrokeshire, on the 22nd instant, and, on the evening of that day, disembarked some troops (reported by deserters to be about 1,200 men, but without any field pieces). Every exertion had been made by the Lord Lieutenant, and gentlemen of that county, and its neighbourhood, for taking the proper steps on this occasion ; and the greatest zeal and loyalty has been shewn by all ranks of people. Immediately, on an account having been received at Plymouth, of this force having appeared in the Bristol Channel, frigates were despatched from Plymouth in quest of them.

I have the honour to be, &c.

PORTLAND.

In the ' Times ' of March 13, 1797, is the following :—

Commodore NELSON's *Receipt to make an Olla-Podrida.*

Take a Spanish first-rate, and an 80 gun ship and after well *battering* and *basting* them for an hour, keep throwing in your *force balls*, and be sure to let them be *well seasoned.* Your *fire* must never *slacken* for a single moment, but must be kept up as *brisk* as possible during the whole time. So soon as you perceive your Spaniards to be well *stewed* and *blended* together you must then throw your own ship on board of the two-decker. Lash your sprit-sail-yard to her mizen-mast : then jump into her quarter gallery, sword in hand, and let the rest of your boarders follow as they can. The moment you appear on the 80 gun ship's quarter deck, the Spaniards will all throw down their arms and fly : you will then have only to take a hop, step and a jump, from your *stepping stone,* and you will find yourself in the middle of the first-rate's quarter-deck with all the Spaniards at your feet. Your Olla Podrida may now be considered as completely *dished* and fit to be set before his MAJESTY.—*Nelson's New Art of Cookery.*

Negotiations for peace with France had been going on during the year, and Lord Malmesbury went over to Lisle to conduct them on the part of the English, but they came to nothing. The French, however, in order to keep us in anxiety, massed large quantities of troops on their coast, which the Directory ordered should be called the ' Army of England,' and they gave Bonaparte the command of it.

It was destined to come to nothing. Napoleon had made peace with the Austrians, and was then given the above command.

> Among themselves [1] they had indeed,
> On Nap's departure all agreed ;
> For, one of his prodigious sway,
> 'Twas policy to send away.
> So Barras, who had such a wise head,
> Albion's immediate fall advised.
> And to send Boney, he thought best,
> To head the army in the West,
> Which had a pompous appellation,
> As 'twas to rouse the English nation ;
> The ' Army of England ' it was named,
> Though never for an action famed ;
> They had, indeed, for the occasion,
> (We mean of the resolv'd invasion),
> Rafts and Balloons, and ships for diving,
> And other matters were contriving.
> The business settled, Barras wrote
> To his *dear* Bonaparte a note.
> ' Your loving friend now reinstates you,
> Another victory awaits you—
> To Albion's shores conduct your army,
> There's nothing there that can alarm ye ;
> I will each necessary thing lend,
> That you may sack the Bank of England ;
> On London's Tower let them see
> The Standard of French Liberty.'
> Some of the Ministers it seems
> Thought this the maddest of all schemes ;
> Tho' Barras with fine words embellish'd it—
> Not even Mr. Boney relish'd it ;
> And very soon, it must be own'd
> The project wisely was postpon'd.

Thus stood things at the end of 1797, a year which left the public pulse—the Three per Cent. Consols—at 49 (they had, in September, dropped to 47⅞), and the quartern loaf about eightpence all the year through.

[1] The Directory.

CHAPTER IX.

CARICATURES ABOUT THE FRENCH INVASION—FOX'S FRENCH PROCLIVITIES
—PATRIOTISM IN THE COUNTRY—EXPEDITION TO EGYPT—NELSON'S
BLUNDERS—LANDING IN EGYPT—NAPOLEON AS A MAHOMETAN—
HIS PROCLAMATIONS.

IN 1798 the caricatures with regard to the relations between France and England became more numerous, and in this year the personal entity of Napoleon is confessed, and his likeness, a somewhat rough one, but still recognisable, is established.   An early one in this year is, the ' Storm Rising, or the Republican Flotilla in danger,' Feb. 1798, by Gillray.   Fox, Sheridan, the Duke of Bedford, and Mr. Tierney are represented as working a windlass, which is used to pull over the Flotilla.   This is represented by a huge raft bristling with cannon ; a large fort is in the centre, and minor ones all around which bear flags inscribed ' Liberty, Atheism, Blasphemy, Invasion, Requisitions, Plunder, Beggary, Murder, Destruction, Anarchy, and Slavery.'   It is represented as coming from Brest, where the devil is seen dancing on a guillotine, fiddling, and singing, ' Over de Vater ! over de Vater to Charley !'   Fox's coat lies on the ground, together with a paper, a ' List of the New Republican Ministry.   Citizen Volpone (Fox) Premier.'   Their designs, however, are being defeated by Pitt, who as Eolus, is raising a storm, and blowing against the Flotilla, the Admirals Duncan, Curtis, Howe, Gardiner, Trollope, Colpoys, St. Vincent, Seymour, Parker, and Onslow.   A somewhat similar idea was worked out in a caricature by Isaac [1] Cruikshank, January 28, 1789.

In March Sir John Dalrymple drew, and Gillray etched, a series of four caricatures.   The first was called the ' Consequences of a successful French Invasion,' and it shows the French clearing out the House of Commons, and the members in fetters.   The second engraving is, ' We explain de Rights of Man to de Noblesse.'   Paine's doctrines are

---

[1] He was the father of our great caricaturist, George ; but there is little doubt from the internal evidence of the pictures, that George either wholly produced, or materially helped in the execution of many caricatures signed with his father's name.

being carried out in far more than their entirety. A guillotine takes the place of the throne, and the French commander orders, à la Cromwell, one of his men, 'Here, take away this bauble! but if there be any gold on it take it to my lodging.'

The next one is a slap in the face for Ireland, and is called, 'We fly on the wings of the wind to save the Irish Catholics from persecution,' and French sympathy is shown by a priest being stabbed, and the holy vessels trampled on.

The fourth is 'Me teach de English Republicans to work,' and the French are represented as cruel taskmasters. Men and women are put to work in the fields, and Republicans, with fearful whips, keep them up to the mark of efficiency. Others are harnessed to a plough, and are kept well to their work by a most cruel lash.

Napoleon gave up all idea of invading England, and in May the expedition to Egypt was formed.

Fox's French proclivities are shown in a caricature (the Shrine of St. Anne's Hill,[1] May 26, 1798, Gillray) where he is seen on his knees before an altar, on which are a cap of liberty, and two busts of Robespierre and Bonaparte. The reredos is composed of a guillotine, and the tables of the ten commandments are labelled 'Droit de l'homme. 1. Right to worship whom we please. 2. Right to create and bow down to anything we chuse to set up. 3. Right to use in vain any name we like. 4. Right to work 9 days in the Week and do what we please on the tenth. 5. Right to honor both Father and Mother when we find it necessary.

[1] Fox's residence.

6. Right to Kill. 7. Right to commit Adultery. 8. Right to Plunder. 9. Right to bear what Witness we please. 10. Right to covet our Neighbour's house and all that is his.' Nichols, Tierney, Lauderdale, Bedford, Lansdowne, and Norfolk, appear in the upper background as Cherubin.

When the invasion panic was abroad, patriotism was rampant, and everybody was very brave—on paper. This was the sort of stuff the people were fed on, of which I will give but two or three verses out of the eight.[1]

> While deeds of Hell deface the World,
> And GALLIA's throne in ruin lies,
> While round the Earth revolt is hurl'd,
> And Discord's baneful Banner flies—
> Loud shall the loyal BRITON sing
> To arms ! to arms ! your bucklers bring,
> To shield our Country, guard our King,
> And GEORGE and ENGLAND save.
>
> Ne'er shall the desolating Woe
> That shades with horror Europe o'er,
> To us her hideous image shew,
> Or steep in blood this happy shore ;
> Firm as our rock-bound Isle we'll stand,
> With watchful eye and iron hand,
> To wield the might of BRITAIN's land,
> And GEORGE and ENGLAND save.
>
> Oh, happy Isle ! wise order'd State !
> Well temper'd work of Freedom's hand !
> No Shock of Realms can touch thy fate,
> If Union bind thy sea-girt Land !
> Vainly the storms shall round thee ring,
> While BRITAIN's sons in concord sing,
> We'll shield our Country, guard our King,
> And GEORGE and ENGLAND save.

To give some idea of the commotion caused by the threat of invasion, and yet not to be wearisome on the subject, I will only give the warlike items in the number of the *True Briton*, from which the above verses are taken, and which may be accepted as a fair sample. ' We understand that the Duke of Bedford has received an answer from his Royal Highness the Commander in Chief to his

---

[1] *The True Briton*, May 11, 1798.

offer of service, that it would be highly acceptable to the Government if he would exert his influence in Devonshire for the defence of the Coast.' 'His Grace the Duke of Grafton has not only offered to furnish his waggons and horses to Government, in case of emergency, but has also expressed his desire to encourage all his neighbours and tenants to assist with their persons and teams as far as may be in their power.' 'Last week there was a respectable Meeting of the Inhabitants of Stowmarket, at which it was unanimously agreed to form a Volunteer Corps of Infantry for the defence of that Town and Hundred.' 'In the county of Bedford, Lord Ongley, Mr. Trevor, and Mr. Whitbread, raise, each of them, a troop of Yeomanry. The town of Bedford raises a troop of Volunteer Cavalry.' 'A Meeting was held at Newmarket on Sunday last, after Divine Service, for aiding Government in case of Invasion, pursuant to the Regulations of Mr. Dundas's Defence Bill ; when the Inhabitants all came forward in a very laudable manner for that purpose, and most of the labourers offered their services as pioneers, or in any other capacity that may be deemed necessary.' 'The farmers of the Parish of Tarvin, in Cheshire, have set a noble example to their brethren throughout the Kingdom, in having entered into an agreement that they will, at a moment's notice, in case of actual invasion, or imminent danger thereof, furnish their respective teams, with able horses and drivers, for the service of Government, free from any payment or gratuity whatever ; and the number of each which they bind themselves to furnish, are 39 waggons, 68 carts, 347 horses, and an adequate number of drivers.'

This is the voluntary, patriotic side of the question ; take next day's paper, and we see, 'There was a sharp press from the ships in Yarmouth Roads on Tuesday evening, by which means some good Seamen were procured.'

There is a vast amount of humour in 'Anticipation, Ways and Means, or Buonaparte really taken' (I. Cruikshank, August 13, 1798). This represents a booth at a country fair, where a Pierrot in tricolour costume (Fox), is showing to a lot of yokels a highly imaginative show canvas of Napoleon, with huge mouth and teeth, goggle eyes, two daggers, and immense boots and spurs. ' To be seen here alive, the noted Bony Parte, from Egypt. ☞ An undoubted likeness.' With tears streaming down his cheeks, he assures his audience that ' he is certainly taken. I never was so pleased at any event in the whole course of my life.'

Pitt, who, suffering from gout, sits down and acts as trumpeter to the show, addresses the people thus: 'Believe me, I do not mean to deceive you this time : he is really *taken*, and in this Booth at this present moment. Out with your pence good people—don't be so shy—Tumble up Mr. Bull—the only booth in the fair! don't be alarm'd —he is perfectly tame I assure you.'

The expedition to Egypt may be said to be the starting-point from which came the numerous caricatures of Napoleon. Before this, he had been known only by his victorious career in Italy, and had never come into active hostility with England ; but now that we were to measure our strength with the Chief of the 'Army of England,' he became an important person, and, consequently, the caricaturists, ever feeling the public pulse, took him up, and found it to their benefit.

The occupation of Egypt by the French, if successful, would have led to their attacking our empire in India, and this was Napoleon's design. Why the flotilla was ever allowed to go on its way unmolested, is hard to conceive ; but it was so, and on May, 19, 1798, sailed out of Toulon 13 sail of the line, 7 frigates, 62 gunboats, and 400 transport vessels, having 20,000 troops and large quantities of military stores on board. There were also 121 men learned in different branches of science, who accompanied the expedition, and the whole was under the supreme command of Napoleon.

On June 11 they reached Malta, which surrendered without resistance, and then went on their way. Nelson followed them, and got to Malta, where he arrived on the 22nd, only to find that the French had left some days before, on which he sailed for Alexandria, getting there on June 28, but found no news of the French fleet ; so, instead of waiting for them, he steered northward for

Caramania, and then went to Sicily ; whence, after refitting, he sailed again for Alexandria.

In the meantime the French, of course, took advantage of his (to them) lucky absence ; and, on July 2, they disembarked the army, and took possession of Alexandria, but not without some loss on the side of the French ; and the bodies of the soldiers thus slain were by Napoleon's orders buried at the foot of Pompey's Pillar, and their names were to be engraved on the Column.

And now, as it will be a frequent article of impeachment against Napoleon in this book, let us examine into the truth of his turning Mahometan, and see, first, what foundation it had in fact from the mouths of his own countrymen. De Bourrienne gives a proclamation made by Napoleon to his soldiers before their arrival in Egypt, from which I extract only those sentences bearing on this subject :—

Head Quarters, on board the ' Orient.'
The 4th Messidor, Year VI. (June 22, 1798.)

Soldiers,—The people amongst whom you are going to live, are Mahometans. The first article of their faith is this : ' There is no God but God, and Mahomet is his Prophet.' Do not contradict this. Behave to them as you have behaved to the Jews— to the Italians. Pay respect to their muftis, and their imams, as you did to the rabbis and the bishops. Extend to the ceremonies prescribed by the Alcoran, and to the Mosques, the same toleration which you showed to the synagogues, to the religion of Moses, and of Jesus Christ. The Roman legions protected all religions.

And again, the same author says : ' On arriving at Alexandria, the General in Chief issued a proclamation to the people of Egypt, which, besides adverting to the insults and extortions experienced by French merchants from the Beys, contained the following passages :—

' " People of Egypt,—You will be told that I am come to destroy your religion—do not believe it. Be assured that I come to restore your rights, to punish the usurpers, and that I respect more than the Mamelukes, God, his prophet, and the Alcoran. Tell them that all men are equal in the eye of God ; wisdom, talents, and virtue make the only difference.

'" Cadis, Sheiks, Imams, Scorbajis, tell the people that we are the friends of the true Mussulmans. Have we not destroyed the Pope, who says that war ought to be made upon Mussulmans? Have we not destroyed the Knights of Malta, because those bigots believed that God required them to raise their swords against the Mussulmans?"'

And again (still quoting from the same authority), in a proclamation to the people of Cairo, dated from Ghizeh, 4th Thermidor, year VI. (July 22, 1798): ' Fear nothing for your families, your houses, or your property; and least of all, for the religion of the prophet, which I respect (*j'aime*).'

In another proclamation to the inhabitants of Cairo, according to ' Buonapartiana,' he is made to say : ' Make known to the people that since the world has been a world, it was written, that having destroyed the *enemies of Islamism, the Cross* should be thrown down ; I have come from the extreme confines of the West, to fulfil the task which has been imposed upon me. Shew your people that in the book of the Koran, in more than twenty passages, that what has happened has been predicted, and that what will happen is equally explained.'

In a French History[1] he is described as conversing with the Muftis and Imams in the Pyramid of Cheops. At p. 171 he says, ' Honour to Allah !' at p. 172, ' Glory to Allah ! There is no other God but God, Mahomet is his prophet, and I am one of his friends ;' and at p. 173, ' Mufti, I thank you, the divine Koran is the joy of my soul, and the occupation of my eyes. I love the prophet ; and I am reckoning, before long, to see and honour his tomb in the Holy City.'

It is not worth while to multiply instances. His policy led him to conciliate the people, and, probably, his utterances were rather more in accordance with their religious ideas than would have been conformable in the mouth of a zealous Christian. But to the English caricaturist and satirist they were *bonnes bouches*, and they twisted and distorted them to suit their purposes. It became almost

[1] *Histoire de Bonaparte, Premier Consul, Depuis sa Naissance, jusqu'à la Paix de Lunéville*, Paris, chez Barba, 1801.

an article of belief with the average Englishman, that Napoleon had embraced the Mahometan religion. Were there not his own proclamations to prove it? Gillray even depicted him as undergoing a ceremony of reception into the Mahometan religion, surrounded as he is by Muftis, one of whom puts a turban on his head, another sonorously reads from the Koran, whilst a third brandishes a fearful knife for circumcision.

DEMOCRATIC RELIGION.
Bonaparte turning Turk at Cairo for Interest, after swearing on the Sacrement to support yᵉ Catholic Faith

CHAPTER X.

CONDUCT OF FRENCH SOLDIERY—NAPOLEON'S HATRED OF ENGLAND—THE EGYPTIAN CAMPAIGN—DESTRUCTION OF THE MAMELUKES—BATTLE OF THE NILE—TARDY NEWS THEREOF.

AFTER the entry into Alexandria, Napoleon, by several proclamations, imposed the strictest discipline upon his soldiers ; and, although it is possible some irregularities may have occurred on the part of the troops, such scenes as were depicted by Cruikshank and Combe, one with his pencil, the other with his pen, were simply impossible.

> He took the City by surprise,
> For he was always very wise,
> And with extreme amaze and dread,
> To mosques the people gladly fled.
> Regenerators yet annoy'd them,
> For they o'ertook and soon destroy'd them ;
> And horrible indeed to tell,
> Both men and women quickly fell ;
> Nay, even the infants at the breast !
> How sad the cries of the distrest !

E

As *trophies* of this *glorious* fight,
The spears held up the babes to sight ;
While this unparalleled ferocity
Was call'd *amazing generosity.*

The *avowed* object of Napoleon's expedition was to punish the Beys, of whom there were twenty-four, who kept up a force of some eight thousand Mamelukes, splendid cavalry, recruited from slaves bought in Georgia, the Caucasus, and even in Europe. The pretence against them was injustice and oppression against French merchants ; but the *real* reason for it is in the proclamation dated on board the ' Orient,' of 4th Messidor, year VI. : ' Soldiers, you

are about to undertake a conquest, the effects of which on civilisation and commerce are incalculable. *The blow you are about to give to England, will be the best aimed, and the most sensibly felt, she can receive, until the time when you can give her her death blow.*[1] . . . The Destinies are with us. The

MASSACRE IN EGYPT.

Mameluke Beys who favour exclusively English commerce, whose extortions oppress our merchants, and who tyrannise over the unfortunate inhabitants of the Nile, a few days after our arrival will no longer exist.'

With what intensity Bonaparte hated England! For example, take this little extract from Madame Junot,[2] to whose brother Napoleon was speaking : ' " England ! " he then rejoined. "So you think in Paris that we are going to attack it at last ? The Parisians are not mistaken ; it is indeed to humble that saucy nation that we are arming. England ! If my voice has any influence, never shall England have an hour's truce. Yes, yes, war with England for ever, until its utter destruction." '

[1] The italics are mine.—J. A.   [2] *Memoirs,* vol. i. p. 209.

Alexandria was taken and garrisoned ; but this was only the commencement of the campaign. Cairo must be reached speedily, and at all hazards. Then came that terrible march across the desert, from the 7th to the 10th of July —with generals all but mutinous, with Lannes and Murat dashing their cocked hats on the sands and trampling upon them in sight of the soldiers; the burning sun, the scarcity of water, harassed by enemies, human and insect—what joy could exceed theirs when they reached the Nile at Rahmanié! That wild rush into the water, without even thinking of the depth, and then the welcome shade and the juicy melons in such abundance ; it must have been a glimpse of heaven to those poor half-maddened, half-starved soldiers.

After a brief rest they pushed on towards Cairo. On July 19 they sighted the pyramids; on the 21st they had to encounter Mourad Bey, who had a force of 8,000 Mamelukes, forty pieces of cannon, and 20,000 infantry Then was it that, pointing to those grand historical monuments, Napoleon addressed his soldiers with the ever-memorable and oft-quoted speech : ' Soldiers ! From the summit of those pyramids forty centuries look down upon you.'

We know the issue of that battle—how, out of 8,000 Mamelukes that proudly sat their steeds that morning, 6,000 bit the dust ere night. The French that day drank deep of blood, for 10,000 of the Egyptian troops lay dead on the field ; they took 1,000 prisoners, and all their artillery and baggage. They could make no further stand, and the way to Cairo was open. A small force under Dupuy took possession of the city, which they found almost deserted, and on July 24, the *Sultan Kebir*, or *King of Fire*, as the natives had christened Napoleon, made his formal entry into Cairo. A brief rest to tranquillise the place and restore confidence to its returning inhabitants, and then, leaving Desaix in charge of the city, Napoleon went in pursuit of Ibrahim Bey, and drove him into Syria.

But what news was to welcome the conqueror back to Cairo? Sad indeed was the tale he heard—nought less than the destruction and capture of his whole fleet, save

two ships, which effected their escape.   Nelson had made
up for lost time, and on August 1 he fought the 'Battle of
the Nile,' when 'L'Orient' was blown up, and young Casa-
bianca, the son of the captain of the ship, with it.   We all
know the poem by Mrs. Hemans commencing, 'The boy
stood on the burning deck.'

De Bourrienne does not disguise the effect this disaster
had upon Napoleon.   He says : ' The catastrophe of Aboukir
came like a thunderbolt upon the General-in-Chief.   In
spite of all his energy and fortitude, he was deeply dis-
tressed by the disasters which now assailed him.   To the
painful feelings excited by the complaints and dejection of
his companion-in-arms, was now added the irreparable misfortune of the burning our fleet.   He measured the fatal
consequences of this event at a single glance.   We were
now cut off from all communication with France, and all
hope of returning thither, except by a degrading capitulation with an implacable and hated enemy.   Bonaparte had
lost all chance of preserving his conquest, and to him this
was indeed a bitter reflection.'

But with what different feelings was the news received
in England !   There was no steam, no electricity, then ;
men did not receive their news red-hot as we do now, but
had to wait for it, more or less calmly, according to their
temperament.   Let us take this battle of the Nile as an
example.   It was fought on August 1.   On September 1
the ' True Briton ' (from which the following extracts are
taken) gives its readers an ' Extract from a letter from
Strasbourg, of the 20th August,' in which a circumstantial
account of the total destruction and capture of the French
fleet by that of England is given, together with a veracious
statement that 'the latter lost their Admiral Nelson, who,
nevertheless, two hours before he died of his wounds,
received General Buonaparte on board his ship (the ' Cul-
loden ') *Prisoner, with all his General Staff.'*   This corre-
spondent's veracity is only equalled by his impartiality.

On September 17 we hear of the sailing of the English
fleet from Syracuse in quest of her enemy.   On September
21 we have a quotation from the ' Redacteur' of September
14: 'The same Letters inform us, that the Squadron of

Admiral Brueys had anchored on the coast of *Bignieres*, and was preparing to return to France, when it was attacked by the English Squadron, which was superior to ours, both in the number and the size of the vessels ; that on both sides the action was maintained with a degree of obstinacy, of which History affords no example ; that during the action the Vessel of the French Admiral was burnt ; that two or three French Ships sunk ; and that some others, both French and English, ran aground after having lost all their Masts ; and that, finally, some other French ships, quite disabled, remained on the spot where the Battle was fought.'

CHAPTER XI.

RECEPTION OF THE NEWS OF THE BATTLE OF THE NILE—NELSON SENDS FRENCH ADMIRAL'S SWORD TO THE CITY OF LONDON—VARIOUS CARICATURES ON THE BATTLE—TYPICAL JOHN BULL.

IT was not till October 2 that a glimmer of the truth, through rather a roundabout channel, appeared in the papers ; and later on that day appeared a 'London Gazette extraordinary,' with Nelson's despatches, which were very brief. Who can wonder at the excessive national rejoicing ? People were drunk with joy. Take a few paragraphs from the ' Times ' of October 3 :—

'DRURY LANE.—After the play, the news of Admiral Nelson's glorious victory produced a burst of patriotic exultation that has been rarely witnessed in a theatre. " Rule Britannia " was unanimously called for from every part of the house, and Messrs. Kelly, Dignum, Sedgewick, Miss Leak, and Mrs. Bland, came forward and sung it, accompanied by numbers of the audience. It was called for, and sung, a second time. The acclamations were the loudest and most fervent we have ever witnessed.

' The following lines, written for the occasion, were introduced by Mr. Dignum and Mr. Sedgewick—

> Again the tributary Strain
> Of grateful Britons let us raise,
> And to the Heroes on the Main,
> Triumphant add a Nelson's praise.

> Though the *Great Nation* proudly boasts
> Herself invincible to be ;
> Yet our bravè NELSON still can prove
> BRITANNIA, Mistress of the Sea.

The audience were not satisfied with this repeated mark of exultation, but in the effusion of enthusiastic loyalty, called for " God save the King," which was received with reiterated plaudits.'

' Immediately that the news of the gallant victory obtained by Admiral NELSON was known at Lloyd's, a subscription was opened for the relief of the widows and orphans of the brave men who perished in fighting for their country.' [1]

' Every man in this country may address Admiral NELSON with SHAKESPEARE,

> Horatio, thou art e'en as *brave* a man
> As e'er my understanding cop'd withal

The Capture of the French Fleet by NELSON has reduced BUONAPARTE to the situation of *Macbeth*,

> There is no going hence, nor tarrying here.'

' A person last night, in the gallery of Drury Lane house, calling frequently for the tune of BRITONS STRIKE HOME,[2] was immediately silenced by the appropriate observation of another at some distance from him, " Why, damn it, they have—have not they ? " '

' An affray happened last night opposite to the Admiralty, where the crowd was very great. The mob, as usual, insisted on every person of genteel appearance pulling off their hats ; six Officers passing along, were ordered to pay the same compliment to the mobility, and, refusing to do so, the populace attempted to force their hats off. The Officers drew their swords, and it was said that some persons were wounded.'

The next day's ' Times ' (October 4) says : ' To shew the zeal for Illumination in honour of our late splendid Victory,

---

[1] Eleven hundred guineas were collected at once on the first day, besides which, the *Times*, October 4, says, ' The Royal Exchange and London Assurance Companies have subscribed 100 guineas each, and the East India Company have voted 1,000*l.* towards this benevolent and patriotic fund.'

[2] From *Bonduca*, by Henry Purcell, A.D. 1710.

a chaise last night passed through the town, in which were three Ladies, with large cockades in their head dresses. The inside of the chaise was lighted up ; a postillion was on each horse with flambeaux in their hands, besides two out-riders, also carrying flambeaux.'

' It was remarked by a loyal Hibernian, on the official news of Admiral Nelson's victory, that nothing on *earth* could resist us by *sea*.'

The mob after a day or two became so uproarious that the magistrates were compelled to order the cessation of the illuminations.

On October 3 the Court of Common Council met, two hundred strong, when the Lord Mayor read the subjoined letter from Nelson—

Vanguard, Mouth of the Nile :
August 8th, 1798.

My Lord,—Having the honour of being a freeman of the City of London, I take the liberty of sending to your Lordship the sword of the commanding French admiral, Monsieur Blanquet, who survived after the battle of the 1st, off the Nile, and request that the City of London will honour me with the acceptance of it, as a remembrance that Britannia still rules the waves ; which that she may for ever do, is the fervent prayer of

Your lordship's
Most obedient Servant
HORATIO NELSON.

Right hon. the Lord Mayor of London.

Naturally, this gratifying memorial of this splendid victory was welcomed with enthusiasm, and orders were given to provide a suitable case, with inscription, for it ; and the Council voted Nelson a sword, value 200 guineas ; also the freedom of the City in a gold box, value 100 guineas, to Captain Berry, who was captain of the admiral's flagship, the ' Vanguard ;' and the thanks of the court to every one concerned.

The caricaturists soon pounced upon the subject, and the way in which the news of the victory was taken by different statesmen is very amusingly shown. (Gillray, October 3, 1798.) Burdett, who is always represented with his crop of hair combed over his eyes, is reading the ' Extraordinary Gazette,' and, in astonishment, exclaims, ' Sure I cannot see clear ? ' Jekyll is telling Lord Lansdowne how nine French ships of war were captured and two burnt ; but his lordship claps his hands to his ears, and calls out, ' I can't hear, I can't hear.' The Duke of Bedford will not believe it, and is tearing up the notification of ' the complete destruction of Buonaparte's Fleet,' exclaiming, ' It's all a damn'd Lye ; ' whilst poor Erskine, with Republican briefs before him, drops the paper which tells him of the capture of Bonaparte's despatches, and, with a smelling-bottle to his nose, plaintively calls out, ' I shall faint, I, I, I.' The poor Duke of Norfolk, whose many empty bottles of port testify to his inebriate condition, is very ill, and gives his opinion that ' Nelson and the British Fleet' is ' a sickening toast.' Tierney is in despair, and with the ' End of the Irish Rebellion ' in his pocket, and on his knees a paper, ' End of the French Navy. Britannia rules the Waves,' calls out, with upturned eyes, ' Ah ! our hopes are all lost.'

Moodily, with his head resting on his hands, sits Sheridan, with a ' List of the Republican Ships taken and destroyed ' before him, and his thoughts are of prudence, ' I must lock up my Jaw.' Black-visaged Fox, wearing a Cap of Liberty, has kicked over the stool that hitherto has supported him, and mournfully bidding ' Farewell to the Whig Club,' says, ' and I—— end with Eciat.'

This victory of the Nile is very graphically depicted (Gillray, October 6, 1798) in the ' Extirpation of the Plagues of Egypt ;—Destruction of Revolutionary Crocodiles ;—or —The British Hero cleansing ye Mouth of ye Nile.' Here Nelson has half-a-dozen crocodiles (typical of captured French ships) hooked and in his power, whilst, with a stout cudgel of ' British Oak,' he is spreading deadly blows and consternation into a quantity of tricoloured crocodiles. The blowing up of the ' Orient' is shown by one crocodile which is thus being destroyed.

Another caricature (October 7, 1798) of the victory of the Nile is ' The Gallant Nellson bringing home two uncommon fierce French Crocodiles from the Nile as a present to the King.' The one-armed hero is leading by a chain Fox and Sheridan, who have their jaws muzzled by rings, and Fox's mouth is also secured by a padlock, 'a mouthpiece for hypocrites.' They are both weeping copiously, after the fabled manner of crocodiles. Nelson is saying, 'Come along you Hypocritical dogs, I dare say your Dam'd sorry now for what you've done. No, no, I shall bring you to my MASTER ;' whilst John Bull, habited as a countryman, exclaims, ' Aye, aye, what ! Horatio has got 'em at *last* Why, these be the Old Cock Deviles. I thought as how he would not go so far for nothing.' This goes well with that of October 3.

A very curious caricature is (Ansell, October 24, 1798) Bonaparte in Egypt, ' A terrible Turk preparing a Mummy for a *present* to the Grand Nation.' A Turk, terrible indeed, has Napoleon by the throat, and, with sword in hand, is going to despatch him, saying, ' As for you, you Dog of no Religion, I'll sacrifice you at the tomb of the Prophet, whose name you have prophaned for the purposes of Murder, Rapine, and Plunder.'

Napoleon, whose defenceless state is typified by his swordless scabbard being broken, is endeavouring to mollify the wrath of the Turk. ' Now, mild and gentle Sir, don't be so rough : do you think I would cut your throat, ravish your wives, or plunder your house ? No, by Mahomet I would not. Sacrè Dieu, I would not. Ah, Diable, you'll choak me.'

Fox, Erskine, Sheridan, and the Duke of Norfolk are kneeling down, begging for Napoleon's life, whilst a Turk, who exclaims, ' You agree together so well, I think I'll fix you together for life,' has a bowstring ready to strangle all four. Pleads Fox, ' Pray don't hurt our dear friend, he would not hurt Man, Woman, or Child.   He can't bear the sight of blood ; as for plunder or deception, he is the determined enemy to both, by —— he is, and we are ready to swear

it.' Sheridan and Erskine say —the one, 'd—n me if he ayn't, and we are ready to swear it ;' the other, ' I'll swear it, I, I, I, swear it.'

' John Bull taking a lun· cheon ' (Gillray, October 24, 1798) is an extremely graphic caricature, and introduces us to the popular idea of John Bull, who, certainly, is never represented in this period with any of the refinement that Leech, Doyle, Tenniel, or any of our modern caricatur- ists depict him ; tastes and habits were coarser then than now, and John Bull was always shown in the rough. The second portion of the title of the picture helps us to realise the popular fancy, 'or— British Cooks cramming old *Grumble Gizzard* with Bonne Chére.' All

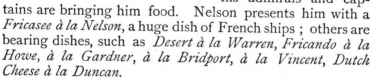

his admirals and cap- tains are bringing him food.   Nelson presents him with a *Fricasee à la Nelson,* a huge dish of French ships ; others are bearing dishes, such as *Desert à la Warren, Fricando à la Howe, à la Gardner, à la Bridport, à la Vincent, Dutch Cheese à la Duncan.*

John Bull is seated, devouring these viands, which are to be washed down with mighty draughts of *True British*

Stout, exclaiming, 'What! more Frigasees ? why you sons o' b——s, you, where do you think I shall find room to stow all you bring in ?' Fox and Sheridan are seen through an open window, running away, calling out, ' Oh curse his Guts, he'll take a chop at us next.'

There is another one with similar *motif* by Ansell, November 1, 1798.

The 'destruction of the French Collossus' (Gillray, November 1, 1798) is a painful picture. The huge creation strides from Egypt to France ; its head being a skull, with vipers crawling in and out—its hands and feet being imbrued in blood ; it clutches the guillotine, and tramples the Bible, Crucifix, and scales of Justice under foot. Round its neck is the bleeding head of Louis XVI. Britannia (typified by a shield of the national flag) hurls a thunderbolt, and shatters the huge statue into pieces.

CHAPTER XII.

REVOLT AND MASSACRE AT CAIRO—CARICATURES OF THE CAPTURE OF
FRENCH SHIPS—FIGHTING FOR THE DUNGHILL, ETC.—PRICE OF
BREAD AND CONSOLS IN 1798.

I HAVE omitted an episode which, to be chronologically correct, should have been introduced earlier ; and here, as usual, we find a French authority for what might seem an English slander : Emile de la Bédoliére, in his ' Tableau Chronologique de l'Histoire de Napoléon,' gives the story of the revolt at Cairo very tersely :—

October 21.—' During two months the Mussulmans patiently supported the yoke of the conquerors ; but the establishment of a registration of landed property became the cause of a violent insurrection.

' On the 30th Vendemaire, year VII. (October 21, 1798), a multitude ran through the streets, and massacred all the French they met. Bonaparte repaired to the scene, and took measures to cut the communications between the different quarters of the city, which were in the hands of the insurgents. Fifteen thousand of them took refuge in the great mosque, and refused to surrender. A hail of bombs, shells, and bullets, threatened to engulph them under the débris of their last asylum. Soon they uttered lamentable cries, implored the mercy of the general-in-chief, and surrendered at discretion.'

Combe thus versifies this event :—

> Mock liberty caus'd disaffection,
> And soon commenc'd an insurrection.
> According to our hero's plan
> Of course a massacre began :
> The streets were clear'd, and all the men
> Ran to the mosques for refuge then.
> The troops, tho', having forc'd the doors,
> Strew'd with combustibles the floors,
> And such indeed the conflagration,
> It was a grand illumination ;
> With screams and groans the air was fill'd,
> For some were burn'd and some were kill'd—
> All indiscriminately slain,
> Who had for quarter begg'd in vain.
> At length our hero was inclin'd
> Tho' somewhat slowly, to be kind ;
> He granted quarter, and he trusted
> All would be quietly adjusted.
> He knew, which certainly was verified,
> They had sufficiently been terrified.

Cruikshank, of course, grossly exaggerates the fact, and represents the French soldiery savagely attacking, even with pickaxes, the Egyptians who are endeavouring to escape from the mosque.

In November (12th) of this year, Rowlandson produced a plate called ' High fun for John Bull, or the Republicans put to their last shift.' This represents him as being in great glee at having captured so many ships, whilst the French are hard at work making fresh ones, which they are baking by batches in a *Dutch Oven* (an allusion to their being built in Holland). A Frenchman, with a large trayful of ships, calls out, ' Sacre dieu, Citoyens, make a Haste wit one autre Fleet, den we will shew you how to make one grande Invasion.' Another, a Spaniard, with a tray of cannon on his head, says, ' How ! That Nelson, wit one Arm and Eye can take our Ships by Dozens, then vat shall we do against the autres, wid two Arms and

Eyes, dey will have two dozen at a time.' A stolid Dutchman is baking a batch, grumbling the while, ' Donder and
Blaxam to dis Fraternization ; instead of smoking mine
Pipes and sacking De Gold, dis French Broders make me
build ships dat Mynheer Jan Bull may have de Fun to
take dem.' Another Frenchman adds, ' Well you may
talk, make haste, when dat English Nelson take our ships
by the Douzaine.'

John Bull, who holds a whip in his hand, says, ' What!
you could not find that out before, you stupid Dupes ; but
since you began the fun, you shall keep on. So work
away, Damn ye, else Jack Tar will soon be idle.' A sailor
carrying a trayful of ships on his head, calls out, ' Push
on, keep moving, I'll soon come for another cargo. Old
England for ever. Huzza ! '

' Fighting for the Dunghill—or—Jack Tar settling
Buonaparte,' is by Gillray, November 20, 1798. Napoleon
is terribly punished, his body being a mass of bruises
and wounds, the worst being a large one in the breast, and
labelled *Nelson.* Blood is streaming from his nose, and

Jack is driving him out of the world altogether, having his
foot upon Malta, whilst Napoleon is insecure in Turkey.
This engraving is an extremely typical one of the burly,
beef-fed Englishman, and the ' skinny Frenchman,' the
' Johnny Crapaud ' of the time, any number of whom an
Englishman was supposed to be a match for—

One skinny Frenchman, two Portugee,
One jolly Englishman beat 'em all three.

Napoleon is depicted by Gillray (December 8, 1798)
as being in a fearful rage—and an extremely diverting
sketch it is. It is called ' Buonaparte hearing of Nelson's
Victory, swears by his sword to extirpate the English from
off the Earth. See Buonaparte's Speech to the French
Army at Cairo, published by authority of the Directory in
Volney's Letters.' His melodramatic pose, and costume,
are superb. A huge cocked hat and feathers, the hat
adorned with a crescent (to show his supposed Mahometan
proclivities), as well as a tricoloured cockade, surmounts his
head, which bears a most ferocious expression, somewhat
heightened by the formidable pigtail which he wears. A
huge green necktie is round his neck, and he wears a tricoloured scarf, in which are stuck a pistol and dagger ; boots,
with huge spurs, add to the dignity of the costume. He
is waving his bloody sword, and stamps upon a paper,
' Nelson's Victory over the Fleet of the Republic,' while he
shouts out : ' What ? our Fleet captured and destroyed by
the slaves of Britain ? by my sword and by holy Mahomet
I swear eternal Vengeance ! yes, when I have subjected
Egypt, subdued the Arabs, the Druses, and the Maronites ;
become master of Syria; turn'd the great river Euphrates,
and sailed upon it through the sandy deserts ; ccmpelled
to my assistance the Bedouins, Turcomans, Kurds, Arme-
nians, and Persians ; formed a million of cavalry, and
pass'd them upon rafts, six or seven hundred miles over the
Bosphorus, I shall enter Constantinople. Now I enter the
Theatre of Europe, I establish the republic of Greece, I
raise Poland from its ruins, I make Prussia bend ye knee
to France, I chain up ye Russian bear, I cut the head from
ye Imperial Eagle, I drive the ferocious English from the
Archipelago, I hunt them from the Mediterranean, and
blot them out from the catalogue of Nations. Then shall
the conquer'd Earth sue for Peace, and an Obelisk be erected
at Constantinople, inscribed " To Buonaparte, conqueror
of the World, and extirpator of the ENGLISH NATION." '

This brings the year 1798 to a close of the prosperity,
or otherwise, of which we may judge by the price of the

quartern loaf, which averaged $8\frac{1}{2}d.$ for the year, and by the three per cent. Consols, which were $49\frac{5}{8}$ in January, and $52\frac{5}{8}$ in December ; but in this, as in other stocks, there was much fluctuation: for instance, in September Consols were $49\frac{7}{8}$; then came the news of the victory of the Nile, and up they went to $56\frac{1}{2}$, only, however, to fall to $50\frac{1}{2}$. But they rose again in November to $57\frac{5}{8}$, fell again to $52\frac{1}{8}$, and rose in December to $56.$

CHAPTER XIII.

REPORTED ATTEMPT TO ASSASSINATE NAPOLEON—HIS AMOUR WITH MADAME FOURÉS—THE EGYPTIAN CAMPAIGN—THE 'SAVANTS'— CARICATURES ON THEM.

THE new year opens with a somewhat curious print by I. Cruikshank, January 1, 1799, of the 'Ghost of Buonaparte appearing to the Directory.' The latter are in fearful dismay at the apparition, which, attired in the airiest of costume, shakes his notched sword at them, saying, ' Regicides, Parricides, Matricides, and Patricides, this is the effect of your insatiable thirst for Conquest ; this is your reward for my glorious Achievements in Italy, Germany, &c.—to die by the hand of an Assassin, a d—d Mussulman : and all my Brave Legions Destroyed by Water melons and the Arabs. Go, Murderers in cold blood, may your conscious guilt ever prey upon your vitals, and may the name of *Nelson* ever haunt you, sleeping and waking ! ' What is meant by his dying ' by the hand of an Assassin,' I do not know ; but probably some rumour was afloat to that effect, as Barre observes : 'Whilst Buonaparte and his army were thus cut off from Europe, the most absurd reports were spread (no doubt by the partisans of the artful Corsican) representing him as a victim of the Directory, who had thought proper to remove so great, famous, and fortunate a general.

' They pretended that the Directory, unable to repay the signal services of Buonaparte, and, fearing, at the same time, his popularity, had contrived, with Talleyrand, to flatter the ambitious vanity of that young conqueror with an expedition, which would raise his fame above the glory acquired by Alexander, or Cæsar. They added, that, as

Buonaparte was sure of being director at the next election, the Directory had resolved to put him out of the way, by sacrificing him and his army ; having even directed that the fleet should be exposed to certain destruction, in order that no possibility could exist of his return.'

The 'Times' of January 2, 1799, has the subjoined :—

The following Epigram has been handed about in Paris. The French points are all that can be remembered by the Gentleman who has put it in an English dress.

> ' France, to get rid of Turbulence,
> Sends her best Soldiers far from hence,
> With promises, and wishes, hearty ;
> Pleas'd and content that what so e'er
> May happen either here or there,
> To hazard all *in Bonâ-parte.*

> ' And still, though rous'd by home alarms,
> Nay, threatened by the world in arms,
> France holds her head up bold and hearty—
> Since now each Directorial Elf,
> By losing *Bonaparte's* self
> Enjoys the loss *in Bonâ-parte.*'

Meanwhile Napoleon was taking things pretty easily in Egypt, enjoying himself after his manner. It is a marvel that none of the English caricaturists ever depicted this portion of his life. True, Gillray, as we have seen, drew him in Turkish costume ; but he never wore it but once, and then but for a very short time. But why did they spare him in his *amour* with Madame Fourés (Pauline, or *Queen of the East*, as the army christened her) ? De Bourrienne makes no secret of it. He says : 'About the middle of September in this year (1798), Buonaparte ordered to be brought to the house of Elfy Bey, half a dozen Asiatic women, whose beauty he had heard highly extolled. However, their ungraceful obesity displeased him, and they were immediately dismissed. A few days after, he fell violently in love with Madame Fourés,[1] the wife of a lieutenant of Infantry. She was very pretty, and

---

[1] There is a long account of this lady in *Amours secrètes de Napoléon, des Princes et Princesses de sa famille, &c.*, by M. de B. . . . 2 vols., Paris, 1844, 12mo.

her charms were enhanced by the rarity of seeing a woman, in Egypt, who was calculated to please the eye of a Euro- pean. Bonaparte engaged, for her, a house adjoining the palace of Elfy Bey, which he occupied. He frequently ordered dinner to be prepared there, and I used to go there with him at seven o'clock, and leave him at nine.

'This connection soon became the general subject of gossip at head-quarters. Through a feeling of delicacy to M. Fourés, the General in Chief gave him a mission to the Directory. He embarked at Alexandria, and the ship was captured by the English, who, being informed of the Cause of his mission, were malicious enough to send him back to Egypt, instead of keeping him prisoner.'

But he was not one to waste much time in dalliance. Turkey was not at all satisfied with the occupation of Egypt, and two armies were assembled, one in Syria, and one at Rhodes ; the former of which had already pushed forward into Egyptian territory as far as El-Arisch, and also a train of artillery had been placed at Jaffa (the ancient Joppa). The commander of this *corps d'armée* (Achmet Pacha) had earned the unenviable title of *Djezzar*, or *the Butcher*. Napoleon, very early in the year 1799, marched against him, his busy brain having schemed the plan of crushing these Turkish troops, a demonstration against Constantinople itself, a forced peace with the Porte, and then hey! for India. To pave the way for this latter he actually wrote to Tippoo Sahib, saying he was coming to deliver him from the English yoke, and requesting his answer, which he might possibly have received, had not Tippoo been killed on May 4 of that year.

Napoleon, by way of conciliating the Egyptians, assisted at the celebration of ' Ramadan,' with great pomp, which, naturally, would afford his detractors another opportunity for outcry at his Mahometan proclivities. As soon as it was over, he set out against Achmet Pacha, and, on Febru- ary 17, El-Arisch capitulated, and the army marched to Gaza. How the vanguard lost their way, and their terrible sufferings in the desert, it boots not to tell. Gaza was taken, its stores were confiscated, and then Jaffa was their bourne, which was reached, and invested, on March 4.

F

Before reading the sad page of history which Jaffa gives us, let us glance at one or two caricatures which appeared in England about this time. Napoleon had taken with him, in his expedition to Egypt, Denon and divers other learned men to investigate the archæology of the country, &c., and most valuable were the services of ' the Institute,' as this body of *savants* was called. They furnished some fun to the army, and the cry, when any danger threatened, of ' the Asses and the *Savants* to the centre,' was naturally productive of mirth; the army also christening the asses ' *Demi savants*.'

Gillray makes great fun of the expedition to Egypt, and satirises the French soldiers unmercifully ; nor do the poor *savants* who accompanied the army fare any better. A good example is the ' Siege de la Colonne de Pompée, or Science in the Pillory,' published March 6, 1799. At the foot of the picture is : ' It appears by an intercepted letter from General Kleber, dated Alexandria, 5 brumaire, 7th year of the Republic, that when the garrison was obliged to retire into the New Town, at the approach of the Turkish Army, under the Pacha of Rhodes, a party of the *sçavans*, who had ascended Pompey's Pillar for scientific purposes, was cut off by a Band of Bedouin Arabs, who, having made a large Pile of Straw, and dry Reeds, at the foot of the Pillar, set fire to it, and rendered unavailing the gallant defence of the learned Garrison, of whose Catastrophe the above design is intended to convey an idea.

' To study Alexandria's store
Of Science, Amru deem'd a bore
And briefly set it burning.
The Man was ignorant, 'tis true,
So sought one comprehensive view
Of the light shed by learning.
Your modern Arabs grown more wise,
French vagrant Science duly prize ;
They've fairly bit the biters.
They've learnt the style of Hebert's Jokes,
Amru to books confined his Hoax ;
These Bedouins roast the writers.'

The *savants* are, indeed, in a parlous state, on the broad

summit of the pillar, exposed to fire from below, and the guns and pistols of the Arabs ; they defend themselves as well as possible by hurling their globes, and scientific instruments, at their assailants, who are exceedingly astonished at them. A balloon, La Diligence d'Abyssinie, is fired at, and struck, the aeronauts, one of whom has a parachute, being precipitated to the ground.

'The Institute,' which was modelled on that of Paris, also gave scope to Gillray's facile pencil, and he published a series of half a dozen plates, in the first one of which it was most amusingly caricatured. It was published on March 12, 1799, and called, ' L'Insurrection de l'Institut Amphibie— The pursuit of Knowledge.' A *savant* is depicted as studying a work ' Sur l'Education du Crocodile,' some plates from which have dropped out. They show how useful the crocodile may become, by training, to tow vessels, and to ride and drive on land. He evidently is intending to put his theories into practice, for he has brought with him, to the river's side, a saddle, a fearfully cruel bridle, and a huge whip, when he is seized by an enormous saurian, and devoured. Another learned man, who has been reading ' Les Droits du Crocodile,' drops it, when he finds one of these creatures asserting its rights by seizing his coat-tails.

CHAPTER XIV.

TAKING OF JAFFA, AND MASSACRE OF SOLDIERS--DE BOURRIENNE'S
ACCOUNT—NAPOLEON'S OWN VERSION.

IT is sad to turn from this rollicking fun to the episode of Jaffa ; but it cannot be dismissed, as it has afforded so much employment to the detractors of Napoleon, and to the English satirists of the time. First of all, let us give the version of an eye-witness (De Bourrienne), friend of, and secretary to, Napoleon. It is rather long, but no word of it can be omitted, as it gives every argument that can be brought forward to palliate the sickening massacre.

' On the 4th of March we commenced the siege of Jaffa. That paltry place, which, to round a sentence, was pompously styled the ancient Joppa, held out only to the 6th of March, when it was taken by storm, and given up to pillage.

F 2

The massacre was horrible. General Bonaparte sent his aides de camp, Beauharnais and Croisier, to appease the fury of the soldiers as much as possible, to observe what was passing, and to report to him. They learnt that a considerable part of the garrison had retired into some vast buildings, a sort of caravanserais, which formed a large enclosed court. Beauharnais and Croisier, who were distinguished by wearing the aide de camp scarf on the arm, proceeded to that place.

'The Arnauts and Albanians, of whom these refugees were almost entirely composed, cried, from the windows, that they were willing to surrender, upon an assurance that they would be exempted from the massacre to which the town was doomed ; if not, they threatened to fire on the aides de camp, and to defend themselves to the last extremity. The two officers thought that they ought to accede to the proposition, notwithstanding the decree of death which had been pronounced against the whole garrison, in consequence of the town being taken by storm. They brought them to our camp in two divisions, one consisting of about two thousand five hundred men, the other of about fifteen hundred.

'I was walking with General Bonaparte, in front of his tent, when he saw this multitude of men approaching, and, before he even saw his aides de camp, he said to me in a tone of profound sorrow, "What do they wish me to do with these men ? Have I food for them ? ships to convey them to Egypt or France ? Why, in the Devil's name, have they served me thus ? " After their arrival, and the explanations which the General in Chief demanded, and listened to with anger, Eugene and Croisier received the most severe reprimand for their conduct.

'But the deed was done. Four thousand men were there. It was necessary to decide upon their fate. The two aides de camp observed, that they had found themselves alone in the midst of numerous enemies, and that he had directed them to restrain the carnage. "Yes, doubtless," replied the General in Chief, with great warmth, "as to women, children, and old men—all the peaceable inhabitants ; but not with respect to armed soldiers. It was your

duty to die, rather than bring these unfortunate creatures
to me. What do you want me to do with them?" These
words were pronounced in the most angry tone.

'The prisoners were then ordered to sit down, and were
placed, without any order, in front of the tents, their hands
tied behind their backs. A sombre fury was depicted in
their countenances. We gave them a little biscuit and bread,
squeezed out of the already scanty supply for the army.

'On the first day of their arrival, a council of war was
held in the tent of the General in Chief, to determine what
course should be pursued with respect to them. The
Council deliberated a long time without coming to any
decision.

'On the evening of the following day, the daily reports
of the generals of division came in. They spoke of nothing
but the insufficiency of the rations, the complaints of the
soldiers—of their murmurs and discontent at seeing their
bread given to enemies, who had been withdrawn from
their vengeance, inasmuch as a decree of death, in conformity with the laws of war, had been passed on Jaffa.
All these reports were alarming, and especially that of
General Bon, in which no reserve was made. He spoke of
nothing less than the fear of revolt, which would be justified by the serious nature of the case.

'The Council assembled again. All the generals of
division were summoned to attend, and, for several hours
together, they discussed, under separate questions, what
measures might be adopted, with the most sincere desire
to discover and execute one which would save the lives of
these unfortunate prisoners.

'Should they be sent to Egypt? could it be done?

'To do so, it would be necessary to send with them
a numerous escort, which would too much weaken our
little army in the enemy's country. How, besides, could
they and the escort be supported till they reached Cairo,
having no provisions to give them on setting out, and,
their route being through a hostile territory, which we had
exhausted, which presented no fresh resources, and through
which we, perhaps, might have to return?

'Should they be embarked?

'Where were the ships? where could they be found?
All our optical instruments, directed over the sea, could
not descry a single friendly sail. Bonaparte, I affirm,
would have regarded such an event as a real favour of
fortune. It was, and I am glad to have to say it, this sole
idea, this sole hope, which made him brave, for three days,
the murmurs of his army. But in vain was help looked
for, seawards—It did not come.

'Should the prisoners be set at liberty?

'They would then proceed to St. Jean d'Acre to rein-
force the Pacha, or else, throwing themselves into the
mountains of Naplouse, would greatly annoy our rear and
right flank, and deal out death to us, as a recompense for
the life we had given them. There could be no doubt of
this. What is a Christian dog to a Turk? It would even
have been a religious and meritorious act in the eyes of
the Prophet.

'Could they be incorporated, disarmed, with our soldiers
in the ranks?

'Here again the question of food presented itself in all
its force. Next came to be considered the danger of
having such comrades, while marching through an enemy's
country. What might happen in the event of a battle
before St. Jean d'Acre? Could we even tell what might
occur during the march? and—finally—what must be done
with them when under the ramparts of that town, if we
should be able to take them there? The same embarrass-
ments with respect to the questions of provisions, and
security, would then recur with increased force.

'The third day arrived without its being possible,
anxiously as it was desired, to come to any conclusion
favourable to the preservation of these unfortunate men.
The murmurs in the camp grew louder—the evil went on
increasing—remedy appeared impossible—danger was real
and imminent.

'The order for shooting the prisoners was given and
executed on the 10th of March. We did not, as has been
stated, separate the Egyptians from the other prisoners.
There were no Egyptians.

'Many of the unfortunate creatures composing the

smaller division, which was fired on close to the sea-coast, at some distance from the other column, succeeded in swimming to some reefs of rocks out of the reach of musket shot. The soldiers rested their muskets on the sand, and, to induce the prisoners to return, employed the Egyptian signs of reconciliation, in use in that country. They came back ; but, as they advanced, they were killed, and disappeared among the waves.'

Thus far De Bourrienne. Now let us hear what Napoleon himself says of the matter.[1] ' He spoke about the measures which he had caused to be taken at Jaffa. "After the assault," said he, "it was impossible to restore any kind of discipline until night. The infuriated soldiers rushed into the streets in search of women. You know what kind of people the Turks are. A few of them kept up a fire in the streets. The soldiers, who desired nothing more, whenever a shot was discharged, cried out that they were fired upon from certain houses, which they immediately broke open, and violated all the women they found."

' I replied[2] that Miot . . . positively asserted that he (Napoleon) had caused between three and four thousand Turks to be shot, some days after the capture of Jaffa. Napoleon answered : " It is not true that there were so many. I ordered about a thousand or twelve hundred to be shot, which was done. The reason was, that amongst the garrison of Jaffa, a number of Turkish troops were discovered, whom I had taken a short time before at El-Arish, and sent to Bagdat upon their parole not to serve again, or to be found in arms against me for a year. I had caused them to be escorted twelve leagues on their way to Bagdat, by a division of my army. But those Turks, instead of proceeding to Bagdat, threw themselves into Jaffa, defended it to the last, and cost me a number of brave men to take it, whose lives would have been spared, if the others had not reinforced the garrison of Jaffa. Moreover, before I attacked the town, I sent them a flag

---

[1] *Napoleon in Exile, or a Voice from St. Helena, &c.*, by Barry E. O'Meara. 2 vols., London, 1822. Vol. ii. p. 127.

[2] Ibid., vol. i. p. 329.

of truce. Immediately afterwards we saw the head of the bearer elevated on a pole over the wall. Now, if I had spared them again, and sent them away upon their parole, they would directly have gone to St. Jean d'Acre, where they would have played over again the same scene that they had done at Jaffa. In justice to the lives of my soldiers, as every general ought to consider himself as their father, and them as his children, I could not allow this.

' " To leave as a guard a portion of my army, already small and reduced in number, in consequence of the breach of faith of those wretches, was impossible. Indeed, to have acted otherwise than I did, would probably have caused the destruction of my whole army. I, therefore, availing myself of the rights of war, which authorise the putting to death prisoners taken under such circumstances, independent of the right given to me by having taken the city by assault, and that of retaliation on the Turks, ordered that the prisoners taken at El-Arish, who, in defiance of their capitulation, had been found bearing arms against me, should be selected out and shot. The rest, amounting to a considerable number, were spared. I would," continued he, " do the same thing again to-morrow, and so would Wellington, or any general commanding an army under similar circumstances! " '

Between these two partial accounts there are grave discrepancies—both parties trying, as far as possible, to excuse the deed ; but, if De Bourrienne can be relied on, his account of the cold-blooded massacre must be the true one, for he says, ' I confine myself to those details of this act of dreadful necessity of which I was an eye-witness.'

CHAPTER XV.

THE MASSACRE AT JAFFA (*continued*)—ENGLISH EVIDENCE THEREON—
SIEGE OF ST. JEAN D'ACRE—CAPTURE OF NAPOLEON'S BATTERING
TRAIN—FAILURE OF THE SIEGE, AND RETREAT TO JAFFA.

IT is a singular thing, that, even in the very meagre accounts, of transactions in Egypt no mention of this should have got into the English newspapers ; but I have searched, and can find none. But when, in 1803, this country was in fear of invasion, it was brought up, and used with great effect, in stimulating patriotism. Take, as an instance, one [1] out of the thousands of broadsides which then flooded the country, and we shall find that the fact, although broadly stated, has not been exaggerated.

' On the 7th that town was taken by assault. This affair is on all hands allowed to have been bloody in the extreme ; but a tale has been brought to light, and attested by persons of undoubted credit, so bloody, so diabolical, as to outstrip everything which such an expression is calculated to describe.

' It is asserted that three days after the capture of the town, three thousand eight hundred prisoners were marched to a rising ground, and there massacred by means of musquetry, grape shot, and the bayonet. This fact was first made known in Europe by Sir Sidney Smith, and Mr. Morier, Secretary to Lord Elgin, now a prisoner in Paris ; its history has been minutely given by Colonel Sir Robert Wilson, of Hompesch's hussars, and its truth has been attested by Dr. Wittman, who accompanied the army of the Grand Vizir.'

This Dr. Wittman was the physician to the British Military Mission, which went with that army through Turkey, Syria, and Egypt, and who wrote a narrative of his travels, in which, at p. 128, he says the unfortunates were dragged ' to the sand hills, about a league distant, in the way to Gaza, and there most inhumanly put to death. I have seen *the Skeletons of those unfortunate victims*, which lie scattered over the hills ; a modern Golgotha, which remains a lasting disgrace to a Nation calling itself civilised.'

Sir Robert Wilson says : ' Vollies of musquetry and grape instantly played against them ; and Buonaparte, who had been regarding the scene through a telescope, when he saw the smoke ascending, could not restrain his joy, but broke out into exclamations of approval ; indeed, he had just reason to dread the refusal of his troops thus to dishonour themselves. Kleber had remonstrated in the most strenuous manner, and the officer of the Etat-Major, who commanded (for the general to whom the division belonged was absent),

[1] *History of Buonaparte*, price 6*d*. Printed by Cox, Son, & Baylis, 75 Great Queen Street.

even refused to execute the order without a written instruction ; but Buonaparte was too cautious, and sent Berthier to
enforce obedience. . . . The bones still lie in heaps, and
are shown to every traveller who arrives ; nor can they be
confounded with those who perished in the assault, since
this field of butchery lies a mile from the town.'

Combe, of course, does not forget this incident.

> Another bloody work ensued
> Which the brave Nap with rapture view'd—
> He near four thousand prisoners had,
> The number almost drove him mad ;
> Because so many men to feed,
> Required a deal of food indeed.
> He chid his troops for being so good,
> And said such mercy was of no good.
> Resolv'd to get rid of his burthen,
> (Tho' Kleber ventur'd to demur then,)
> He bade his troops the men surround,
> And march them to a rising ground ;
> The soldiers did as he directed,
> And they by Boney were inspected ;
> It seems our hero was inclin'd
> If *'twas his interest*, to be kind ;
> Now Nap, among these Captives rude,
> An aged Janizary view'd ;
> And, with a contumacious sneer,
> Said he 'Old man, what brought you here !'
> The Janizary, no way frighten'd,
> Although unconscious how it might end,
> Replied 'That question soon I can, Sir,
> By asking you a like one, answer,
> To serve your Sultan, you'll rejoin—
> And the same answer now is mine.'
> This frankness all around delighted,
> And admiration, too, excited.
> Behold—our very hero smiled,
> As if he had been reconciled.
> That smile, some whispered, is a gracious one,
> This guess was not, tho', a sagacious one ;
> The Janizary was not spared,
> His fellow-prisoners' fate he shared ;
> But previously brave Nap withdrew,
> And at a distance had a view ;

The signal given—none dared to stop—
The musquetry went pop—pop—pop.
Nap thro' his spy glass marked the fun,
And cried out ' bravo ' when 'twas done—
His soldiers, who the dead surrounded,
Humanely stabbed and killed the wounded.

Napoleon now turned his attention to the siege of St. Jean d'Acre, where the garrison had the advantage of European aid, besides which, Sir Sydney Smith cruised about the fort, and Napoleon's battering-train, which had been captured, was duly pointed at the besiegers. He was, besides, called off to help Kleber, who was in an awkward situation at Mount Thabor, and had been fighting Achmet Pasha, who had a considerably superior force, from six in the morning till one in the afternoon. Not one moment too soon did Napoleon make his appearance ; but he turned the tide of battle, and the Turks were defeated with the loss of 5,000 or 6,000 men, and all their stores, &c.

Back they went to St. Jean d'Acre, and did their best at the siege ; but it was not to be. Reinforcements were thrown into the town, Napoleon's army grew smaller, provisions got scarcer, the plague was in their midst ; so, sending his sick and wounded to Jaffa, he raised the siege and began to retreat on May 20.

O'Meara tells us Napoleon's version of the causes which led to this.[1] ' " The chief cause of the failure there was that Sir Sydney Smith took all my battering-train, which was on board of several small vessels. Had it not been for that, I would have taken Acre in spite of him. He behaved very bravely, and was well seconded by Phillipeaux, a Frenchman of talent, who had studied with me as an engineer. . . . The acquisition of five or six hundred seamen as cannoniers, was a great advantage to the Turks, whose spirits they revived, and whom they showed how to defend the fortress.

' " But he committed a great fault in making sorties, which cost the lives of two or three hundred brave fellows, without the possibility of success. For it was impossible he could succeed against the number of the French who were

[1] Vol. i. p. 209.

before Acre. I would lay a wager, he lost half of his crew in them. He dispersed proclamations among my troops which certainly shook some of them, and I, in consequence, published an order, stating that he was *mad*, and forbidding all communication with him. Some days after, he sent, by means of a flag of truce, a lieutenant, or a midshipman, with a letter containing a challenge to me, to meet him at some place he pointed out, in order to fight a duel. I laughed at this, and sent him back an intimation that when he brought Marlborough to fight me I would meet him. Notwithstanding this, I like the character of the man." '

The French reached Jaffa on May 24, and found the hospitals full of wounded and those sick of the plague. Compelled still to retreat, it was necessary to remove the sick ; and, to encourage his soldiers in the task, and to show them how little was the risk, Napoleon is said to have handled several of the infected.

CHAPTER XVI.

RETREAT FROM JAFFA—POISONING OF FIVE HUNDRED SOLDIERS—DIF-
FERENT ENGLISH AUTHORITIES THEREON—NAPOLEON'S OWN STORY,
ALSO THOSE OF LAS CASES AND O'MEARA—RETREAT TO CAIRO.

BUT this retreat became the subject of a dreadful accusation against Napoleon, which must have hit him hard
at the time of his projected invasion in 1803—aye, quite as
hard as the massacre at Jaffa. It was nothing less than
that he poisoned, with opium, 500 of his sick soldiers, before
he left Jaffa. There was a solid foundation for this fearful
charge, as will be shown hereafter. Combe speaks of it
thus—

Another great thing Boney now did,
With sick the hospitals were crowded,
He therefore planned, nor planned in vain,
To put the wretches out of pain ;
He an apothecary found—
For a physician, since renown'd,
The butchering task with scorn declined,
Th' apothecary, tho', was *kind*.
It seems that Romeo met with such a one,
This is a mournful theme to touch upon,

Opium was put in pleasant food,
The wretched victims thought it good ;
But, in a few hours, as they say,
About six hundred, breathless lay.

The truth of this has never been accurately established, but I fancy, at that time, there were very few Englishmen who did not thoroughly believe it. Sir Robert Wilson wrote: 'Buonaparte finding that his hospitals at Jaffa were crowded with sick, sent for a physician, whose name should be inscribed in letters of gold, but which, from important reasons, cannot be here inserted ; on his arrival, he entered into a long conversation with him respecting the danger of contagion, concluding at last with the remark, that something must be done to remedy the evil, and that the

POISONING THE SICK AT JAFFA.

destruction of the sick at present in the hospital, was the only measure which could be adopted. The physician, alarmed at the proposal, bold in the confidence of virtue and the cause of humanity, remonstrated vehemently, respecting the cruelty, as well as the atrocity, of such a murder ; but, finding that Buonaparte persevered and menaced, he indignantly left the tent, with this memorable observation : " Neither my principles, nor the character of my profession, will allow me to become a murderer ; and, General, if such qualities as you insinuate are necessary to form a great man, I thank my God that I do not possess them."

'Buonaparte was not to be diverted from his object by moral considerations ; he persevered, and found an apothecary, who (dreading the weight of power, but who since has made an atonement to his mind, by unequivocally confessing the fact) consented to become his agent, and to administer poison to the sick. Opium, at night, was distributed in gratifying food, the wretched, unsuspecting.

victims banqueted, and, in a few hours, five hundred and
eighty soldiers, who had suffered so much for their country,
perished thus miserably by the order of its idol. . . .

'If a doubt should still exist as to the veracity of this
statement, let the Members of the Institute at Cairo be asked
what passed in their sitting after the return of Buonaparte
from Syria; they will relate, that the same virtuous physician,
who refused to become the destroyer of those committed to
his protection, accused Buonaparte of high treason, in the
full assembly, against the honour of France, her children,
and humanity ; that he entered into the full details of the
poisoning of the sick, and the massacre of the garrison,
aggravating these crimes by charging Buonaparte with
strangling, previously, at Rosetta, a number of French and
Copts, who were ill of the plague ; thus proving that this
disposal of his sick was a premeditated plan, which he
wished to introduce into general practice.   In vain Buonaparte attempted to justify himself; the members sat petri-
fied with terror, and almost doubted whether the scene
passing before their eyes was not an illusion.'

Dr. Wittman assures his readers that whilst he was in
Egypt with the army, a man was pointed out to them as
having been the executioner of Napoleon's commands to
poison the sick and wounded French soldiers in the hospitals of Jaffa.

Barre says : ' Although neither Sir Robert Wilson nor
Dr. Wittman mention the name of the worthy physician
who refused with horror, and of the infamous wretch, who
basely consented to become the executioner of the sick
soldiers, it is now well known that the former was the
worthy physician Dr. Desgenettes, and the latter, one
Rouyer, an infamous apothecary, who thus became the
murderer of his own countrymen, in compliance with the
wishes of a Corsican assassin.'

In a little periodical, called ' Ring the Alarum Bell ! '
(which only ran four numbers), published in 1803, is the
following, written by a General Danican : ' In 1801 I met,
at a lazaretto in Sicily, with a number of French Soldiers
just come from Alexandria.   With one of them I contracted habits of intimacy during my stay, and who fre-

quently related to me some curious particulars of the conduct of Buonaparté in Egypt. . . . Having been witness to the poisoning scene at Caiffa he related to me the following anecdote. A grenadier, who had lost two brothers, was amongst the unfortunate wretches slightly affected with the pestilential disease. From what he had previously observed in the hospital, he had become more suspicious than his companions in distress, and he had scarcely taken the *Corsican physic*, than he immediately discharged it, made his way out of the hospital, and escaping the guard, whom he contrived to knock down, he gained the column under the command of Kleber, at whose feet he threw himself, and, in the intercession, almost of despair, conjured him to let him mount one of the camels, describing what he had escaped from, and venting the most energetic maledictions on the *Poisoner in Chief*. The poor wretch, in the most piteous manner, assured General Kleber that he would keep at a distance from the army, so that no one should be in any danger of catching his disorder, except the camel. Kleber granted his request; the grenadier was saved and recovered, and was alive when the English landed under the brave Abercrombie.'

Now let us hear the Emperor's side of the question, beginning with De Bourrienne. 'Orders were given directly to undermine the fortifications and blow them up ; and, on the 27th May, upon the signal being given, the town was in a moment laid bare. An hour afterwards, the General in Chief left his tent and repaired to the town, accompanied by Berthier, some physicians and surgeons, and his usual staff. I was also one of the party. A long and sad deliberation took place on the question, which now arose, relative to the men who were incurably ill of the plague, or were at the point of death. After a discussion of the most serious and conscientious kind, it was decided to accelerate a few moments, by a potion, a death which was inevitable, and which otherwise would be painful and cruel. . . .

'I cannot say that I saw the potion administered. I should state an untruth if I did. I cannot name any person concerned in the matter, without hazarding a

misrepresentation. But I well know that the decision was
come to after that deliberation, which was due to so important a measure ; that the order was given, and that the
infected are dead. What ! shall that which formed the
subject of the whole conversation of the head quarters, on
the day after leaving Jaffa, and was spoken of without any
question of its reality ; which was regarded by us as a
dreadful, but unavoidable, misfortune ; which was never
mentioned in the army but as a fact, of which there was no
doubt, and only the details of which were inquired after—
I appeal to every honourable man who was present, for the
truth of what I state—shall that, I say, be now stigmatized
as a malignant calumny, fabricated to injure the reputation
of a hero, who, were this the only reproach that might be
addressed to him, would go down with little blemish on
his character, to posterity ?'

Las Cases is specially wroth with Sir Robert Wilson,
but even he, cannot successfully whitewash his beloved
emperor. His attempted vindication is too long to be reproduced *in extenso*, but it goes to prove how widely spread
in the army was the belief that the sick were hurried to their
rest at Jaffa. 'A circumstance, which will not a little surprise those who have yet to learn how little credit is due to
public report, and which will serve to show the errors that
may creep into history, is that Marshall Bertrand, who
was himself with the army in Egypt, (though certainly in
a rank which did not enable him to come into immediate
contact with the General in Chief) firmly believed, up to
the period of his residence at Saint Helena, the story of
poison having been administered to sixty invalids. The
report was circulated, and believed, even in our army
therefore, what answer could be given to those who tri-
umphantly asserted, " It is a fact, I assure you, I have it
from officers who served in the French army at the time."
Nevertheless, the whole story is false. I have collected
the following facts from the highest source, from the
mouth of Napoleon himself.

'1st. That the invalids in question who were infected
with the plague, amounted, according to the report made
to the General in Chief, only to *seven* in number.

' 2nd. That it was not the General in Chief, but a professional man, who, at the moment of the crisis, proposed the administering of opium.

' 3rd. That opium was not administered to a single individual.

' 4th. That the·retreat having been effected slowly, a rear-guard was left behind in Jaffa for three days.

' 5th. That on the departure of the rear-guard, the invalids were all dead, except one or two, who must have fallen into the hands of the English.'

But Las Cases, in his zeal, tries to prove too much; for, in a later passage, he says, that since his return to Paris he has had opportunities of conversing with those whose situation and profession naturally rendered them the first actors on the scene, and he finds 'that no order was given for the administering of opium to the sick,' and ' That there was not at the period in question, in the medicine chest of the army, a single grain of opium for the use of the sick.' So he admits that the emperor had the proposition made to him, by a man who must have known he had not the means to carry it out.

Is Barry O'Meara to be trusted? Let us hear what his testimony is (also professedly from the emperor's own lips). ' " Previously to leaving Jaffa," continued Napoleon, " and after the greatest number of the sick and wounded had been embarked, it was reported to me that there were some men in the hospital so dangerously ill, as not to be able to be moved. I ordered, immediately, the chiefs of the medical staff to consult together upon what was best to be done, and to give me their opinion on the subject. Accordingly they met, and found there were seven or eight men so dangerously ill, that they conceived it impossible to recover, and also that they could not exist twenty-four or thirty-six hours longer; that, moreover, being afflicted with the plague, they would spread that complaint amongst all who approached them. Some of them, who were sensible, perceiving they were about to be abandoned, demanded with earnest entreaties, to be put to death. Larrey was of opinion that recovery was impossible, and that those poor fellows could not exist many

G

hours ; but as they might live long enough to be alive when the Turks entered, and experience the dreadful torments which they were accustomed to inflict upon their prisoners, he thought it would be an act of charity to comply with their desires, and accelerate their end by a few hours. Desgenettes did not approve of this, and replied, that his profession was to cure the sick, and not to despatch them.

'"Larrey came to me immediately afterwards, informed me of the circumstances, and of what Desgenettes had said ; adding, that perhaps Desgenettes was right. ' But,' continued Larrey, 'those men cannot live more than a few hours, twenty-four, or thirty-six at most ; and, if you will leave a rear-guard of cavalry to stay and protect them from advanced parties, it will be sufficient.' Accordingly I ordered four or five hundred cavalry to remain behind, and not to quit the place until all were dead. They did remain, and informed me that all had expired before they had left the town ; but I have heard since, that Sydney Smith found one or two alive when he entered it. This is the truth of the business. . . .

'"You have been amongst the Turks, and know what they are ; I ask you now, to place yourself in the situation of one of those sick men, and that you were asked which you would prefer, to be left to suffer the tortures of those miscreants, or to have opium administered to you ?" I replied, "Most undoubtedly I would prefer the latter." "Certainly, so would any man," answered Napoleon ; "if my *own son* (and I believe I love my son as well as any father does his child) were in a similar situation with those men, I would advise it to be done ; and, if so situated myself, I would insist upon it, if I had sense enough, and strength enough to demand it. . . .

'"If I had thought such a measure, as that of giving opium, necessary, I would have called a council of war, have stated the necessity of it, and have published it in the order of the day." He afterwards goes on to say that if he had done so, some of his soldiers would have been sure to have shot him.'

I have gone thus at length into these occurrences at

Jaffa, to show how widely spread was the belief in them, and also to prove that these scandals were not of British origin. Whatever amount of truth there may be in them, readers must judge, as I have laid both sides fairly before them. That there was foundation for them, there can be no doubt—but we know that a tale does not lose in telling.

The return to Cairo, and the battle of Aboukir, are soon dismissed by the satirist, and not chronicled by the caricaturist.

CHAPTER XVII.

THE OLD RÉGIME AND THE REPUBLICANS—THE ' INCROYABLES '—NAPOLEON LEAVES EGYPT—HIS REASONS FOR SO DOING—FEELING OF THE ARMY—ACCUSED OF TAKING WITH HIM THE MILITARY CHEST.

IT is refreshing, and like going among green pastures and cool streams, to leave for a while political caricature, with its ambitions, and its carnage, and find a really funny social skit, aiming at the follies of the times, even if it be only in ridiculing extravagance in dress.

Exceedingly droll is a social caricature by Gillray (August 15, 1799), where a courtly old gentleman of the Court of Louis XVI. bows low, saying, ' Je suis votre très humble serviteur,' whilst the ruffianly French ' gentleman of the Court of Égalité ' replies with a sentence unfit for reproduction. (See next page.)

Littré, in his magnificent dictionary, gives a very terse definition of these ' Incroyables ' : ' s. *m.* Nom donné aux petits-maîtres sous le Directoire, parce qu'on les entendait s'écrier à tout propos : c'est vraiment incroyable ; et, parce que leur costume était tellement exagéré qu'il dépassait la croyance commune.' They were Napoleon's detestation, according to Madame Junot, and she describes them with feminine minuteness. ' They wore grey greatcoats with black collars and green cravats. Their hair, instead of being *à la Titus*, which was the prevailing fashion of the day, was powdered, plaited, and turned up with a comb, while on each side of the face hung two long curls, called dog's ears (*oreilles de chien*). As these young men were

G 2

very frequently attacked, they carried about with them
large sticks, which were not always weapons of defence ;
for the frays which arose in Paris at that time were often
provoked by them.'

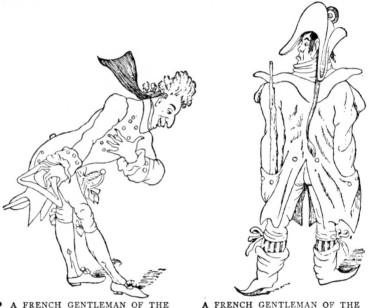

' A FRENCH GENTLEMAN OF THE   A FRENCH GENTLEMAN OF THE
COURT OF LOUIS XVI.   COURT OF ÉGALITÉ.

Pardon must be begged for this digression, and the
matter in hand strictly attended to.

Napoleon left Egypt on August 23, 1799, and reached
France October 8 of that year. The causes for this step
will be detailed a little later on. Meanwhile the caricaturist was watching events on the Continent, and, after his
lights, depicting them. With those not personally affecting Napoleon we have nothing to do ; and of him—Egypt
being a far cry—we have but few, until after his return,
when he was brought prominently before European notice.
Gillray thought he saw his power declining, and on
September 1, 1799, he published 'Allied Powers, Un-
booting Égalité.' In this picture Napoleon is being badly
treated. One foot is on a Dutch cheese, which a Hollander

is plucking away ; a British tar has him fast round the waist, and arms ; whilst a Turk, of most ferocious description, his dress being garnished with human ears, is pulling his nose, and slashing him with his scimitar, St. Jean d'Acre, which is reeking with blood. Prussia, backed up by Russia, is drawing off Italy, which serves as a boot for one leg, and, with it, a large quantity of gold coin.

The causes which induced Napoleon to leave Egypt cannot better be made known, and understood, than by quoting from De Bourrienne, who was an actor in this episode. He says : ' After the battle,[1] which took place on the 25th July, Bonaparte sent a flag of truce on board the English Admiral's ship. Our intercourse was full of politeness, such as might be expected in the communications of the people of two civilised nations. The English Admiral gave the flag of truce some presents, in exchange for some we sent, and, likewise, a copy of the French Gazette of Francfort, dated 10th June, 1799.[2] For ten months we had received no news from France. Bonaparte glanced over this journal with an eagerness which may easily be conceived.

' " Heavens ! " said he to me, " my presentiment is verified : the fools have lost Italy. All the fruits of our victories are gone ! I must leave Egypt ! "

' He sent for Berthier, to whom he communicated the news, adding that things were going on very badly in France —that he wished to return home—that he (Berthier) should go along with him, and that, for the present, only he, Gantheaume, and I, were in the secret. He recommended him to be prudent, not to betray any symptoms of joy, nor to purchase, or sell, anything.

' He concluded by assuring him that he depended on

---

[1] Of Aboukir.

[2] Which probably gave details of the defeats of the French by Suwaroff, who is thus described in the *Vienna Gazette* (according to his portrait by Gillray, May 23, 1799) : ' This extraordinary man is now in the prime of life, six feet ten inches in height, never tastes either wine or spirits, takes but one meal a day, and every morning plunges into an ice bath ; his wardrobe consists of a plain shirt, a white waistcoat and breeches, short boots, and a Russian cloak ; he wears no covering on his head either by day or night ; when tired, he wraps himself up in a blanket, and sleeps in the open air ; he has fought twenty-nine pitched battles, and been in seventy-five engagements.'

him. " I can answer," said he, " for myself and Bourrienne."
Berthier promised to be secret, and he kept his word. He
had had enough of Egypt, and he so ardently longed to
return to France, that there was little reason to fear he
would disappoint himself by any indiscretion.

'Gantheaume arrived, and Bonaparte gave him orders
to fit out the two frigates, the *Muiron* and the *Carrère*,
and the two small vessels, the *Revanche* and the *Fortune*,
with a two months' supply of provisions for from four,
to five, hundred men. He enjoined his secrecy as to the
object of these preparations, and desired him to act with
such circumspection that the English cruisers might have
no knowledge of what was going on. He afterwards
arranged with Gantheaume the course he wished to take.
Nothing escaped his attention.'

Bonaparte concealed his operations with much care ;
but still some vague rumours crept abroad. General
Dugua, the commandant of Cairo, whom he had just left,
for the purpose of embarking, wrote to him on August 18
to the following effect :—

'I have this moment heard, that it is reported at the
Institute, you are about to return for France, taking with
you Monge, Berthollet, Berthier, Lannes, and Murat.
This news has spread like lightning through the city, and
I should not be at all surprised if it produced an unfavour-
able effect, which, however, I hope you will obviate.'

Bonaparte embarked five days after the receipt of
Dugua's letter ; and, as may be supposed, without replying
to it.

On August 18, he wrote to the Divan of Cairo as
follows : ' I set out to-morrow for Menouf, from whence I
intend to make various excursions to the Delta, in order
that I may, myself, witness the acts of oppression which
are committed there, and to acquire some knowledge of
the people.'

He told the army but half the truth : ' The news from
Europe,' said he, 'has determined me to proceed to France.
I leave the command of the army to General Kleber. The
army shall hear from me forthwith. At present I can say
no more. It costs me much pain to quit troops to whom

I am so strongly attached. But my absence will be but temporary, and the general I leave in command has the confidence of the government, as well as mine.'

At night, in the dark, on August 23, he stole on board : and who can wonder if the army expressed some dissatis-faction at his leaving them in the lurch ? From the many works I have consulted, whilst writing this book, I can believe the words of General Danican (who has been before quoted) in ' Ring the Alarum Bell ! '—' Immediately after Buonaparte's midnight flight from Egypt, with the Cash of the army, he was hung in effigy by the Soldiers ; who, in dancing round the spectacle, sang the coarsest couplets (a copy of which I have now in my possession) written for the occasion, to the tune of the *Carmagnole*, beginning : " So, Harlequin has at length deserted us !— never mind my boys, never mind ; he will at last be really hanged ; he promised to make us all rich ; but, instead, he has robbed all the cash himself, and now's gone off : oh ! the scoundrel Harlequin, &c., &c." '

FLIGHT FROM EGYPT.

This charge against Napoleon, of running away with the treasure-chests, is, like almost all the others, of French origin. Hear what Madame Junot says, as it shows the feeling of the French army on this point, that some one had taken them (for Napoleon's benefit) : 'A report was circulated in the army that Junot was carrying away the treasures found in the pyramids by the General in Chief. He could not carry them away himself' (such was the language held to the soldiers), 'and so the man who possesses all his confidence is now taking them to him.' The matter was carried so far that several subalterns, and soldiers, proceeded to the shore, and some of them went on board the merchantman which was to sail with Junot the same evening. They rummaged about, but found nothing ; at length they came to a prodigious chest, which ten men could not move, between decks, " Here is the treasure ! " cried the soldiers ; "here is our pay that has been kept from us above a year; where is the key?" Junot's valet, an honest German, shouted to them in vain, with all his might, that the chest did not belong to his chenerâl. They would not listen to him.

' Unluckily, Junot, who was not to embark till evening, was not then on board. The mutineers seized a hatchet, and began to cut away at the chest, which they would soon have broken up, had not the ship's carpenter come running out of breath. " What the devil are you at ? " cried he, " mad fellows that you are : stop ! don't destroy my chest— here's the key." He opened it immediately, and lo !—the tools of the master carpenter.'

Barre, of course, alludes to this alleged robbery, and Combe writes of his desertion of his troops as follows :—

> Aboukir castle having won,
> Our hero thought it best to run.
> The bravest man will run away,
> When it is dangerous to stay ;
> But, as he to his troops declared,
> By him all dangers should be shared,
> And that on no account he'd leave them,
> 'Twas proper he should now deceive them.
> The cunning he display'd in fight,
> He manifested in his flight.
> On some pretence, it seems, he wrote
> To certain generals a note,
> Acquainting them with what he wanted,
> The time and place, too, he appointed.

These generals, so well they fared,
The *fame* of his desertion shared.
When to th' appointed place they got,
Nap was already on the spot ;
And, what of all things made them glad,
The military chest he had !

BUONAPARTE LEAVING EGYPT.

For an Illustration of the above see the intercepted Letters from the Republican General Kleber to the French Directory respecting the Courage, Honor,
and Patriotism of ——, the Deserter of the Army of Egypt.

He left his army,—but we find
He left these words for them behind :
' This parting grieves me sore, altho' meant
To be for only a short moment.'

This caricature is presumably by Gillray, although it is
not signed by him ; and, as it was published on March 8,
1800, it is absolutely prophetic, for Napoleon is pointing
to a future imperial crown and sceptre. This is especially
curious, as it shows how, even then, the public opinion of
England (of which, of course, the caricaturist was but a
reflex) estimated him.

CHAPTER XVIII.

NAPOLEON'S ARRIVAL IN PARIS—HIS POPULARITY—DISSOLUTION OF THE
COUNCIL OF FIVE HUNDRED—GRAPHIC DESCRIPTION OF THE SCENE
—NAPOLEON, SIÈYES, AND DUCOS NAMED CONSULS.

NAPOLEON arrived in Paris at, for him, a happy moment,
for the Directory was then as good as defunct. There was
a feeling that a strong hand was needed to guide the affairs
of the nation, and Generals Moreau and Jubert had
already been offered the post of First Magistrate of the
Republic, and each had declined the honour. When
Napoleon landed, he was hailed as THE MAN, and his
arrival was telegraphed to Paris, where it created an
immense sensation.

On the day after his arrival, he had an interview with
the Directors, to whom he explained the state of the army
in Egypt, and told them, how, having heard of the disasters
that had befallen their armies, he had returned home to
help them ; but, although he was offered his choice of
commands, he would have none of them, and lived quietly
at Paris. The Council of Five Hundred even gave him a
public dinner [1]—but he was steadily working out the ends
he had in view.

What that was, was evident to the English people, for

[1] In the *Times* of November 15, 1799, we read of this dinner (November
7) that ' Buonaparte gave the toast, " To the union of all Frenchmen." '   The
same paper records that Bonaparte had presented Moreau with a robe
enriched with diamonds, which he brought from Egypt, and was valued at
10,000 livres.   This probably purchased his aid in the *coup d'état* of the
18th Brumaire.

his aim was shown very amusingly in a caricature by an unknown artist (November 1799). Napoleon, who, even then, is represented as crowned, appears as a crocodile, in jackboots and sword, squeezing the life out of two frogs, whilst the dismay of the others is most comically rendered: a body-guard of crocodiles, in military uniform, back up their leader.

On November 9, he was made commandant of the forces in Paris, which prepared him for the explosion of the 18th Brumaire, year 8 (November 10, 1799). The expulsion of the Council is most graphically told in the 'Times' of November 18, eight days after the event, showing how slowly news travelled then. The scene must have been painted by an eye-witness, for it gives the whole previous debate—which at last turned on Napoleon's appointment as commandant. It is so well told, I cannot help giving it in its entirety.

'*Grandmaison.* "We are only offering crossing and contradicting propositions, without coming to any decision: I move that you begin by declaring the appointment of Buonaparte to be unconstitutional."

'"Yes, yes," was resounded from several parts of the Hall.

'L. (*ucien*) Buonaparte quitted the Chair, which he gave up to Chazal, and said, "I entreat the Council calmly to reflect on the commotion that has manifested itself. It may not be needless to represent"—(Here he was interrupted by a loud voice, who said, "Do not attempt to amuse us")—"I propose" (continued Lucien Buonaparte) "that you summon the General who commands to appear before you."

'"We do not acknowledge him," exclaimed several Members.

'"When cool consideration" (observed Buonaparte) "shall have stilled in your breasts the extraordinary emotion which you have testified" (*murmurs*), "you will, perhaps, be sensible of the injustice done General Buonaparte. Whatever may be the event, I now, in your presence, lay down on the altar of the Country, the badge of Magistracy with which the people had invested me."

'On saying these words, he laid down his badge of office on the President's table : upon which the doors of the Hall were opened, and twenty Grenadiers entered. They advanced towards the Bureau, took L. Buonaparte into custody, and, placing him in the midst of them, they conducted him out of the Hall.

'The Council was seized with extreme agitation. Cries, vociferations, and tumultuous confusion, arose from the Members suddenly quitting their places. Not a word could be distinctly heard.

'Grandmaison, Blin, Delbrel, Bigonnet, Sherlock, Crochon, and several other Members, pressed forward towards the tribune.

'Sherlock made an effort to speak, but could scarcely make himself heard among the tumult. "I move," said he, "that you call back your President, whose resignation you have not accepted."

'"He could have done nothing better," exclaimed several Members, "than to have given it in."

'Meantime, at a distance was heard the sound of drums that beat the *pas de charge.* . . . Soon after, for the third time, the doors of the Hall were thrown open ; and a third time the spectators endeavoured precipitately to escape by leaping out of the windows.

'An officer came forwards, followed by a numerous guard, exclaiming with a loud voice, "*General Buonaparte orders the Hall to be cleared.*" Upon which, the troops advanced into the Hall, the further part of which remained occupied by the Deputies, who had not retired. The soldiers suspended their march for a moment, in order to afford time for the Hall to be cleared. About a Dozen of Members, among whom was Blin, remained near the Tribune, or at the Bureau ; one of them who was at the Tribune, exclaimed,

'"What are you, Soldiers? are you anything else than guardians of the National Representation ; and do you dare to menace its safety, to incroach on its independence —is it thus that you tarnish the laurels which your courage has won ? "

'This harangue was coldly listened to by the soldiers,

who advanced into the Hall with drums beating. The Members who stood near the Bureau and the Tribune, were at length obliged to yield their places to the soldiers, who took possession of them. As the latter advanced into the Hall, these members went out at the opposite door. In a few minutes the Hall was completely cleared. It was then five o'clock.

'Several members set out immediately for Paris, others remained at St. Cloud to observe the deliberations of the Council of Elders, and the extraordinary movement of the troops who filled the square of the palace. From time to time were heard the cries of *Vive Buonaparte*! *Vive la République*!

'General Buonaparte, on hearing the Council of Five Hundred had withdrawn, advanced towards the soldiers and harangued them.

'He entreated them to remain calm, and to rest assured that the good cause should triumph. They all answered by shouts of *Vive Buonaparte*!'

The scene depicted in the accompanying illustration is somewhat dramatically told by Napoleon himself in his proclamation of 19th Brumaire: 'I presented myself before the Council of Five Hundred, alone, unarmed, my head uncovered, just as the Ancients had received and applauded me. My object was to re-store to the majority the expression of its will, and to secure to it its power.

DISSOLUTION OF THE COUNCIL OF FIVE HUNDRED.

'The stilettos which had menaced the Deputies, were instantly raised against their deliverer. Twenty assassins rushed upon me, and aimed at my breast. The grenadiers of the legislative body, whom I had left at the door of the hall, ran forward, and placed themselves between me and the assassins. One of these brave grenadiers (Thorne [1]) had his clothes pierced by a stiletto. They bore me off.'

> Th' appointed meeting now took place,
> Producing tumult and disgrace,
> Some of the members, when desired,
> Refused to take the oath required,
> Insisting Nap should not be spared
> But as an outlaw be declared.
> As President Nap's brother sat,
> So Lucien *hemm'd* and *haw'd* at that.
> But so outrageous was the strife,
> He found it hard to save his life ;
> His eloquence he now display'd,
> 'Napoleon must be heard,' he said.
> Then Boney came—in great dismay ;
> Th' Assembly ordered him away—
> But such an order was mere *fudge*,
> The brave Napoleon scorn'd to budge ;
> And several began to push in,
> To tear to pieces Nap and Lucien.
> Nap gave the word—his troops attended,
> By grenadiers he was defended ;
> Tremendous now the hurly-burly,
> Each phiz appear'd confounded surly ;
> They drew their daggers in a rage,
> And civil war began to wage.
> Amidst these violent attacks,
> Now some were thrown upon their backs,
> And others fell upon their faces,
> And others, on their —— proper places ;
> While many, uttering sad groans,
> Were found upon their marrow bones.

Gillray, of course (November 21, 1799), touched on it but not very effectively, his picture 'Exit Liberté à la Française !—or—Buonaparte closing the Farce of Égalité, at Saint Cloud, near Paris, November 10, 1799,' being the weakest caricature of any on this subject. Napoleon is directing his troops, who are charging the Council with fixed bayonets.

The Council met again at night, but simply to do as

---

[1] A gross exaggeration, for he only had his coat torn by a Deputy who had sufficient courage to collar him.

they were bid. Thorne, the grenadier with the torn coat, was decreed to have deserved well of his country, as were also Napoleon, Lefebvre, Murat, Berthier, and many others. Sixty-one members of the Council were expelled, and Article two of the Resolution, passed that night, says,—

'The Legislative Body creates provisionally an Executive Consular Committee, composed of Citizens Syeyes and Roger Ducos, Ex-Directors, and Buonaparte, General. They shall bear the name of Consuls of the French Republic.'

CHAPTER XIX.

NAPOLEON TAKES THE LEAD—SIÈYES AND DUCOS ARE DEPOSED—CAM-
BACÉRÈS AND LEBRUN NAMED SECOND AND THIRD CONSULS—
NAPOLEON'S LETTER TO GEORGE THE THIRD—REPLY TO SAME.

NAPOLEON had now got his foot fairly on the ladder, but it was he alone who was to mount it. At the first meeting of the Consuls, Sièyes asked, ' Which of us is to preside ? ' Ducos had grasped the position, and replied, ' Do you not see that the General presides ? '

There is a caricature by Cawse (November 30, 1799) of ' Satan's return from ~~Egypt~~ Earth. Discovered in Council with Belzebub and Belial—a Sketch after Fuseli [1] ! ! ! ' Here Napoleon forms the centre figure, one foot resting on a skull, the other on the Marseillaise hymn and the Council of Five Hundred. Behind him is a glory, with a trinity formed of three daggers—Sièyes, Ducos, and Buonaparte. Devils surround him, and, at his feet, is a howling French mob.

> Our hero, now, the people guided,
> And a new government provided.
> First Consul, *modestly* he claim'd,
> Two others were Sub-Consuls named ;
> But these were not in Boney's way,
> For the first Consul had full sway.
> And now these Consuls took an oath,
> For Nap to swear was never loth.
> Thus elevated, Josephine
> Imagin'd she would be a queen ;

[1] This was one of Fuseli's celebrated 'Milton Gallery,' a series of 47 pictures, produced between the years 1790 and 1800.

But she by Nap was harshly told,
That six and forty was too old ;
His mother, who the lady hated,
Advised him to be separated ;
By her persuasions, Nap, of course
Began to think of a divorce.
He ponder'd ev'ry afternoon,
And rubbing once his forehead, soon
The lady's banishment decreed,
Because—their tempers disagreed.
In fact, her faults he recollected,
And her caresses now rejected.
But, as 'twill not improve our morals,
We'll pass these matrimonial quarrels.
    As Nap a love of pow'r betray'd,
He great munificence display'd ;
For he rewarded with donations,
His friends, especially relations.
He to his mother acted handsome,
As he bestowed on her a grand sum ;
For Joe, and Lucien, he provided,
Who, at this time, in France resided—
How suddenly success awaits men !
Both Joe, and Lucien, he made Statesmen.

It was not probable that Napoleon would rest con-tented with the provisional position he occupied. A fresh government had to be constituted, of which he must be the head : and so the Constitution of December 13 was manu-factured, and afterwards passed into law. Article 23 provided, ' The sittings of the Senate are not to be public.' Article 24, ' The Citizens Sièyes, and Roger Ducos, the Consuls quitting their functions, are appointed members of the Conservative Senate. They shall assemble along with the second and third Consuls nominated by the present Constitution. These four Citizens shall appoint the Majority of the Senate, which shall then complete itself, and proceed to the elections entrusted to it.'

Article 39. ' The Government is entrusted to three Consuls appointed for ten years, and indefinitely re-eligible. Each of them is to be elected individually with the distinct quality of Chief, Second, or Third Consul. The first time the Third Consul shall only be named for five years. For the present time General Bonaparte is appointed Chief Consul, Citizen Cambaceres, now Minister of Justice, Second Consul, and Citizen Lebrun, Member of the Committee of Antients, Third Consul.' Article 41. ' The Chief Consul is to promulgate the laws : he is to name and revoke at pleasure the Members of the Council of State; the Ministers, Ambassadors, and other principal foreign agents, the officers of the army by land and sea, the members of local administration and the Commissioners of the Government

CAMBACERES, LE-BRUN. BUONAPARTE.

at the Tribunals. He is to appoint all Judges, Criminal and Civil, as well as Justices of the Peace, and the Judges of Cassation, without the power of afterwards revoking them.' Article 43. ' The salary of the Chief Consul shall be 500,000 francs for the 8th year' (ending September 22, 1800). ' The salary of the other two Consuls shall be equal to three-tenths of that of the first.' So that we see Napoleon fully knew how to take care of himself.

On January 1, 1800, Gillray published ' The French

H

Triumvirate settling the New Constitution'—and mighty wise they look. (See preceding page.)

In the year 1799, Consols ranged from 55 in January to 62¼, the closing price in December. Bread, however, was dear, the average of the quartern loaf being 13*d.*

It was in the latter part of this year that Napoleon notified to George the Third his elevation to the dignity of First Consul, and appropriately chose Christmas Day on which to date his letter, which breathed (sincerely or not) ' Peace on earth, goodwill towards men.'

Bonaparte, First Consul of the Republic, to His Majesty the King of Great Britain and Ireland.

Paris 5 Nivôse year VIII. of the Republic.

Called by the wishes of the French Nation to occupy the first magistracy of the French Republic, I deem it desirable, in entering on its functions, to make a direct communication to your Majesty.

Must The War, which for four years, has ravaged every part of the world, be eternal? Are there no means of coming to an understanding?

How can the two most enlightened nations of Europe, more powerful and stronger than is necessary for their safety and independence, sacrifice to the idea of a vain grandeur, the benefits of commerce, of internal prosperity, and domestic happiness? How is it they do not feel that peace is as glorious as necessary?

These sentiments cannot be strangers to the heart of your Majesty, who rules over a free nation, with no other view than to render them happy.

Your Majesty will only see in this overture my sincere desire to effectually contribute to a general pacification, by a prompt step, free and untrammeled by those forms, which, necessary, perhaps, to disguise the apprehensions of feeble states, only prove in the case of strong ones, the mutual desire to deceive.

France and England, by abusing their strength, may for a long time yet, to the misery of all other nations, defer the moment of their absolute exhaustion ; but I will venture to say that the fate of all civilised nations, depends on the end of a war which envelopes the whole world.

signed BONAPARTE.

The British Government did not quite see it, but considered that the claws of the French eagle required yet more cutting. They had been partially operated on at the Nile, and at Acre. Italy was no longer under French rule. Suwarrow's victories had severely crippled the French, who were, besides, very weak financially. Add to this, that there were 140,000 Austrians gathering along the Rhine. But still it was judged they were yet too sharp for the peace of Europe.

> The answer from the English Court,
> Vex'd Nap, according to report :
> 'Twas to the Minister address'd,
> It being candidly confess'd
> That there appear'd not the least cause
> To break through ceremonial laws ;
> In this his Majesty agreed,
> Peace was desirable indeed,
> If that his Majesty were able
> T' obtain one permanent and stable ;
> But that at present there was poor hope
> For England, and indeed for Europe,
> Till France her lawful princes own'd
> The Bourbons—whom she had dethron'd.

This, really, was the tenor of Lord Grenville's reply, dated January 4, 1800, which is far too long, and uninteresting, to reproduce.

Gillray caricatured this letter of Napoleon's (February 24, 1800) in ' *The Apples and the Horse dung, or Buonaparte among the Golden Pippins* ; from an old Fable. Explanation. — Some horse dung being washed by the current from a neighbouring dunghill, espied a number of fair apples swimming up the stream, when, wishing to be thought of consequence, the horse dung would every moment be bawling out, " Lack-a-day, how we apples swim ! " *See* Buonaparte's " Letter to his Majesty," and Mr. Whitbread's " Remarks upon the Correspondence between Crowned Heads." ' Although Gillray did not choose a very savoury subject to illustrate his caricature, yet there is much humour in it.

CHAPTER XX.

BATTLE OF MARENGO—DEATH OF DESAIX—SAID TO HAVE BEEN ASSAS-
SINATED—NAPOLEON'S LOVE FOR HIM—SOUP KITCHENS AT PARIS—
LAVISH EXPENDITURE OF NAPOLEON'S GENERALS.

THERE was very little caricature of Napoleon in the year
1800, for the best of reasons, that we had very little to do
with him, as he was occupied till May in settling his
Government, and then he left for his Italian campaign.
But in this year (May 12) Gillray issued a series of eight
plates, 'Democracy, or
a Sketch of the life of
Buonaparte,' of which
I have already given
three — 'Democratic
Innocence,' 'Demo-
cratic Humility,' and
'Democratic Religion.'
As four are not very
interesting, I have not
given them, only the
last of the series, which,
evidently, was meant
to be extended.

DEMOCRATIC CONSOLATIONS.

Buonaparte on his Couch surrounded by the
Ghosts of the Murder'd—the dangers which
threaten his Usurpation, and all the Horrors
of Final Retribution.

Combe, even, had
very little to say of
this time, lightly touch-
ing the passage of the Alps, the occupation of Milan and
Pavia, the defeat of the Austrians at Montebello, and the
battle of Marengo, where he makes an assertion I cannot
find elsewhere, nor trace to any French source, except De
Bourrienne.

> Soon after this the gallant fellow
> The Austrians drove from Montebello,
> And then did he, with all his men go,
> To aid the battle of Marengo ;
> Here was indeed a bold resistance,
> Brave Boney saw it at a distance :
> And at this time, it is not doubted,
> Nap's army was completely routed ;

Indeed, it grieves the muse to say,
Our hero cried, and ran away ;
But brave Desaix, who was not idle,
His horse soon grappled by the bridle,
And turning round the Consul's phiz,
He said, while anger ruffled his,
' Citizen Consul, look before ye—
That is the road to fame and glory.
Nap bit his lip, and swore by heaven,
Th' offence was not to be forgiven ;
Indeed, as many understand,
That hour the Gen'ral's fall he plann'd.
By Victor and Desaix defeated,
The Austrians in their turn retreated.
This Victor, who destruction hurl'd
Made always a great noise in the world,
For he had been a drummer, so
The way to *beat* he'd cause to know.
But, while victorious, now we find
Desaix received a shot behind,
His Aid-du-camp was bribed to do it,
And well, too, the First Consul knew it ;

Besides the shot, a base attack !
He got a stab, too, in the back ;
He fell, and instantly expir'd—
His death by Boney was desired :
Yet when they told him he was dead,
' Why can't I weep ? ' he faintly said.

This scandalous accusation is too contemptible to be thought true for a moment; but I must reproduce it, to show what was said of Napoleon in England. Yet, in a portion of it, there is a small substratum of truth. Hear what De Bourrienne says: 'The death of Desaix was not perceived at the moment it took place. He fell without saying a word, at a little distance from Lefebvre-Desnouettes. A battalion-sergeant of the ninth brigade of light infantry, commanded by Barrois, seeing him extended on the ground, asked permission to pick up his cap. It was found to be perforated behind; and this circumstance leaves it doubtful whether Desaix was killed by some unlucky inadvertency while advancing at the head of his troops, or by the enemy when turning towards his men to encourage them.'

Other accounts speak of his being shot in the breast.

How Napoleon loved Desaix, is best told by them who knew him well, and let them bear witness against this gross calumny. De Bourrienne says: 'After supper, the First Consul dictated to me the bulletin of the battle. When we were alone, I said to him, " General, here's a fine victory. You recollect what you said the other day, about the pleasure with which you would return to France after striking a grand blow in Italy : surely you must be satisfied now ? "—" Yes, Bourrienne, I am satisfied. But Desaix ! . . . Ah, what a triumph would this have been if I could have embraced him to-night on the field of battle ! " As he uttered these words, I saw that Bonaparte was on the point of shedding tears, so sincere and profound was his grief for the death of Desaix. He certainly never loved, esteemed or regretted, any man so much.'

O'Meara writes : ' Asked him if it were true that Desaix had, a little before his death, sent a message of the following purport to him : " Tell the First Consul that I regret dying before I have done sufficient to make my name known to posterity." Napoleon replied, " it was true," and accompanied it with some warm eulogiums on Desaix.'

As a matter of fact Napoleon could not sufficiently honour the memory of his comrade, so highly did he esti- mate him. He spoke, in his bulletins, of the irreparable loss his death caused him ; he took for his own aides-de-camp, Rapp, and Savary, who had acted in this capacity to Desaix. A medal was struck in his honour, his statue should have been erected on the Place des Victoires, solemn ceremonies were ordered, masses were said, and a monument was raised, by subscription, on the Place Dauphine, Paris.

It is amusing to read in the newspapers of the day (with the exception of the ' Times ') the spiteful things said against Napoleon. But Cobbett, in the ' Porcupine,' outdoes them all, and spits his venom on the most harmless deeds. ' The late establishment of Soup shops in Paris, naturally excites some curious ideas. Madame Bonaparte, their patroness, who is also a sprig of nobility, seems in no small degree attached to the ancient regimen ; hence probably her wish to revive soup meagre, frogs, &c. Nor is it less remarkable that the French should wish to establish soup shops, just at the time when they were falling into disuse in this country.' [1] ' The *Morning Post* tells us that " the Chief Consul has taken a thousand sub-scription tickets for the *soup establishments* at Paris." This is at once a proof of that *plenty* which we have been told exists in France, and of the Charity of the Chief Consul. If ever there was a country more degraded than all others, it is France. Should there be, amongst the people of that country, one man left, who entertains antient notions, what must be his mortification and shame to see his countrymen not only ruled, but actually fed like paupers, by a low bred upstart from the contemptible island of Corsica ! And this, ye gods ! is the *Grand Nation* ! This is the nation who is to change the public law of Europe ! This is the nation to whom Britons are requested to bow down their heads ! To return to the " *soup establishments*," we should be glad to know how the Corsican came by the money to purchase a thousand tickets. Was it part of the dower which Barras gave him with his bride ? We rather think he wrung it from the hands of the sovereign people. What a base, what a despicable, race of slaves ! They submit to assessments, forced loans, requisitions, and con-

[1] No. 8, Nov. 7, 1800.

fiscations ; they see their treasure seized on by millions
upon millions, and they applaud the " *charity* and *generosity* "
of the plunderer in chief, because he bestows on them the
fractions in soup maigre ! ' [1]

Cobbett did not write with ink, but with gall, and was
not at all particular as to the veracity of his statements.
Take the following examples : [2] ' *Lucien Buonaparte* is
holden in detestation in France.   His office, as Minister of
the Interior, gives him the command of very large sums,
which he wastes in every kind of dissipation, and in the
most scandalous manner, in order, forsooth ! to support his
rank as a *Prince of the Blood* ! ! ! He is protected by
the whole power of his brother, whose *vanity*, the leading
foible in his character, leads him to confer on the members
of his family, all the advantages and prerogatives of
Sovereign princes.   This conduct has rendered him the
object of incessant ridicule, and considerably diminished
his popularity.

' Another species of evil peculiar to a corrupt military
government, prevails in a very great degree, and has
become particularly offensive to the French, viz. the influence and insolence of generals.

' All the generals attached to Buonaparte, those who
supported him in his usurpation, and those who were with
him in Egypt, bear an exact resemblance to the minions
and favourites of the Roman Emperors.   These men have
the public treasure almost entirely at their disposal.
General Lasnes, one of the Consul's chief friends, spends
the enormous sum of *five hundred thousand livres* (upwards
of twenty thousand guineas ! ! !) a month, at Paris, where
he and his aids de camp occupy one of the most magnificent *hotels* in that capital.   Buonaparte, not being able to
supply his favourites with sufficient specie for defraying
their unbounded expences, grants them *congées d'exportation*, i.e. an exclusive permission to export various articles
the exportation of which is prohibited by law ; these *congées* are sold to mercantile men, who purchase them at a
very high price.'

' To the facts, which we stated on Monday, respecting

---

[1] The *Porcupine*, No. 13, Nov. 13.   [2] *Ibid.* No. 28, Dec. 1.

the prodigality of Buonaparte and his creatures, we may add the instance of General Ney. This Republican Bashaw has fixed his head-quarters at Neubourg, at the expence of which place, his table is furnished at the rate of *ninety pounds sterling a day!* The French have a proverb, the truth of which they and their neighbours now experience to their sorrow : "Il vaut mieux qu'une cité soit brûlée, q'un parvenu la gouverne"—A city had better be burnt to ashes, than submit to the rule of an upstart vagabond.'[1]

CHAPTER XXI.

PLOTS AGAINST NAPOLEON'S LIFE—THAT OF OCTOBER 10, 1800—THAT
OF DECEMBER 24, 1800—NUMBER OF PEOPLE KILLED AND INJURED
—NAPOLEON'S PORTRAIT.

THE two plots against Napoleon's life which occurred in this year must not be forgotten. Let us have Combe's version, which does not much exaggerate the facts of the cases :—

It seems the Jacobins against
Our hero greatly were incensed :
His levées, drawing-rooms, and so forth,
They look'd upon as deeds of no worth ;
The pageantry he held so dear,
Did not Republican appear ;
And, at such goings on distrest,
Their indignation they exprest ;
Our hero consequently saw
The need of keeping them in awe ;
So he contrived a plot, which seems
The masterpiece of all his schemes ;
And in this plot, too, he resolved
His greatest foes should be involved.
Fouché pretended, on th' occasion,
(For Nap allow'd of no evasion)
That some conspirators had got
Daggers and pistols, and what not,
To make the Conqueror their aim,
When from the Opera he came.
Nap to the Opera went indeed,
One gave the signal, as agreed ;

[1] The *Porcupine*, No. 30, Dec. 3, 1800.

Three men were instantly arrested,
Three whom great Bonaparte detested.
They got it seems a dagger from one,
But carrying daggers now was common ;
He was from Nap at a great distance,
This proof, tho', was of no assistance ;
When the supposed assassination
Had undergone examination,
They seiz'd on others, as directed,
For having such a scheme projected ;
One prov'd at home that night he slept,
For being ill, his bed he kept ;
All this, however, had no weight,
For Nap's resentment was too great.
They suffered by the guillotine,
Which was his favourite machine ;
Save one, th' Italian too, I wot,
From whom the dagger had been got,
Nap banish'd him, and with him too,
Th' Italian patriotic crew ;
Four thousand, as historians say,
For no offence were swept away.

The first plot was that of October 10, 1800, and it has, certainly, somewhat of a police 'get up' about it. The First Consul knew all about it through an ex *chef de bataillon* named Harrel, who used to come every night to De Bourrienne, and tell him what the so-called conspirators had done. He supplied Harrel, at Napoleon's request, with money, &c. Napoleon was never in any danger, and four men perished by the guillotine.

Barre says : ' Still the persons designed, and arrested, on the very spot of the premeditated murder, were strictly searched about their proper persons, and neighbouring places, and not an arm, nor even a pin, was found. With what, then, could those pretended conspirators commit a murder, since, at the very moment, and on the very spot where it was to have been perpetrated, no kind of arms were found about them ?

'That such was the case, it was asserted, and never denied, in the course of the trial.

'The only witness was one Harel, an acknowledged spy of the police, holding the rank of Captain.

'And on the single evidence of a spy, devoted to, and paid by, the police, four men (Arena, Ceracchi, Demerville, and Topino-Lebrun,) were condemned to death. . . .

'Those unfortunate men having appealed from such iniquitous judgment, as grounded on many erroneous statements, and irregular proceedings, the court of appeals divided, when it was found that eight judges were for repealing, and eight for confirming, the judgment.

'The division being equal, five more judges were added to the sixteen, when the iniquitous judgment was confirmed.'

The other attempt upon Napoleon's life was genuine enough. On December 24, 1800, Haydn's Oratorio of the 'Creation' was to be performed at the Opera. He was sleepy, and disinclined to go, but was overpersuaded, and went. Luckily his coachman was drunk, and drove faster than usual. In the Rue St. Nicaise there was a loud explosion, two or three seconds after he had passed the place where it had occurred.

A barrel of gunpowder, surrounded by grapeshot, and pieces of iron, was fixed in a cart, and fired when Napoleon passed. He escaped, but twenty people were killed, and fifty-three wounded, including St. Regent who fired the train. The coachman was so drunk that he drove on, thinking it was only a salute that had been fired. There are several, and contradictory, versions of this event, but this seems to be the most authentic—

> For this conspiracy ideal
> Was soon succeeded by one real.
> While the First Consul, with delight,
> Was going to the play one night ;
> His carriage pass'd a narrow way,
> Where an infernal barrel lay—
> This barrel of a sudden blew up,
> And the combustibles all flew up.
> With great dismay was Boney filled,
> No wonder—some were hurt and kill'd ;
> The windows of the carriage broke,
> And most tremendous was the smoke :
> The coachman luckily enough,
> Had taken plenty of strong stuff ;

And, not regarding any evil,
Drove thro' the passage like a devil ;
His whip applied when there was need,
And saved his master by his speed.
Had coachee been of drink no lover,
With Nap it would have been all over.
The Jacobins (for, as related,
This party the brave Consul hated,)
Were mark'd for this assassination,
And many suffered transportation.
Indeed our hero firmly swore,
(As he had often done before,
For he would swear thro' thick and thin),
The British had a hand therein—
It seems the gentleman forgot
John Bull disdains a wicked plot.

Cobbett, of course, improves the occasion.[1] 'Miserable
slaves ! For an instance of base flattery, surpassing anything we have hitherto seen, take the following from the
Chef du Cabinet : " The explosion of the infernal machine
broke *twenty-nine* pictures, out of *thirty*, which ornamented
an apartment in the street of St. Thomas. The single
picture which escaped, was that of the Chief Consul. One
would be ready to affirm (mark this) *that the same God,
who watches over the life of the first Consul, protected even his
likeness*" ! ! ! What Emperor was it that talked of making
his horse a Consul? An English blood horse would be
disgraced by becoming the successor of Buonaparte.'

And again :[2] 'Buonaparte's embracing the Parisian
addressers, puts us in mind of the good old ceremony of
the *thief's kissing the hangman*.'

CHAPTER XXII.

GENERAL FAST—ADULTERATION, AND COMPULSORY SALE OF STALE BREAD
—WAR IN EGYPT—THE BOULOGNE FLOTILLA—NEGOTIATIONS FOR
PEACE—RATIFICATION OF PRELIMINARIES—RECEPTION IN ENGLAND
—GENERAL REJOICINGS.

IT is sad to take up the very first number of the ' London
Gazette ' for 1801, and find ' A Proclamation for a general
Fast,' which was to be held on February 13, the reason

[1] The *Porcupine*, No. 60, Jan. 7, 1801.   [2] *Ibid.* No. 61, Jan. 8, 1801.

wherefore is stated thus: 'WE, taking into Our most serious consideration the heavy Judgments with which Almighty God is pleased to visit the Iniquities of this land, by a grievous Scarcity and Dearth of divers Articles of Sustenance, and Necessaries of Life &c.'

The war bore grievously on the Commons, and, consequently, Napoleon was in like measure abhorred. Nothing short of the thought of approaching famine could have caused Parliament to pass, and the king give his royal assent to,[1] 'An Act to prevent until the Sixth Day of November, One Thousand Eight Hundred and One, and from thence to the End of Six Weeks from the Commencement of the then next Session of Parliament, the manufacturing of any fine Flour from Wheat, or other Grain, and the making of any Bread solely from the fine Flour of Wheat; and to repeal an Act, passed in the Thirty-Sixth Year of the Reign of His present Majesty, for permitting Bakers to make and sell certain Sorts of Bread, and to make more effectual Provision for the same.' This took effect on January 31, 1801.

'An Act to prohibit, until the First Day of October, One thousand eight hundred and one, and from thence to the End of Six Weeks next after the then next Session of Parliament, any Person or Persons from selling any Bread which shall not have been baked Twenty-four Hours.' This Act was 41 Geo. III. cap. 17, and it recites the reason in the preamble: 'Whereas it is expedient to reduce as much as possible, at the present moment, the consumption of Wheat flour. And whereas it appears a considerable saving would arise if Bread was prohibited from being sold until it had been baked a certain time, &c.' The penalties of non-compliance ranging from 5s. to 40s.

Here is a receipt given for adulterated bread: 'Improvement of bread, with economy of flour, and saving of expense:—Take one pound of ground rice, put it in cold water sufficient to cover it, and something more, boil it, and it will absorb all the water, and weigh four pounds; mix four pounds of flour with it, knead them well together.

[1] Dec. 31, 1800.

and lighten them with yeast, like common bread, and they will produce ten pounds ten ounces of excellent bread, which will not cost more than twopence halfpenny per pound, and will save one half in the consumption of flour. N.B. this bread will keep moist a week.'

When we remember that bad bread was on January 1, 1801, 1*s*. 9¼*d*. per quartern loaf, on March 5, 1*s*. 10½*d*., and although it dropped after harvest as low as 10¼*d*., yet closed December 31 at 1*s*. 0¼*d*., and that this bad bread had to be eaten stale, all through Boney, we cannot wonder that the people did not love him. His direct presence was brought home to all and every one daily, by means of that most susceptible bodily organ, the stomach. It was hitting John Bull in a very vulnerable part.

The war in Egypt still kept on, and in February re- inforcements of 15,330 men, under the command of Sir Ralph Abercrombie, set sail in a fleet of 175 vessels or ships. In March they defeated the French under Menou, the rene- gade, but at the cost of the life of the brave Abercrombie.

On April 19, Rosetta surrendered to our forces, and on June 27 Cairo capitulated, on condition that General Belliard, with all his troops, arms, and baggage, should be taken back to France. On their march back to the coast, Menou, finding his cause hopeless, surrendered on the same terms, and thus ended the French oecupation of Egypt.

With Napoleon's concordat with the Pope we have nothing to do, except that his satirists here did not forget to contrast his attendance at the solemn *Te Deum* at Notre Dame with his pseudo-Mahometanism in Egypt. What more affected us, was the arming along the Channel coast, and the Flotilla at Boulogne, which was to act as transport for the army for the invasion of England. The French themselves laughed at these little cockle-shells of boats, *teste* Madame Junot:—

' Boulogne was designated from the year 1801, as the chief station of the enterprise against England. The greatest activity suddenly prevailed in all ports of the Channel ; camps were formed on the coast, divisions of light vessels were organised, and multitudes were built. The

Flotilla, as it was called, created apparently with the greatest exertion, and all the apparatus of preparation, spread, as was intended, alarm on the opposite shore. The Boulogne Flotilla was composed of extremely light boats, so small, that at Paris, where everything forms the subject of a jest, they were called walnut shells. Brunet, who at this time was a truly comic actor, performing in some piece which I do not remember, was eating walnuts, the shells of which, after a little preparation, he launched upon some water in a tub by his side. " What are you doing ? " said his fellow actor. " Making des péniches," replied Brunet. This was the name by which the flat-bottomed boats of the flotilla were known at Paris. But poor Brunet was made to atone by twenty-four hours' imprisonment for his unseasonble joke on the Government ; and the day after his release the same piece was performed. When Brunet should have made the interdicted reply, he was silent. The other actor repeated the inquiry as to what he was doing. Still Brunet made no answer, and the other with an air of impatience proceeded : " Perhaps you do not know what you are about ? " " Oh yes ! " said Brunet, " I know very well what I am about, but I know better than to tell." The laugh was general, and so were the applauses ; and, in truth, nothing could be more droll than the manner in which this was uttered ; Brunet's countenance in saying it was of itself sufficient to provoke universal hilarity.'

But, in very truth, John Bull was not much frightened : there was Nelson, and his fleet, and people had great faith in them. But Nelson could do little against this passive fleet. On August 3 he bombarded Boulogne, sunk five gun-boats, and damaged others ; and on the 15th of the same month he tried to capture, or destroy, these gun-boats, but was unsuccessful in his attempt, as the French had chained them to the shore.

We now come to the principal event of the year, the Peace—over which there was much coquetting. As early as March, Lord Hawkesbury, the then Secretary of State for Foreign Affairs, addressed a letter to M. Otto, signifying King George's desire to enter into negotiations for the restoration of peace.

These negotiations for peace were naturally noticed, and one very good etching, by Roberts, 'Negotiation See Saw,' shows Napoleon and John Bull engaged in that pastime seated on a plank ' Peace or War.' Bonaparte says, 'There Johnny, now I'm down, and you are up—then I go up and you go down Johnny—so we go on.' John Bull does not enjoy the situation so much, but grumbles, ' I wish you would settle it one way or other, for if you keep bumping me up and down in this manner I shall be ruined in Diachilem Plaster.'

A somewhat elaborate etching, also by Roberts (no date, 1801), depicts ' John Bull's Prayer to Peace, or the flight of Discord.' He is on his knees praying the following to Peace : ' Sublime Descendant of Happiness, incline thine ear to the Petition of thy poor Patient, worn out oppressed I. Bull, who humbly prayeth thee that thou would'st in the first place exert thy influence, and be the means of restoring to me again those lost Liberties and Privileges I have been so basely rob'd of, and that you would'st be pleased also to put a speedy stop to cruel monopolizing, and e'er it be long, send me thy attendant Plenty, to comfort me and my long suffering numerous Family, and may that horrid Demon Discord never return again.' Peace, whom the eye of Providence watches over, replies : ' Thy Prayer shall be fulfill'd, Plenty awaits thee with all her blessings, her pace is slow but sure.' Bonaparte and Pitt, who is represented as covered with serpents, are retreating.

On October 1, preliminary articles of peace with France were signed at Lord Hawkesbury's office at Downing Street, by his Lordship, and M. Otto on the part of the French Government, and great were the rejoicings at the event, although not so great as they might have been. The ' Times ' of October 3 says : ' The public were so impatient to express their feelings on the occasion of the News of the Preliminaries of Peace being signed, that almost all the public streets were illuminated last night. This was evidently not the wish of the Government, who have deferred a general illumination until the ratification of them comes back from France. Accordingly, none of the Public

Offices were illuminated, nor either of the Theatres. The ratification of the Preliminaries is expected from Paris on Tuesday next.'

No wonder 'the public were so impatient to express their feelings,' their joy must have been so great. Long-suffering, they had borne the burden and heat of a long war, cheerfully too, and gladly must they have welcomed its conclusion.

In Paris the joy was the same. The 'Times,' October 10, says : 'The Intelligence . . . was announced to the inhabitants of Paris by discharges of Artillery, and was proclaimed by torch light throughout the streets. At night there was a general illumination. Never was joy more fervently expressed.'

One of the most practical tests of renewed confidence was the great variation of 3 per cent. Consols –in September $58\frac{1}{4}$; in October $69\frac{1}{2}$.

On October 10 came the preliminaries, ratified. Let us see the 'Times'' account :—'London October 12th. On Saturday morning, at ten o'clock, General Daurostan,[1] *Chef de Brigade* in the Artillery, and Aide de Camp to General Bonaparte, arrived at M. Otto's house in Hereford Street, with the ratification of the French Government of the Preliminaries of Peace signed on the 1st inst. between Lord Hawkesbury and M. Otto in Downing Street.

'The Preliminaries were ratified in Paris on the 5th ; but General Daurostan was not dispatched till Wednesday evening, in order to give time for a magnificent gold box to be made, in which the ratification was enclosed to Lord Hawkesbury. The General was also delayed by his carriage breaking down upon the road.

'After breakfasting at M. Otto's, the General, accompanied by the Minister, and Mr. St. John (Mrs. Otto's brother), proceeded to *Reddish's* Hotel, in St. James's Street, where he dressed, and afterwards went to Downing Street. On their way thither, the populace took the horses from the carriage, and drew it through the principal streets. As soon as the Ratifications had been exchanged, Lord Hawkesbury sent a letter to the Lord Mayor. . . .

[1] Lauriston.

I

General Daurostan cannot fail to communicate to his Court the very flattering manner in which he had been received in London. His carriage having been drawn to St. James's Street, he alighted and came forward to the window, and bowed to the populace. On his way to Downing Street, they drew his carriage through the Park. Lord St. Vincent happening to be at the garden-gate of the Admiralty, the mob gave the gallant Admiral three hearty cheers, who, in return, recommended them to take care of the strangers, and not to overturn the carriage. . . . It is understood that there will be another illumination this evening. The Bank and Post Office have given notice of their intending to do so.'

Cobbett foamed at the mouth over this Peace, and his utterances are so caustic as to be well worth reproduction.[1] 'We request our readers to observe, that henceforth we shall be very particular in what we say about the most illustrious Sovereign Consul Buonaparte. Oh ! how we shall extol him ! We shall endeavour to give our readers the earliest information, when he rises, breakfasts, dines, sups, and spits. With all reverence, we shall treat of his lovely, chaste, and bonny Queen—thus by way of a touch :

' It is with superlative pleasure we inform our readers, that the last news from France represents the health of the First Consul to be improving. This glory of the world, is returned to his country palace at Malmaison.'

But it was after October 10, when the Ratification had arrived, that Cobbett's wrath boiled over, and he appears at his finest. In the number for October 12, he gives vent to his impassioned feelings in words like these :[2] 'On Saturday last, such a scene was exhibited in this metropolis, as we never expected to have lived to witness, and having witnessed it, we care not how soon we resign our existence ! . . . a vile degraded rabble, miscalled Britons, took the horses out of the carriage which contained the two French Citizens, Otto and Lauriston—the latter of whom they mistook for the brother of Buonaparte—and dragged it from Oxford Street to Downing Street ; then back through the Park, and, not content with taking the usual

[1] *Porcupine*, No. 291, Oct. 3, 1800.   [2] *Ibid.*, No. 298.

carriage road, dragged it through the Mall, a place appropriated, exclusively, as a carriage road, to the use of the
ROYAL FAMILY!!!'

But Cobbett had good reason to be sore, for the mob had
smashed the windows of his dwelling-house in Pall Mall,
and at his office in Southampton Street, because he would
not illuminate; so he takes his revenge in a peculiar manner. ' He did not know that there existed in the country,
any force whatever, to compel his Majesty's subjects to
exhibit, at night, manifestations of joy at an event which,
in the morning, he had stated his reasons for believing to be
a subject of deep concern. But he has unfortunately found
himself mistaken; and he is, therefore, under the necessity
of apprizing his readers, that, until the principles of the
British Constitution, and the laws of the realm, which have
ever been objects of his fervent admiration, and most
zealous support, can rise superior to the destructive rage of
a senseless and infuriate rabble; until he can derive that
protection from the Police of the Country, which every
subject has a right to claim, but which he has, hitherto,
been unable to obtain; until, in short, that " *tumult* of
exultation," and that "*delirium* of joy," which a Ministerial
writer so emphatically described, and so earnestly wished,
might *increase*, shall have subsided, the publication of The
Porcupine will cease, and the mob be left to exercise their
vengeance on an empty office.'

But he did not long leave the populace thirsting for his
utterances, for the paper was resumed on October 15.

> At length all parties pleased to yield,
> A treaty was in London seal'd;
> And Nap with pleasure had to say
> That England own'd his Cons'lar sway.
> The Royalists were vex'd at this,
> They took the treaty much amiss;
> It seem'd (as for a time it was)
> Destructive of the Bourbon cause.
> This Amiens treaty, as 'twas termed
> Was in October month confirm'd;
> And London, tho' so ill repaid,
> Illuminations grand display'd.

CHAPTER XXIII.

THE PEACE OF AMIENS—CESSION OF TRINIDAD AND CEYLON—INTER-
NATIONAL VISITS—FOX'S TRIP TO FRANCE, AND RECEPTION BY
NAPOLEON.

AN unknown artist, probably Ansell, produced on October
26, 1801, a caricature of 'The Child and Champion of
Jacobinism new Christened (vide Pitt's Speech).' Bonaparte
is bending over a font, which is supported by Egyptian
sphinges, whilst a bishop calls out, ' Name this Child.' Addington and Pitt are the godfathers, and Lord Hawkesbury
is the godmother. Pitt replies, ' Deliverer of Europe and
Pacificator of the World.' Addington says, ' I hope he will
abolish the Slave Trade'; and the godmother mentions,
' You need not say anything about the march to Paris.'

Gillray (November 9, 1801) gives us a very elaborate
picture of ' Political Dreamings—Visions of Peace!—Perspective Horrors!' Windham, who was the leader of the war

party, is asleep,
and his dreams
are full of inci-
dent — too full,
indeed, to re-
capitulate here.
But the princi-
pal scene in the
sleeping man's
vision is Napo-
leon dragging
to the guillotine by a halter, Britannia, whose trident is
broken, as also is her shield.

' The Balance of Power,' by Ansell (December 1, 1801),
shows a pair of scales, in which Bonaparte weighs down Pitt
and the Lord Chancellor. Pitt ruefully exclaims, ' So this is
the Balance of Power we have been making such a fuss about
—a pretty piece of business we have made of it. Curse
that sword of his, 'tis that has made us kick the Beam.'

Hostilities with France having ceased with the ratification of the preliminaries of peace, there was but little cari-

caturing of Napoleon, and none of an offensive character. Napoleon occupied his time in attending to home affairs, as also did the British Government. But the peace was not absolutely concluded, and much diplomatic wrangling took place, as usual, before the Peace of Amiens was really signed on March 27, 1802. Its principal articles must be briefly enumerated here, as they will be found of use in understanding forthcoming caricatures.

England restored to France, Spain, and Batavia, all the possessions which had been occupied or conquered during the war, with the exception of Trinidad and Ceylon. Malta was to be restored to the Order of St. John of Jeru-salem—the British troops to evacuate the island within three months, or sooner ; but Malta was to be independent, such independence being guaranteed by the Great Powers, and the ports to be open to the vessels of all nations, with the exception of those belonging to the Barbary Powers. These are the principal articles necessary for us to bear in mind.

Due credit was given to Bonaparte's astuteness and our plenipotentiary, Lord Cornwallis, was considered no match for him.

The Caricature year of 1802 seems to open with one by Ansell (January 9), ' A Game at Chess ' between Bona-parte and Lord Cornwallis. Bonaparte says, ' Check to your King. Remember this is not the first time, and I think a very few Manœuvres more will compleatly con-vince you that I am better acquainted with the Game I am playing, than you are aware of.' Cornwallis, tearing his hair, exclaims, ' Curse it, I shall lose this game. You are too much for me.'

This was followed by another from the same pencil (February 8), called ' Cross examination,' where Lord Cornwallis is button-holing Bonaparte, and saying, ' There is great delay in our negociation comeing to a conclusion, and I understand our People are very uneasy lest you should be Humbugging us—Your fleet having sail'd, has given cause for many conjectures, and to tell you the truth it puzzles me a little to know what your intention is. Bonaparte's reply is plain and simple, ' I have to tell you,

Sir, that I do not desire to give you the information you seem to wish for, and whether I sign or not, is of little consequence to the Republican government; our fleet I am in hopes will pick up something.'

In March 1802 Woodward produced a somewhat dreary picture called 'The National Institute's first Interview with their President.' Napoleon, seated under a canopy, says to Sheridan, Fox, Bedford, and Burdett, 'Gentlemen, you are welcome, and I invite you to the Honors of the sitting.' Sheridan, who is kneeling, holds a phial and box in his hands, and begs that Napoleon will 'Be pleased to accept some true poetic Tincture, and a small Box of Pizarro[1] Pills.' Fox, who has a money bag under his arm, says, 'I have brought a pound and a half of Patriotism for your eminence.' The Duke of Bedford opines that 'He'll not be displeased with a few Bedford biscuits;' and Burdett, with his hair, as usual, combed over his eyes, refers to his present, 'I have brought him a Phial of Genuine Bastile Balsam.'

But when once the peace was signed, much show was made of shaking hands and being friends. Englishmen went over to France in numbers; Frenchmen reciprocated, but not to the same extent. This feeling is shown by the caricaturist, for on April 14, 1802, was published (artist unknown) a picture entitled 'A Peaceable Pipe, or a Consular Visit to John Bull.' Napoleon and John Bull are in amicable converse, smoking, and drinking beer. John Bull says, 'Here's to you, Master Boney Party; come, take another whiff, my hearty!' To this hospitable invitation Napoleon replies, 'Je vous remercie, John Bull, I think I'll take another pull.' Mrs. Bull is hard at work mending John's breeches, which are wofully dilapidated: says she, soliloquising, 'Now we are at Peace, if my Husband does take a drop extraordinary I don't much mind, but when he was at war, he was always grumbling. Bless me, how tiresome these old breeches are to mend; no wonder he wore them out, for he had always his hands in his pockets for something or other.'

As before said, with the peace came mutual intercourse

[1] An allusion to his play of that name.

between England and France, and there is a picture by
Ansell (May 14, 1802), which represents 'A Trip to Paris,
or Iohn Bull and his Spouse, invited to the Honors of the
Sitting !!' Napoleon receives John Bull and Ireland, and
when seated, Napoleon addresses them thus : ' Indeed, Mr.
Bull, I am quite charmed with you—there is something so
easy and polite in your manners.'

John Bull, however, is not to be taken in by such palp-
able ' *blarney*,' and replies, ' Come—come Mounseer Bonny
party, that's all gammon d'ye see. D—n me if I know
more about politeness than a Cow does of a new shilling !!'
Ireland looks very angrily at her spouse, and remonstrates :
' For shame, Mr. Bull, what will the Jontleman think of
your Blarney about gammon and cows, and Bodder and
nonsense ; by St. Patrick, I must send you to Kilkenny to
larn good breeding.'

Some of these caricatures were rather dreary ; take, for
example, ' The Consular Warehouse or a Great Man nail'd
to the Counter' (Cawse, May 20). Napoleon is keeping a
shop, selling, among other things, ' Preserved Promises,
Pickled Piety from Rome, Oil of Lodi, Marengo Olio, Bullet
Bolusses. advice gratis. N.B. One Pill is a dose. also Islands
for Home Consumption Martinique—St. Lucia.' John Bull
has just bought two, paid for in good hard cash, and takes
his goods home with him. Under one arm he carries the
' Island of Indemnity, ci-devant Ceylon '—under the other
is the ' Island of Security, ci-devant Trinidad.' They hardly
seem to be John Bull's idea of a bargain, for he is saying,
' They be very light to be sure—but harkee, my worthy,—
you'll not forget to carry on a little trade with the Old
Shop ; if you don't, you know, a Rowland for an Oliver,
that's all.' Napoleon, however, reassures him with ' We'll
not talk of that at present, Mr. Bull ; all you have to do,
is to take care of your new Islands ; mind you don't tumble
down, and break them, before you get home—They are
very brittle, but a very good article for all that.'

As the year grew older, the *entente cordiale* grew colder.
Suspicions of Napoleon's intentions were aroused, and
Malta was not evacuated as per treaty. One or two warn-
ing caricatures, stormy petrels, made their appearance, and

in the autumn of this year appeared 'The Corsican Conjurer raising the plagues of Europe.' He is shewn with
huge cocked hat and an ample robe, which is held up by
the Devil, who encourages him, 'That's right my fine fellow
—If you don't kick up a pretty dust in the world, never
trust the Devil again—that's all.' Napoleon is waving a
rod over a caldron, in which are serpents, and a devil, the
steam from which is labelled, in different clouds, 'Anarchy,
Pride, Murder, Confusion, Treason, War, Plunder, Revenge,
Massacre, Avarice, Cruelty, Usurpation, Hatred, Horror,
Envy, Blasphemy, Malice, Craft, Falsehood, and Terror.'

There is another one, 'Parcelling out John Bull,' which
is a queer conceit. Napoleon has a huge pair of Com-
passes, with which he is measuring John Bull—congratulating himself that 'He really will make a pretty addition
to my departments—he cuts out extremely well indeed.'
There is the Wig Department, Department of the Head,
Arm Department, Department of the Body, Fob Department, Breeches pocket Department, Right and Left Leg
Divisions. But John Bull assures his friend, in no kindly
spirit, 'Harkee Young one, you have forgotten the Fist
Department, and if you don't take away your d—d Com-
passes, I'll give you a relish of it. Cut me out, indeed!
why, I'll fight you with one hand tied behind me.' This
caricature is neither signed nor dated, but it was undoubtedly issued in the autumn of 1802.

We have seen that it was fashionable for Englishmen
to run over to France after the conclusion of peace, and
Charles James Fox was no exception to the rule ; but he
had to wait a little, until after the Westminster election,
when, on July 15, he was returned head of the poll. He
did not long delay the trip, and on July 29 he set out on
his journey, accompanied by his wife, the Hon. St. Andrew
St. John (afterwards Lord St. John) and a young Irishman
named Trotter,[1] who wrote an exhaustive account of their
journey. On the 4th of August, Napoleon had been elected
Consul for life, a step which might probably tend to con-

[1] *Memoirs of the Later Years of the Right Honourable Charles James Fox*,
by John Bernard Trotter, Esq., late private secretary to Mr. Fox, London,
1811.

solidate peace, and which rendered his position equal to any other European sovereign. When Fox reached Paris, it was rumoured that this was only preliminary to his taking a higher rank, with the title of Emperor of the Gauls. Just then, Englishmen were in great favour at Paris, and Fox's arrival created a great commotion. All vied with each other to pay him attention, and it was settled he should be presented to the First Consul at his next *levée*, which took place on September 3.

Caricaturists, like poets, must needs be allowed some licence, and Gillray (November 15), in his picture of the 'Introduction of Citizen Volpone,[1] and his Suite, at Paris,' draws slightly upon his imagination as to Napoleon's state at this reception ; still the allegorical globes, and the introduction of Rûstan the Mameluke, add a fictitious dignity to the picture.

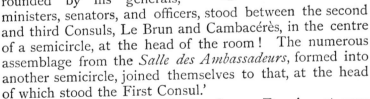

The actual scene, as it was viewed by an eyewitness,[2] is thus described : ' We reached the interior apartment, where Buonaparte, First Consul, surrounded by his generals, ministers, senators, and officers, stood between the second and third Consuls, Le Brun and Cambacérès, in the centre of a semicircle, at the head of the room ! The numerous assemblage from the *Salle des Ambassadeurs*, formed into another semicircle, joined themselves to that, at the head of which stood the First Consul.'

Gillray's portrait of Charles James Fox is not very much exaggerated. Let us hope that of Mrs. Fox is. This lady, although she was married to Fox on September 28, 1795, was never introduced to his friends as his wife until

[1] Fox.   [2] Trotter.

this journey. She was always believed to be his mistress, Mrs. Armistead.[1]   She made him a good and loving wife, and he was very fond of her.

Trotter describes the actual presentation thus: ' Buonaparte, of a small, and by no means commanding figure, dressed plainly, though richly, in the embroidered consular coat, without powder in his hair, looked like a private gentleman, indifferent as to dress, and devoid of all haughtiness in his air. . . . The moment the circle was formed, Buonaparte began with the Spanish Ambassador, then went to the American, with whom he spoke some time, and so on, performing his part with ease, and very agreeably ; until he came to the English Ambassador, who, after the presentation of some English Noblemen, announced to him Mr. Fox ! He was a good deal flurried, and after indicating considerable emotion, very rapidly said, "Ah! Mr. Fox ! I have heard with pleasure of your arrival—I have desired much to see you—I have long admired in you the orator, and friend of his country, who in constantly raising his voice for peace, consulted that country's best interests—those of Europe—and of the human race. The two great nations of Europe require peace ;—they have nothing to fear ; they ought to understand and value one another. In you, Mr. Fox, I see, with much satisfaction, that great statesman who recommended Peace, because there was no just object of war ; who saw Europe desolated to no purpose, and who struggled for its relief."

'Mr. Fox said little, or rather, nothing, in reply,—to a complimentary address to himself, he always found in-

[1] Her real name, *vide his Marriage Register*, was Elizabeth B. Cane.

vincible repugnance to answer; nor did he bestow one word of admiration or applause upon the extraordinary and elevated character who addressed him. A few questions and answers relative to Mr. Fox's tour terminated the interview.'

Other caricaturists took the matter up, for Fox's visit to Paris was naturally commented on; and there is an engraving by Anseil (November 8, 1802), 'English Patriots bowing at the Shrine of Despotism.' These 'Patriots' are Fox, Erskine, and Combe, the brewer, who was Lord Mayor. They are represented as bowing in the most lowly fashion—so low, indeed, that Fox has burst his trousers behind; and with one voice they assure Napoleon that they 'are, with the highest consideration, your Super Royal Consulship's most Devoted, most Obsequious, and most honored Servants.' Bonaparte, seated in almost regal state, criticises them : 'Oh, from the World ! O'Connor's friends—Fox, ha ! how old are you ? A Brewer ; Lord Mayor, ha ! great pomp. Mr. Brief, ha ! a great Lawyer can talk well. There, you may go.'

Thus we see they did not quite get hold of the right version of this interview, as 'Taking leave' was satirised by a nameless artist (November 12, 1802), and represents Fox bowing very humbly to the First Consul, who is crowned with death's-head and cross-bones, daggers, pistols, and swords, and regards him in an extremely haughty manner.

CHAPTER XXIV.

LORD WHITWORTH AS PLENIPOTENTIARY—HIS EQUIPAGE—ENGLISH VISIT
    PARIS—UNSETTLED FEELING—NAPOLEON BEHAVES RUDELY TO LORD
    WHITWORTH.

IN June, Lord Whitworth was appointed ambassador extraordinary, and minister plenipotentiary, to the French Republic, and the state he then kept up was a striking contrast to the plainness of Republican equipages. It was different under the Empire; but then the word Citizen had not been dropped, and there was a certain affectation of simplicity. The English attracted great attention by the

splendour of their equipages, and there is a caricature
(nameless, December 14, 1802) of 'Lord Whitworth's
Coachman at Paris.' His get-up is, certainly, 'exceeding
magnifical,' and is the wonder of the Parisians. It is
almost too much for his equanimity, for he is shown as
saying, 'How the Mounseers stare at me! D—n me, if I
don't think they take me for the Ambassador.'

The effects of the peace were hardly realisable for a
time, and Woodward gives us an amusing caricature of the
state of the empire (December 20, 1802). It is called 'A
Peep at the Lion,' which is supposed to be on show. Outside the Exhibition Pitt is inviting Europe, generally, to
'Walk in Ladies and Gentlemen, and see the famous Lion.
Though I have some share in the concern, I have nothing
to do with showing him, I assure you—I am not his keeper ;
the Lion I used to show was very fierce, but this is quite quiet
and peaceable.' Inside, the Lion is shewn as lying down,
but with one eye open, Napoleon patting him on the head,
saying, 'Poor fellow, poor fellow, what a beautiful Animal,
—how sound he sleeps.' But the Chancellor, Lord Eldon,
warns him, 'You had better not be too free with him Sir,
In case of an accident. He is now asleep with one eye, and
awake with the other.'

At the opening of the year 1803, although the storm

clouds of war were
ominously gathering,
yet all seemed peace.
The English enjoyed
the rare treat of visit-
ing France, and, gene-
rally, being of the
better class, were well
received. The year
opens in a kindly spirit
with 'The first kiss
these ten Years ! or the
meeting of Britannia
and Citizen François'
(Gillray, January 1, 1803), which is a remarkably good
caricature. Britannia, owing to the peace, has grown

prosperous, and stout; her trident and shield are put away in a corner, and the portraits of Napoleon and George the Third repose, in loving juxtaposition, on the wall, intertwined with palm-branches. Says Citizen François (his sword and cocked hat being laid aside), 'Madame, permettez me to pay my profound esteem to your engaging person! and to seal on your divine Lips my everlasting attachment.' Madame Britannia replies, 'Monsieur, you are so truly a well bred Gentleman! and tho' you make me blush, yet you kiss so delicately, that I cannot refuse you; tho' I was sure you would deceive me again !!!'

A most amusing picture (Gillray, January 1, 1803) is that called 'German Nonchalance, or the vexation of Little Boney. vide the Diplomatique's late Journey through Paris.' It represents the Austrian ambassador being driven furiously through Paris, his luggage being directed 'à Londres.' With the utmost *insouciance*, he is taking a pinch of snuff, calmly regarding Napoleon, who is standing on some steps, and is in a fearful rage. With arms and legs outstretched, and his hat fallen off, he yells out, 'Ha, diable! va t'en, Impertinent! va t'en! is dere von Man on Earth who not worship little Boney? Soldats! aux Armes! revenge! ah! Sacre Dieu, je suis tout tremblant.' The soldiers, however, although preparing to draw their swords, do not appear to be particularly anxious to avenge their insulted leader.

This incident arose from the Austrian minister neglecting to pay his respects to the First Consul, whilst passing through Paris.

As an evidence of the uneasiness of public political feeling, take the following. In January 1803 was published a caricature by Raymond, called 'Leap Frog.' Napoleon has already jumped over the bowed backs of Holland and Spain. The poor Dutchman exclaims, 'He has left the Swiss and Italians a Mile behind—and as for me he has knocked my hat off and broken my pipe—pretty encouragement this to play at Leap-frog.' The don ruefully says that 'By St. Jago—my back is almost broken.' Napoleon is now jumping over Hanover, who plaintively asks, 'Why did I submit to this?' but the conqueror only says, 'Keep down your head Master Hanoverian, my next leap shall be over John Bull.' But that individual, who looks uncommonly belligerent, with clenched fists, exclaims, 'I'll be d—d if you do Master Corsican.'

FROM INDIGENCE IN CORSICA TO AFFLUENCE IN FRANCE.   FROM ASPIRING AMBITION TO THE SUMMIT OF POWER.   FROM CALAIS TO DOVER, WHERE LITTLE JOHN BULL DOES THE CORSICAN OVER.[1]

The English Government, seeing how Napoleon was aggrandising himself, and seeing also that this country, alone, could save the liberty of Europe, did not hurry to conform with the treaty of Amiens, and surrender all the advantages gained by the late long struggle ; and although, with reluctance, the Cape, and other Batavian settlements, were given up, excuses were always to be found for not evacuating Malta.

On January 25, Lord Whitworth and Talleyrand had an interview, and the latter, after bitterly complaining of the licence of the British press, which he said ought to be curbed, or suppressed, asked plainly what were the intentions of the British Government with regard to Malta ? It is to this interview, probably, that the following caricature owed its existence. How Cobbett lashed Addington, for his nepotism, in his 'Annual Register'!!

'The Evacuation of Malta' (Gillray, February 9, 1803) is vividly, almost too graphically, depicted. Ferocious little Bonaparte has hold of poor frightened Addington by his

[1] January 1, 1803. Artist unknown.

necktie, and, by flourishing his enormous sword, compels him to evacuate Malta, Egypt, Cape of Good Hope, St. Domingo, Guadaloup, and Martinique. In vain Addington pleads, 'Pray do not insist upon Malta! I shall certainly be turned out! and I have a great many Cousins and Uncles and Aunts to provide for yet.' But his merciless enemy will hear of no compromise, and yells out ' All! All! you Jean F—t—e! and think yourself well off that I leave you Great Britain!!!' A French officer mildly remonstrates, and suggests, 'My General, you had better not get him turned out, for we shall not be able to humbug them any more.'

Ansell executed an engraving (February 10, 1803) of the 'Rival Gardeners,' which represents Napoleon, and George III., tending their respective gardens, which are divided by the Channel. Napoleon has a number of plants labelled 'Military poppies,' which flourish well; but he is greatly concerned about his principal flower, which has a very drooping head and flagging leaves. He cannot understand it. 'Why, I don't know what is the reason; my Poppies flourish charmingly; but this *Corona Imperialis* is rather a delicate kind of a plant, and requires great judgment in rearing.' His rival, however, points with pride to the sturdy British Oak, whose vigour is matchless, and is in full bloom, with a royal crown. He replies, ' No, No, Brother Gardener, though only a ditch parts our grounds, yet this is the spot for true Gardening; here the *Corona Britanica* and yᵉ *Heart of Oak* will flourish to the end of the world.'

On March 8, the king sent a message to Parliament, respecting military preparations in the ports of France and Holland, and acquaints the House of Commons that 'he has judged it expedient to adopt additional measures of precaution for the security of his dominions;' and this gives us the key to the next caricature—

' Physical Aid, or, Britannia recover'd from a Trance, also the Patriotic Courage of Merry Andrew, and a peep thro' the Fog,' was published by Gillray, March 14, 1803, and is a very amusing picture. Bonaparte, and his flotilla, are crossing the Channel, and Sheridan, with fool's cap and bell, a tattered harlequin suit, a lathen sword, ' Dramatic

Loyalty,' a shield with a Medusa's head, the snaky hair of which is labelled ' Envy, abuse, bouncing, puffing, detrac-

tion, stolen jests, malevolence, and stale wit,' and a paper, in his sash, endorsed ' Ways and means to get a living,' calls out, ' Let 'em come ! dam'me ! ! ! Where are the French Buggabos ? single-handed I'd beat forty of 'em ! ! ! dam'me I'd pay 'em like Renter's shares, sconce off their half-crowns ! ! ! mulct them out of their benefits, and come ye Drury Lane Slang over 'em.'

A THEATRICAL HERO.

Britannia, suddenly aroused from her trance, screams out, 'Doctors and ministers of disgrace defend me,' and attempts to rise. Addington is attempting to recover her, by holding a bottle of gunpowder to her nose, saying ' Do not be alarm'd, my dear Lady! The Buggabos (the Honest Gentlemen, I mean) are avowedly directed to Colonial service, they can have nothing to do Here, my lady—nothing to do with US ! do take a sniff or two to raise your Spirits, and try to stand, if it is only upon one leg.' Lord Hawkesbury is presenting, in a feeble manner, to Britannia, her spear—with broken point, and her shield, which is sadly cracked, and bleats forth, ' Yes, my lady, you must try to stand up, or we shall never be able to march to Paris.' Fox, who is wilfully screening his face with his hat, exclaims, ' Dear me—what can be the reason of the old lady being awaked in such a fright ? I declare I can't see anything of the Buggabos ! ' On the ground lies the treaty of peace, torn.

On March 13, Napoleon behaved in a very rude, and intemperate, manner to Lord Whitworth respecting the non-evacuation of Malta—which scene is thus versified :—

> Our hero now, with great chagrin,
> Begg'd of Lord Whitworth to call in.

Agreeably to his request,
Th' Ambassador became his guest,
And in the Cab'net of the Thuilleries
Napoleon play'd off all his fooleries.
'What is the cause,' he cried, 'of this?
How comes it England acts amiss?
I swear that every provocation,
Daily augments my indignation ;
Why are these libels to annoy me,
Pensioned assassins to destroy me?
Why Malta's non-evacuation,
And Alexandria, by your nation?
You'd fain keep Malta—I believe you,
But part of France I'd rather give you.
Why all these provocations? why o' late,
The Amiens treaty dare to violate?'
Nap ask'd so many questions now,
That not an answer he'd allow.
Lord Whitworth moved his lips, but then
Our hero wagged his tongue again.
It seems Lord Whitworth wish'd to say,
France for infringements led the way ;
But when that she was pleased to stop,
And all her base aggressions drop,
The treaty England would fulfil,
For that, indeed, was England's will.
In spite of Nap's vociferation,
His Lordship made this observation :
' My sovereign's actions ne'er have been
Insidious, treacherous, or mean,
Because it is the king's desire
More to *preserve* than to *acquire.*'

CHAPTER XXV.

GENERAL UNEASINESS—CARICATURES THEREON—ADDINGTON'S NEPOTISM
—NAPOLEON'S DISCOURTESY TO LORD WHITWORTH—TRIAL OF JEAN
PELTIER.

'THE Political Cocks' (by Ansell, March 27, 1803) is very
graphic. Napoleon, a game cock armed with terrific spurs,
is calling across the Channel to Pitt, who, standing on the
British Crown, is crowing lustily. Napoleon says, ' Eh
Master Billy, if I could but take a flight over this brook, I

K

would soon stop your Crowing. I would knock you off
that Perch, I swear by Mahomet, the Pope, and all the Idols

THE POLITICAL COCKS.

I have ever worshipped.' Pitt, however, replies, 'Tuck-a-
roo—too—that you never can do !!!'

This was a fine time for the caricaturists, and their works
came thick and fast. Telling their own tale, they need no
explanation. 'An Attempt to swallow the World' (artist
unknown, April 6, 1803) shows Napoleon attempting this
difficult feat—John Bull looking on, and remarking, ' I'll
tell you what, Mr. Boneypartee, when you come to a little
spot I have in my eye, it will stick in your throat and
choak you.'

West (April 6, 1803) engraved 'John Bull teased by
an Earwig.' Napoleon, drawn very small, is on John Bull's
shoulder, pricking his cheek with his little sword. This
annoys the old man, and, looking up angrily from his meal
of bread (Ceylon), and cheese (Malta), he says, ' I tell you
what, young one—if you won't let me eat my bread and
cheese in peace and comfort, I'll blow you away, you may
depend upon it.' To which the *Earwig* replies, ' I will
have the Cheese, you Brute, you ; I have a great mind to
annihilate you, you great overgrown Monster.'

'Easier to say than to do' (I. Cruikshank, April 14,
1803) shows Bonaparte seated before a *New Map of the
World*, attempting to erase the British Isles. A Dutchman, with a lighted candle, suggests, 'Got for d—n de ting

—here take te candle, and burn tem out.' On the other side, a Spaniard says, ' Here, my friend, take the paste-brush, and stick a piece of your three-coloured flag over them.' Whilst a Jew, who has a label coming out of his pocket, ' Subscription to new loan,' says, ' I tink if I lend a little more monish at Turty per shent, it will soon annihilate dem.' Bonaparte reflects : ' I cannot scrape these little islands out of the map. As for your plan, Mynheer, we did try to burn them once, but they would not take fire ; and let me tell you, Don Diego, they are not so easily over-run with any flag as you may think! I believe Moses's plan the best ; that, and a threat now and then may probably do the business.'

' An Attempt to undermine John Bull, or working through the Globe ' (Roberts, April 16, 1803), shows Napoleon standing on ruins, surrounded by ' Territories pickaxed with impunity '—Switzerland, Italian Republic, Batavian Republic ; and he is now commencing operations with his pickaxe on John Bull, saying, ' O, the Pick axe is infinitely the best way—I shall soon be at the little fellow, that's his abode, I know it by the white cliffs.' John Bull is lying down, sword in hand, with his ear on the ground, and says, ' I hear you burrowing away, my fine fellow ; but it won't do.—As soon as you pop your head above the surface, you shall be saluted with a few of John Bull's pop-guns.'

Another caricature (artist unknown, April 16, 1803), called ' A stoppage to a Stride over the Globe,' shows a colossal Napoleon bestriding the World, whilst a small John Bull, on England, is hacking at his foot, with a sword. Napoleon, in disgust, is calling out, ' Ah ! who is it dares to interrupt me in my progress ? ' ' Why, 'tis I, little Johnny Bull, protecting a little spot I clap my hand on, and d—n me if you come any farther—that's all.'

Ansell, too, the same date (April 16, 1803), drew ' The Governor of Europe, Stoped in his career, or Little B——n too much for great B——te.' Here a huge Bonaparte has attempted to put his foot on Britain, and John Bull has cut it off. Napoleon, dancing with pain and loss of blood, drops his sword, yells out, ' Ah, you tam John Bull ! ! You

have spoil my *Dance*!! You have ruined all my Projets.'
Little John Bull, pointing to his native land, says, 'I ax
pardon, Master Boney, but as we says, *Paws off, Pompey*,
we keep this little spot to ourselves, you must not dance
here Master Boney.'

Rowlandson (May 1, 1803), brought out 'John Bull
listening to the quarrels of State affairs.' Napoleon is
talking to the Chancellor, and says, 'And so—if you do *so*,
I do *so*.' The Chancellor, in an evident fright, exclaims
tremulously, 'Oh! Oh!!' whilst old John Bull looks on,
listening, all eyes and expectation, with his hair on end,
'I declare my very wig stands on end with curiosity. What
can they be quareling about? O that I could but be let
into the secret! If I ax our gentleman concerning it, it is
ten to one if he tells me the right story.'

On May 2, 1803, Gillray produced a very effective caricature called 'Doctor Sangrado curing John Bull of Re-
pletion, with the kind offices of young Clyster pipe[1] and
little Boney. A hint from Gil Blas.' John Bull is seated,
very weak indeed, held up by Lord Hawkesbury. Fox

and Sheridan are
behind, bringing
warm water, and
everybody in the
drawing is ex-
horting the pa-
tient to 'Courage.'
Addington is per-
forming the ope-
ration, and the
blood streams forth
copiously. Napoleon catches in his cocked hat, Ceylon,
Malta, Cape of Good Hope, and West Indies; whilst
young Clyster pipe holds out his hat, labelled 'Clerk
of the Pells,' and catches a stream '3,000*l.* per annum.'
This scandalous job, his father having given him this lucra-
tive sinecure when he was very young, excited much adverse
comment at the time.

'Britannia repremanding a Naughty Boy!' (artist un-

[1] A name bestowed on young Addington.

known, May 3, 1803). Britannia, with a helmet on her
head, her shield by her side, a spear in one hand, and a
birch rod in the other, stands on the shore at Dover. On
the top of the cliffs is a crown on a cushion. Napoleon,
attired, as usual, in an enormous cocked hat, stands on the
shore at Calais, whimpering, 'I'm tired of this great hat, I
will have that crown.' But says Britannia: 'Stay where
you are, you little troublesome Urchin. If once you cross
the Dyke you'll get a good birchin!'

'Lunar Speculations' is the whimsical title of a picture
by Ansell, May 3, 1803. Bonaparte is looking through a
large telescope, mounted on a tripod, at the moon ; and he
is saying: 'I wonder the Idea never struck me before!
The place would easily be taken, and has undoubtedly
great capabilities—Besides they would make me Emperor :—and then, the sound of the Title EMPEROR OF
THE FULL MOON—oh ! delightful ! I'll send for Garner [1]
and his balloons and set about the scheme immediately.'
John Bull, looking at him quizzically, and holding his very
fat sides, says : 'What! going to revolutionize the Moon,
Bonny ? That's a good one, however—To be sure, you
talk'd of paying a visit to my little island, and one should
certainly be as easily accomplished as the other.'

The situation was getting more strained daily, and
Napoleon did not mend matters by his studied discourtesy
to Lord Whitworth.

'Indeed,' said Whitworth, 'you mistake,
We wish a lasting peace to make.'
'Pay more respect to treaties, then.'
Cried Nap, and raised his voice again ;
'What use are treaties?—all my eye—
If violated—fie—oh fie—
What use are treaties? woe to those
Who don't respect them—they're my foes ;
Yes, they're my foes—I tell you flat,
And I don't value them—not that.'
This said, his argument to back,
He with his fingers gave a crack,

[1] Garnerin, the aeronaut.

The Company were all ashamed,
And his indelicacy blamed ;
His manners were so ungenteel,
That each now turn'd upon his heel.
England's Ambassador was bent
The Consul's conduct to resent.
He sent a note of all that pass'd
From the beginning to the last,
Then sought for passports, as advis'd ;
At this the Consul was surpris'd ;
But England now was irritated,
For in the *Moniteur* 'twas stated,
That she could never, single handed,
Contend with France—so he demanded
His passports—likewise he averr'd,
That war, he to suspense, preferr'd.
His lordship's wish they strove t' evade,
The passports daily were delay'd.
Lord Whitworth, soon as they were granted,
Set off for London, as he wanted.

By way of parenthesis, I may say that Napoleon made
loud complaint about the libels published about him in
England ; and, to show the impartiality of the Government,
and their desire to do justice, even at a time when war
between the two countries was almost morally certain, a
Frenchman, named Jean Peltier, was prosecuted for libelling
him, the indictment being 'That peace existed between
N. Bonaparte and our Lord the King ; but that M. Peltier,
intending to destroy the friendship so existing, and to despoil said Napoleon of his consular dignity, did devise, print,
and publish, in the French Language, to the tenor following, &c.'

It is never worth while to go into the words of the libel
(which appeared in a periodical called *L'Ambigu*), which
is purely political, and which would never be noticed
nowadays. I only introduce the episode to shew that the
English Government even went out of their way to conciliate Bonaparte, and that the libel, as usual, sprang
from French sources.

He was unanimously found guilty, and judgment was to
have been delivered next term, but, war being renewed, he
was never called upon to appear.

CHAPTER XXVI.

THE *ULTIMATUM*—LORD WHITWORTH LEAVES PARIS—DECLARATION OF
WAR—CARICATURES PREVIOUS THERETO—SURRENDER OF HANOVER.

NOW came the *ultimatums* on both sides. The presentation of an *ultimatum* is hardly a personal caricature of Napoleon, but it belongs to the history of the times. One picture was published May 3, 1803, by an unknown artist, and was called 'Waste Paper.' A French officer holds four *ultimatums* in his hand, and presents John Bull with No. 1. A servant, behind, carries a huge sack of *ultimatums*. The Frenchman thus speaks : 'Monsieur Jean Bull, I am come from De Grand Nation to present you vone *Ultimatum*. If you not like dat—I present you vone oder—I have got seventy tree Tousand *Ultimatum*, and you must agree to vone or de oder.—or, begar, I sal kick you out of de Europe. My lacquey has got Dem in de Sac, and will leave dem for your consideration. Health and Fraternity, Citizen Bull !' John Bull uplifts his cudgel, and his bulldog growls. Says the old man, ' Hark ye, Mr. Frog ! I was just feeling in my pocket, for a little bit of waste paper, and you have just supplied me in time : so now get you gone, or I'll shew you the use of my Horns, by tossing you out of old ENGLAND.'

But this giving of *ultimatums* was not all on one side. I. Cruikshank (May 14, 1803) drew ' Ultimatum, or the Ambassador taking proper steps.' Our ambassador[1] is just stepping into his carriage, and, whilst doing so, presents Napoleon with an *ultimatum*, saying, with national courtesy, ' Be quick, or d— me I'm off.' Napoleon is depicted as being deeply affected by this conduct. He weeps copiously, and wrings his hands, whimpering, ' Pray stop, and I will agree to anything.'

There is a caricature by an artist unknown (May 18, 1803), called ' The Bone of Contention,' which is labelled MALTA. Bonaparte, looking very fierce, menaces John Bull with his sword, exclaiming ' By the Bridge of Lodi ! by the plains of Marengo !! by everything that is great and

[1] Lord Whitworth.

terrible—I command you to surrender that bone ! ! ! !' John
Bull, however, has set his foot upon that bone, and is prepared to defend it with his oaken cudgel.   He laconically
replies 'You be d—d.'

   This subject waʊ also treated by Ansell (June 14, 1803)
in 'The Bone of Contention, or the English Bulldog and
the Corsican Monkey.'   The monkey, in a fearful and
wonderful cocked hat, calls out, 'Eh! you Bull Dog, vat
you carry off dat Bone for?   I vas come to take dat
myself.   I vas good mind to lick you, but for dem Dam
Tooths.'   Whilst John Bull, typified as a bulldog, has the
bone, Malta, firmly between his teeth, and growls defiance.

   Lord Whitworth left Paris on May 12, and arrived at
Dover on the 17th,[1] where he met General Andreossi, the
French minister, on the point of returning to France.   On
the 18th, George III. sent his Declaration of War to both
Houses of Parliament, and Nelson hoisted his flag on
board the *Victory*, at Portsmouth, the same day.   Thus
ended a peace which had existed only one year and sixteen
days.

   Of course, the caricatures were, necessarily, prepared
a day or two before their publication, so the dates do

ARMED HEROES.

not depend upon the
events which took
place.   Such an one is
'Armed Heroes,' Gill-
ray, May 18, 1803,
which is amusing.   It
is Addington who is
bestriding the Roast
Beef of Old England.
Lord Hawkesbury sits
behind him ; whilst
the two other figures
respectively represent
Hely Addington and
Bragge Bathurst, who

were members of the Addington family, and had been
provided with good places by their powerful relative.

   [1] *St. James's Chronicle*, May 17/19, 1803.

Napoleon looks with hungry eyes on the beef, and exclaims :—

> Ah, ha ! sacrè dieu ! vat do I see yonder ?
> Dat look so invitingly Red and de Vite ?
> Oh by Gar ! I see 'tis de Roast Beef of Londres
> Vich I vill chop up, at von letel bite !

Addington is in a curious state of mind, between bluster
and fear, calling out, 'Who's afraid ? damme ?—*O Lord, O
Lord,— what a Fiery Fellow he is !*—Who's afraid ? damme ?
—*O dear ! what will become of y*^e *Roast Beef ?* Damme !
who's afraid ?—*O dear !—O dear !*'

The medicine bottles peeping out of his pockets are a
delicate allusion to Addington's parentage, his father having
been a physician.

The caricatures which follow are simply dated May ;
but, from their internal evidence, they precede the declaration of war. Bonaparte is represented as being excessively
frightened at the prospect of a rupture with England, and,
in May 1803, an etching (artist unknown) was produced,
shewing 'A Little Man Alarmed at his own Shadow.' He
is cowering, and trembling, and looking back at his length-
ened shadow on a wall, saying ' Mercy on us—what tall
figure is that. It surely can't be Johnny Bull ? No, no,
that cannot be, it is not lusty enough for him.'

A very graphic caricature is 'Maniac Ravings, or Little
Boney in a strong Fit. Vide Lord W——'s[1] account of a
visit to the Thuilleries.' Here he is depicted in a fearful
state of frenzy ; he has kicked over the consular chair, a
globe (with all Europe expunged, except the British Isles),
dashed his hat to the ground, upset a table, with all his
writings on it, broken his sword and scabbard ; and, whilst
tearing his hair, stamps frantically on such papers as
' Wyndham's Speeches,' ' Cobbett's Weekly Journal,' 'Anti-
Jacobin Review,' ' Wilson's Egypt,' &c. His ' Maniac Ravings ' are veritably so. ' Oh Egypt, Egypt, Egypt ! Oh,
St. Domingo, Oh ! Oh, the liberty of the English Press !
English Bloodhounds ! Wyndham ! Grenville ! Pitt ! Oh
I'm murdered ! I'm assassinated !! London Newspapers !
Oh ! Oh ! Oh ! Revenge ! Revenge ! come Fire ! Sword !

[1] Whitworth.

Famine! Invasion! Invasion! Four Hundred and Eighty
Frenchmen! British Slavery and everlasting Chains! ever-
lasting Chains! O Diable! the Riches! Freedom! and
Happiness of the British Nation! Ah! Diable Diable,
Diable! Malta! Malta! Malta! Oh, cursed Liberty of the
British Press! Insolence of British Parliament! Treaty of
Amiens! Damnation! British trade and commerce! Oh!
Oh! Oh! English calumniating Newspapers! Oh, Sebas-
tiani! Sebastiani! Oh, Georges! Arras! de Rolle! Dutheil!
O Assassins! Treason! Treason! Treason! Hated and
Betray'd by the French! Despised by the English! and
laughed at by the whole world!!! Oh, English Newspapers!!!
English Newspapers!!!! English Newspapers!!!!!'

Woodward drew a picture (May 1803) of 'A great Man
Intoxicated with Success,' and depicted Boney with a very
'how came you so?' expression of countenance, reeling
along, and saying, 'Ah Johnny Bull, how are you my
Boy—I am going to re-establish slavery—I am grown very
Pious. I—I—I'll double my guards. I—I—I don't know
what I'll do.' John Bull is utterly astonished at such conduct. 'Why, bless your heart, my fine fellow, you be
Muzzy—I dare say you find it difficult to stand. Now,
let me advise you—take a little Nap—if it's only for a
quarter of an hour, you can't think how much it will refresh
you.'

Another caricature, apparently by Woodward, was
published in May 1803, 'Bonaparte and the Quaker.'
Bonaparte's attitude is decidedly aggressive and bullying:
'So they are all Great Men in your Country, eh!—but I
suppose they are like you—not very fond of fighting—is
not that the case Master Quaker?' Brother Broadbrim
replies, 'Little Man, it is not the case. I myself encourage
not fighting. But if thou, or any of thy Comrades, darest
to cross the great waters, my Countrymen shall make
Quakers of you all.'

The national feeling was well expressed in a caricature
(May 1803)—Bonaparte is represented as a mighty mushroom, looking, with no very benign expression of countenance,
on John Bull, who, embracing the British Oak, exclaims,
'You may look as cross as you please, master Mushroom :

but here stands the British Oak, and by St. George and the Dragon, not a leaf of it shall fall to the Ground.'

On May 28, George III., as Elector of Hanover, issued a proclamation, in which he said that, abiding by the treaty of Luneville, he would, as Elector of Hanover, take no part in the war. But, notwithstanding this, the Electorate of Hanover surrendered, by capitulation, to General Mortier on June 3. This prologue is necessary for us to understand the following halfpenny broadside : —

A PEEP INTO HANOVER,

OR

A faint Description of the Atrocities committed by the French in that City.

IT will be remembered, that the Electorate surrendered without Resistance. This we do not mention, as increasing our Compassion for the Inhabitants, which it certainly does not ; but as increasing our abhorrence of the Invaders, who, without Provocation, or Pretext of Resistance, have perpetrated the Atrocities, of which the following is a faint outline :

Ever since the Conquest, the whole Electorate has been a scene of Pillage and Butchery, which is said to yield only to the fate of Switzerland, in Spring 1798. The French Soldiers have the most unbounded Indulgence of their ruling passions of Rapacity, Cruelty and Lust ;—*In the City of Hanover, and even in the Public Street, Women of the Highest Rank have been violated by the lowest of that brutal Soldiery, in presence of their Husbands and Fathers, and subjected, at the same time, to such additional and undescribable Outrages, as the brutal Fury of the Violators, enflamed by Drunkenness, could contrive.* We have seen the names of some of these unfortunate Ladies : but the Honour of their Families, and the Peace of their own future Lives (if they can have peace) forbid us to publish them. The Baron de K——, a well known partisan of French Philosophy and Politics, went to the Commandant of Hanover, and claimed his Protection, as an admirer of the French Revolution ! but he found no more favour in the Sight of the *Aga of Sultan* BONAPARTE'S Janisaries, than the most loyal *Noblemen in Hanover.* The French Officer told him, '*All that Jacobinism is now out of Fashion—Go about your business !*' Nor have we heard that the Philosophers of Gottingen, the Enthusiasts of *Equality and Perfectability*, have been at all better treated.—

Such are the tender Mercies of the Wicked ! Such are the
Gangs of ferocious Banditti, whom the MURDERER OF JAFFA let
loose on the civilized World ! Such, and ten thousand times
worse, is the Fate prepared *for England, if the valour of her people
do not avert it ; for England will assuredly be more oppressed, in
proportion as she is more dreaded, envied, and hated.* To shew any
symptom of Neutrality in such a Cause, not to support it with all
our might, IS THE FOULEST TREASON AGAINST THE PEOPLE OF
ENGLAND ; and the poorest honest Labourer, who has a Mother,
or a Sister, a Wife, or a Daughter, has, in truth, as much reason
as the highest Duke in the Land to detest the Traitor. Englishmen think of this and profit by Example.

These were the kind of handbills (of which there are
hundreds in variety) which were circulated, to arouse and
stimulate martial fire and patriotic ardour in the Britannic
mind. Their name is Legion, and I have had to read
them all, in order to pick out the examples given in this
book. They are curious, and help us, more than any other
history, to gauge the temper of the times. It was a veritable scare. Hardly having felt any of the benefits of
peace, the English were once more involved in war, with
the almost certainty, this time, of having their, hitherto
almost inviolate, islands invaded by the French. We can
hardly wonder, therefore, at the hearty hatred our forefathers felt for the 'Corsican Ogre,' to whom all this tur-
moil was due ; and, to do them justice, they did hate him
with a thoroughly genuine detestation—so much so, that
they did not always scrupulously investigate the truth of
some of the very questionable statements dished up for
them (and they were highly spiced). There can be no
manner of doubt but that these broadsides and handbills,
together with the caricatures, had the desired effect in
rousing the nation to a fervid patriotism, and, as they did
so, it is perhaps hardly right to question the legality of
their statements, but accept them according to the doctrine
that ' the end justifies the means.'

CHAPTER XXVII.

PATRIOTIC HANDBILLS.

ON June 10, 1803, Gillray published an extra-sized picture of 'French Invasion—or Buonaparte Landing in Great Britain.' The French fleet is nearing land, and boats, full of armed men, are putting off. Bonaparte, and a large body of troops, including cavalry, have landed ; but, before they can scale the cliffs, and are yet on the shore, a few artillerymen, with two guns, have utterly routed them. It is *Sauve qui peut.* Napoleon, joining in the flight, throws away his sword ; the army is utterly demoralised, the ground being strewn with dead.

I. Cruikshank drew a not very interesting caricature, (June 10, 1803) of ' The Scarecrow's arrival, or Honest PAT giving them an Irish Welcome.' Napoleon, as a skeleton, is leading an army of skeletons, who are wading through the sea. He is just putting his foot on the shore, and, to encourage his troops, calls out, ' Now, my boys, halloo away —vil frighten Mr. Bull out of his wits, we vil make them quake like the Dutch, the Italian, the Swiss, and the rest of our Friends.' But a sturdy Irishman receives them with a shovel-full of mud in their faces. ' Och it is your own pratty figure it is, Master Bonny, d'ye think that Pat was to be blarney'd by such Scare Crows. No, no, Bother, the time is gone by : Pat's Eyes are wide open, and, look ye, if you don't imme-diately jump into the Sea to save your lives, I will shovel you all there to save mine.'

Here is a stirring appeal to the army :—

BRAVE SOLDIERS.
Defenders of your COUNTRY.

THE road to glory is open before you.—Pursue the great career of your forefathers, and rival them in the field of honour. *A proud and usurping* TYRANT (a name ever execrated by English-men) dares to *threaten our shores with* INVASION, *and to reduce the free born Sons of Britain to* SLAVERY *and* SERVITUDE. For-getting what English Soldiers are capable of, and ranking them with the hirelings of the powers who have fallen his prey on the Continent, he supposes his threat easily executed. *Give him a lesson, my brave Countrymen, that he will not easily forget, and that France may have by heart, for a Century to come!* Neither the vaunting Hero (who deserted his own Comrades and Soldiers in Egypt), nor the French Army, have ever been able to cope with British valour when fairly opposed to it. Our Ancestors declared that ONE ENGLISHMAN *was ever a match for* THREE FRENCHMEN—and that man to man was too great odds in our favour. We have but to feel their sentiments, to confirm them— you will find that their declaration was founded on experience ; and that even in our day, within these three years, an army of your brave Comrades has convinced its admiring Country, that the balance is still as great as ever, against the enemy. Our EDWARD, *the illustrious Black Prince, laid waste the country of France, to the Gates of Paris, and, on the Plains of Cressy, left* 11 *Princes and* 30,000 *men dead upon the Field of Battle—a greater number than the whole English Army boasted at the beginning of the action.* The same heroic Prince, having annihilated the Fleet of France, *entirely routed her Army at Poictiers, took her King prisoner, and brought him Captive to London, with thousands of his Nobles and People, and all this against an Army* SIX TIMES AS NUMEROUS AS THAT OF THE ENGLISH ! Did not our Harry the Fifth invade France, and at Agincourt *oppose an Army of* 9,000 *men, sickly, fatigued, and half starved, to that of the French, amounting to* 50,000 ; and did he not leave 10,000 of the enemy dead upon the field, and take 14,000 prisoners, with the loss of only 400 men ?

Have we not, within this century, to boast a MARLBOROUGH, who, (besides his other victories) at Blenheim slew 12,000 of the French, and made 14,000 Prisoners, *and in less than a month conquered* 300 *miles of Territory from the Enemy?* Did not the gallant WOLFE, in the year 1759, gain the Heights of Abraham with a handful of British Troops, and, afterwards, *defeat the whole French Army, and gain possession of all Canada, &c. ?*

And are not the glories of our ABERCROMBY *and the Gallant* ARMY *of* EGYPT fresh in your minds? *An Army of* 14,000 *Britons, who landed in the face of upwards of* 20,000 *troops of France,* and drove from a country, with whose strongholds they were acquainted, and whose resources they knew how to apply, a host of Frenchmen, enured to the Climate, and Veterans in arms? *Did they not cut in pieces that vaunted Corps of Buonaparte's, whose successes against other Powers had obtained for it the appellation of* INVINCIBLE—And is not their Standard (all that is left of it) a trophy, at this moment, in our Capital ?

The Briton fights for his Liberty and Rights, the Frenchman fights for *Buonaparte,* who has robbed him of both ! Which, then, in the nature of events, will be most zealous, most active, and most terrible in the Field of Battle? the independent supporter of his country's cause, or the Slave who trembles lest the arms of his comrades should be turned against himself ; who knows that his Leader, his General, his *Tyrant, did not hesitate, after having* MURDERED 4,000 *disarmed Turks, in cool blood, to* POISON 300 *of his own sick Soldiers, of men who had been fighting his battles of ambition, and been wounded in his defence*—English Soldiers will scarcely credit this, but it is on record, not to be doubted, never to be expunged. But more ; read and blush for the depravity even of an enemy. It is not that these bloody deeds have been perpetrated from necessity, from circumstances however imperious at the moment ; they were the acts of cool and deliberate determination, and his purpose, no less sanguinary, is again declared in the event of success in his enterprise against this Country. Feeling that even the slavish followers of his fortune were not to be forced to embark in this ruinous and destructive expedition, he declares to them, in a public proclamation, or decoy, that *when they have landed in this Country, in order to make the booty the richer,* NO QUARTER *shall be given to the* BASE ENGLISH *who fight for their perfidious Government—that they shall be* PUT TO THE SWORD, *and their Property distributed among the Soldiers of the Victorious Army ! ! !* Say, is this the conduct of a Hero? is this the man who is destined to break the spirit of Englishmen? *shall we suffer an* ASSASSIN *to enter our blessed Country, and despoil our fields of their produce—to massacre our brave Soldiers in cool blood, and hang up every man who has carried arms ?* Your cry is vengeance for the insult—and Vengeance is in your own hands. It must be signal and terrible ! Like the bolt from Heaven, let it strike the devoted Army of Invaders ! *Every Frenchman will find his Grave where he first steps on British ground, and not a Soldier of Buonaparte's boasted Legions shall escape the fate his ambitious Tyrant has prepared for him !*

BRITONS STRIKE HOME !

Or your Fame is for ever blasted,—Your Liberties for ever lost ! ! !

This is very bombastic and 'high-falutin,' but Englishmen were in a very grievous fright, nevertheless.

Still harping on the prospect of a French landing, we have a caricature by T. West (June 13, 1803) of ' Britannia correcting an Unruly Boy.' Britannia has got Boney across her knee, and, having taken down his breeches, is administering such a sound castigation with a birch rod, called the *United Kingdom*, as to bring forth copious streams of blood. Needless to say, our hero is repentant, and prays 'Oh forgive me this time and I never will do so again. Oh dear! Oh dear! you'll entirely destroy the *Honors of the Sitting.*' But the stern matron still keeps on, with 'There take that, and that, and that, and be more careful not to provoke my anger more.'

We have an illustration of the homely proverb of 'Set a beggar on horseback &c.,' in 'The Corsican Beggar Riding to the Devil,' by Ansell (June 15, 1803). Here we have Hell treated in the mediæval manner, a huge, grotesque, dragon-like head, with outstretched jaws, vomiting flames. Napoleon, on a white charger, hugging himself with the idea that 'Sure they will make me Emperor,' is riding straight to it; whilst two devils are in a high state of jubilation. One opines that 'He is sure to come; we will finish your ambition,' the other politely calls out, 'Shew him in.' Ireland asks John Bull, 'Hey Johnny, who's that?' and gets as a reply, 'Tis Boney going Post, brother Pat.' The Gallic Cock, crowing on its dunghill, screams, 'This is nothing new.'

Here is a passionate appeal, supposed to come from one of the softer sex :—

MEN OF ENGLAND.

IT is said that some of you are so discontented, that you would join the Enemies against your Country—Is it possible that you are so misled as to believe that the Enemies to England would, whatever they pretend, be friends *to you*. Be assured, if you are so persuaded, that you are grossly imposed upon. What should make them your friends—What ties should bind them? Think a little—and a very little proper reflection will be sufficient to make you see, that the Invaders of your Country, in their hearts, hate the inhabitants of it ; and will, in the end, themselves betray the Traitors to it.

The Invaders would nearly desolate your Country—and if Provisions are dear now, what would they be when numberless stacks of hay and corn were burnt—the cattle destroyed, and a horrid legion of desperate, faithless, lawless Invaders, to be maintained? who would trample upon every tie, break all promises, make *tools* of you first, but soon sacrifice your wives, your daughters, your families, and yourselves, when you have served their purpose. If any few among you were guilty of plunder, you would, yourselves, soon be plundered and destroyed.

It has been the necessity of defending our country against its enemies that has made provisions dear ; but your wages have been increased in proportion—and though you may sometimes, in the course of events, suffer some hardships, as *everybody*, in their turn, must do, you may, unless it be your own faults, enjoy the greatest comforts—a peaceable home—a happy family—a quiet country, whose trade and consequence is envied by all the world—plentiful harvests—a government which respects you, and that your forefathers would have defended with the last drop of their blood—you have an excellent and lawful King, who will protect you ; and above all, you may have a blessing from God, who will reward you hereafter if you do your duty *here*. But from an Usurper, and Invader, you can have nothing to expect, but the being slaves to his lawless schemes for power. Let who will tell you the contrary, he comes only for plunder, and revenge, upon the only nation he fears. Will you be his instruments, his tools? Can you, as Englishmen, lower yourselves in such a manner—to such a mean Usurper ? Heaven, from the beginning, intended you should have Kings and superiors—Equality was never in-tended—it never can be, on this earth—Heaven and reason forbid it—and Bonaparte, himself, has shewn you how little he intended to establish it. Your forefathers call to you from their graves— their warning voice tells you, that you would soon find the perfidy of his heart. The wretched condition you would bring yourselves and your families into, you would repent too late—deprived of every friend, but sure of ample punishment here, and hereafter.

People of England ! Sons of my beloved glorious Country ! You are now called upon by the women of your Country to protect them – Can you refuse to hear us ? Can you bear the thought of not only seeing *us* used with insult and barbarity,—of seeing your country bleed at every pore, but of being the occasion of these dreadful evils, in consequence of your mistaken opinions, and by suffering yourselves to be deceived, and cajoled, by foreign, ill designing wretches, who have only our, and your, ruin at heart.

Attend, Men of England,—you who may give conquest to your Country, safety to us, and everlasting glory to yourselves— Attend, Men of England, to the *solemn* truths told you by an honest

ENGLISHWOMAN.

It is a weak spot in these lucubrations that very few of them are dated, so that it is impossible to arrange them,

L

like the illustrations, in chronological sequence. But this is of little matter ; the situation was the same, whatever might be the month.

J. Smith (June 25, 1803) etched King George 'Playing at Bubbles.' The monarch is seated before a large tub of soap-suds, amusing himself by blowing bubbles, which are *Napoleon, flat-bottomed boats, invasion, and little ships*—and, judging by the king's placid countenance, caring very little for his creations.

A very excellent example of caricature is Gillray's

'King of Brobdingnag and Gulliver' (June 26, 1803). The burly king has the diminutive Bonaparte in the palm of his hand and is critically examining him through his glass. Says he, 'My little friend Grildrig you have made a most admirable panegyric upon yourself and country, but from what I can gather from your own relation, and the answers I have with much pains wring'd and extorted from you, I cannot but conclude you to be one of the most pernicious little odious reptiles that nature ever suffered to crawl upon the surface of the Earth.'

And, indeed, he well deserved this character, if he were anything like the demon the English sought to make him out. In one of the handbills, however, is a quotation from 'Denon's Travels in Egypt,' which is wrested to serve its purpose in fomenting the Invasion furor.

To the infamous WREïCH, if there be such an one in England, who dares to talk of, or even hopes to find *Mercy* in the Breast of the *Corsican Bonaparte*, the *eternal sworn Foe of England*, the Conqueror and Grand Subjugator of France.

If there be any Englishmen so base, or so foolish, as to wish to trust to the *Mercy* of a French *Invading Army*, let him read that which follows :—The accuracy and veracity of the account cannot be doubted, it being an Extract from a Book, not only written under the inspection of the French Government, but, moreover, dedicated to the *Grand Consul.*

I shall make no comment on this most scandalous public avowal, or rather, boast, of so inhuman and atrocious a proceeding, as the simple Fact sufficiently speaks for itself.

' We, who boasted that we were more just than the Mamelukes, committed daily, and *almost necessarily*, a number of iniquities : the difficulty of distinguishing our Enemies by their Form and Colour, made us, every day, *kill innocent Peasants* ; the Soldiers took Caravans of *poor Merchants* for enemies, and, before justice could be done them, *(when there was time to do it)* *two or three of them were shot*, a part of their cargo was *pillaged or destroyed*, and their camels exchanged for those of ours, which had been wounded. The Fate of the People, *for whose happiness we no doubt came to Egypt*, was no better. If, at our approach, terror made them leave their houses, they found on their return, nothing but *the Mud of which the Walls were composed* ; utensils, ploughs, gates, roofs, everything served as fuel to boil our Soup ; their pots were broken, their grain was eaten, their fowls and pigeons roasted, and nothing was left but the carcases of their dogs, *when they defended the Property of their Masters.* If we remained in their Villages, the wretches were *summoned to return*, under pain of being treated as *Rebels*, and, in consequence, *double Taxed* ; and when they yielded to these Menaces, came *to pay their Tax*, it sometimes happened, that, from their great number, they were taken for a body of Revolters, their sticks for arms, and they received *some discharges of Musketry before there was time for explaining the Mistake* ; the Dead were interred, and we remained friends, till a safe opportunity for revenge occurred. It is true, that when they staid at home, *paid the Tax, and supplied all the Wants of the Army*, they were saved the trouble of a Journey to a Residence in the Desert, *saw their Provisions consumed with regularity*, and *were allowed* a Part of them, preserved some of their gates, sold their eggs to the Soldiers, AND HAD BUT FEW OF THEIR WIVES AND DAUGHTERS VIOLATED ! '

Such was the Treatment which Egypt experienced ; a Country which the French were desirous to possess, and to conciliate ; very Different is their Design upon Great Britain, which it is their avowed Intention to Ravage, Plunder and Destroy.

CHAPTER XXVIII.

ATTEMPT AT MEDIATION BY RUSSIA—MARTIAL ENTHUSIASM IN ENGLAND
—ENROLMENT OF VOLUNTEERS—PATRIOTIC HANDBILLS AND SONGS.

INEFFECTUAL attempts at mediation seem to have been made, but, situated as the two opposing Powers were, this could not be.

'Bruin become mediator' (artist unknown, June 1803) represents the Emperor of Russia as a bear, joining the hands of a Bull and a Monkey. The peacemaker thus addresses them, 'I wonder you civilized folks could not agree upon matters without reference to me, whom you have ridiculed as a Barbarian—but I suppose you think I must have more sense than yourselves, because I come further North.' The Monkey is giving his hand with 'I promise on the faith of a Frenchman (which is as any Birmingham Sixpence) to let you graze quietly in the Malta Paddock—and to love you with all my heart, as much as I do the Liberty of the French Nation.' The Bull says, 'Well Nappy, if you will leave off your Pranks and not think of skipping over to Egypt, and if you will promise not to hop the twig to Hanover, I will be reconciled.'

And again, a month later, is another caricature, called 'Olympic Games, or John Bull introducing his new Ambassador to the Grand Consul,' by I. Cruikshank (July 16, 1803), shewing us the little Corsican giving an ambassador a blow in the face with his clenched fist, saying, 'There Sir, take that, and tell your master, I'll thrash every one who dares to speak to me : I'll thrash all the World. D— me I'll, I'll, I'll, be King of the Universe.' The astonished Ambassador exclaims, 'Why this is Club Law ! this is the Argument of force indeed. The little Gentleman is Derangé.' John Bull, however, is introducing a prize-fighter as his representative, telling Napoleon, 'There, my Boy, is an Ambassador who will treat with you in your own way— but I say, be as gentle with him as you can.' The pugilist looks on his adversary with contempt, 'What! is it that little whipper snapper I am to set to with ? Why I think the *first round* will settle his hash.' The Austrian ambassador meanwhile remarks, ' The Monarch I represent, will return this insult with becoming Dignity.'

Martial enthusiasm was at its height, corps of volunteers were enrolled everywhere. The militia, 80,000 strong, had been called out on March 25 ; there was the regular army of 130,000, and, on June 28, the House of Commons agreed to the raising of 50,000 more, by means of conscription—of which England was to furnish 34,000, Ireland 10,000, and Scotland 6,000 ; whilst, on June 30, the Court of Common Council for the City of London resolved to raise, and equip, 800 men for the national service. This, be it remembered, only represented that portion of London within the city walls. Factions were for a time done away with, and men, of all shades of politics, stood shoulder by shoulder, as now, in the ranks of the different volunteer corps. Stirring broadsides were not needed, although they appeared, and the following may be taken as a good sample :—

ENGLISH MASTIFFS.

WE by this Address, publicly and solemnly, before God and our Country, pledge our Fortunes, Persons, and Lives, in the Defence of our Sovereign, and all the Blessings of our glorious Constitution.

There is not a Man that hears me, I am persuaded, who is not prompt and eager to redeem that pledge. There is not, there cannot be a Man here, who would leave undefended, our good, tried, and brave OLD KING in the Hour of Danger.

No, Sir ! we need now no Warning-voice ; no string of Eloquence ; no Thoughts that heat, and Words that burn, are necessary to raise a Host of hardy Men, when the King, the Parliament, and the Country are in Distress.[1] CALL OUT TO YORKSHIREMEN, ' COME FORTH TO BATTLE ! ' our Answer will be—One and All— ' WE ARE READY !—*There is the Enemy !*—Lead on ! ' Sir, that Enemy is not far off ; a very numerous, well appointed, ably commanded Army, to whom is promised the Plunder of England, are now hovering round, and Part of them in daily Sight of the Promised Land. They view it, like so many famished Wolves,

---

[1] Is from Mr. Stanhope's speech at a meeting of Yorkshire noblemen and gentlemen, at the Castle, York, July 28, 1803, for the purpose of addressing the king on the situation of the country.

Cruel as Death, and Hungry as the Grave, panting for an Opportunity, at any Risk, to come into our Sheep Fold ;—*but*, and if they should, is it not our Business, our first Duty, to have such a Guard of old, faithful ENGLISH MASTIFFS, of the old Breed, as shall make them quickly repent their temerity.

The Chief Consul of France tells us, that we are but a Nation of Shopkeepers : let us, Shopkeepers, then melt our Weights, and our Scales, and return him the Compliment in Bullets. Sir ; we may have a firm Reliance on the Exertions of as gallant a Fleet as ever sailed ; but the Fleet cannot perform Impossibilities ; it cannot be in two places at once ; it cannot conquer the Winds, and subdue the Storms. Though our old Tars can do much, they cannot do everything ; and it would be unsafe and dastardly to lie skulking behind them. With the Blessing of GOD, and a good Cause, we can do Wonders ; but if we depend upon our Naval Prowess only, we have much to fear. NO, SIR : England will never be perfectly safe, until she can defend herself as well by *Land*, as by *Sea* ; until she can defy the haughty Foe : if there was *even a Bridge* between Calais and Dover, and that Bridge in Possession of the Enemy, still can she say, in the Language of a good *English Boxing Match*, ' A FAIR FIELD AND NO FAVOUR.'

'Our good, tried, and brave OLD KING, in the Hour of Danger,' had made all snug, at least as far as human foresight could act. When the dreaded invasion came, he was to go either to Chelmsford or Dartford ; whilst the Queen, with the Royal Family and the treasure, were to go to Worcester, the city whose motto is ' Civitas in bello, et in pace, fidelis.' All the stores at Woolwich, including the artillery, were to be sent into the Midlands by means of the Grand Junction Canal ; in fact, every precaution was taken that forethought could devise : and there is but little doubt that, had Napoleon made good a landing, he would have had a warmer reception than he expected. Yet what disadvantages they laboured under compared to our days! no Telegraphs, no Railways, no Steam. Of course it may be said that the enemy was in no better position ; but still a lucky wind might favour their crossing, and hinder our preventing it.

Loyal and patriotic poetry abounded ; here is a specimen :—

THE VOICE OF THE BRITISH ISLES.

TUNE —' *Hearts of Oak.*'

Away, my brave boys, haste away to the shore ;
Our foes, the base French, boast they're straight coming o'er,
To murder, and plunder, and ravish, and burn —
Let them come—we'll take care they shall never return ;
For around all our shores, hark ! the notes loudly ring,
    United, we're ready,
    Steady, boys, steady,
To fight for our Liberty, Laws, and our King.

They boast in the dark they will give us the slip :
The attempt may procure them a dangerous dip ;
Our bold Tars are watching in Ocean's green lap,
To give them a long *Jacobinical* nap.[1]
But should they steal over, with one voice we'll sing,
    United, we're ready, &c.

They knew, that united, we sons of the waves
Would ne'er bow to Frenchmen, nor grovel like Slaves ;
So ere they dare venture to touch on our strand,
They sent black Sedition to poison our land.
But around all our shores let the notes loudly ring,
    United, we're ready, &c.

They swore we were slaves, all lost and undone ;
That a Jacobine nostrum, as sure as a gun,
Would make us all equal, and happy, and free ;
'Twas only to dance round their Liberty's tree.
No, no ! round our shores let the notes loudly ring,
    United, we're ready, &c.

'Twas only to grant them the kiss call'd fraternal—
A kiss which all Europe has found most infernal ;
And then they maintained the effect could not miss —
We should all be as blest as the Dutch and the Swiss.
No, no ! round our shores let the notes loudly ring,
    United, we're ready, &c.

With lies, and with many a Gallican wile,
They spread their dread poison o'er Erin's green Isle ;
But now each *shillalah* is ready to thwack,
And baste the lean ribs of the Gallican Quack.
All around Erin's shores, hark ! the notes loudly ring,
    United, we're ready, &c.

[1] ' Death is an eternal sleep,' *vide* Robespierre's Decree.

Stout Sandy, our brother, with heart, and with hand,
And his well-try'd *Glaymore*, joins the patriot band.
Now Jack, Pat, and Sandy thus cordial agree,
We sons of the wave shall for ever be free.
While around all our shores, hark ! the notes loudly ring,
  United, we're ready, &c.

As they could not deceive, now they threaten to pour
Their hosts on our land, to lay waste and devour ;
To drench our fair fields, and our cities in gore,
Nor cease to destroy till Britannia's no more.
Let them come if they dare—hark ! the notes loudly ring,
  United, we're ready, &c.

My sweet rosy Nan is a true British wife,
And loves her dear Jack, as she loves her own life ;
Yet she girds on my sword, and smiles while I glow,
To meet the proud French, and to lay their heads low,
And chants 'tween each buss, while the notes loudly ring,
  My Jack, art thou ready ?
  Steady, boy, steady,
Go fight for thy Liberty, Laws, and thy King.

And Ned, my brave Lad, with a true British heart,
Has forsaken his plough, has forsaken his cart ;
E'en Dolly has quitted, to dig in a trench,
All, all, for the sake of a cut at the French ;
While he sings all day long, let the notes loudly ring,
  I'm ready, I'm ready !
  Steady, boy, steady,
To fight for my Liberty, Laws, and my King.

Away then, my boys ! haste away to the shore,
Our foes, the base French, boast they're straight coming o'er,
To murder, and plunder, and ravish, and burn—
They may come,—but, by Jove, they shall never return ;
For around all our shores, hark ! the notes loudly ring,
  United, we're ready,
  Steady, boys, steady,
To fight for our Liberty, Laws, and our King.

'The Final Pacification of Europe' (artist unknown,
June 1803) shews that this desirable thing could only be
accomplished by the death of Napoleon—so he is represented as being suspended from a gallows, whilst postboys,

duly equipped with horns, and dressed in their different national garbs, are shouting, 'Good News for Russia, Prussia, Old England, Germany, and Switzerland.' Holland is excessively joyful: Mynheer calling out, 'Good news for Holland, ti-lol-de-riddle-lol.'

A very amusing caricature is 'Green Spectacles, or Consular Goggles' (artist unknown, June 1803), where Napoleon is represented as sitting on a rock called *Usurped Power*, and wearing an enormous pair of green goggles labelled 'Green eyed Jealousy,' through which he darts envious glances at Great Britain, West Indies, East Indies, Malta, and Egypt.

CHAPTER XXIX.

PATRIOTIC HANDBILLS, ETC.

WE meet with a slight notice of Toussaint l'Ouverture, and the war in St. Domingo, in a broadside dwelling on the consequences of a successful invasion: 'Here then there would be no *volunteering*, no *balloting*, unless, indeed, such Volunteers as were raised in France for the conquest of St. Domingo. And how were they raised? Why, by every man having a bayonet put to his breast, being seized by force, and then *chained in couples like dogs*, and drove down in a string to the coast, for embarkation, like so many *Galley slaves*. This, though it may sound incredible to an Englishman's ear, is a fact known to all Europe.

'Such my brave Countrymen, would be your dreadful fate, could this blessed island be once subjugated to that haughty and merciless Tyrant, the Corsican Bonaparte. Where then, is the Man who would not die a thousand, and a thousand deaths sooner than submit to so cruel and unnatural a fate?'

July was very prolific of these broadsheets, some of them taking the form of theatrical announcements, two of which are here given.

THEATRE ROYAL, ENGLAND.

IN REHEARSAL, AND MEANT TO BE SPEEDILY *ATTEMPTED*,

A FARCE

IN ONE ACT, CALLED THE

INVASION OF ENGLAND.

Principal Buffo .   . MR. BUONAPARTE,

Being his FIRST (and most likely his Last) Appearance on this Stage.

Anticipated Critique.

The structure of this Farce is very *loose*, and there is a moral, and radical, Defect in the Ground work. It boasts, however, considerable Novelty, for the Characters are ALL MAD. It is probable it will *not* be played in the COUNTRY, but will certainly never be *acted* in TOWN ; where ever it may be represented, we will do it the justice to say, it will be received with *Thunders* of . . . CANNON ! ! ! but we will venture to affirm will never equall the Success of

JOHN BULL.

It is however likely that the Piece may yet be put off on account of the Indisposition of the Principal Performer, Mr. BUONAPARTE. We don't exactly know what this Gentleman's Merits may be on the Tragic Boards of France, but he will never succeed here ; his Figure is very diminutive, he struts a great deal, seems to have no Conception of his *Character*, and treads the Stage very badly ; notwithstanding which defects, we think, if he comes here, he will get an ENGAGEMENT, though it is probable that he will, shortly after, be reduced to the situation of a SCENE SHIFTER.

As for the Farce, we recommend it to be withdrawn, as it is the opinion of all Political Critics, that if played, it will cer-tainly be

DAMN'D.

' *Vivant Rex et Regina.*'

The other is :—

THEATRE ROYAL OF THE UNITED KINGDOMS.

Some Dark, Foggy Night, about November next, will be ATTEMPTED, by a Strolling Company of French Vagrants, an Old Pantomomic Farce, called

HARLEQUIN'S INVASION

OR THE

DISAPPOINTED BANDITTI.

WITH NEW MACHINERY, MUSIC, DRESSES, AND DECORATIONS.

HARLEQUIN BUTCHER, BY MR. BUONAPARTE

FROM CORSICA.

(Who Murdered that Character in *Egypt, Italy, Switzerland, Holland,* &c.)

THE OTHER PARTS BY

MESSRS. SIEYES, LE BRUN, TALLEYRAND, MARET, ANGEREAU, MASSENA, AND THE REST OF THE GANG.

In the Course of the Piece will be introduced a Distant View of *Harlequin's Flat-Bottomed Boats*

WARMLY ENGAGED BY THE

WOODEN WALLS OF OLD ENGLAND.

THE REPULSE.

OR, BRITONS TRIUMPHANT.

The Parts of John Bull, Paddy Whack, Sawney Mac Snaish, and Shone-ap-Morgan, by Messrs. NELSON, MOIRA, ST. VINCENT, GARDNER, HUTCHINSON, WARREN, PELLEW, S. SMITH, &c. &c. &c.

The Chorus of '*Hearts of Oak,*' by the JOLLY TARS and ARMY of OLD ENGLAND,

Assisted by a Numerous Company of Provincial Performers, Who have VOLUNTEERED their Services on this Occasion.

The Overture to consist of 'Britons Strike Home'—'Stand to your Guns'—'Rule Britannia' and

GOD SAVE THE KING.

The Dresses will be splendid ; the Band numerous and compleat. The whole to conclude with a GRAND ILLUMINATION, and a TRANSPARENCY displaying BRITANNIA receiving the Homage of GALLIC SLAVES.

** No Room for Lobby Loungers. *Vivant Rex et Regina.*

According to the caricaturist, Hanover had no special attractions for Bonaparte. 'Boney in possession of the Millstone' (Ansell, July 5, 1803) shews him as having a fearfully large and weighty millstone hung round his neck, called Hanover. He totters under the weight, and calls out that 'It's cursed heavy! I wish it had been Malta!' John Bull, dressed as a countryman, jeers him: 'What! thee hast got it, hast thee? The Devil do thee good with it—Old Measter Chatham used to say it was a Millstone about my neck—so perhaps I may feel more lightsome without it.'

'Flags of Truth and Lies' (artist unknown, July 10, 1803) is a representation of a typical Frenchman and Englishman, as then imagined. The Frenchman holds a tricoloured flag, and intimates that 'Mon grande Maître bid-a you read dat, Monsieur!' and points to the following text on the flag: 'Citizen first Consul Buonaparte presents Compliments and Thanks to the Ladies and Gentlemen of Great Britain, who have honored him with their visits at Paris, and intends himself the pleasure of returning it in person, as soon as his arrangements for that purpose can be completed.' John Bull replies, 'And let your Grand Master read that, Mounseer,' and points to his flag, the Union Jack, on which is written 'John Bull does not rightly understand the Chief Consul's lingo—but supposes he means something about Invasion; therefore the said John Bull deems it necessary to observe that if his Consular Highness dares to invade any Ladies or Gentlemen on his coast, he'll be damn'd if he don't sink him.'

THE DEVIL AND THE CONSUL.
A New Song.

As the Devil thro' Paris one Day took a Walk,
BUONAPARTE he met,—and they both had some Talk ;
Great Hero, says *Satan*, pray how do you do?
I am well, cried the Consul, my Service to you.
Derry down, down, down, derry down!

What News do you bring from your Empire below,
How is OLIVER CROMWELL? But very so, so !
I fancy he envies your *glories* so great ;
For he vows he ne'er reigned in such Splendor and State—
Derry down, &c.

Tho' he often exerted himself in *my* Cause,
Still Britons from him, had some excellent Laws ;
How much below yours all his Merits must fall,
Who rules this *Republic* without Laws at all ! ! !

              Derry down, &c.

ALEXANDER, and CÆSAR, fine Heroes in Story,
Are jealous, I know, of your Deeds, and your Glory ;
Tho' they push'd thro' the Globe all their Conquests pell mell,
And rul'd *Monarchs* on Earth, now they're *Subjects* in Hell.

              Derry down, &c.

'Bout Religion at Rome you once made a great Pother,
Have pulled down one *Pope*, and then set up another !
In *Egypt* I've heard of your *wonderful* Works,
How Mahomet you worshipp'd, to flatter the Turks !

              Derry down, &c.

The Deeds you there acted with *Poison* and Ire,
On my Realms are recorded in Letters of Fire ;
Not an *Imp* in my Service, but boasts of your Fame,
And 'grins, horribly' grins—when he mentions your name.

              Derry down, &c.

You boast much, dear CONSUL, of Liberty's Tree,
You say that the *Dutch* and the *Swiss* are quite free !
If such Freedom as this to give Britain's your aim,
Try your skill, that I soon to yourself may lay claim !

              Derry down, &c.

When the Time shall arrive that's determin'd by Fate—
That you quit for INVASION your Consular Seat ;
Fear not—if bold Britons should prove your o'erthrow,
You're sure of a *Seat* in my Kingdom below !

              Derry down, &c.

Gillray (July 20, 1803) produced the 'Death of the Corsican Fox—Scene, the last of the Royal Hunt,' in which George III. holding his horse's bridle, with one hand holds up the Corsican Fox, to throw to his hounds, St. Vincent, Nelson, Sydney Smith, Gardner, Cornwallis, and others— shouting merrily, meanwhile, 'Tally ho ! Tally ho ! ho ! ho ! ho !'

DEATH OF THE CORSICAN FOX.

CHAPTER XXX.

INVASION SQUIBS, CONTINUED—BONAPARTE'S TEN COMMANDMENTS, ETC

THE NEW MOSES
OR
BONAPARTE'S TEN COMMANDMENTS.
Translated from a French Manuscript,
BY SOLIMAN THE TRAVELLER.

And when the great man came from Egypt, he used cunning, and force, to subject the people. The good, as well as the wicked, of the land trembled before him, because he had won the hearts of all the fighting men ; and, after he had succeeded in many of his schemes, his heart swelled with pride, and he sought how to ensnare the people more and more, to be the greatest man under the Sun.

The Multitude of the people were of four kinds ; some resembled blind men, that cannot see ; some were fearful, who trembled before him ; others courageous, and for the good of the people, but too weak in number ; and others yet, who were as wicked as the great man himself. And when he was at the head of the deluded nation, he gave strict laws, and the following commandments, which were read before a multitude of people, and in a full congregation of all his priests :

1. Ye Frenchmen, ye shall have no other commander above me, for I, Bonaparte, am the supreme head of the nation, and will make all nations bow down to you, and obey me, as your Lord, and Commander.

2. Ye shall not have any graven images upon your coin, in marble, wood, or metal, which might represent any person above me ; nor shall ye acknowledge any person to excel me, whether he be among the living or the dead ; whether he be in the happy land of the enlightened French, or in the cursed island of the dull English ; for I, the Chief Consul of France, am a jealous hero, and visit disobedience of an individual upon a whole nation, and of a father upon the children, and upon the third and fourth generation of them that hate me ; and shew mercy unto those that love me, and humble themselves.

3. Ye shall not trifle with my name, nor take it in vain; nor shall you suffer that any other nation treat it disrespectfully, for I will be the sole commander upon earth, and make you triumph over your enemies.

4. Remember, that ye keep the days of prayers, and pray for me as the head of the Nation and the future Conqueror of the base English. Ye shall pray fervently, with your faces cast upon the ground, and not look at the priest when he pronounces my name ; for I am a jealous hero, and delight in my priests, because they are humble, and I have regarded the lowliness of their hearts, and forgiven them all their past iniquities. And ye priests, remember the power of him, who made you his creatures, and do your duty.

5. Respect and honour all French heroes, that ye may find mercy in mine eyes for all your iniquities, and that ye may live in the land, in which I, the Lord, your Commander, live.

6. Ye shall not murder each other, save it be by my own commands, for purposes that may be known to me alone ; but of your enemies, and all those nations that will not acknowledge your, and my, greatness, ye may kill an infinite number ; for that is a pleasing sight in the eyes of your supreme commander.

7. Ye shall not commit adultery at home, whatever ye may do in the land of infidels, and the stiff-necked people ; for they are an abomination to the Lord, your Commander.

8. Ye shall not steal at home, but suppress your covetousness, and insatiable desire of plunder, until ye may arrive in the land of our enemies. Ye shall neither steal from them with indiscretion, but seem to give with the left hand, when the right taketh.

9. Ye shall not bear false witness against your neighbour, if he should distinguish himself in the land of the enemies.

10. Ye shall not covet any thing of your neighbour, but every-

thing of your enemies ; his jewels, his gold, his silver, his horse or
ass, his maid, his daughter, his wife, or anything in which your
hearts find delight ; and ye may take it, but still with cunning ;
for the Lord, your Commander, loveth mildness, more than
strength, to please the people when he plunders.—Use the sword
in battle, cunning after it, look for plunder, but subject the people
to me ;—herein lie all my commandments, and those who keep
them shall be protected by my power and prosper in all my under-
takings.

MASTER BONEY'S
HEARTY WELCOME TO ENGLAND.

Being the Song of Songs, and worth all the Songs in the World put together.
To be sung, or said, by every Jovial Fellow, who is a
True Lover of our good King and most happy
Constitution.

Should Boney come hither, our Britons declare,
They'd flog the dog well—you may surely guess where :
While others have vow'd, they would hang him as high,
As Haman the Jew—'twixt the earth and the sky.
    Boney down, down, down, Boney down.

Some say they will treat him no better than fleas,
And 'twixt thumb and finger they'll give him a squeeze ;
Whilst some by the ears, the vile Ruffian they'll lug,
And others will give him a good Cornish hug.
    Boney down, &c.

Nay, many would clap him in cage for a show,
At two pence a piece, Sirs—the price is too low :
Whilst others would drive him post haste to the Tower,
A *tit-bit* for tygers and wolves to devour.
    Boney down, &c.

Stand by, says young Snip, don't you see my bold shears ?
For the least I will have, is his nose or his ears ;
Says the Cook, I will baste him, and humble his pride,
Cries the Tanner, Pox take him, I'll tan his vile hide.
    Boney down, &c.

Says the Butcher, I'll knock down the dog like an ox,
Cries the Constable bold—put the knave in the Stocks ;
Says the Chandler, when once to the Pill'ry he hies,
Rotten eggs will I furnish to bung up his eyes.
    Boney down, &c.

Says the Doctor, I'm ready to give him a pill,
For the doctors, like Boney, they know how to kill ;

Says the Lawyer, I'll make the cur presently mute,
When once I shall bring him the cost of his suit.
Boney down, &c.

Cries the Huntsman, I long on his shoulders to ride,
I warrant a good pair of spurs I'll provide.
Says the Welchman, I'll toast him as I would toast cheese ;
Says Paddy, I'll whack him, as long as you *plase.*
Boney down, &c.

Cries a brave bonny Scot, Mon, gee mee his *lug,*
And I'll squeeze him as flat as a *bonnock* or bug ;
Says old Suds, I will shave him with razor so notch'd,
As shall leave his black muzzle most famously scotch'd.
Boney down, &c.

Says the Dust-man, I'll *dust* him—you know what I mean,
I'll give him a hide, all black, blue and green ;
Says the Mason, I'll case him in good bricks and mortar,
No, no, says Jack Ketch—don't you see this nice *halter ?*
Boney, down, &c.

Says the Baker, the Rogue in my oven I'll poke ;
Cries young Sweep—in the chimney I'll give him a smoke ;
The Cobler will give him a stitch in the heel,
And here's Moll, who would skin him as clean as an eel.
Boney down, &c.

But here's Tom the Miller, who swears he'll have Boney,
And grind him as close as—Old Hunks keeps his money,
Nay, stop, cries the Joiner, I'll saw off his head,
Cries the Surgeon, we'll have him as soon as he's dead.
Boney down, &c.

Then stretch the Dog out, and when flat on his back,
We'll cut out his heart to see if it's black ;
For sure such another, no mortal e'er saw,
Unless vomited forth, from old Belzebub's maw.
Boney down, &c.

But now for his flesh—we must lay bare his bones,
And then let him stand clear of Old *Davy Jones,*[1]
But Davy will have him, as sure as a gun,
So now Master Boney, here ends all your fun.
Boney down, &c.

The Soldiers will stick him—the Sailor he cries,
He'll never come hither, the Rascal's too wise ;

[1] Another name for old Nick.

M

He knows that the Tars of Old England ne'er shrink,
But him, and his flat-bottom'd boats they will sink.
          Boney down, &c.
'Twou'd weary your patience to hear folks repeat,
How Boney the *Pigmy* they're anxious to treat ;
So let him come hither, we'll soon make a ring,
Then fight till we die, for our Country and King.
          Boney down, &c.

Among the caricatures, West gives us (July 1803) 'A British Chymist Analizing a Corsican Earth Worm ! !' Bonaparte is in a retort, being distilled, and George the Third is examining a cup of his extract, with a magnifying glass, saying, ' I think I can now pretty well ascertain the ingredients of which this insect is composed—viz.—Ambition and self sufficiency, two parts—Forgetfulness—one part—some light Invasion Froth, on the surface, and a prodigious quantity of fretful passion, and conceited Arrogance is the residue ! ! '

' Little Ships, or John Bull very Inquisitive ' (artist unknown, July 1803), shews us Napoleon employed in cutting toy ships out of bits of wood ; he has already filled a large basket with them, and has two or three before him, on a table. John Bull, with a terrific oaken cudgel, comes suddenly upon him, saying, ' I ax Pardon for coming in with my hat on, without knocking—but, hearing a nation thumping in your workshop—thought I may as well step up stairs, and see what the youngster is about.' Napoleon replies, ' Don't be alarm'd Johnny—I am only making a few little Ships, for my own Private Amusement.'

The following broadside was printed with different headings, so as to sell in different counties—

TWENTY THOUSAND POUNDS
REWARD.

MIDDLESEX (to wit)
To all Constables, Head boroughs, Tithing Men, and other Officers of the County of Middlesex, and to every of whom it may concern,

WHEREAS a certain ill disposed Vagrant, and common disturber, commonly called, or known by the name of NAPOLEON BONAPARTE, *alias* Jaffa Bonaparte, *alias* Opium Bonaparte, *alias*

Whitworth Bonaparte, *alias* Acre Bonaparte, still continues to go about swindling and defrauding divers Countries, Cities, Towns, and Villages, under divers, various, and many false and wicked pretences, out of their Rights, Comforts, Conveniences, and Cash; AND WHEREAS the said NAPOLEON BONAPARTE, *alias* Jaffa Bonaparte, *alias* Opium Bonaparte, *alias* Whitworth Bonaparte, *alias* Acre Bonaparte, hath been guilty of divers Outrages, Rapes, and Murders, at *Jaffa, Rosetta,* and elsewhere ; AND WHEREAS It is strongly suspected that the said NAPOLEON BONAPARTE, *alias* Jaffa Bonaparte, *alias* Opium Bonaparte, *alias* Whitworth Bonaparte, *alias* Acre Bonaparte, hath in contemplation at the Day of the Date of these presents, to land in some, (but in what, part is not yet known) of Great Britain or Ireland : WE DO hereby will and require, that in case the said NAPOLEON BONAPARTE, *alias* Jaffa Bonaparte, *alias* Opium Bonaparte, *alias* Whitworth Bonaparte, *alias* Acre Bonaparte, shall be found to *lurk,* and *wander* up and down your Bailiwick, that you bring before us the body of the said NAPOLEON BONAPARTE, *alias* Jaffa Bonaparte, *alias* Opium Bonaparte, *alias* Whitworth Bonaparte, *alias* Acre Bonaparte, on or before the Morrow[1] of All Souls, that he may be forthwith sent to our Jail for WILD BEASTS, situate, standing, and being, over Exeter 'Change in the Strand, without *Bail* or *Mainprize* ; and that he be there placed in a certain Iron Cage, with the Ouran Outang, or some other ferocious and voracious animal like himself, for the purpose of being tamed, or until a warrant shall issue to our beloved subject *Jack Ketch,* to deal with him according to Law and the *Virtue* of his Office ; and this in no-wise omit at your peril. Witness our hands

JOHN DOE and RICHARD ROE.

The said NAPOLEON BONAPARTE, *alias* Jaffa Bonaparte, *alias* Opium Bonaparte, *alias* Whitworth Bonaparte, *alias* Acre Bonaparte, is a Corsican by birth, about five feet four inches in height, of a swarthy black complexion, dark hair and eye brows, and resembles a great deal in person, a Bear-leader, or one of the Savoyards who play on the reeds at Vauxhall : he is remarkable for walking fast, and taking long strides, and has been thought to squint, though it is, in fact, no more than a *cast* in the left eye, with looking too much at one object—Old England—to which over application, he also owes being afflicted with the Jaundice.

The above reward will be paid by the County immediately on apprehension.

[1] November 3.

CHAPTER XXXI.

INVASION, *continued*—'BRITONS, STRIKE HOME'—BONAPARTE'S WILL.

AT this time much use was made of the phrase 'Britons, strike home!' which first appears in an adaptation of Beaumont and Fletcher's play of 'Bonduca,' or Boadicea—which was set to music by Henry Purcell in 1695. The few words are not in the original drama, but are interpolated with other songs, and form a solo and chorus.

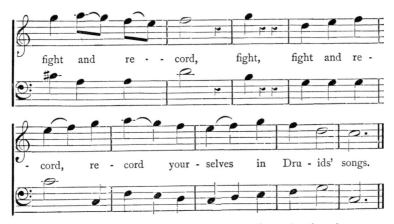

fight and re - - cord, fight, fight and re - - cord, re - cord your - selves in Dru - ids' songs.

But these simple words would hardly suit the times, so a brand new patriotic song was evolved, embodying the title

BRITONS, STRIKE HOME !

A New Song.

Should Frenchmen e'er pollute Britannia's strand,
Or press with hostile hoof this sacred land ;
The daring deed should every Briton arm,
To save his native land from dire alarm ;
Her free born Sons should instant take the field,
The Altar and the Throne at once to shield.
  Britons, strike home ! avenge your Country's cause,
  Protect your *King*, your *Liberties*, and *Laws !*

Repel the Foe, that, desperate, dares invade
The land protected by great Sydney's shade ;
And in the cause for which your Hampden bled,
Should ev'ry Briton's blood be freely shed ;
A cause no less than Liberty and Life,
The poor Man's Home, his Children and his Wife.
  Britons, strike home ! &c.

The base Usurper comes—his troops advance,
And line, with threat'ning front, the shores of France ;
Already has the Despot given the word ;
Already has he drawn his blood stain'd sword ;
While *Jaffa's* plains attest th' Assassin's skill,
Poison and blood—the dagger and the pill.
  Britons, strike home ! &c.

No common war we wage, our *native land*
Is menac'd by a murderous, ruthless band ;
The Throne and Altar by their Chief o'erturn'd,
And at his feet one half the prostrate world !
' Plunder and Rape and Death ' 's the hostile cry,
' Fire to your towns—to Britons slavery ! '
        Britons, strike home ! &c.

Come, Bonaparte, come ! we are prepar'd ;
No British heart a foreign foe e'er fear'd.
What ! tho' an abject world in arms should rise,
In *England's* cause, a Briton death defies ;
If to herself she prove but firm and true,
Gaul, and her frantic Chief, she'll make to rue.
        Britons, strike home ! &c.

Plung'd in the deep, her navy we'll confound,
Or with French blood manure our British ground ;
Drive backward to the sea the Gallic slaves,
And whelm their host, like Pharaoh's, in the waves ;
Restore lost Peace and Plenty to our isle,
And make the land again with gladness smile.
        Britons, strike home ! &c.

There is an amusing picture by West (July 1803) called ' Amusement after Dinner, or The Corsican Fairy displaying his Prowess.' George the Third and Queen Charlotte are at dessert, which is, as was their whole *ménage*, frugal, consisting only of a blancmange—the top ornament of which is a fleet of ships, behind which is a pineapple (the *King fruit*, as it was called on its introduction into England), the summit of which bears a crown. The royal pair are highly amused by the antics of the Corsican fairy (Napoleon) who vapours about the table in huge cocked hat and enormous sword. Pointing to the blancmange, he says, ' If I could but get over this dish of Blanche Mange, I would soon invade the Pine Apple.'

In ' A Monstrous Stride,' by I. Cruikshank (July 25, 1803), Bonaparte is represented as flourishing his sword and, having one foot on Turkey and Poland, is attempting to put the other on Great Britain, but steps short, and comes among the fleet guarding the English shores. Underneath the picture is ' He will put his foot in it.'

There was a somewhat amusing political squib on

Napoleon, published some time in July of this year, entitled

BONAPARTE'S WILL.

In the name of my Trinity, the Goddess of Reason, Mahomet the Prophet, and Pius the Pope ; We the most great, most magnanimous, and most puissant BRUTUS ALY NAPOLEON BONAPARTE, son to a Spy, grandson to a Butcher, and great-grandson to a Galley Slave, Emperor of the Gauls, First Consul of France, President of Italy, Landamman of Switzerland, Director of Holland, King of Etruria, Protector of Emperors, Dictator and Creator of Kings, Electors, Princes, Cardinals, Senators, Generals, Bishops, Prefects, Actors, Schoolmasters, &c., &c., &c., do declare, that notwithstanding the adulation of our Slaves, and their assurances of immortality, the pangs of our conscience, the decay of our body, the fear of recoiling daggers, the dreadful anticipation of infernal machines emitting fire and smoke, invented at Jaffa, and the hissing breath of the poisonous serpents generated at El Arish, remind us that we soon must die, and that our power must die with us. We, therefore, according to the *Senatus Consultum* of our free Senate, do declare this to be our last Will and Testament, as follows :
Imprimis.

To our most beloved, and dearest *Ibrahim Rostan*, Mameluke, we give and bequeath after our decease, the crown of Henry IV., the sceptre of Saint Louis, and the throne of France and Navarre, the sovereignty and sovereign disposal of the lives and fortunes of thirty millions of Frenchmen, of six millions of Italians, of seven millions of Spaniards, of two millions of Helvetians, and of three millions of Batavians, (except as is hereafter excepted) and we enjoin and charge all the world to acknowledge, adore, and respect this Mameluke, *Ibrahim Rostan*, the African, as the natural and legal successor of us, *Brutus Aly Napoleon Bonaparte*, the Corsican.

We give and bequeath in reversion, to Citizen *Barras*, our dear Consort, much improved, and more enriched, but reserving to ourselves the disposal of her virtuous Maids of Honour, whom we give and bequeath to our *Legion of Honour*, as a reward due as well to the virtues of the one, as to the valour of the other.

We give and bequeath to our dearly beloved brother *Joseph*, the presidency of the Italian Republic, together with our dearly bought Minister *Talleyrand*, to be disposed of as his own property, in all future negociations.

To our dearly beloved brother *Lucien*, we give and bequeath our Batavian Republic, and our Minister *Chaptal*, who, hereafter, shall write his speeches, dictate his letters, and correct his spelling.

To our dearly beloved brother *Louis*, we bequeath our Helvetian Republic, and our Minister *Berthier*, accompanied with the sense of his Secretary *Achambau*, whose instructions, in some time, may enable him to become a good Corporal of Grenadiers.

To our dearly beloved brother *Jerome*, we bequeath, *in petto*, the sovereignty of the seas, with our minister of Marine, and all the admirals of our navy, doubting, however, if their united efforts will make him a good midshipman.

To our dearly beloved *Mother*, we give and bequeath his Holiness, the *Pope*, and our uncle, Cardinal *Frere*[1]; with a Pope, and a Cardinal, in her possession, her stay in purgatory must be short, and in Heaven long.

To our dearly beloved sisters, Mistresses *Bacchiocchi, Murat, Santa Cruce*, and *Le Clerc*, we give and bequeath our family honours, chastity, modesty, and moderation.

To our dear son in law, *Eugenius Beauharnais*, we give and bequeath *Parma* and *Plaisance*,[2] with our dear countryman *Sebastiani*, who will instruct him to drive like a coachman, and ride like a postillion.

To our much beloved daughter in law, Madame *Fanny Beauharnais*, as a reward for her loyalty, we bequeath a representation, in wax, of the scaffold of her father, and the throne of her mother, both designed by the revolutionary modellers, *Barras* & Co.

To our dear uncle, Cardinal Frere,[1] we give and bequeath the triple crown of St. Peter, *in petto*, and to all our nameless known and unknown relatives, we give and bequeath the kingdom of *Etruria*, to be disposed of to the highest bidder, and its value laid out in mourning rings, to be equally distributed amongst them, and certain Continental Princes hereinafter mentioned.

We give and bequeath to our dear friend the King of *Spain*, an Etrurian mourning ring, and four family pictures, representing the Bourbons dethroned, the Bourbons degraded, the Bourbons repenting, and the Bourbons forgiven.

We give and bequeath to the King of *Naples*, three marble statues, after a model by his Queen, representing Faith, Loyalty, and Constancy; and to the Kings of *Sardinia*, we bequeath our promises of honour, to be equally divided between them.

We give and bequeath to his Holiness the *Pope*, the doctrines of the Goddess of Reason, the Alcoran of Mahomet, and the atheism of our Institute; all true relics; besides, to himself, his successors, and College of Cardinals, we bequeath concordant mourning rings, from the manufactory of our Counsellor of State *Portalis*.[3]

[1] Fesch.   [2] Placentia.
[3] Who had the chief share in promoting the Concordat with the Pope.

We give and bequeath to his Imperial Majesty the Emperor of *Germany*, two drawings, representing Hope amongst the ruins of *Turkey*, and Desire contemplating *Bavaria*, designed by Citizen *Dupe*, and sold by Citizen *Plot*.

We give and bequeath to his Imperial Majesty the Emperor of *Russia*, three pictures, representing Louis XVI. upon the Throne, Louis XVI. in the Temple, and Louis XVI. upon the Scaffold ; by Citizens *Loyalty*, *Monarchy*, and *Warning*.

We give and bequeath to our dearest friend the King of *Prussia*, the landscape of Hanover, with the Imperial Crown in perspective, by Citizens *Royalty*, *Jacobin*, and *Rebel*.

We give and bequeath to our natural Ally the Emperor of the *Turkish Empire*, the description of our Conquests of *Egypt*, our flight from *Egypt*, and our future return to *Egypt*, by Citizens *Treachery*, *Cowardice*, and *Design*.

We give and bequeath to his Majesty the King of the United Kingdoms of *Great Britain*, and *Ireland*, the United Navy of Holland and France, commanded by Citizen *Envy*, mann'd by Citizen *Coalition*, and lost by Citizen *Invasion*.

We give and bequeath to his Majesty the King of *Sweden*, the French original representation of the assassination of *Gustavus III.* to remind him of vengeance, honour and duty.

We give to our dear friend the King of *Denmark*, an original painting, of the insults, torments, and death, of his Queen *Caroline Matilda* ; designed and executed by two celebrated French artists, Citizens *Intrigue* and *Crime*.

We give and bequeath to the Regent of *Portugal*, a Code of our Revolutionary Laws of Nations, and a chapter of the Rebel Etiquette of Grenadier Ambassadors, explained and illustrated by Citizens *Sans Culottes*, *Rudeness*, and *Impudence*.

We give and bequeath to our friend the Elector of *Bavaria* the Bible of the *Theophilanthropes*, and the Concordat of *Portalis*, as an assistance to his patriotic illuminated ministers, in their political reformations, and religious innovations.

We give and bequeath to our chosen Grand Master of *Malta*, the Musical Opera of the Capture of *Malta*, performed in 1798 with a Concerto by Citizen *Treason*, and in 1800 with a Bravura, by Citizen *Valour*, with the farcical afterpiece of the *Recapture*, performed at *Amiens*, by Citizens *Fraud* and *Treaty*.

To all other *Continental Sovereigns*, who have accepted more or less of our bountiful indemnities, we give and bequeath our mourning rings of honour ; and to all other ambassadors, ministers, agents, and deputies, who have negociated, intrigued, bribed, or begged indemnities, we give and bequeath, with our consciences of honour, the revolutionary principles of *Necker*, the ex-minister, the probity, and disinterestedness of *Talleyrand*, our minister, and the honour and virtue of *Fouché* our senator, to be equally divided amongst them, share and share alike.

We give and bequeath to all *Sovereigns* upon earth, who have acknowledged our Corsican Kingdom of *Etruria*, and to their ministers and counsellors, *Iron* mourning rings, from the axe of the Guillotine, of the *Luneville* manufactory, bearing the following inscription, '*Monarchy degraded, and Monarchy dishonoured, Feb.* 1801.'[1]

We give and bequeath to the *Citizens of the Republics* in *Italy*, *Switzerland*, and *Holland*, our Corsican Mourning rings, with an inscription, '*Liberty lost*, 1801, *and unrevenged*, 1803.'

N.B.—We give and bequeath to the *Citizens* of the *United States* of *America*, the funeral speeches on the tombs of the Liberty of *France*, *Germany*, *Switzerland*, *Italy*, and *Holland*, translated and published by Citizen *Plot*, in *Louisiana*.

To all our *Senators, Legislators, Tribunes, Counsellors, Ministers, Generals, Cardinals, Bishops, Prefects*, &c., &c., &c., and to all other of our *Slaves* of every denomination and description, whether *Rebel, Royalist*, or *Regicide Jacobins* ; either *Traitors, Apostates, Murderers*, or *Plunderers*, we give and bequeath the Cannon of *St. Napoleon*, the dagger of *St. Brutus*, the poison of *St. Aly*, the Guillotine of *St. Robespierre*, and the halter of *St. Judas* ; all true relics, to be equally divided amongst them.

We give and bequeath to the Manes of all the Citizens butchered by us at Toulon, murdered by us at Paris, and poisoned by us in Egypt ; our confession to our Cardinal Bishop at Paris, and our absolution from his Holiness the *Pope*.

We command, and desire most earnestly, not to be buried in any Church or Church-yard, in any mosque or pantheon, but in the common sewer of *Montmartre*, where the corses of our worthy predecessors, *Marat* and *Robespierre*, were deposited ; but for the quiet of our soul, we do order, and put into requisition, *La Revalliere*, high priest to the *Goddess* of *Reason*, *Mercier*, the atheist of the Institute, *Amarat*, the mufti of *Constantinople*, and *Pius* the *Pope* of *Rome*, to say prayers over our tomb, and to read '*Domine salvum fac Consulem*,' *sic transit Gloria mundi !*

Lastly, to *Louis* the XVIII. commonly called the Pretender, and to all Princes of the *House* of *Bourbon*, their heirs, executors, administrators, and assigns, we give and bequeath our everlasting hate ; and it is our further will and pleasure, that, if any potentate or power, shall harbour the said *Louis* XVIII. or any of the said princes, such harbouring shall be a good cause of war ; and the

[1] The Treaty of Luneville was signed Feb. 9, 1801.

potentate and power guilty of such humanity, and hospitality, shall be punished by a Coalition of Powers as a violater of the law of nations, and contrary to the rights of man.

In Witness whereof, we have hereunto set our hand and seal the 25th day of Prairial, (14 June, 1803) in the eleventh year of the French Republic, one and indivisible.

BRUTUS ALY NAPOLEON
BONAPARTE.

As a specimen of the bombast of the time, we may take the subjoined illustration of what our Tars would do with Napoleon.

INVASION.

CHAPTER XXXII.

INVASION SQUIBS, *continued*—' BRITONS TO ARMS '—BRAGGADOCIO— NAPOLEON'S EPITAPH.

A MOST ghastly picture, which should not be called a caricature, yet is meant so to be, is by Gillray (July 26, 1803), and is called ' Buonaparte forty-eight Hours after Landing ! ' A crowd of rural volunteers are assembled, and one of them hoists the head of Napoleon upon a pitchfork, calling out ' Ha, my little Boney ! what do'st think of Johnny Bull, now ? Plunder Old England ! hay ? make French slaves of us all! hay? ravish all our Wives and Daughters ! hay? O Lord, help that silly Head ! To think that  Johnny Bull would ever suffer those lanthorn Jaws to become King of Old England Roast Beef and Plum pudding.' Whilst on the top of the engraving is inscribed, 'This is to give information for the benefit of all Jacobin Adventurers, that Policies are now open'd at Lloyd's— where the depositer of One Guinea is entitled to a Hundred if the Corsican Cut throat is alive 48 Hours after Landing on the British Coast.'

Ansell also takes up this gruesome subject (August 6, 1803) in 'After the Invasion. The Levée en Masse, or Britons Strike Home.' The French have landed, but have been thoroughly defeated ; the British soldiers driving them bodily over the cliffs, into the sea. The women are plundering the dead, but complain bitterly of the poverty of their spoil. ' Why, this is poor finding, I have emptied the pockets of a score and only found garlic, one head of an onion, and a parcel of pill boxes.' A rural volunteer, who has Bonaparte's head on a pitchfork, addresses two comrades thus : ' Here he is exalted, my Lads, 24 Hours after Landing.' Says one of the countrymen, ' Why, Harkee, d'ye zee, I never liked soldiering afore, but, somehow or other, when I thought of our Sal, the bearns, the poor Cows, and the Geese, why I could have killed the whole Army, my own self.' The other remarks, ' Dang my Buttons if that beant the head of that Rogue Boney—I told our Squire this morning, What do you think, says I, the lads of our Village can't cut up a Regiment of them French Mounseers ? and, as soon as the Lasses had given us a Kiss for good luck, I could have sworn we should do it, and so we have.'

Of loyal and patriotic songs, there are enough and to spare, but one was very popular, and therefore should be reproduced :—

BRITONS TO ARMS ! ! !

Written by WM. THOS. FITZGERALD, Esqr.,
And Recited by him at the ANNUAL MEETING of the
LITERARY FUND, at GREENWICH.
14 July, 1803.

Britons to Arms !—of apathy beware,
And let your Country be your dearest care ;
Protect your Altars ! guard your Monarch's throne,
The Cause of GEORGE and FREEDOM, make your own !

What ! shall that England want her Sons' support,
Whose Heroes fought at Cressy—Agincourt ?
And when great MARLBOROUGH led the English Van,
In France, o'er Frenchmen triumphed to a man !
By ALFRED's great, and ever honoured, Name !
By EDWARD's prowess, and by HENRY's fame !
By all the generous Blood for Freedom shed,
And by the Ashes of the Patriot Dead !
By the bright Glory Britons lately won,
On Egypt's Plains, beneath the burning Sun !
Britons to Arms ! defend your Country's Cause,
Fight for your King ! your Liberties ; and Laws !
Be France defied, her slavish yoke abhor'd,
And place your safety only on your Sword.
The Gallic Despot, sworn your mortal Foe,
Now aims his last,—but his most deadly blow ;
With England's Plunder tempts his hungry Slaves,
And dares to brave you, on your Native Waves !
If Briton's right be worth a Briton's care,
To shield them from the Son of Rapine—swear !
Then to Invasion be defiance giv'n—
Your Cause is just—approv'd by Earth and Heaven
Should adverse winds our gallant Fleet restrain,
To sweep his 'bawbling [1] vessels' from the main ;
And Fate permit him on our Shores t' advance—
The Tyrant never shall return to France ;
Fortune, herself, shall be no more his friend,
And *here* the Hist'ry of his Crimes shall end—
His slaughter'd Legions shall manure our shore,
And England never know Invasion more.

This was the stilted sort of stuff given to our forefathers,
to inflame their patriotic zeal, and this example is of good
quality compared to most. Here is another one, which I
give, as having the music, published July 30, 1803 :—

BRITONS TO ARMS !

Cheerly my hearts of cour - age true, The hour's at hand to

[1] 'A bawbling vessell was he Captain of,
For shallow draught and bulk unprizable.'—*Twelfth Night*, act 5, sc. i.
Trifling, insignificant, contemptible.

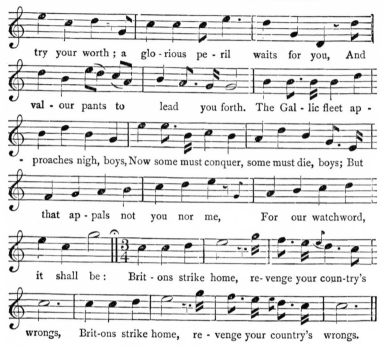

try your worth; a glo-rious pe-ril waits for you, And val-our pants to lead you forth. The Gal-lic fleet ap-proaches nigh, boys, Now some must conquer, some must die, boys; But that ap-pals not you nor me, For our watchword, it shall be: Brit-ons strike home, re-venge your coun-try's wrongs, Brit-ons strike home, re-venge your country's wrongs.

2.

Undaunted Britons now shall prove
   The Frenchman's folly to invade
Our dearest rights, our country's love,
   Our laws, our freedom, and our trade ;
On our white cliffs our colours fly, boys ;
Which we'll defend, or bravely die, boys ;
For we are Britons bold and free,
And our watchword it shall be
       Britons strike home, &c.

3.

The Tyrant Consul, then too late,
   Dismayed shall mourn th' avenging blow.
Yet vanquish'd, meet the milder fate
   Which mercy grants a fallen foe :
Thus shall the British banners fly, boys,
On Albion's cliffs still rais'd on high, boys,
And while the gallant flag we see,
We'll swear our watchword still shall be
       Britons strike home, &c.

About the last caricature in this month was by I. Cruikshank, who depicted Napoleon (July 28, 1803) as 'Preparing to invade.' He is pouring himself out a bumper, and soliloquising, 'I must take a little Dutch Courage, for I am sure I shall never attempt it in my sober senses! Besides, when John Bull catches me, I can plead it was only a Drunken Frolick! Diable! if I not go, den all my Soldiers call me one Braggadocio, and one Coward, and if I do, begor, dey vil shew me in the Tower, as one very Great Wild Beast.'

I. Cruikshank (July 28, 1803) tells us 'How to stop an invader.' Napoleon, and his army, are represented as having landed, and he is asking 'Which is the way to London?' A countryman replies, giving emphasis to his words by driving his pitchfork deeply into the Consul's breast, 'Why, thro' my Body—but I'se be thro' yourn virst.' His wife, as a type of what was expected of the women of England, is emptying the offensive contents of a domestic utensil over him. Bulldogs are let loose, and are rapidly making an end of their enemies, in which laudable enterprise they are materially assisted by prize-fighters and carters.

The month of August was very fruitful in caricature, for in that month, and in September, the Invasion scare was at its height.

There was an immense amount of Gasconading and Braggadocio going about, as senseless as it was improbable. Take this for example: 'The Consequence of Invasion, or the Hero's Reward. None but the brave deserve the fair. The Yeomanry Cavalry's first Essay' (Ansell, August 1, 1803). A stout yeoman is swaggering about, with his sword drawn, and carrying a pole, on the top of which is Bonaparte's head, and, lower down, he grasps some fifteen or twenty bleeding heads of decapitated Frenchmen. He is saying, 'There, you Rogues, there! there's the *Boney parts* of them. Twenty more; Killed them!! Twenty more; Killed them too!! I have destroyed half the army with this same Toledo.' Women from all parts are coming to hug and caress him, saying, 'Bless the Warrior that saved our Virgin Charms.' 'Ah! bless him, he has saved us from

Death and Vileation.' 'Take care, I'll smother him with kisses.' One lady says to a man, not a Volunteer : 'There you Poltroon look how that Noble Hero's caressed !' whilst the poor wretch thus addressed exclaims, 'Ods Niggins, I wish I had been a Soldier too, then the Girls would have run after me, but I never could bear the smell of Gun-powder.'

'John Bull offering Little Boney fair play' is the title of one of Gillray's pictures (August 2, 1803), and depicts the fortified coasts on both sides of the Channel, with John

Bull, as a Jack Tar, stripped to the waist for action. He wades half across to hurl defiance at his foe. 'You're a coming? You be d—d! If you mean to invade us, why make such a rout? I say little Boney, why don't you come out? yes, d—n ye, why don't ye come out?' Meanwhile Boney, secure in his fortress, and with his flotilla safe on shore, looks over the parapet, and says, 'I'm a coming! I'm a coming !!!'

His epitaph was even obligingly written for him during his lifetime, and here it is :—

EPITAPH

Underneath a GIBBET, *over a* DUNGHILL *near* HASTINGS,
close by the SEA BEACH.

Underneath this Dunghill
Is all that remains of a mighty Conqueror,
NAPOLEON BUONAPARTE.
Who, with inflexible Cruelty of Heart,
And unexampled depravity of Mind,
Was permitted to scourge the Earth, for a Time,
With all the Horrors of War :
Too ignorant, and incapable, to do good to Mankind,
The whole Force of his Mind was employed
In oppressing the Weak, and plundering the Industrious :
He was equally detested by all ;
His enemies he butchered in cold Blood ;
And fearing to leave incomplete the Catalogue of his Crimes
His friends he rewarded with a poison'd Chalice.
He was an Epitome
Of all that was vicious in the worst of Tyrants ;
He possess'd their Cruelty, without their Talents ;
Their Madness, without their Genius ;
The Baseness of one, and the Imbecility of another.
Providence, at last,
Wearied out with his Crimes,
Returned him to the Dunghill from which he sprung ;
After having held him forth
On the neighbouring Gibbet,
As a Scare-crow to the Invaders of the British Coast.
This Beach,
The only Spot in our Isle polluted by his footsteps ;
This Dunghill
All that remains to him of his boasted Conquest.
Briton !
Ere you pass by
Kneel and thank thy God,
For all the Blessings of thy glorious Constitution ;
Then return unto the peaceful Bosom of thy Family, and continue
In the Practice of those Virtues,
By which thy Ancestors
Merited the Favor of the Almighty.

I. Cruikshank, in 'Johnny Bull giving Boney a Pull'
(August 7, 1803), brought out a caricature in which is

N

˙ graphically depicted the total annihilation of the French
flotilla, and John Bull is dragging Napoleon, by a cord round
his neck, to a gallows, surrounded by people waving their
hats in token of joy. Napoleon, not unnaturally, hangs
back, remarking, 'Ah! Misericordi! Ah! Misericordi! Jean
Bool, Jean Bool, hanging not good for Frenchmen.' But
John pulls along manfully, exclaiming, 'I shant *measure
the Cord*, you F——. I am sure it is long enough for a
dozen such Fellows as you.'

A picture by West (August 8, 1803), 'Resolutions in
case of an Invasion,' is divided into six compartments. A
tailor, with his shears, says, 'I'll trim his skirts for him.' A
barber, 'I'll lather his wiskers.' An apothecary, with a
pestle and mortar, 'I'll pound him.' A cobbler, 'I'll strap
his Jacket.' A publican, 'I'll cool his Courage in a pot of
Brown Stout.' An epicure, 'I'll eat him.'

The punishment, for any attempt at invasion, was pro-
phesied as being his certain downfall, and a nameless artist
(August 12, 1803) produced an engraving of 'A rash attempt, and woful downfall'—Bonaparte snatching at the
British Crown.

> But as he climb'd to grasp the Crown,
> She knock'd him with the Scepter down,
> He tumbled in the Gulph profound,
> There doom'd to whirl an endless Round.

Britannia is represented as standing on a cliff, with a
crown upraised in her left hand, and a sceptre in her right.
Napoleon is shewn as tumbling into the infernal regions, to
the great joy of attendant demons.

'Observations upon Stilts' is by an unknown artist
(August 12, 1803), and represents Bonaparte upon a huge
pair of stilts. He is looking over to England, through a
telescope, and is saying, 'How very diminutive everything
appears from this astonishing elevation. Who is that little
man, I wonder, on the Island, the other side the ditch? he
seems to be watching my motions.' John Bull, the person
referred to, is also using his telescope, exclaiming, 'Why
surely that can't be Bonny, perch'd up in that manner.
Rabbit him! if he puts one of his Poles across here, I'll
soon lighten his timbers.'

CHAPTER XXXIII.

INVASION SQUIBS, *continued*—'HARLEQUIN INVASION'—'BOB ROUSEM'S
EPISTLE'—NAPOLEON'S TOUR TO BELGIUM.

'HARLEQUIN Invasion' is by West (August 12, 1803).
Napoleon is a Harlequin, and points with his wooden sword
'Invincible' to Great Britain, which is surrounded by goodly
ships of war. Pantaloon, as the Pope, typifying Italy, lies
dead, and Holland, dressed as a Pierrot, does not relish the
command of his master, who tells him, 'As Pantaloon is no
more, I insist on your joining me to invade that little island.'
Poor Holland replies, 'D—m me—if I do, Master—for I
don't like the look of their little ships—can't you let me be
at quiet—whisking me here, and there, and everywhere.'

1.

Ladies and Gentlemen, to day
    With scenes adapted to th' occasion
A Grand new Pantomime we play,
    Entitled—Harlequin's Invasion.

2.

No comic Pantomime before
    Could ever boast such tricks surprising;
The Hero capers Europe o'er,
    But hush ! behold the Curtain rising.

3.

And first that little Isle survey,
    Where sleeps a Peasant boy, so hearty ;
That little Isle is Corsica,
    That peasant boy is Bonaparte.

4.

Now lightnings flash and thunders roar,
    Dæmons of witchcraft hover o'er him ;
And rising thro' the stage trap door,
    An evil genius stands before him.

5.

His arms in solemn state are cross'd,
    His voice appalls th' amaz'd beholders ;
His head in circling clouds is lost,
    And crimson pinions shade his shoulders.

6.

Mortal, awake ! the phantom cries,
    And burst the bonds of fear asunder !
My name is *Anarchy* ; arise !
    Thy future fortunes teem with wonder.

N 2

7.

To spread my reign the earth around,
    Here take this sword, whose magic pow'r,
Shall sense, and right, and wrong confound,
    And work new wonders ev'ry hour.

8.

Throw off that peasant garb, begin
    T' assume the party colour'd rover,
And, as a sprightly Harlequin,
    Trip, lightly trip, all Europe over.

9.

He spoke, and instant to the view
    Begins the curious transformation ;
His mask assumes a sable hue,
    His dress a pantomimic fashion.

10.

Now round the Stage, in gaudy pride
    Capers the renovated varlet,
Shakes the lath weapon at his side,
    And shines in blue, and white, and scarlet.

11.

High on a rock, his cunning eye
    Surveys half Europe at a glance ;
Fat Holland, fertile Italy,
    Old Spain, and gay, regenerate France.

12.

He strikes, with wooden sword, the earth,
    Which heaves with motion necromantic ;
The nations own a second birth,
    And trace his steps with gestures antic.

13.

The *Pope* prepares for war, but soon
    All pow'rful Harlequin disarms him,
And changing into *Pantaloon*,
    Each motion frets, each noise alarms him.

14.

With trembling haste he seeks to join
    His daughter *Gallia*, lovely rover !
But she, transform'd to *Columbine*,
    Her father scorns, and seeks her lover.

15.

The *Dutchman* next his magic feels,
  Chang'd to the *Clown*, he hobbles after ;
Blund'ring pursues the light of heels,
  Convulsing friends and foes with laughter.

16.

But all their various deeds of sin,
  What mortal man has ever reckon'd?
The mischief plann'd by Harlequin,
  Fair Columbine is sure to second.

17.

They quickly kill poor *Pantaloon,*
  And now our drama's plot grows riper,
When e'er they frisk it to *some tune,*
  The Clown is forc'd to *pay the piper.*

18.

Each foreign land he dances through,
  In some new garb behold the Hero,
Pagan and Christian, Turk and Jew,
  Cromwell, Caligula and Nero.

19.

A Butcher, Harlequin appears,
  The rapid scene to Egypt flying,
O'er captive Turks his steel up rears,
  The stage is strew'd with dead and dying.

20.

Next by the crafty genius taught,
  Sportive he tries Sangrado's trick,
Presents a bowl, with poison fraught,
  And kills his own unconscious sick.

21.

Hey pass ! he's back to Europe flown,
  His hostile foll'wers disappointed :
Kicks five old women from the throne,
  And dubs himself the Lord's Anointed.

22.

In close embrace with Columbine,
  Pass, gaily pass, the flying hours ;
While prostrate at their blood stained Shrine,
  Low bow the European powers.

23.

Touch'd by his sword, the morals fly,
  The virtues, into vices dwindling,
Courage is turn'd to cruelty,
  And public faith, to private swindling.

24.

With Atheist Bishops, Jockey Peers,
  His hurly burly Court is graced ;
Contractors, Brewers, Charioteers,
  Mad Lords, and *Duchesses disgraced.*

25.

And now th' Invasion scene comes on ;
  The patch'd and pyeball'd renegado,
Hurls at Britannia's lofty throne
  Full many an Insolent bravado.

26.

The trembling Clown dissuades in vain
  And finds too late, there's no retreating,
Whatever Harlequin may gain,
  The Clown is sure to have a beating.

27.

They tempt the main, the canvas raise,
  A storm destroys his valiant legions ;
And lo ! our closing scene displays
  A grand view of th' infernal regions.

28.

Thus have we, gentlefolks, to day,
  With pains proportion'd to th' occasion,
Our piece perform'd : then further say,
  How like you Harlequin's Invasion ?

BOB ROUSEM'S
EPISTLE TO
BONYPART.

This comes hoping you are well, as I am at this present ; but
I say, Bony, what a damn'd Lubber you must be to think of getting *soundings* among us English. I tell ye as how your Anchor
will never hold ; it isn't made of good Stuff, so luff up, Bony, or
you'll be *fast aground* before you know where you are. We don't
mind your Palaver and Nonsense ; for tho' 'tis all Wind, it would
hardly fill the Stun' sails of an English Man of War. You'll
never catch a Breeze to bring ye here as long as you live, depend
upon it. I'll give ye a Bit of Advice now ; do *try* and Lie as

near the *Truth* as possible, and don't give us any more of your
Clinchers. I say, do you remember how Nelson came *round* ye
at the Nile? I tell ye what, if you don't take Care what you are
about, you'll soon be afloat in a way you won't like, in a High
Sea, upon a Grating, my Boy, without a bit of soft Tommy to put
into your lanthorn jaws. I tell you now, how we shall fill up the
Log-Book if you come ; I'll give ye the Journal, my Boy, with an
Allowance for *Lee way* and *Variation* that you don't expect.
Now then, at Five A.M. Bonypart's Cock-Boats sent out to amuse
our ENGLISH MEN-OF-WAR with *fighting*, (that we like). Six A.M.
Bonypart lands, (that is, if he can); then we begin to blow the
Grampus ; Seven A.M. Bonypart in a Pucker ; Eight A.M. Bonypart
running away ; Nine A.M. Bonypart on board ; Ten a.m. Bonypart
sinking ; Eleven a m. Bonypart in *Davy's locker ;* Meridian,
Bonypart in the North Corner of ——, where it burns and freezes
at the same time ; but you know, any port in a storm, Bony, so
there I'll leave ye. Now you know what you have to expect ; so
you see you can't say I didn't tell ye. Come, I'll give ye a Toast:
Here's Hard Breezes and Foul Weather to ye, my Boy, in your
Passage ; here's *May you be Sea Sick ;* we'll soon make ye *Sick of
the Sea* ; Here's, May you never have a Friend here, or a Bottle
to give him. And to conclude : Here's the French Flag where
it ought to be, under the ENGLISH. his

Bob + Rousem.

mark

P.S. You see as I coudn't write, our Captain's Clerk put the
Lingo into black and white for me, and says *he'll charge it to you.*

Woodward (August 13, 1803) illustrated a very amusing
little ballad. The picture is simple. Napoleon, as usual,
with an enormous cocked hat and sword. John Bull, of
ample rotundity, with his oaken cudgel. It is called ' John
Bull and Bonaparte !! to the tune of the Blue Bells of
Scotland.'

When, and O when, does this little Boney come?
Perhaps he'll come in August, perhaps he'll stay at home ;
But it's O in my heart, how I'll hide him should he come.

Where, and O where, does this little Boney dwell?
His birth-place is in Corsica—but France he likes so well,
That it's O the poor French, how they crouch beneath his spell.

What cloathes, and what cloathes, does this little Boney wear?
He wears a large cock'd hat, for to make the people stare ;
But it's O my oak stick ! I'd advise him to take care !

What shall be done, should this little Boney die?
Nine cats shall squall his dirge, in sweet melodious cry ;
And it's O in my heart, if a tear shall dim my eye !

Yet still he boldly brags, with consequence full cramm'd,
On England's happy island his legions he will land ;
But it's O in my heart, if he does, may I be d—d.

In June of this year, Bonaparte, and Josephine, took a
tour into Belgium, and the Côtes du Nord.   What it was
like, cannot better be told than in the words of De Bourrienne.   'Bonaparte left Paris on June 3 : and, although
it was not for upwards of a year afterwards, that his brow
was encircled with the imperial diadem, everything connected with the journey, had an imperial air.   It was
formerly the custom, when the kings of France entered the
ancient capital of Picardy, for the town of Amiens to offer
them, in homage, some beautiful swans.   Care was taken
to revive this custom, which pleased Bonaparte greatly, because it was treating him like a king.   The swans were
accepted, and sent to Paris, to be placed in the basin of the
Tuileries, in order to show the Parisians, the royal homage
which the First Consul received, when absent from the
Capital.'   So it was all through his progress.   The caricature
here described is, of course, exaggerated, but it shows the
feeling which animated the popular breast on this particular journey.

'Boney at Brussels' is by I. Cruikshank (August 14,
1803), and here he is represented seated on a throne, with
a Mameluke, armed with sword and pistol, on each side of
him.   He is provided with a huge fork in each hand, with
which he is greedily feeding himself from dishes provided
in the most humble and abject manner by all kinds of
great dignitaries.

He has his mouth full of an 'Address to the Deified
Consul.'   The next morsel, which is on one of the forks, is
'To the Grand Consular Deity,' and the other fork is dug well
into ' We burn with desire to lick the Dust of your Deified
feet.'   A prelate begs him to 'Accept the Keys of Heaven
and Hell ; ' and other dishes are labelled ' Act of Submission,' 'Your most abject Slave, Terror of France,' and 'The

Idol of our Hearts, Livers, Lights, Guts, and Garbage, Souls and all.'

' John Bull out of all Patience !!' is by Roberts (August 16, 1803), and represents him in a Cavalry uniform, and a most towering rage, astride of the British Lion, which is swimming across to France. He is shouting out, ' I'll be after you, my lads—do you think I'll stay at home waiting for you ? If you mean to come, d—n it, why don't you come ? do you think I put on my regimentals for nothing ?' Boney and his army are running away, the former calling out ' Dat is right my brave Friends, take to your heels, for here is dat dam Jean Bool coming over on his Lion.'

The subjoined illustration also does duty for ' The Sorrows of Boney, or Meditations in the Island of Elba, April 15, 1814,' but, having priority, it appears here as :—

CROCODILE'S TEARS
OR
BONAPARTE'S LAMENTATION
A NEW SONG.
Tune ' Bow, wow, wow.'

By gar, this Johnny Bull—be a very cunning elf, Sir,
He by de Arts and Commerce thrive, and so he gain de pelf, Sir ;
But he no let us rob de land—or else, with naval thunder,
He'll send dat lion bold, Jack Tar, and make us all strike under.
    Lack, lack a day, fal lal, &c.

By gar, de British Bulvarks be—a very grand annoyance,
I'm told, against all EUROPE join'd, they've often dar'd defiance!
Then what can France and Holland do? By gar, dat day me rue,
     Sir,
When I de peaceful Treaty broke—to England prov'd untrue, Sir.
     Lack, lack a day, fal lal, &c.

And then, when in von passion thrown, by gar, I took occasion,
To shew de *Gasconade de France!* and threat them with Invasion !
John Bull, he made at me de scoff, and call'd me Gasconader,
By gar, me find he ne'er will flinch—from any French Invader!
     Lack, lack a day, fal lal, &c.

And now, what vex me worse than all, John Bull prepare for war,
     Sir,
For, fraught with vengeance, he send out that valiant dog, Jack
     Tar, Sir,
By gar, he sweep de Channel clean, and den he mar our sport,
     Sir,
He either take de ships of France, or block them in de port, Sir,
     Lack, lack a day, fal lal, &c.

This spoil'd my scheme for sending troops from Gallia's shore to
     Dover,
So then, by gar, me send them off, and then they took Hanover ;
But, for to ratify the terms, th' ELECTOR did not choose, Sir,
Because, I'm told, the British King, to sign them did refuse, Sir.
     Lack, lack a day, fal lal, &c.

O ! next I make more gasconade, and then most loudly boast,
     Sir,
That I would send flat-bottom'd boats, and soon invade de coast,
     Sir,
' *That all the men in arms I found, by gar, I'd take their lives,*
     Sir,
And put to sword the Britons all, their children, and their wives,
     Sir ! ! !'
     Lack, lack a day, fal lal, &c.

I found my boasting threats are vain, for now, all ranks, by gar, Sir,
From fifteen, up to fifty-five, are all prepar'd for war, Sir,
They swear, ' no Gallic yoke they'll bear, or Corsican's proud
     sting, Sir,
But, bravely for their Freedom fight, their Country, and their
     King ! Sir.'
     Lack lack a day, fal lal, &c.

And then they talk of warlike deeds—of *Edward the Black
Prince,* Sir,
And how their *Harries* fought of old—true courage to evince,
Sir,
In modern times, a *Nelson* brave ! and *Abercrombie's* fame, Sir,
O er Gallia's fleets and armies too, have spread eternal shame,
Sir.
Lack, lack a day, fal lal, &c.
By gar, me always thought, till now, I was a mighty *Hero* !
But then, I'm told, the people say, me cruel was as Nero,
Because *three thousand Turks* I slew, they say I was to blame,
Sir,
As also when at Jaffa I—did poison sick and lame, Sir.
Lack, lack a day, fal lal, &c.
By gar, I find my ardor fail, and all my courage cool, Sir,
De *World* confess I am de *knave*—de *English* call me *fool,*
Sir ;
Hard fate ! alas, that I am both ! my heart, of grief, is full, Sir,
By gar, me wish I was at *peace !* with honest *Johnny Bull !* Sir.
Lack, lack a day, fal lal, &c.

CHAPTER XXXIV.

INVASION SQUIBS, *continued*—THE BOTTLE CONJUROR—PIDCOCK'S
MENAGERIE.

IN order to understand the next caricature, it is necessary to go back to January 16, 1749, when a famous hoax
was played on the public. The 'Gentleman's Magazine' for
that month says, ' A person advertised that he would, this
evening, at the *Theatre* in the *Hay-market,* play on a common walking cane the music of every instrument now used,
to surprising perfection ; that he would, on the stage, get
into a tavern quart bottle, without equivocation ; and while
there, sing several songs, and suffer any spectator to handle
the bottle ; that, if any spectator should come mask'd, he
would, if requested, declare who they were ; that, in a private room, he would produce the representation of any
person dead, with which the party requesting it could converse some minutes as if alive, &c.'
    The bait took, and the theatre was crowded : patience
was exhausted, and some one in the pit calling out that

'For double prices, the conjurer will go into a pint bottle,' an uproar began, which ended in the wreckage of the house, which was made into a bonfire outside, and the carrying off of the treasury.

With this introduction we can the better understand 'Britannia blowing up the Corsican Bottle-Conjurer,' by I. Cruikshank (August 17, 1803), which represents Napoleon being violently ejected into the air, in an extremely disorganised condition, from the mouth of a bottle which is labelled 'British Spirits composed of True Liberty, Courage, Loyalty and Religion,' and in which is seated Britannia, helmed, and armed with spear and shield. Woodward designed 'The Corsican Moth' (August 22, 1803), which, flying towards the candle,

THE CORSICAN MOTH!

exclaims: 'It is a very fierce flame; I am afraid I shall singe my wings!' George III. consoles himself with: 'Thou little contemptible insect, I shall see thee consumed by-and-by.'

This very vivid caricature explains itself. The French Court are consuming all the good things to be got by the invasion of England in anticipation, when the fearful 'Mene, Mene, Tekel Upharsin,' the mystic handwriting on the wall, appears.  Napoleon is in consternation, but his wife and the assembled guests do not seem to notice it. Josephine is here, as generally, de- picted as being very fat. She was not so at this

THE HANDWRITING ON THE WALL.

time, nor for some time after. Madame Junot says : 'I ob- served that Josephine had grown very stout since the time of my departure from Spain. This change was at once for the better and the worse. It imparted a more youthful ap- pearance to her face ; but her elegant and slender figure, which had been one of her principal attractions, had en- tirely disappeared. She was now decidedly *embonpoint*, and her figure had assumed that matronly air which we find in the statues of Agrippina, Cornelia, &c.' The three ladies behind her chair are supposed to represent Pauline, who was afterwards the Princess Borghese, the Princess Louise, and the Princess Joseph Bonaparte.

'A Knock Down blow in the Ocean, or Bonaparte taking French leave,' is by some unknown artist (August 24, 1803). John Bull, stripped to the waist in true pugi- listic style, has encountered Bonaparte in the Channel, and, with one well-directed blow, has sunk him, leaving only his hat and boots to tell the tale. With great satisfaction the old man says : 'There, my lad, I think that blow will settle the business. D—n me, he is gone in such a hurry he has left his hat and spurs behind him.' The English give ringing cheers: 'John Bull for ever! Huzza! Huzza! Bravo! Bravo!' But the French look very rueful, and, wringing their hands and weeping, exclaim : 'Ah!

misericorde, pauvre Bonaparte. O dat Terrible Jean Bool.'

AN INVASION SKETCH.

If there be one Person so lost to all Love for his Country, and the British Constitution, as to suppose that his Person or his Property, his Rights and his Freedom, would be respected under a Foreign Yoke, let him contemplate the following Picture—not Overcharged, but drawn from Scenes afforded by every Country : Italy, Holland, Switzerland, Germany, Spain, Hanover, which has been exposed to the Miseries of a French Invasion.

LONDON, 10 *Thermidor— Year*——.

General BONAPARTE made his public entrance into the capital, over London Bridge, upon a charger from his BRITANNIC MAJESTY'S Stables at Hanover, preceded by a detachment of Mamelukes. He stopped upon the bridge for a few seconds, to survey the number of ships in the river ; and, beckoning to one of his Aid-de-camps, ordered the French flags to be hoisted above the English—the English sailors on board, who attempted to resist the execution of this order, were bayonetted, and thrown overboard.

When he came to the Bank, he smiled with complaisance upon a detachment of French grenadiers, who had been sent to load all the bullion in waggons, which had previously been put in requisition by the Prefect of London, Citizen MENGAUD, for the purpose of being conveyed to France. The Directors of the Bank were placed under a strong guard of French soldiers, in the Bank parlour.

From the Bank, the FIRST CONSUL proceeded, in grand procession, along Cheapside, St. Paul's, Ludgate Hill, Fleet Street, and the Strand, to St. James's Palace. He there held a grand Circle, which was attended by all his officers, whose congratulations he received upon his entrance into the Capital of these once proud islanders. BONAPARTE, previous to his arrival, appointed two Prefects, one for London, and one for Westminster. Citizen MENGAUD, late Commissary at Calais, is the Prefect of London, and Citizen RAPP, of Westminster. He also nominated Citizen Fouché to the office of Minister of Police. The Mansion-house has been selected for the residence of the Prefect of London, and Northumberland House for the residence of the Prefect of Westminster. As it has been deemed necessary to have the Minister of Police always near the person of the FIRST CONSUL, Marlborough House has been given to Citizen Fouché. Lodgings have been prepared elsewhere, for the late owners of that splendid Palace.

London was ordered to be illuminated, and detachments of French Dragoons paraded the principal streets, and squares, all night.

11 *Thermidor.*

BONAPARTE, at five o'clock in the morning, reviewed the French Troops on the Esplanade at the Horse Guards. A Council was afterwards held, at which the following Proclamations were drawn up, and ordered to be posted in every part of the City :

BY ORDER OF THE FIRST CONSUL.

PROCLAMATION.

St. James's Palace.

Inhabitants of London, be tranquil. The Hero, the Pacificator, is come among you. His moderation, and his mercy, are too well known to you. He delights in restoring peace and liberty to all mankind. Banish all alarms. Pursue your usual occupations. Put on the habit of joy and gladness.

The FIRST CONSUL orders,

That all the Inhabitants of London and Westminster remain in their own houses for three days.

That no molestation shall be offered to the measures which the French Soldiers will be required to execute.

All persons disobeying these Orders, will be immediately carried before the Minister of Police.

(signed)   BONAPARTE.

The Minister of Police   FOUCHÉ.

PROCLAMATION
To the French Soldiers.

Soldiers ! BONAPARTE has led you to the Shores, and the Capital of this proud island. He promised to reward his brave companions in arms. He promised to give up the Capital of the British Empire to pillage. Brave Comrades take your reward. London, the second Carthage, is given up to pillage for three days.   (signed)   BONAPARTE.

The Minister of War, par interim   ANGEREAU.

The acclamations of the French soldiery—*Vive Bonaparte—le Heros—le Pacificateur—le Magnanime*—resound through every street.

12th, 13th, 14th, Thermidor.

LONDON PILLAGED ! The doors of private houses forced. Bands of drunken soldiers dragging wives, and daughters, from the arms of husbands, and fathers. Many husbands, who had the *temerity* to resist, butchered in the presence of their Children— Flames seen in a hundred different places, bursting from houses which had been set fire to, by the *vivacity* of the troops. Churches broken open, and the Church plate plundered—The pews and altars converted into stabling—Four Bishops murdered, who had taken refuge in Westminster Abbey—The screams of women, and of children, mix with the cries of the soldiers—*Vive la Republique! Vive Bonaparte!*

St. Martin's Church converted into a *depôt* for the property acquired by the pillage of the soldiery.

15 *Thermidor.*

A proclamation published by the FIRST CONSUL, promising *protection* to the inhabitants.

The houses of the principal Nobility and Gentry, appropriated to the use of the French Generals. Every house is required to furnish so many rations of bread and meat for the troops.

At a Council of State, presided over by BONAPARTE, the two Houses of Parliament are solemnly abolished, and ordered to be replaced by a Senate, and a Council of State. General MASSENA appointed Provisional President of the former, and General DESSOLLES of the latter. The Courts of Law are directed to discontinue their sittings, and are replaced by Military tribunals.

16 *Thermidor.*

A contribution of twenty millions ordered to be levied upon London. A deputation was sent to BONAPARTE to represent the impossibility of complying with the demand, the Bank and the Capital having been pillaged. After waiting in the ante-chamber of the Consul for four hours, the deputation are informed by a Mameluke guard, that BONAPARTE will not see them. Two hundred of the principal citizens ordered to be imprisoned till the contribution is paid.

17 *Thermidor.*

A plot discovered by FOUCHÉ against the FIRST CONSUL, and three hundred, supposed to be implicated in it, sent to the Tower.

Insurrections in different parts of the Capital, on account of the excesses of the soldiers, and the contribution of twenty millions. Cannon planted at all the principal avenues, and a heavy fire of grape-shot kept up against the insurgents.

Lords NELSON, ST. VINCENT, and DUNCAN, Messrs. ADDING- TON, PITT, SHERIDAN, GREY, twenty Peers and Commons, among the latter is Sir SIDNEY SMITH, tried by the Military tribunals, for having been concerned in the *insurrection* against France, and sentenced to be shot. Sentence was immediately carried into execution in Hyde Park.

17 *Thermidor.*

The Dock-yards ordered to send all the timber, hemp, anchors, masts, &c., to France. The relations of the British sailors at sea, sent to prison till the ships are brought into port, and placed at the disposal of the French. Detachments dispatched to the different Counties to disarm the people.

The Island ordered to be divided into departments, and military divisions—the name of London to be changed for *Bona-part-opolis*—and the appellation of the country to be altered from Great Britain, to that of *La France insulaire*—Edinburgh to take the name of *Lucien ville*—Dublin, that of *Massen-opolis.*

BRITONS ! can this be endured ?—Shall we suffer ourselves thus to be parcelled off ?—I hear you one and all say, No ! No ! No !—To your Tents, O Israel !—for BRITONS NEVER WILL BE SLAVES.

PIDCOCK'S GRAND MENAGERIE,

With an exact representation of

BUONAPARTE,

THE LITTLE CORSICAN MONKEY,

As he may probably appear at the above Receptacle of Foreign Curiosities, on, or before, Christmas 1803.

Ladies and Gemmen !

THIS surprising Animal was taken by Admiral JOHN BULL, of the TRUE BRITON, one of his Majesty's principal Line of Battle Ships. He possesses the Cunning of the Fox, the Rapacity of the Wolf, the bloodthirsty *Nater* of the Hyena, the tender Feelings of the Crocodile, and the Obstinacy of an Ass. He has rambled over several parts of the world, where he played a number of wicked and ridiculous Tricks, particularly in Egypt; there he had like to have been *nabbed* by Sir Sidney Smith, but contrived to steal away to France, where, after a Time, exerting all the bad Qualities he possesses, he so far got the better of his own species as to reign King Paramount over Thirty Millions of poor deceived Monkeys. 'Come, come, Jacko ; don't look Melancholy, you shall have your Gruel with a Crust in it presently.' Ladies and *Gemmen*, if I was to quit him an Instant, he would play a thousand *figaries* ; break all your Crockery, drink up your Wine, play the Devil and Doctor Faustus with your Wives and *Darters* ; eat your Provisions, steal your Goods and Chattels, and commit more

O

Mischief here, than he did in Egypt. He's of unbounded Ambition, and, by some fortunate Strokes of good Luck, more than by his Abilities, proved very successful in his Deceptions ; but this Luck was not to last for ever. Puf't up, as full as a blown bladder, with conceit, he thought he *coud* conquer the four Quarters of the Globe : when, sailing with a party of large Baboons, who were

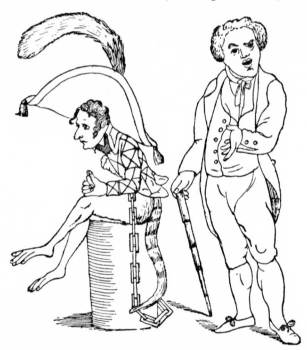

called his body Guard, he stole, one dark Night, out of Boulogne Harbour, to make an attack, and seize the Island of Great Britain ; where he assured his Companions of immense Wealth by their Plunders. But Admiral BULL coming up with him by break of day, when he was half Seas over, gave them a Broad Side, and *woud* have sunk them outright; but seeing the Crew were nothing but a Collection of miserable, deluded, poor, Brutes, he turned them adrift, and only seized their Leader to shew. him as *Curiosity.*[1]

[1] Pidcock's Menagerie was one of the best and largest that used to exhibit in Bartholomew and other fairs : the animals being hired from Cross's famous collection in Exeter 'Change. At this time (1803) Pidcock was probably dead, as he exhibited in 1769. The show was afterwards known as Polito's.

A suggestion was made that two could play at the game of Invasion, and 'John Bull landed in France' is a caricature by West (August 29, 1803). He is in cavalry uniform, and, mounted on his lion, is pursuing the French troops, who, bestriding frogs, are in full flight. The terrible old man roars out, 'D—m me, but I'll put your Cavalry to the hop—I only wish I could find out your Commander.' But Boney is looking out of a cottage chimney, remarking, 'Mercy on me, what a terrible fellow. I think I am tolerably safe here!'

West (August, 1803) describes the 'Three plagues of Europe.' Bonaparte figures as 'The Turberlent Mr. Fightall'; Pitt as 'The Honourable Mr. Taxall'; and the Devil as 'The Worshipful Mr. Takeall.'

CHAPTER XXXV.

INVASION SQUIBS AND CARICATURES, *continued.*

SONG.

THE INVASION.

Come listen every Lord and Lady,
   'Squire, Gentleman, and Statesman,
I've got a *little Song* to sing,
   About a *very great Man !*
And, if the Name of BONAPARTE
   Should mingle in my Story,
'Tis with all due submission
   T' his Honour's Worship's Glory.
      Bow, wow, wow, &c.

The kindness of this philanthropic
   Gentleman extending,
From Shore to Shore, Colossus like,
   Their grievances amending,
To Britain would reach, if he could,
   From fancied Ills to save ye;
But tho' he likes us vastly well,
   He *does not like our Navy !*
      Bow, wow, wow, &c.

With Egypt, once, he fell in Love,
   Because it was the high Road,

O 2

To India, for himself and friends
　To travel by a nigh Road ;
And after making mighty Fuss,
　And fighting Day and Night there,
'Twas vastly ungenteel of us,
　Who would not let him stay there.
　　　　　Bow, wow, wow, &c.

A Nobleman was sent to him,
　For Negotiation able,
And BONAPARTE kindly set
　Him down at his own Table,
And in a Story, two Hours long,
　The Gentleman was heard in,
Whilst our Ambassador declar'd
　He could not get a word in.
　　　　　Bow, wow, wow, &c.

With Belles and Beaux the drawing-room
　One morning it was quite full,
And BONA, like *a Bantam cock,*
　Came crowing rather spiteful ;
He then began to huff and bluff,
　To show that War his Trade is ;
He scolded all the Englishmen,
　And frighten'd all the Ladies ! ! !
　　　　　Bow, wow, wow, &c.

From Malta, next, he took his Text,
　My Lord look'd rather blue on 't ;
For every Trick the Consul had,
　My Lord had one worth *two* on 't ;
Why, Gen'ral, says he, 'Sdeath and Fire,
　Unless you cease these Capers,
They'll publish every word you say
　In all the English Papers.
　　　　　Bow, wow, wow, &c.

My Lord, says he, you needs must see,
　I pity British Blindness,
And wish to open all your Eyes,
　Out of pure Love and Kindness,
To make a generous People free,
　My Legions shall pell mell come,
What think you then ?—Why, Sir, I think
　They'd be more free than welcome.
　　　　　Bow, wow, wow, &c.

When I come o'er, I'll make all Britons
    Live in perfect bliss, Sir,
I'm sure they will receive me just
    As kindly as the Swiss, Sir.
The Odds an hundred are to one
    I fail, tho' Fortune's Minion.
Says our Ambassador to him,
    I'm quite of your opinion.
              Bow, wow, wow, &c.

My Lord, says he, I'll take the Field.
    You'd better take the Ocean.
My plans are deep.—*Why, yes, they'll reach*
    The Bottom, I'; e a Notion.
What would the English think to see
    Me 'twixt Boulogne and Dover?
Why, General, they'd surely think
    Your Worship half seas over!
              Bow, wow, wow, &c.

Your Government I'll tame, says he,
    Since War you are so fond on ;
I've got my will in Paris here,
    And wish the same in London ;
I'll rule your great *John Bull!* says he,
    I have him in the Ring, Sir.—
Says John, I'll not be rul'd by you,
    Nor any such a *Thing*, Sir.
              Bow, wow, wow, &c.

Then bring my Flag, invincible,
    A Scot took it long ago, Sir.
For now I think, your ships I'll sink,
    And never strike a Blow, Sir,
A clever Man has found a plan,
    A plan he's surely right in,
For if you beat the British Fleet,
    It must not be at Fighting.
              Bow, wow, wow, &c.

Quite frantic now, he vows Revenge,
    The Moment that he's landed,
And proudly boasts, we cannot hope
    To fight him single handed.
What, single handed, we can do,
    His troops shall know full well soon ;

For him, he learn'd it long ago,
From *single handed* Nelson.
Bow, wow, wow, &c.

Now, since their Minds are quite made up,
Let me on this Occasion,
Make one request to Neptune : Should
They dream of an Invasion ;
To bring them safely out of Port,
On gentle Billows guide them,
To where a set of British Boys
May anchor close beside them.
Bow, wow, wow, &c.

Reference is made to Napoleon's attempts to stir up sedition in Ireland in 'An attempt on the Potatoe bag,' by some artist unknown (August 1803). It shows an Irishman trudging along towards Dublin, having on his back a huge sack of potatos, which Napoleon is slitting, allowing the potatos to escape. Says Bonaparte : 'I say, Paddy, Give up the bag quietly, and you shall have this Purse of Gold.' But Paddy replies : 'I see what you are at, you sly Teaf of the World ; you may cut out a few of the Potatoes that are rotten at the core—but, by St. Patrick, you'll never get the whole bag—so you may pocket your Cash, and march home and be D—d.'

Dean Swift's 'Gulliver' is very frequently used as a *motif* for caricature, and Charles etched (August 1803) 'Gulliver and his Guide, or a Check String to the Corsican.' King George, as King of Brobdingnag, is seated in a gallery, looking through the invariable glass at Gulliver (Napoleon), who is climbing a flight of steps to get at him ; but he has a rope round his neck, which is held by a sailor armed with a stout oak cudgel. Says the King : 'Ay, what ! what ! Does the little Gulliver want my C * * * n ! Let him come, and he will soon find how 'tis protected. Hearts of oak are our ships, Jolly tars are our men, &c. &c.' Napoleon, throttled by the rope, exclaims : 'If these fellows did not keep such a tight hand over me, I would soon try how that Ornament would fit my head.' Whilst the sailor, who has him in hand and checks his advance, calls out : 'Avast there, my littie fellow ; for, D—n my

Timbers, if I don't take you Aback before you reach the end of your Intended travels.   So pull away, pull away, I say, for the tight little bit of land in the Ocean.'

There is a charming libel on Napoleon in a periodical publication, called ' Ring the Alarum Bell,' No. 3, August 27, 1803 (I believe it only reached four numbers), the heading of which is, ' Atrocities of Brutus Napoleone Ali Buona-parté, who now pretends to be at war for restoring the Knights of Malta, and who told the Egyptians ' (July 1798), 'that he was a true Mussulman, and had been to Malta, on purpose to drive from thence those Christian Infidels, the Knights ! ! ! '

After a most scurrilous and incorrect version of his life, this precious paper gives us a thrilling account of ' *The Corsican's Drowning his own wounded Soldiers, and his Thievery.*

' During the early engagements at Mantua with General Wurmsur, the hospital for the French who were wounded was at Como.   Some officers, who are ready to swear to the truth of their assertion, passing through this town in the month of April 1800, were informed by the inhabitants that one morning they beheld, with unspeakable horror, the dead bodies of a number of French soldiers floating upon the surface of the lake, whom this infamous assassin, Buonaparté, had ordered to be cast into it on the pre-ceding night.   Every one of these unfortunate wretches were soldiers who had suffered amputation of some member or other !   This monster caused, at the same time, not only the dead, but even the sick, in the hospitals to be thrown pell-mell into a ditch at Salo, on the Lake of Guarda.   It is a fact, well-known in Upper Italy, that the Curate of Salo died with grief at the sight of this horrible trans-action.

' The pecuniary robberies of the Corsican are innumer-able.   At Leghorn he caused a servant of the Grand Duke to bring him all the plate belonging to that Prince, and kept himself an inventory, in order to examine whether any article was missing.   At Pisa a British nobleman (the Marquis of D——) was robbed of his carriage, and other effects, by a party of French Hussars.   Buonaparte appro-

priated the carriage to himself, and afterwards made use of
it at Milan. France was then in a state of profound peace
with the Grand Duke. At Milan, Buonaparte imprisoned
the Nobles, and, in order to procure their release, their con-
sorts brought their diamonds to the wife of the Usurper.'

The following might well go as companion to 'Pidcock's
Menagerie':—

Most Wonderful
WONDER OF WONDERS.

Just arrived, at Mr. BULL'S MENAGERIE, in British Lane, the
most renowned and sagacious MAN TIGER, or Ourang Outang
called

NAPOLEON BUONAPARTE;

HE has been exhibited through the greatest Part of Europe, particularly in Holland, Switzerland, and Italy, and lately in Egypt—
He has a wonderful faculty of Speech, and undertakes to reason
with the most learned Doctors in Law, Divinity, and Physic—He
proves, incontrovertibly, that the strongest POISONS are the most
Sovereign Remedies for Wounds of all kinds ; and by a Dose or
two, made up in his own Way, he cures his Patients of all their Ills
by the Gross—He PICKS the POCKETS of the Company, and by a
Rope,[1] suspended near a Lantern, shews them, as clear as Day, that
they are all richer than before—If any Man in the Room has
empty Pockets, or an empty Stomach, by taking a Dose or two of
his POWDER of HEMP, he finds them on a sudden full of Guineas,
and has no longer a Craving for Food ; If he is rich, he gets rid
of his tædium vitæ ; and, if he is over-gorged, finds a perfect Cure
for his Indigestion.—He proves, by unanswerable Arguments, that
Soupe Maigre, and *Frogs*, are a much more wholesome food than
Beef and *Pudding*—and that it would be better for OLD ENGLAND,
if her Inhabitants were all *Monkeys* and *Tigers* as, in times of
Scarcity, one half of the Nation might devour the other half.—He
strips the Company of their Cloaths, and when they are stark
naked, presents a PAPER on the POINT of a BAYONET, by reading
which they are all presently convinced that it is very pleasant to
be in a state of Nature.—By a kind of hocus-pocus Trick, he
breathes on a Crown, and it changes suddenly into a Guillotine.—
He deceives the eye most dexterously ; one Moment he is in the
Garb of the MUFTI : the next of a JEW, and the next Moment
you see him the POPE.—He imitates all Sounds ; bleats like a

[1] Hanging them. A revival of the old Revolutionary cry of 'À la
Lanterne !'

Lamb; roars like a *Tiger*; cries like a Crocodile; and brays most inimitably like an Ass.

He used also to perform some wonderful Tricks with *Gunpowder*; but he was very sick in passing the Channel, and has shewn great aversion to them ever since.

Admittance, One Shilling and Sixpence.

N.B. If any Gentleman of the *Corps Diplomatique* should wish to see his Ourang Outang, Mr. Bull begs a Line or two first; as on such Occasions, he finds it necessary to bleed him, or give him a Dose or two of cooling Physic, being apt to fly at them, if they appear without such preparation.

'John Bull and the Alarmist' is as well drawn as any of Gillray's caricatures (September 1, 1803). Sheridan, in the character of a bill-sticker, having under his arm a sheaf of 'Loyal Bills, Sherry Andrew's Address, Playbills,' &c., and, with a *bonnet rouge* peeping out of his pocket, is telling John Bull the two last lines of the first verse of the subjoined song.

The old boy stands resolutely before the throne, which he is ready to defend with his huge oak cudgel carved with a bulldog's head, and, whilst nourishing himself on a tankard of ale, tells his informant his opinion of his intelligence in the words of the second verse :—

John Bull as he sat in his old Easy Chair,
An Alarmist came to him, and said in his Ear,
' A Corsican Thief has just slipt from his quarters,
And is coming to Ravish your Wives and your Daughters !'

'Let him come, and be D—d !' thus roar'd out John Bull,
'With my Crab-stick assured I will fracture his Scull,
Or I'll squeeze ye vile reptile twixt my Finger and Thumb,
Make him stink like a Bug, if he dares to presume.'

' They say a full Thousand of Flat bottomed Boats,
Each a Hundred and Fifty have, Warriors of Note ;

All fully determin'd to feast on your Lands,
So I fear you will find full enough on your hands.'
John smiling arose, upright as a post,
' I've a Million of Friends bravely guarding my Coast,
And my old Ally, Neptune, will give them a dowsing,
And prevent the mean rascals to come here a lousing.'

I know not from what source the statistics relative to
the strength of the French flotilla, contained in the subjoined broadsheet, are taken.   It purports to be an extract from a French letter :—

CITIZENS OF ENGLAND
YOU HAVE BEEN TOLD THAT
BONAPARTE
WILL NOT ATTEMPT
INVASION :

*Read the following detailed Account of his Preparations, and ask
yourselves whether those who tell you so, are your Friends or your
Enemies.*

' The Alertness of our People, employed in the several
Yards along the Coasts, never had a parallel.   I reckon 11,000
Ship-Carpenters,   and   their   necessary   Assistants,   Labourers,
&c., employed here, and at *Calais*, *Dunkirk*, and *Ostend*, besides
those at Work on the Boats preparing at *Ghent*, *Bruges*, and
Antwerp.

' At *Boulogne*, we have 36 Gun Boats ready, each carrying
three heavy Pieces of Ordnance, Two fore, and One aft ; besides 152 of what are called *Flat Bottomed* Boats ; but they
are now generally *rounded below*, and *keeled*.   In three Weeks
Time, we expect to have as many more in a State of perfect
Readiness.

' At *Calais*, several of the *Floating Batteries*, that opposed LORD
NELSON, when he attacked Boulogne, are now fitting up, and
about seventy boats that will carry 150 Men each.

' At *Dunkirk*, and the adjacent Canals, there are 47 *Gun
boats ready*, with remarkable heavy Ordnance ; and not less
than 220 Boats for carrying men.   They count upon being able
to send 400 of these vessels (great and small) to Sea, in less than
Three Weeks.

' At *Ostend*, the *Gun Boats*, *Floating Batteries*, and *Vessels for
carrying Soldiers*, that are now, and will be, completed during the
present month, amount to 487.   They work here during the Whole
of the Moonlight nights.

' I cannot, at present, exactly ascertain what Number of Men are employed, at *Bruges* and *Ghent*; but they are extremely numerous. Such is the case at Antwerp.'

But not one of these vessels dared shew her nose out of harbour, for every French port in the Channel was blockaded by English men-of-war, of which there were some five hundred, of different sizes, afloat. Sometimes this blockading business got tiresome, and it was relieved by an occasional landing, on which occasions mischief to the French, in some shape or other, was always included in the programme ; or a vessel would be cut out, or a few shells would be thrown into a town such as Dieppe or Havre— anything to vary the monotony. At home they were bragging and blustering of what they would do ; afloat they were *doing*, and we cannot tell from what fate their action saved us.

Woodward drew an amusing sketch of ' John Bull shewing the Corsican monkey ' (September 3, 1803), who is represented as seated on a Russian bear, which is muzzled and led by John Bull, who thus expatiates on his charge to the delighted audience : ' My friends and neighbours, this is no monkey of the common order ; he is a very cholerick little gentleman, I assure you. I had a vast deal of trouble to bring him to any kind of obedience—he is very fond of playing with globes and scepters—so you may perceive, I let him have one of each made of Gingerbread—in order to amuse him in a strange country.'

A not very witty picture, ' Buonaparte on his Ass,' by an unknown artist (September 14, 1803), represents Bonaparte on a donkey, which has got itself in a terrible mess through trampling on Italy, Switzerland, Holland, and Hanover, and is endeavouring to reach Malta, which, however, is protected by the British Lion. Napoleon opines that, ' This d—d ass gets so entangled and unruly, I'm afraid I shall never be able to reach Malta.'

> O'er countrys I'll trample, where threats may prevail,
> But must let those alone where they will not avail,
> For on looking around me to find where to prance,
> To touch Malta, might be destruction to France.

Woodward drew (September 16, 1803) 'The Corsican Macheath,' with Napoleon singing :—

> Which way shall I turn me ?
> How can I decide
> The Prospects before me ?
> I long for to stride.
> But 'tis this way—or that way,
> Or which way I will,
> John Bull at his Post,
> Is prepared with a Pill.

CHAPTER XXXVI.

INVASION SQUIBS, *continued*—TALLEYRAND'S DISINCLINATION TO INVADE ENGLAND.

'A FULL and particular Account of the Trial of Napoleon Buonaparte before John Bull,' drawn by Woodward, etched by Cruikshank (September 14, 1803), is a broadside not remarkable for artistic merit ; it does not even give a fair idea of Napoleon's features. The letterpress is as follows :—

The Court being opened, and John Bull on the bench, Napoleon Buonaparte was put to the Bar, charged with various high crimes, thieving, and misdemeanours. Counsellor Tell Truth opened the case on the part of the prosecution, as follows :

Counsellor. May it please your worship Mr. John Bull, and Gentlemen of the Jury, From the Indictment now before you, you will perceive the prisoner stands charged as follows : that he, Napoleon Buonaparte, on the 28th of December, 1793, caused at Toulon, when the siege was over, fifteen hundred men, women, and children, to be fired upon with grape shot ; that by these means he became a favourite of Robespierre, and, in concert with that destroyer, did on the 13th Vendemaire, October 4, 1795, sweep the streets of Paris near the Pont Neuf with artillery, and covered the steps of St. Roch with heaps of slaughtered bodies ; the persons massacred on the whole amounted to about eight thousand. At Pavia, the magistrates having interfered to save the people from the bayonet, were bound together, and shot by his order ; he also burnt the town of Benasco, and massacred the inhabitants. At Alexandria he gave up the city to his soldiers for four hours ; the old people, women, and children, flew to the mosques, but the mosques were no protection from brutal fury, though Buonaparte professed himself a Turk ;—at Jaffa, horrid to relate ! three thousand eight hundred prisoners were marched to a rising ground, and there destroyed by means of musquetry, grape shot, and the bayonet ; in short, his various massacres, robberies, and pillage, are too numerous to bring forward. I shall only observe, that this gentle, this merciful man, at the above place, Jaffa, finding his hospitals crowded with sick of his own army, caused the whole to be poisoned ; thus, in a few hours, five hundred and eighty soldiers died miserably by order of their General—; so says Sir Robert Wilson.

John Bull. Mercy on me, Mr. Tell Truth, let me hear no more, it will lift my wig off with horror ! ! !

Counsellor T. T. I shall briefly observe, that this man, after overrunning all Italy, France, Holland, Switzerland, stealing our beloved George's horses at Hanover, and various other sacrifices to his unbounded ambition, had the audacity to declare he would invade the happy shores of Great Britain, and disturb the fireside of honest John Bull and his children ; but he was stopped in his career by a single English seaman, who will lay the particulars before the Court.   Crier, call in Tom Mizen.

Crier. Tom Mizen, come into Court.

John Bull. Now, Mister Mizen, what have you to say ?

Tom Mizen. You must know, Mr. Bull, having, as it were, lashed myself to a love of my King and Country, and hearing the land lubber at the bar was about to bring over his Cock boats ; I thought myself, in duty bounden, to see what sort of game he was after ; so, rigging out my little skiff the Buxom Kitty, I clapped a few pounders aboard, with an allowance of grog, and set sail ; when I got near Bull-hog-ney—I think they call it so in their palaver—but I never can think of their outlandish palaver, not I—howsomdever I soon spied a little gun boat or two, and on board one of them I saw a little pale-faced olive-coloured man in a large cocked hat, taking measure of the sides : may I never set sail again, said I, if that is not little Boney—so I made no more ado, but got ready my cordage and grappling irons, and after one broadside, towed the little gentleman into Brighton.

John Bull. Bravo, Mister Mizen—now let us hear what Mynheer Dutchman has to say.

Dutchman. Indeed, Mynheer Bool, I have nothing to say in his favour—he has robbed me of my liberty, my money, and everything that is dear to me.

Italian. I am precisely in the same position.

Swiss. And I.

The Pope. I once had a voice in the senate, but he has totally abridged my power.

Hanoverian, &c.   We are one and all tired of his tyrannical usurpation.

John Bull. Then it appears to me no one will speak in his favour.

From the Court. Not one.

John Bull. Well then—what has the prisoner to say in his own defence?

Buonaparte. I am a man of few words, and leave my defence entirely to my counsel.

The Devil, as Counsellor for the Prisoner. Mr. Bull, and Gentlemen of the Jury, I blush for the first time in my life ; it is well known I am the father of lies and mischief, and have had the prisoner at the bar a considerable time in training, but he really goes so much beyond my abilities, that I entirely give up to the discretion of the Jury.

John Bull. I shall very briefly, gentlemen, sum up the evidence ; you have heard a long and serious detail of the prisoner's cruelties in different parts of the world. The conduct of our worthy countryman, Tom Mizen, you must all admire ; you perceive there is not one person to speak in his favour ; and even his old counsel the Devil will have nothing to do with him— I therefore leave him to your verdict.

The Jury, without leaving the Court, pronounced the prisoner *Guilty.*

John Bull then passed sentence, as follows :

NAPOLEON BUONAPARTE—after a fair trial, you have been found guilty of various high crimes and misdemeanours, in different parts of this world. I am a man that delights not in blood ; I therefore sentence you to be turned over to the care of my trusty and beloved friend, Mr. Pidcock, proprietor of the Wild beasts over Exeter 'Change in the Strand ; there to be publicly shewn to my fellow citizens, inclosed in an iron cage for three months; after the expiration of which time, I sentence you to be transported to your native town of Ajaccio in Corsica for three months, and, for the remainder of your life, to be hung up by your legs in the mines of Mexico.

Mr. Pidcock attended with a cage, and disposed of the prisoner according to his sentence ; he appeared extremely hardened during the whole of the trial. The Court was uncommonly crowded.

'Buonaparte's Soliloquy at Calais, written and designed by G. M. Woodward,' was published September 21, 1803. It is as follows :—

To go or not to go? that is the question ;—
Whether 'tis better for my views to suffer
The ease and quiet of yon hated rival,
Or to take arms against the haughty people,
And by invading, end them?   T' invade,—to fight,—
No more ! and by a fight, to say we end
The envy and the thousand jealous pangs

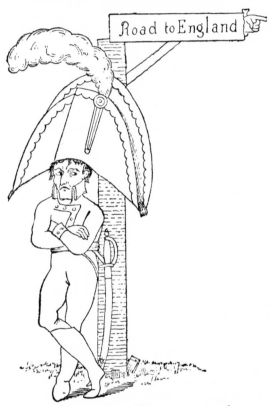

We now must bear with ; 'tis a consummation
Devoutly to be wish'd.   T' invade—to fight—
To fight ?—perchance be beat : aye, there's the rub ;
For in our passage hence what ills may come,
When we have parted from our native ports,
Must give us pause ;—there's the respect
That makes th' alternative so hard a choice.
For who would bear their just and equal laws,

Their sacred faith, and general happiness,
That shew in contrast black our tyrant sway,
Our frequent breach of treaty, and the harms
Devouring armies on the people bring,
When he himself could the dark shame remove
By mere invasion? Who would tamely view
That happy nation's great and thriving power,
But that the dread of falling on their coast,
(That firm and loyal country, from whose shores
No enemy returns,) puzzles the will,
And makes us rather bear the ills we have,
Than fly to others that we know not of?
Thus conscience does make cowards of us all ;
And thus the native hue of resolution
Is sicklied o'er with the pale cast of thought ;
And enterprises of great pith and moment,
With this regard, their currents turn awry,
And lose the name of action.

'The Fable of the Bundle of Faggots exemplified, or Bonaparte baffled,' by an unknown artist (September 20, 1803), shows Napoleon unable to break the bundle of *Britons.* His foot rests on a heap of broken faggots, all conquered nations, but this is too hard a job for him, as he confesses : 'Au diable ! all I can do, they'll neither bend or break.'

An unknown artist (September 1803) gave us, 'A Peep at the Corsican Fairy.' Here little Boney is chained to a table and padlocked by *The British Navy.* An Italian, Swiss, Dutchman, and Spaniard are looking curiously at him, thus making their remarks : 'Monsieur John Bull, I think I have seen this little Gentleman before – he was with us in Italy.' 'We shall never forget him in Switzerland.' ' My frow once persuaded me to show our house, and he took possession of the whole premises.' ' By St. Diego, he is a curious little fellow.' John Bull is showing him, and has a sweetmeat labelled ' Malta ' in his hand: ' Oh yes, sir, he is a great Traveller—but don't come too near him ; he is very cholerick ; he put himself into a great passion with me about the sugar plumb I hold in my hand—indeed, if it was not for my little chain and padlock, I could not keep him in any sort of order.

It is well known that Talleyrand was averse to the intended invasion of England, and some time in September 1803, Gillray produced 'The Corsican Carcase Butcher's Reckoning Day, New Style, *No Quarter* Day !' a portion of which is here given.

Talleyrand (his ecclesiastical status expressed by the cross on his partially military cocked hat) restrains Napoleon from invading England, although the Conqueror has on his seven-league boots. In the distance are the white cliffs of Albion, surrounded by ships of war, and a huge bull bellows defiance. At the open door the Russian bear looks in, enraging Napoleon almost to frenzy. On the ground is a coop full of foxes labelled 'From Rome, not worth killing.' 'The Germanic Body' lies in a sadly mutilated condition, having lost its head, feet, and hands ; one of the latter—the right hand—lies close by, labelled 'Hanover.' A poor, lean, gaunt dog, 'Prussia,' is in a kennel 'put up to fatten.' The food provided for it is blood, or 'Consular Whipt Syllabub.' In a trough lie the bodies of six Mamelukes, 'Jaffa Cross breeds,' whose blood drains into a receptacle 'Glory.'

P

On the walls are hung a sheep, 'True Spanish Fleec'd '; a dead Monkey, 'Native Breed '; an ass 'from Switzerland,' and a pig 'from Holland.'

BONEY AND TALLEY.
THE CORSICAN CARCASE BUTCHER'S RECKONING DAY.

NEW STYLE. *No QUARTER* DAY !

1.

Says Boney the Butcher to Talley his man,
One settling day as they reckon'd,
 'Times are hard—'twere a sin,
 Not to keep our hand in '—
Talley guessed at his thoughts in a second.

2.

Then he reach'd the account book—turn'd over awhile ;
'I have it—see here are the Dutch, Sir.'
 Boney cries 'It appears
 That they're much in arrears.'
Quoth Talley ' *They don't owe us much, Sir !* '

3.

'Here's Parma, Placentia ; there's Naples and Rome.'
Talley smil'd ' They are nothing but bone, Sir ! '
 ' For the present pass Prussia ;
 What think you of Russia?'
'*'Twere as good that we let her alone, Sir !* '

4.

' My ambition unsated, my fury unquenched,
Let Europe now shake to her bases :
 For my banner unfurl'd,
 I defy all the world,
And *spit in th' ambassadors' faces.* '

5.

Seeing raw-head and bloody bones wondrous irate,
Talley turn'd o'er the leaf with his finger ;
 ' Here's Hanover—if—'
 ' If what ?' in a tiff
Cries Boney, ' Tell Mortier to bring her.

6.

' Let her bleed till her life strings are ready to burst,
To drain her let Massena shew you ;

The job being done,
And all her fat run,
We'll give up her trunk to—*you know who.*

7.

' This will do for a breakfast—read on.'   Talley read,
Each page they conn'd over and over,
   ' I can find nothing here ;
   We must stop, Sir, I fear.'
Boney scowl'd, *and then pointed to Dover.*

8.

' Shall I want employ—whilst a breed there exists
So sleek, and so tempting to slaughter ?
   Reach my cleaver and steel,
   I'll not sit at a meal—
Till '—Talley cries ' Think of the *Water.'*

9.

' A soul such as mine, by the Koran I swear
Such childish impediment scorns, Sir ;
   I will bait this great Bull,
   And his crest I will pull.'
Cries Talley ' *Remember his horns, Sir.'*

10.

' Psha ! my mouth 'gins to water, and yearns for the feast,
Such dainty, such delicate picking ;
   By his horns I will seize him,
   Goad, worry, and teaze him :'
Quoth Talley—'*He's given to kicking.'*

11.

' Let him kick, let him toss, and for mercy implore,
Be mine the proud task to refuse it ;
   The fates shall obey,
   I will have my way ;'
Talley mutters, ' *I hope you won't lose it.'*

12.

' Sound the cleaver and marrow bones,' Boney exclaims,
' Strait this herd in my power shall be, Sir ;'
   ' Should you once reach the shore,'
   (Talley said somewhat lower,)
' You'll soon be at top of the tree, Sir.'

13.

' Don't jest with thy master, thou recreant knave
Am I, Sir, or am I, Sir, no king ?

By the Prophet I swear '—
'Cry you mercy—forbear !'
Quoth Talley, ' *I thought you were joking.*

14.

'Am I such a lover of jibes or of jests,
Do I ever smile ? ' Boney cried, 'Sir ; '
'No, that I may say
But to blast or betray ; '
(But this, Talley uttered aside, Sir.)

15.

He calls on Great Mahomet, swears by his beard,
The Lama he begs to be civil ;
Now tells all his complaints
To the Calendar Saints,
And now sends them all to the Devil.

16.

Thus prepared, he clasp'd firm the dread steel in his hand,
And wielded his cleaver on high, Sir ;—
'Oh thou Bull, thou *Grand Bête* !
Oh thou barb of my Fate !
This day thou most surely shalt die, Sir ! '

17.

Tho' artful and cunning some madmen appear,
The simplest expedient will turn 'em ;
Talley saw what he meant ;
On the schemes he was bent,
And fully resolv'd to adjourn 'em.

18.

Now Boney grown wilder, his eyes seem'd to start,
And loudly began he to bellow ;
When Talley seized hold
Of this hero so bold,
And pinion'd *the poor little fellow.*

19.

'Oh, brave, great, and noble, magnanimous man ! ! ! ! ! !
To save thee thy servant is bound, Sir ;
The Sea it is deep,
And the shores they are steep,
Most certainly you will be drown'd, Sir.

20.

'Think how precious your life is to France and to me,
Obey then your fate, and don't mock it ;

Think what we shou'd do,
Mighty Sir, without you,
With our *liberties all in your pocket*

21.

' Nay—*sweet, gentle* Sir ' (Boney kick'd with all might),
' Oh !—this chivalry's quite out of fashion ! '
　　Talley had his own way,
　　Not a word did Bo say,
For speak he could not for his passion.

22.

' Dread Sir, your great project is worthy yourself,
Your knife shall soon hit the bull's throat, Sir,
　　I'd only premise,
　　Were I fit to advise,
'*Twould be better to order a boat,* Sir.'

23.

' A boat, aye, a boat ! why there's reason in that,'
Boney cries with a scowl of delight, Sir ;
　　For the truth must be told,
　　He knew Talley of old,
And felt in a devilish fright, Sir.

24.

Boney thought that the boat was a much safer plan,
He voted the counsel discreet, Sir ;
　　Quoth Talley ' 'Tis done,
　　And the day is your own,
Just—take—care—to avoid the Fleet, Sir.'

25.

Talley cautiously then let the little man down,
When the little man softened his features ;
　　Yet though little in size, Sir,
　　His soul is as high, Sir,
As the cross at the top of Saint Peter's.

26.

Little Boney shook hands then with Talley the good ;
(*And thought how he best might dispatch him*)
　　Whilst Talley as meek,
　　Kiss'd the Mussulman's cheek,
(*And swore in his heart to o'er match him.*)

27.

They drank to their hopes—hob a nobb'd to their scheme,
Which promis'd such royal diversion ;

Thus cordial they sat,
And, in *harmless chit chat,*
Sketch'd the *plan of this water excursion.*

28.

When the boat will be ready we none of us know,
Talley swears 'twill be here in a trice, Sir ;
But it must be confess'd,
Boney's not in such haste,
Since he thought of the business twice, Sir.

29.

Then a health to the Butcher ! and life long enough,
That he once of the Bull may a view get,
For, whenever we meet,
If he *skulk from the* FLEET,
We will find him head quarters in NEWGATE.

CHAPTER XXXVII.

INVASION SQUIBS—VOLUNTEERS.

, THE Corsican Locust ' (West, September 1803) shows him hovering ovei a picnic party, saying : ' Bless me, how comfortably these People live.' The party consists of an Englishman, Irishman, and a Scotchman. The first has roast beef, plum-pudding, and a foaming tankard, before him, and, regarding the insect, says : ' As sure as I'm alive, that Corsican locust smells the Roast Beef and Plumb pudding.' Paddy has only ' praties,' but looks up at it, and asks : ' Perhaps, my Jewel, 'tis a potatoe or two you want, but the divil a halfpeth do you get from me.' The Scotchman, with his basin and spoon in his hands, thinks : ' Perhaps the Cheeld would like a little o' my Scotch Broth—but Sandy is too cunning for that.'

' The Grand Triumphal Entry of the Chief Consul into London ' is by an unknown artist (October 1, 1803). He is escorted by volunteer cavalry, and is seated, bareheaded and handcuffed, with his face towards the tail of a white horse,[1] his legs being tied under its belly. The horse is led by two volunteers, one of whom carries a flagstaff with the tricolour under the Union Jack, and on the summit is

[1] Indicative of Hanover.

perched Boney's huge hat, labelled 'For Saint Pauls.' One
of the mob is calling out : 'We may thank our Volunteers
for this glorious sight.'

Of 'The Corsican Pest, or Belzebub going to supper,' by
Gillray (October 6, 1803), only a portion is given in the

THE CORSICAN PEST, OR BELZEBUB GOING TO SUPPER.

illustration, but nothing of moment is omitted. The following are the lines under this broadsheet :—

> Buonaparte they say, aye good lack a day !
> With French Legions will hither come swimming,
> And like hungry Sharks, some night in the dark,
> Mean to frighten our Children and Women.
> Tol de rol.

> When these Gallic Foisters gape wide for our Oisters,
> Old Neptune will rise up with glee,
> Souse and Pickle them quick, to be sent to old Nick,
> As a treat from the God of the Sea.
> Tol de rol.

Belzebub will rejoice at a Supper so nice,
And make all his Devils feast hearty ;
But the *little tit bit*, on a fork, he would spit,
The Consular Chief, Buonaparté !
Tol de rol.

Then each Devil suppose, closely stopping his nose,
And shrinking away from the smell,
' By Styx,' they would roar, ' such a damn'd Stink before
Never entered the kingdom of Hell.'
Tol de rol.

Full rotten the heart of the said Buonaparte,
Corrupted his Marrow and Bones,
French evil o'erflows, from his Head to his Toes,
And disorder'd his Brains in his Sconce !
Tol de rol.

His pestiferous breath, has put Millions to Death,
More baneful than Mad dog's Saliva,
More poisonous he, all kingdoms agree,
Than the dire Bohan-Upas of Java—
Tol de rol.

By the favour of Heaven, to our Monarch is given
The power to avert such dire evil,
His subjects are ready, all Loyal and Steady,
To hurl this damn'd Pest to the Devil.
Tol de rol.

An unknown artist (October 11, 1803) gives us ' The
Ballance of Power or the Issue of the Contest.' The hand
of Providence is holding the balance, and John Bull, whose
good qualities are named ' Valour, Justice, Honor, Integrity, Commerce, Firmness, Trade, Heroism, Virtue,' is
rapidly ascending ; and, according to his own account,
' There's a sweet little Cherub that sits up aloft, will take
care of the fate of John Bull. But poor Boney, with a
heavy burden on his back of ' Shame, Disgrace, Obloquy,
Cruelty, Murder, Plunder, Rapine, Villainy, and Hypocrisy,'
is sinking into the earth, which emits flames to consume
him.

' Thoughts on Invasion, both sides the water,' by
Charles (October 11, 1803), shows us the English coast
defended by volunteers. John Bull, laughing, is seated in
a chair, under which is a cornucopia, running over with

corn, wine, beef, and all kinds of provisions. The old boy is chuckling : ' I can't help laughing at the thought of Invasion, but there is no knowing what a mad man may attempt, so I'll take care to have my coast well lined, and I think 80,000 such men as me, able to eat all the Boney rascals in France, and if they mean Invasion, I have sent a Specimen of Bombs into Calais ! ' The ships are shown in the act of bombarding that place, while Boney sits very miserable, with a tricolour foolscap on his head, moaning : ' I wish I had never promis'd to Invade this terrible John Bull, but how shall I avoid it, with Credit to myself and honour to the French Nation ? and this bombarding Calais gives me the Bl—— Blu—— Blue Devils.' A blue devil behind him is saying : ' You must go now, Boney, as sure as I shall have you in the end.'

' The little Princess and Gulliver ' is by Ansell (October 21, 1803), and, of course, the Gulliver is Napoleon, whom a Brobdingnagian princess (Charlotte of Wales) has plunged into a basin of water, and, with her fist, keeps beating him as he rises to the top, saying : ' There you impertinent, boasting, swaggering pigmy—take that. You attempt to take my Grandpapa's Crown indeed, and plunder all his subjects ; I'll let you know that the Spirit and Indignation of every Girl in the Kingdom is roused at your Insolence.'

' The Centinel at his Post, or Boney's peep into Walmer Castle !! ' (Ansell, October 22, 1803) shows Boney, with a boat-load of troops, arrived on the English Coast, but they are at once disconcerted by the appearance of the sentinel, Pitt, who challenges, ' Who goes there ? ' With abject fear depicted on the countenance of Bonaparte and his followers, the former exclaims : 'Ah ! Begar—dat man alive still. Turn about, Citoyens—for there will be no good to be done—I know his tricks of old !! '

There are two caricatures on the same subject, one attributed to Gillray, but signed C.L.S. (October 25, 1803), the other by I. Cruikshank, to which the same date is attributed. One is evidently copied from the other, for the *motif* is the same in both. I prefer the former, and therefore describe it. It is called ' French Volunteers marching

to the Conquest of Great Britain, dedicated (by an Eye
Witness) to the Volunteers of Great Britain.' A mounted
officer leads a gang of chained, handcuffed, and pinioned,
scarecrow-looking conscripts, some of them so weak that
they have to be carried in paniers on donkey-back, or
drawn on a trolley ; whilst a poor, dilapidated, ragged
wretch, also chained by the neck, and with his hands tied
behind him, brings up the rear of the procession.

'John Bull guarding the Toy Shop' (J. B., October 29,
1803) shows a shop-window containing such toys as the
India House, St. James's, the Bank, Custom House, Tower,
and the Treasury. Little Boney, with his handkerchief to
his eyes, is weeping, and crying : ' Pray, Mr. Bull, let me
have some of the Toys, if 'tis only that little one in the
Corner ' (the Bank). But John Bull, who is in full regimentals, and armed with his gun, replies, in his rough,
insular way : ' I tell you, you shan't touch one of them—so
blubber away and be d—d.'

The volunteer force was a great factor in face of the
Invasion, and it was computed to number 350,000 men.[1]
We know, in our own times, that, at a mere whisper of invasion, men enrolled themselves as volunteers by thousands,
and we have never heard that whisper repeated. The
enthusiasm of the citizen army was very great, and twice
in October 1803 (on the 26th 14,500 men, and on the 28th
about 17,000), the King reviewed these volunteers in Hyde
Park. It will be curious briefly to note some particulars
respecting the pay and clothing of volunteers. They are
taken from the circular papers of regulations which were
sent from Lord Hobart's office to the Lords Lieutenant of
the different counties.

8. When not called out on actual service, constant pay to be
allowed for 1 Sergeant and 1 Drummer per Company, at the same
rates as in the disembodied Militia ; the pay of the Drummer to
be distributed at the discretion of the Commandant ; pay (as disembodied Militia) for the rest of the Sergeants and Drummers,
and for the Corporals and private men, to be allowed for two days

[1] The Marquis of Hartington in a speech in the House of Commons, March
17, 1884, said 'there were now 209,365 volunteers enrolled, of whom 202,478
were efficient.'—*Morning Post*, March 18, 1884.

in the week, from the 25th of February to the 24th of October, and for one day in the week from the 25th day of October to the 24th of February, both inclusive, being 85 days pay per annum, but for effectives only, present under arms, on each respective day. Pay may, however, be charged for persons absent by sickness, for a period not exceeding three months, on the Commanding Officer's Certificate to that effect. Sergeants 1/6, Corporals 1/2, Drummers and Privates 1/.

9. If a Corps, or any part thereof, shall be called upon, in case of any riot or disturbance, the charge of constant pay to be made for such services must be at the rates before specified, and must be supported by a Certificate from his Majesty's Lieutenant, or the Sheriff of the County ; but, if called out in case of actual Invasion, the Corps is to be paid and disciplined in all respects as the Regular Infantry, the Artillery Companies excepted, which are then to be paid as the Royal Artillery.

10. The whole to be clothed in Red, with the exception of the Corps of Artillery, which may have Blue clothing, and Rifle Corps, which may have Green, with black belts.

Allowance for Clothing.

£3 3 9 for each Sergeant,
2 12 0 for each Corporal,
2 3 6 for each Drummer,
1 10 0 for each Private Man,

and to be repeated at the end of three years ; the Sergeant Major, and 1 Sergeant, and 1 Drummer per Company, to have clothing annually.

11. An annual allowance to be made for each Company in lieu of every contingent expense heretofore defrayed by Government, viz. £25 for companies of 50 Private men, with an additional allowance of £5 for every 10 Private Men beyond that number.

There is an amusing caricature (October 18, 1803) illustrating Talleyrand's disinclination to the projected invasion of England.

In his 'Voyage to Brobdingnag,' Lemuel Gulliver, speaking of his enemy the King's Dwarf, says : ' He had before served me a scurvy trick, which set the queen a-laughing, although at the same time she was heartily vexed, and would have immediately cashiered him, if I had not been so generous as to intercede. Her majesty had taken a marrow-bone upon her plate, and, after knocking out the marrow, placed the bone again in the dish erect, as it stood before ; the dwarf, watching his opportunity when Glumdalclitch was gone to the sideboard, mounted the stool that she stood on to take care of me at meals, took me up in both hands, and squeezing my legs

THE KING'S DWARF PLAYS GULLIVER A TRICK.

together, wedged them into the marrow bone above my waist, where I stuck for some time, and made a very ridiculous figure. I believe it was near a minute before any one knew what was become of me ; for I thought it below me to cry out. But, as princes seldom get their meat hot, my legs were not scalded, only my stockings and breeches in a sad condition. The dwarf, at my entreaty, had no other punishment than a sound whipping.'

There was also a squib about the same master and man :—

BUONAPARTE

AND

TALLEYRAND.

It is well known that Monsieur TALLEYRAND always objected to the Invasion of England, as a mad Attempt, that must end in the destruction of the Invaders. Having been favoured with a Note of a Conversation between him and the Chief Consul on this Subject, I have attempted, for the Entertainment of my Country-men, to put it into Rhyme.

A. S.

BUONAPARTE.

TALLEYRAND, what's the state of my great preparation,
To crush, at one stroke, this vile, insolent nation,
That baffles my projects, my vengeance derides,
Blasts all my proud hopes, checks my arrogant strides.
Boasts a *Press unrestrained*, points its censure at ME,
And while Frenchmen are Slaves, still presumes to be free ?

TALLEYRAND.

In a Month, Sire, or less, your magnanimous host,
Their standards shall fix on the rude British Coast.

BUONAPARTE.

'Tis well—let the troops be kept hungry and bare,
To make them more keen—for that Island's good fare.
Give them *drafts upon London*, instead of their pay,
And rouse them to *ravish, burn, plunder*, and *slay*.
Prepare, too,—*some draughts*, for the sick and the lame
You know what I mean.

TALLEYRAND.

As in Syria ?

BUONAPARTE.

The same !

That *England I hate*, and its armies subdued,
The *slaughter of Jaffa* shall there be renew'd.
Not a wretch that presumes to oppose, but shall feel
The flames of my fury, the force of my steel.

Their daughters, and wives, to my troops I consign ;
So shall vengeance, sweet vengeance, deep-glutted, be mine,
Their children —

TALLEYRAND.

What ! massacre them, my dread Lord ?

BUONAPARTE.

Why not ? with *me* PITY *was never the word !*
That island once conquer'd, the world is my own,
And its ruins shall furnish the base of my throne.

TALLEYRAND.

What a project ! how vast !—yet allow me one word ;
Sir, the English are brave, and can wield well the sword.
In defence of their freedom, their *King*, and their soil,
Not a man but would dare the most perilous toil.
Should our troops but appear, they will rush to the field,
And will die on the spot to a man e'er they yield.
In defence of their honour, their women will fight,
And their navy, triumphant, still sails in our sight.

BUONAPARTE.

Hush, hush, say no more lest some listeners should hear,
And our troops should be taught these fierce Britons to fear.
They are brave ; and my soldiers have felt it—what then ?
Our numbers are more—to their five, we are ten.
Say their sailors are skilful, oak hearted, and true,
One army may fail, yet another may do.
And though thousands should fatten the sharks in the sea,
There are thousands remaining, *to perish for me.*
In a night, or a fog, we will silent steal over,
And surprise unexpected, the Castle of Dover.
Then to gull the poor dupes of that navy bound land,
You have lies ready coin'd—*'tis your trade,* at command.
We will tell them, and swear it, our sole end and aim,
Is to make them all equally rich—all the same.
I see by your smile you interpret my meaning,
That where my troops reap, they leave nothing for gleaning.
They soar at a palace, they swoop to a cot.
And plunder—not leaving one bone for the pot.
Now, Sir, to your duty, your business prepare,
Leave the rest to *my* Genius, *my* fortune, *my* care.
      [*Exit Buonaparte, Talleyrand looking after him.*

TALLEYRAND.

Your fortune, I fear, Sir, will play you a trick :—
Notwithstanding his vaunts, he is touch'd to the quick.
What folly ! what madness, this project inspires,
To conquer a nation, whom liberty fires.
Even now from their shores, loudly echoed, I hear
The song of defiance appalling mine ear.
Their spirit once rous'd, what destruction awakes !
What vengeance, the wretched invaders o'ertakes.
Prophetic, I plead, but my warning is vain,
Ambition still urges, and maddens his brain :
Fired with hopes of rich booty, his soldiers all burn,
THEY MAY GO, SOME MAY LAND, BUT NOT ONE WILL RETURN.

J. B. (November 5, 1803) produced 'Boney in time for
Lord Mayors Feast.' At this banquet a sailor produces
Napoleon chained, and with a collar round his neck. He
thus introduces him : 'Here he is, please your Honors.
We caught him alive, on the Suffolk Coast. He was a
little queerish at first, but a few Stripes at the Gangway
soon brought him about. I told him he was just in time
for the Lord Mayor's Show. What does your honor think
of him for the Man in Armour ?' The Lord Mayor, glass
in hand, says : ' Ay, you see how we live at this end of the
town, but you get no Roast beef here, Master Boney—Let
him have plenty of Soup Maigre—and in the evening take
him up to the Ball Room for the amusement of the Ladies
—Come, heres the glorious Ninth of November.'

' Destruction of the French Gun Boats—or Little Boney
and his friend Talley in high Glee' is presumably by
Gillray, though not signed by him (November 22, 1803).
It represents the total destruction of the French flotilla by
the English fleet—which Napoleon, mounted on Talleyrand's shoulder, is watching with great glee through a
rolled-up paper (Talleyrand's plan for invading Great
Britain), which is being used in lieu of a telescope. He
shouts out, in great delight, ' Oh my dear Talley, what a
glorious sight ! We've worked up Johnny Bull into a fine
passion ! My good fortune never leaves me ! I shall now
get rid of a Hundred Thousand French Cut Throats whom
I was so afraid of ! Oh, my dear Talley, this beats the

Egyptian Poisoning hollow! Bravo Johnny! pepper 'em Johnny!'

Ansell is answerable for ' Boney's Journey to London, or the reason why he is so long in coming, i.e. because he travels like a Snail with his house at his back' (November 23, 1803). He is portrayed as being in a wooden house, drawn by his soldiers, who are being unmercifully whipped with a knout-like weapon. Napoleon, calling out to the officer who is administering the punishment, ' You Vagabones, make haste, Vite, Vite, or I shall not get to London by Christmass. Give them more of the Fraternal Whip, the dam Rascals do not know the value of Liberty.'

CHAPTER XXXVIII.

INVASION SQUIBS—CADOUDAL'S CONSPIRACY—EXECUTION OF THE
DUC D'ENGHIEN—CAPTAIN WRIGHT.

THE Volunteer movement was well shown in a print by A. M., November 1803 : ' Boney attacking the English Hives, or the Corsican caught at last in the Island.' There are many hives, the chief of which has a royal crown on its top, and is labelled ' Royal London Hive. Threadneedle Street Honey'—which Napoleon is attacking, sword in hand. George the Third, as Bee Master, stands behind the hives, and says, ' What! what! you plundering little Corsican Villain, have you come to rob my industrious Bees of their Honey? I won't trust to your oath. Sting, Sting the Viper to the heart my good Bees, let Buz, Buz be the Word in the Island.' The bees duly obey their master's request, and come in clouds over Napoleon, who has to succumb, and pray, kneeling, ' Curse those Bees they sting like Scorpions. I did not think this Nation of Shopkeepers could sting so sharp. Pray good Master of the Bees, do call them off, and I will swear by all the three creeds which I profess, Mahometan, Infidel, and Christian, that I will never disturb your Bees again.'

' Selling the Skin before the Bear is caught, or cutting up the Bull before he is killed,' is by I. Cruikshank (December 21, 1803), and represents a Bull reposing calmly on the English shore, whilst on the opposite or French coast is Bonaparte, Talleyrand, and several Generals. Bonaparte, pointing to the Bull, says : 'I shall take the Middle part, because it contains the Heart and Vitals— Talley, you may take the head, because you have been accustomed to take the Bull by the horns.' Britannia stands, fully armed, behind the Bull, by an 'alarm post,' on which hangs a bell, 'British Valor,' which she is preparing to ring : 'When these Mounseers have settled their plan, I will just rouse the Bull, and then see who will be cut up first.'

'New Bellman's Verses for Christmas 1803 !' is an extremely inartistic work of an unknown man (December 1803) ; the only thing worth quoting about it are these verses :—

> This little Boney says he'll come
> At Merry Christmas time,
> But that I say is all a hum,
> Or I no more will rhyme.

> Some say in wooden house he'll glide,
> Some say in air Balloon,
> E'en those who airy schemes deride,
> Agree his coming soon.

> Now honest people list to me,
> Though Income is but small,
> I'll bet my Wig to one Pen—ney,
> He does not come at all.

'More than expected, or too many for Boney' (artist unknown, December 1803), shows him as an Ass, on whose back is John Bull, Russia, Prussia, and Germany. Says Russia, 'We all depend upon you Mr. Bull—give him a little more spurring, and we'll soon make him feel the Rowels.' John mildly expostulates with his quadruped : 'Come—come, don't be sulky—if you won't go in a snaffle, you must be forced to go in a curb.'

Dean Swift's immortal book did yeoman's service to the caricaturists, and we find it again employed in a print by West, December 1803 : 'The Brobdingnag Watchman preventing Gulliver's landing.' It is very feeble, and merely consists of George the Third as a watchman turning the

Q

light of the 'Constitutional Lanthorn' upon Bonaparte and his companions, who are attempting a landing.

Another print, by West (December 1803), shows 'Mr. and Mrs. Bull giving Buonaparte a Christmas Treat!' The latter is bound to a post in sight of, but beyond reach of, the national fare of this festival. John Bull says, holding up a piece of beef, in derision, 'Yes, yes—the Beef is very good, so is the pudding too—but the deuce a morsel do you get of either, Master Boney.' Mrs. Bull too, who is drinking from a frothing tankard, says : 'Your health Master Boney, wishing you a merry Christmas,' but offers him none.

An unknown artist gives an undated picture of 'a Cock and Bull Story.' Napoleon, as the Gallic Cock, on his side of the Channel, sings

Cock a dudle doo, I shall come over to you.
I'll fight true game, and crow my Fame,
And make you all look blue.

John Bull, who is peacefully reposing in his pastures, rejoins :—

You impertinent Cock, I'll have you to know
On this side the Brook, you never shall Crow,
And if you're not quick, and give up your jaw,
I'll teach you the nature of English Club Law.

In 1803 was published an amusing squib, in which the names of various plays are very ingeniously made into a patriotic address :—

THE GREEN ROOM OPINION
OF THE
THREATENED INVASION.

SHOULD the Modern *Tamerlane* revive the tragedy of *England Invaded*, and, in the progress of his *Wild goose Chace*, escape the *Tempest*, he will find that, with us, it is *Humours of the Age* to be *Volunteers*. He will prove that we have many a *Plain Dealer*, who will tear off *the Mask*, under which *the Hypocrite*, this *Fool of Fortune*, this *Choleric man*, has abused a credulous world. Should he, to *a Wonder*, attempt a *Trip to Scarborough*, to set them *all alive at Portsmouth*, or to get *on both sides of the gutter*, he will assuredly meet a *Chapter of Accidents* on his *Road to Ruin* ; for *Britannia and the Gods are in Council*, to make him a *Castle*

Spectre : he will, too late, discover *the Secret* of *Who's the Dupe* ; and that it is *the Custom of the Country* of *John Bull*, to shew *the Devil to pay* to any *Busybody*, who seeks to enforce on us *Reformation.*

This *Double Dealer*, who has excited dismay *Abroad and at Home*, and gained *Notoriety* by the magnitude of the mischiefs he has achieved, still presumes, by *the Wheel of Fortune*, like another *Pizarro*, to satiate his *Revenge*, and to learn *How to grow Rich*, by renewing the distressing scenes of *the Siege of Damascus* ; until amongst the desolated ruins of our City, he should establish himself like *a London Hermit.* That *he Would if he Could*, is past all doubt ; but if he will take *a Word to the Wise*, from *a Man of the World*, he will believe *He's much to blame*, and *All in the Wrong* ; for *the Doctor and the Apothecary* are in *the Committee* ; and by good *Management*, are forward in *the Rehearsal* of the lively Comedy of *the Way to keep Him* under *Lock and Key.* They may not be able to produce for him *a Cure for the Heartache*, or for *the Vapourish Man*, but they will shew him at least *Cheap Living*, and prove that he has sown his *Wild Oats*, in *a Comedy of Errors.*

The Poor Soldier, whose generous heart expands to render *Love for Love*, is like the gallant and gay Lothario, armed for either field, and prepared to give *Measure for Measure* ; and to convert the *Agreeable Surprize*, which the Acre *Runaway* antici-pates in *the Camp*, from *the Beaux Stratagem* into *a Tale of Mystery.* *Appearances are against him*, as well as *the Chances* ; but he is a desperate *Gamester* ; and although his schemes of Conquest will end in *Much ado about Nothing*, like a *Midsummer's night's Dream*, or *a Winter's Tale*, yet he is *Heir at Law* to our hate ; and *Every one has his Fault*, if he does not unite to revive the splendid scenes of *Edward the Black Prince*, and *Henry the Fifth*, when France trembled beneath our arms at Cressy and Agincourt ; and give to this unprincipled *Bajazet* an exit corresponding with his crimes.

A NEW SONG OF OLD SAYINGS.

Bonaparte the Bully resolved to come over,
With flat bottomed Wherries, from Calais to Dover ;
No perils to him in the billows are found,
'*For if born to be hang'd, he can never be drown'd*

From a Corsican dunghill this fungus did spring
He was soon made a Captain and would be a King ;
But the higher he rises the more he does evil,
'*For a Beggar, on horseback, will ride to the Devil.*'

To seize all that we have and then clap us in jail,
To devour our victuals, and drink all our ale,
And to grind us to dust is the Corsican's will—
'*For we know all is grist that e'er comes to his mill.*'

To stay quiet, at home, the First Consul can't bear,
Or, mayhap, '*he would have other fish to fry there*';
So, as fish of that sort does not suit his desire,
'*He leaps out of the frying pan, into the fire.*'

He builds barges and cock boats, and craft without end,
And numbers the boats which to England he'll send;
But in spite of his craft, and his barges and boats
'*He still reckons, I think, without one of his hosts.*'

He rides upon France and he tramples on Spain,
And holds Holland and Italy tight in a Chain;
These he hazards for more, though I can't understand,
'*How one bird in the bush is worth two in the hand.*'

He trusts that his luck will all danger expel,
'*But the pitcher is broke that goes oft to the well*';
And when our brave soldiers this Bully surround,
'*Though he's thought* Penny Wise, *he'll be foolish in* Pound.'

France can never forget that our fathers of yore,
Used to pepper and baste her at sea and at shore;
And we'll speedily prove to this mock-Alexander,
'*What was sauce for the goose, will be sauce for the Gander.*'

I have heard and have read in a great many books,
Half the Frenchmen are Tailors, and t'other half Cooks;—
We've fine Trimmings in store for the Knights of the Cloth,
'*And the Cooks that come here, will but spoil their own broth.*'

It is said that the French are a numerous race,
And perhaps it is true—for '*ill weeds grow apace*';
But come when they will, and as many as dare,
'*I expect they'll arive a day after the fair.*'

To invade us more safely these warriors boast
They will wait till a storm drives our fleet from the Coast,
That 'twill be an '*ill wind,*' will be soon understood,
For a wind *that blows* Frenchmen, '*blows nobody good.*'

They would treat Britain worse than they've treated Myn-
heer,
But they'll find '*they have got the wrong sow by the ear.*'
Let them come then in swarms, by this Corsican lead,
And I warrant '*we'll hit the right nail on the head.*'

The year 1804 was a most eventful one for Napoleon. With all his hatred of England, and his wish for her invasion, he was powerless in that matter, and had plenty to employ him at home. The English had got used to their bugbear the flotilla, and the caricaturist had a rest. Napoleon had his hands full. First and foremost was that conspiracy against his life and government, in which Georges Cadoudal, Moreau, and Pichegru figure so prominently, and which entailed the execution of the Duc d'Enghien.

> The Bourbon house he so detested,
> He had the Duke d'Enghien arrested;
> A sort of trial then took place,
> And sentence passed—the usual case.
> 'Tis said that Boney chose a spot,
> To see the gallant fellow shot.

Whatever may have been Napoleon's conduct in this affair, these two last lines are undoubtedly false. The duke had been residing at Ettenheim, in the duchy of Baden, and was thought to be there in readiness to head the Royalists in case of need, that his hunting was but a pretext to cover flying visits to Paris, and that he was the person whom Georges Cadoudal and his fellow conspirators always received bareheaded. He was seized, brought to Paris, and lodged in the Château de Vincennes. A few hours' rest, and he was roused at midnight to go before his judges. It was in vain he pleaded the innocence of his occupations, and begged to have an interview with the First Consul; yet he declared he had borne arms against France, and his wish to serve in the war on the English side against France; and owned that he received a pension of one hundred and fifty guineas a month from England. He was found guilty and condemned to death, and two hours afterwards was led out into the ditch of the fortress, and there shot, a priest being refused him. O'Meara, describing a conversation with Napoleon on this subject, says: 'I now asked if it were true that Talleyrand had retained a letter written by the Duc d'Enghien to him until two days after the duke's execution? Napoleon's reply was, "It is true; the duke had written a letter offering his services, and asking a command in the Army from me, which that *scelerato*, Talleyrand, did not make known until two days after his execution." I observed that Talleyrand, by his culpable concealment of the letter, was virtually guilty of the death of the duke. " Talleyrand," replied Napoleon, " is a *briccone*, capable of any crime. I," continued he, " caused the Duc d'Enghien to be arrested in consequence of the Bourbons having landed assassins in France to murder me. I was resolved to let them see that the blood of one of their princes should pay for their attempts, and he was accordingly tried for having borne arms against the republic, found guilty, and shot, according to the existing laws against such a crime." '

Ansell (June 2, 1804) gives us 'The Cold Blooded Murderer, or the Assassination of the Duc d'Enghien,' in which the duke is represented as being bound to a tree, a soldier on either side holding a torch, whilst Napoleon is running his sword into his heart. D'Enghien bravely cries out, 'Assassin! your Banditti need not cover my Eyes, I fear not Death, tho' perhaps a guiltless countenance may appall your bloodthirsty soul.' Napoleon, whilst stabbing his victim, says : 'Now de whole World shall know de courage of de first grand Consul, dat I can kill my enemies in de Dark, as well as de light, by Night as well as by Day,—dare—and dare I had him—hark, vat noise was dat ? ah ! 'tis only de Wind—dare again, and dare—Now I shall certainly be made Emperor of de Gulls.'[1] Devils are rejoicing over the deed, and are bearing a crown. They say : ' This glorious deed does well deserve a Crown, thus let us feed his wild ambition, untill some bold avenging hand shall make him all our own.'

A Captain Wright figures in this plot ; and, as he was an Englishman, and his name is frequent both in the caricature and satire of the day, some notice of him must be given. He was a lieutenant in the Royal Navy, and somehow got mixed up with this conspiracy. He took Georges Cadoudal and others on board either at Deal or Hastings, and crossed over to Beville, where there was a smuggler's rope let down from an otherwise inaccessible cliff. By means of this they were drawn up, and went secretly

[1] Gauls.

to Paris. The plot failed, and they were thrown into prison, Wright being afterwards captured at sea. Cadoudal went to the scaffold, Pichegru was found strangled in his cell ; and Wright, the English said, after being tortured in prison, to compel him to give evidence against his companions, was assassinated by order of Napoleon.

The latter, however, always indignantly denied it, saying that Captain Wright committed suicide. In O'Meara's book he denies it several times, and an extract or two will be worth noting. ' In different nights of August, September, and December 1803 and January 1804, Wright landed Georges, Pichegru, Rivière, Costa, St. Victor, La Haye, St. Hilaire, and others at Beville. The four last named had been accomplices in the former attempt to assassinate me by means of the infernal machine, and most of the rest were well known to be chiefs of the Chouans,' &c. ' There was something glorious in Wright's death. He preferred taking away his own life, to compromising his government.' ' Napoleon in very good spirits. Asked many questions about the horses that had won at the races, and the manner in which we trained them ; how much I had won or lost ; and about the ladies, &c. " You had a large party yesterday," continued he. " How many bottles of wine ? Drink, your eyes look like drink," which he expressed in English. " Who dined with you ? " I mentioned Captain Wallis amongst others. " What ! is that the lieutenant who was with Wright ? " I replied in the affirmative. " What does he say about Wright's death ? " I said, " He states his belief that Wright was murdered by orders of Fouché, for the purpose of ingratiating himself with you. That six or seven weeks previous, Wright had told him that he expected to be murdered like Pichegru, and begged of him never to believe that he would commit suicide ; that he had received a letter from Wright, about four or five weeks before his death, in which he stated that he was better treated, allowed to subscribe to a library, and to receive newspapers." Napoleon replied, " I will never allow that Wright was put to death by Fouché's orders. If he was put to death privately, it must have been by my orders, and not by those of Fouché. Fouché knew me too well.

He was aware that I would have had him hanged directly, if he attempted it. By this officer's own words, Wright was not *au secret*, as he says he saw him some weeks before his death, and that he was allowed books and newspapers. Now, if it had been in contemplation to make away with him, he would have been put *au secret* for months before, in order that people might not be accustomed to see him for some time previous, as I thought this * * * intended to do in November last. Why not examine the gaolers and turnkeys? The Bourbons have every opportunity of proving it, if such really took place. But your ministers themselves do not believe it. The idea I have of what was my opinion at that time about Wright, is faint; but, as well as I can recollect, it was that he ought to have been brought before a military commission, for having landed spies and assassins, and the sentence executed within forty-eight hours. What dissuaded me from doing so, I cannot clearly recollect. Were I in France at this moment, and a similar occurrence took place, the above would be my opinion, and I would write to the English Government: ' Such an officer of yours has been tried for landing brigands and assassins on my territories. I have caused him to be tried by a military commission. He has been condemned to death. The sentence has been carried into execution. If any of my officers in your prisons have been guilty of the same, try, and execute them. You have my full permission and acquiescence. Or, if you find, hereafter, any of my officers landing assassins on your shores, shoot them instantly.'"'

CHAPTER XXXIX.
NAPOLEON PROCLAIMED EMPEROR—THE FLOTILLA—INVASION SQUIBS.

THE most important event of the year to Napoleon himself, was his being made Emperor. Although First Consul for life, with power to appoint his successor, it did not satisfy his ambition. He would fain be Emperor, and that strong will, which brooked no thwarting, took measures to promote that result. In the Senate M. Curée moved, ' that the First Consul be invested with the hereditary power, under the title of Emperor,' and this motion was but feebly fought against by a few members, so that at last an address was drawn up, beseeching Napoleon to yield to the wishes of the nation. A *plébiscite* was taken on the subject, with the result that over three millions and a half people voted for it, and only about two thousand against it. On May 18, Cambacérès, at the head of the Senate, waited upon Napoleon, at St. Cloud, with an address detailing the feelings and wishes of the nation. It is needless to say that Napoleon ' accepted the Empire, in order that he might labour for the happiness of the French.'

The brave First Consul now began
To set on foot his fav'rite plan ;
The Senate, when the door was clos'd,
As Emperor of France, propos'd
Brave Boney, and his heirs, and then
They call'd him worthiest of men ;
So much accustom'd down to cram a lie,
They prais'd, too, his *illustrious* family.
What *sweet* addresses, what *kind* answers,
A proof mankind, too, oft in France errs ;
All these were equally prepared
In Boney's closet, 'tis declared.
Addresses from the army came,
Which were in tendency the same.
Nap manag'd matters with facility,
Such was the people's instability.
A deputation waited on him,
And by *solicitation* won him ;
In a fine sentimental speech,
Began they Boney to beseech,
That he would graciously agree
The Emperor of France to be ;
Elected by the general voice,
They said he was the people's Choice
And begg'd the title to confer
On one who was not *prone to err.*
Nap much humility pretended,
But to accept it *condescended.*
The business settled thus, *nem. con.*
He put th' imperial purple on,

More gay appear'd his lovely wife,
Than e'er she did in all her life ;
It was enough to make her grin,
As she was Empress Josephine.
Nap now sent letters by the dozens,
To the French Bishops, his new *cousins*,
Informing them that Heav'n, indeed,
His elevation had decreed ;
And, trusting for the same, that they
Wou'd order a thanksgiving day.
As Nap—'twas wise we must allow—
A Roman Catholic was now ;
A prayer had been, to this intent,
By the Pope's legate to them sent.
Moreover, all the Christian Nations,
Received the same notifications.
Soon made they every preparation
For a most brilliant Coronation.

The flotilla, on the other side of the Channel, was still looked upon with uneasiness, and watched with jealous care. Still, we find that it was only at the commencement of the year that it was caricatured, Napoleon's being made Emperor proving a more favourite subject ; and, besides, a feeling sprung up that there was not much mischief in it.

One of the most singular caricatures, in connection with the projected invasion, that I have met with is by Ansell, January 6, 1804. 'The Coffin Expedition, or Boney's Invincible Armada Half seas over.' The flotilla is here represented as gunboats, in the shape of coffins : all the crews, naval and military, wearing shrouds ; whilst at the masthead of each vessel is a skull with *bonnet rouge.* It is needless to say they are represented as all foundering, one man exclaiming, ' Oh de Corsican Bougre was make dese Gun boats on purpose for our Funeral.' Some British vessels are in the mid distance, and two tars converse thus : ' I say Messmate, if we dont bear up quickly, there will be nothing left for us to do.' ' Right, Tom, and I take them there things at the Masthead to be Boney's Crest, a skull without brains.'

' Dutch Embarkation ; or Needs must when the Devil

drives!!' (artist unknown, January 1804) represents Bonaparte, with drawn sword, driving fat, solid Dutchmen each into a gun-boat about as big as a walnut-shell. One remonstrates: 'D—n such Liberty, and D—n such a Flotilla !! I tell you we might as well embark in Walnut Shells.' But Bonaparte replies : ' Come, come, Sir, no grumbling, I insist on your embarking and destroying the modern Carthage —don't you consider the liberty you enjoy—and the grand flotilla that is to carry you over !'

As good a one as any of Gillray's caricatures is the King of Brobdingnag and Gulliver, February 10, 1804—

THE KING OF BROBDINGNAG AND GULLIVER.

scene, 'Gulliver manœuvring with his little boat in the cistern.' The king and queen (excellent likenesses) and two princesses are looking on at Bonaparte sailing, whilst the young princes are blowing, to make a wind for him. Lord Salisbury stands behind the royal chair, and beefeaters and ladies of the court complete the scene. This, however, is specially described as ' designed by an amateur, etched by Gillray.'

'A French Alarmist, or John Bull looking out for the

Grand Flotilla!!' (West, March 1804.) He is on the
coast, accompanied by his bull-dog, and armed with a
sword, looking through a telescope. Behind him is a
Frenchman, who is saying, 'Ah! Ah! Monsieur Bull,—
dere you see our Grande flotilla—de grande gon boats—ma
foi—dere you see em sailing for de grand attack on your
nation—dere you see de Bombs and de Cannons—Dere
you see de Grande Consul himself at de head of his Legions. Dere you see——' But John Bull replies, 'Mounseer, all this I cannot see—because 'tis not in sight.'

We now come to the caricatures relating to the Empire.

A print, attributed to Rowlandson (May 1804?), shows
'A Great Man on his Hobby Horse, a design for an Intended Statue on the Place la Liberté at Paris.' Napoleon
is riding *the high horse* 'Power,' which prances on a Globe.

'A new French Phantasmagoria' is by an unknown
artist (May 1804). John Bull cannot realise the fact of
Napoleon being Emperor, but stares at him through an
enormous pair of spectacles. 'Bless me, what comes here
—its time to put on my large spectacles, and tuck up my
trowsers. Why, surely, it can't be—it is Bonny too, for all
that. Why what game be'st thee at now? acting a play
mayhap. What hast thee got on thy head there? always
at some new freak or other.' Bonaparte, in imperial robes,
and with crown and sceptre, holds out his hand, and says:
'What! my old Friend, Mr. Bull, don't you know me?'

Ansell gives us (May 28, 1804) 'The Frog and the Ox,
or The Emperor of the *Gulls* in his stolen gear.' Napoleon, very small, is depicted as capering about in imperial
robes, with an enormous crown made of coins, daggers,
and a cup of poison; his sceptre has for its top a guillotine.
George the Third is regarding him through his glass.
Napoleon says, 'There Brother! there! I shall soon be as
Big as you, it's a real Crown, but it's cursed heavy, my Head
begins to ache already. I say Can't we have a grand meeting like Henry the 8th and Francis the 1st?' King George
cannot quite make out the mannikin. 'What have we got
here, eh? A fellow that has stolen some Dollars, and
made a Crown of them, eh? and then wants to pass them
off for Sterling; it won't go, it won't pass Fellow. Beside

the King is a bull, and behind Napoleon is a frog, who is trying to swell to the bull's proportions, whilst John Bull laughingly remarks, 'Dang it, why a looks as tho a'd burst: a'l nerr be zo big as one of our Oxen tho.'

'Injecting blood Royal, or Phlebotomy at St. Cloud,' shews Napoleon, in his new phase of power, having the blood of a Royal Tiger infused into his veins. He says, 'It's a delightful operation! I feel the Citizenship oozing out at my fingers' ends.—let all the family be plentifully supplied! Carry up a Bucket full to the Empress immediately!!!'

In June 1804 I. Cruikshank drew a picture called 'the Right Owner.' Louis the Eighteenth appears to Napoleon, and, pointing to his crown, says, 'That's Mine.' Napoleon who is seated on his throne, armed with sword, pistols, and dagger, shrinks back in violent alarm, exclaiming, 'Angels and Ministers of Grace defend me.'

'A Proposal from the New Emperor' is a caricature by Ansell (July 9, 1804). He comes, cap, or rather crown, in hand, to John Bull, saying, 'My Dear Cousin Bull—I have a request to make you—the good people whom I govern, have been so lavish of their favors towards me—that they have exhausted every title in the Empire—therefore, in addition, I wish you to make me a Knight of Malta.' John Bull replies, 'I'll see you d—d first!! You know I told you so before.'

'The Imperial Coronation' is a very inartistic sketch by an unknown artist (July 31, 1804). Napoleon is being crowned by the Pope, who says, 'In a little time you shall see him, and in a little time you shall not see him,' and then lets down the crown, with cruel force, by a rope and pulley from the gibbet from which it has been suspended. Its weight crushes him through the platform on which he has been sitting, and he exclaims, 'My dear Talleyrand, save me ; My throne is giving way. I am afraid the foundation is rotten, and wants a deal of mending.' Talleyrand sympathisingly answers, 'Oh, Master, Master, the Crown is too heavy for you.'

I. Cruikshank drew 'Harlequin's last Skip' (August 23, 1804). Bonaparte is represented in a harlequin's suit, enormous cocked hat, boots, and a blackened face. His sword is broken, and, with upraised hands, in a supplicating attitude, he exclaims, 'O Sacre Dieu! John Bull is de very Devil.' John Bull, with upraised cudgel, says: 'Mr. Boney Party, you have changed Characters pretty often and famously well, and skipped about at a precious rate. But this Invasion hop is your last—we have got you snug —the devil a trap to get through here—Your conjuration sword has lost its Power; you have lied till you are black in the face, and there is no believing a word you say—so now you shall carry John Bull's mark about with you, as every swaggerer should.'

'British men of war towing in the Invader's Fleet,' artist unknown (September 25, 1804), shows a number of English sailors seated on the necks of French and Dutch men, whom they are guiding over the sea to England. One sailor, evidently a Scotchman, is pulling his opponent's ears; the poor Frenchman cries out, 'Oh Morbleu! de salt water make me sick; O mine pauvre Ears!' but his ruthless conqueror has no pity, 'Deil tak your soul, ye lubberly Loon, gin ye dinna mak aw sail, I'll twist off your lugs.' An English sailor rides the redoubtable Boney, and pulls his nose: 'Steady Master Emperor, if you regard your Imperial Nose. Remember a British Tar has you in tow—No more of this wonderful, this great and mighty nation who frighten all the world with their buggabo invasion.' But Boney pleads, 'Oh! mercy, take me back, me will make you all Emperors; it will be Boney here, Boney there, and Boney everywhere, and me wish to my heart me was dead.' An Irish sailor on a Dutchman yells out, 'By Jasus, my Jewel, these bum boats are quizzical toys and sure—heave ahead, you bog trotting spalpeen, or I shall be after keel hauling you. Huzza, Huzza, Huzza, my boys, Huzza! 'Tis Britannia boys, Britannia rules the waves.' Another Dutchman complains, 'O Mynheer Jan English you vill break my back.' But the relentless sailor who bestrides him takes out his tobacco-box, and says, 'Now for a quid of comfort! pretty gig for Jack Tars. Good bye to your bombast, we're going to Dover, Was ever poor Boney, so fairly done over.'

A most remarkable caricature by Ansell (October 25, 1804) shows to what length party spirit will lead men— making truth entirely subservient to party purposes. It probably paid to vilify Napoleon, and consequently this picture was produced. It is called 'Boney's Inquisition. Another Specimen of his Humanity on the person of Madame Toussaint.' Whatever may be our opinion of his treatment of Toussaint l'Ouverture, the only record we have in history (and I have expended much time and trouble in trying to find out the truth of the matter) is that his family, who were brought to France at the same time as himself, took up their residence at Agen, where his wife died in 1816. His eldest son, Isaac, died at Bordeaux in 1850. Now to describe the picture. Madame l'Ouverture is depicted as being bound to a stretcher nearly naked, whilst three Frenchmen are tearing her breasts with red-hot pincers. Another is pulling out her finger-nails with a similar instrument. She exclaims : ' Oh Justice ! Oh Humanity; Oh Deceitfull Villain, in vain you try to blot the Character of the English : 'tis their magnanimity which harrasses your dastard soul.' One of the torturers says : ' Eh ! Diable ! Why you no confess noting ?' Napoleon is seated on his throne, watching the scene with evident delight, chuckling to himself, ' This is Luxury. Jaffa, Acre, Toulon and D'Enghien was nothing to it. Slave, those pincers are not half hot, save those nails for my Cabinet, and if she dies, we can make a confession for her.'

' The Genius of France nursing her darling ' is by a new hand, T. B. d——lle (November 26, 1804). France, whilst dandling her darling, and amusing him with a rattle, sings—

> There's a little King Pippin
> He shall have a Rattle and Crown ;
> Bless thy five Wits,[1] my Baby,
> Mind it don't throw itself down !
> Hey my Kitten, my Kitten, &c.

---

[1] False of Heart, light of Ear, bloody of Hand,
Fox in Stealth, Wolf in Greediness, Dog in Madness,
Lion in Prey ;—bless thy five Wits.
King Lear, act iii. scene 4.

An unknown artist (December 11, 1804) gives us 'The death of Madame Republique.' Madame lies a corpse on

her bed. Sieyès, as nurse, dandles the new emperor. John Bull, spectacles on nose, inquires, 'Pray Mr. Abbé Sayes— what was the cause of the poor lady's Death? She seem'd at one time in a tolerable thriving way.' Sieyès replies, 'She died in Child bed, Mr. Bull, after giving birth to this little Emperor.'

'The Loyalist's Alphabet, an Original Effusion,' by James Bisset (September 3, 1804), consists of twenty-four small engravings, each in a lozenge.

'A, stands for Albion's Isle,'—Britannia seated.
'B, for brave Britons renown'd.'—A soldier and sailor shaking hands.

'C, for a Corsican tyrant,'—Napoleon, with a skull, the guillotine, &c., in the background.

'D, his dread downfall must sound.'—Being hurled from his throne by lightning.

'E, for embattl'd we stand,'—A troop of soldiers.

'F, 'gainst the French our proud Foes,'—shews England guarded by her ships, and the flotilla coming over.

'G, for our glorious Gunners,'—Three artillerymen, and a cannon.

'H, for Heroical blows,'—shews a ship being blown up.

'I, for Invasion once stood,'—Some soldiers carousing. The English flag above the tricolour.

'J, proves 'twas all a mere Joke.'—A soldier laughing heartily, and holding his sides.

'K, for a favorite King, to deal against Knaves a great stroke.'— Medallion of George the Third.

'L, stands for Liberties' laws,'—A cap of liberty, mitre, pastoral staff, crown, and open book.

'M, Magna Charta's strong chain.'—A soldier, sailor, Highlander, and civilian, joining hands.

'N, Noble Nelson, whom Neptune, near Nile crown'd the Lord of the Main,'—is a portrait of the Hero.

'O, stands for Britain's fam'd Oak,'—which is duly portrayed.

'P, for each brave British Prince.'—The three feathers show the Prince of Wales, in volunteer uniform.

'Q, never once made a Question, Respecting the Deeds they'd evince,'—is an officer drawing his sword.

'If R, for our Rights takes the field,'—is a yeomanry volunteer.

'Or S, should a signal display,'—The British Standard.

'They'd each call with T for the Trumpet. To Horse my brave boys and away.'—A mounted Trumpeter.

'U, for United, we stand, V for our bold Volunteers,'—represents one of the latter.

'Whom W welcomes in War, and joins loyal X in three Cheers.'— A soldier and sailor, with hands clasped, cheering.

'With Y all our Youths sally forth, the standards of Freedom advance,'—is a cannon between two standards.

'With Z proving Englishmen's Zeal, to humble the Zany of France,'—shews Napoleon with a fool's cap on, chained to the wall in a cell.

CHAPTER XL.

NAPOLEON'S CORONATION.

NAPOLEON'S coronation was the great event of the year; but some time before it was consummated the English caricaturist took advantage of it, and J. B. (West), in September 1804, produced a ' Design for an Imperial Crown to be used at the Coronation of the New Emperor.' A perusal of the foregoing pages will render any explanation unnecessary.

Napoleon omitted no ceremony which could enhance the pageant of his coronation. The Pope must be present: no meaner ecclesiastic should hallow this rite, and he was gently *invited* to come to Paris for this purpose. Poor Pius VII. had very little option in the matter. His master wanted him, and he must needs go; but Napoleon gilded the chain which drew him. During the whole of his journey he was received with the greatest reverence, and could hardly have failed to have been impressed with the great care and attention paid to him. For instance, the dangerous places in the passage of the Alps were protected by parapets, so that his Holiness should incur no danger. On his arrival at Paris he was lodged in the Tuileries, and a very delicate attention was paid him—his bedchamber was fitted as a counterpart of his own in the palace of Monte-Cavallo, at Rome.

The eventful 2nd of December came at last; but, before we note the ceremony itself, we must pause awhile to see how the English caricaturist treated the procession.

Hardly any one of Gillray's caricatures (January 1, 1805) is as effective as 'The Grand Coronation Procession of Napoleone the 1st, Emperor of France, from the Church of Notre Dame, Dec. 2nd, 1804. Redeunt SATANIA regna, Iam nova progenies cœlo demittitur alto!' Huge bodies of troops form the back-ground, whose different banners are—a comet setting the world ablaze; an Imperial crown and the letters S P Q N; un Dieu, un Napoleon; a serpent biting its tail, surrounding a crowned N. and a Sun, 'Napo-leone yᵉ 1st le Soleil de la Constitution.'

THE THREE GRACES.

The procession is headed by ' His Imperial Highness Prince Louis Buonaparte Marbœuf ' (a delicate hint as to his paternity), ' High Con-stable of the Empire,' who, theatrically dressed, struts, carrying a drum-major's staff fashioned like a sceptre. Behind him come ' The Three Imperial Graces, viz. their Imp.

R 2

High. Princess Borghese, Princess Louis (cher amie of ye Emperor) & Princess Joseph Bonaparte.' These ladies are clad in a most diaphanous costume, which leaves little of their forms to the imagination, and they occupy themselves by scattering flowers as they pass along.

After them comes Madame Talleyrand, (ci-devant Mrs. Halhead the Prophetess),' a stout, Jewish-looking woman, who is 'Conducting the Heir Apparent in ye Path of Glory' —and a most precocious little imp it looks. After them hobbles 'Talleyrand Perigord, Prime Minister and King at Arms, bearing the Emperor's Genealogy,' which begins with 'Buone Butcher,' goes on with 'Bonny Cuckold,' till it reaches the apex of 'Boney Emperor.' Pope Pius VII. follows, and under his cope is the devil disguised as an acolyte, bearing a candle; Cardinal Fesch is by, and acts as thurifer. The incense is in clouds: 'Les Addresses des Municipâlités de Paris—Les Adorations des Badauds—Les Hommages des Canailles—Les Admirations des Fous—Les Congratulations des Grenouilles—Les Humilités des Poltrons.'

TALLEYRAND, KING AT ARMS.

Then comes the central figures of the pageant, 'His Imperial Majesty Napoleone y^e 1st and the Empress Josephine,' the former scowling ferociously, the latter looking blowsy, and fearfully stout. Three harridans, 'ci-devant Poissardes,' support her train, whilst that of Napoleon is borne by a Spanish don, an Austrian hussar, and a Dutchman, whose tattered breeches testify to his poverty. These are styled 'Puissant Continental Powers—Train Bearers to the Emperor.' Following them come 'Berthier, Bernadotte, Angerou, and all the brave Train of Republican

Generals ;' but they are handcuffed, and their faces display, unmistakably, the scorn in which they hold their old comrade. Behind them poses a short corpulent figure, 'Senator Fouché, Intendant General of ye Police, bearing the Sword of Justice.' But Fouché is not content with this weapon. His other hand grasps an assassin's dagger, and both it, and the sword, are well imbrued in blood. The rear of the procession is made up of a 'Garde d'Honneur,' which consists of a gaoler with the keys of the *Temple* and a set of fetters ; a *mouchard* with his report, ' Espionnage de Paris ;' *Mon-*

NAPOLEON IN HIS CORONATION ROBES.

sieur de Paris, the executioner, bears a coil of rope with a noose, and a banner with a representation of the guillotine —and a prisoner, holding aloft two bottles respectively labelled Arsenic and Opium. More banners and more soldiers fill up the background.

What a sight that must have been on the morning of the 2nd of December! Visitors from all parts of France were there ; and the cathedral of Notre-Dame must have presented a gorgeous *coup d'œil*, with its splendid ecclesiastical vestments, its magnificent uniforms, and the beautiful dresses and jewels of the ladies. It can hardly be imagined, so had better be described in the words of an eyewitness, Madame Junot.[1]

' Who that saw Notre-Dame on that memorable day, can ever forget it ? I have witnessed in that venerable pile the celebration of sumptuous and solemn festivals ; but never did I see anything at all approximating in splendour to the *coup d'œil* exhibited at Napoleon's Coronation. The vaulted roof re-echoed the sacred chanting of the

[1] *Memoirs*, vol. ii. p. 345.

priests, who invoked the blessing of the Almighty on the ceremony about to be celebrated, while they awaited the arrival of the Vicar of Christ, whose throne was prepared near the altar. Along the ancient walls of tapestry were ranged, according to their rank, the different bodies of the State, the deputies from every City ; in short, the representatives of all France assembled to implore the benediction of Heaven on the sovereign of the people's choice. The waving plumes which adorned the hats of the Senators, Counsellors of State, and Tribunes ; the splendid uniforms of the military ; the clergy in all their ecclesiastical pomp ; and the multitude of young and beautiful women, glittering in jewels, and arrayed in that style of grace and elegance which is only seen in Paris ;—altogether presented a picture which has, perhaps, rarely been equalled, and certainly never excelled.

'The Pope arrived first ; and at the moment of his entering the Cathedral, the anthem *Tu es Petrus* was commenced. His Holiness advanced from the door with an air at once majestic and humble. Ere long, the firing of cannon announced the departure of the procession from the Tuileries. From an early hour in the morning the weather had been exceedingly unfavourable. It was cold and rainy, and appearances seemed to indicate that the procession would be anything but agreeable to those who joined it. But, as if by the especial favour of Providence, of which so many instances are observable in the career of Napoleon, the clouds suddenly dispersed, the sky brightened up, and the multitudes who lined the streets from the Tuileries to the Cathedral, enjoyed the sight of the procession, without being, as they had anticipated, drenched by a December rain. Napoleon, as he passed along, was greeted by heartfelt expressions of enthusiastic love and attachment.

'On his arrival at Notre-Dame, Napoleon ascended the throne, which was erected in front of the grand altar. Josephine took her place beside him, surrounded by the assembled sovereigns of Europe. Napoleon appeared singularly calm. I watched him narrowly, with the view of discovering whether his heart beat more highly beneath the imperial trappings, than under the uniform of the guards ; but I could observe no difference, and yet I was at the distance of only ten paces from him. The length of the ceremony, however, seemed to weary him ; and I saw him several times check a yawn. Nevertheless, he did everything he was required to do, and did it with propriety. When the Pope anointed him with the triple unction on his head and both hands, I fancied, from the direction of his eyes, that he was thinking of wiping off the oil rather than of anything else ; and I was so perfectly acquainted with the workings of his countenance, that I have no hesitation in saying that was really the thought that crossed his mind at that moment. During the ceremony of anointing, the Holy Father delivered that impressive prayer which concluded with these words :—" Diffuse, O Lord, by my hands, the treasures of your grace and benediction on your servant, Napoleon, whom, in spite of our personal unworthiness, *we this day anoint Emperor, in your name.*" Napoleon listened to this prayer with an air of pious devotion ; but just as the Pope was about to take the crown, called the *Crown of Charlemagne*, from the altar, Napoleon seized it, and placed it on his own head. At that moment he was really handsome, and his countenance was lighted up with an expression, of which no words can convey an idea. He had removed the wreath of laurel which he wore on entering the church, and which encircles his brow in the fine picture of Gérard. The crown was, perhaps, in itself, less becoming to him ; but the expression excited by the act of putting it on, rendered him perfectly handsome.

' When the moment arrived for Josephine to take an active part in the grand drama, she descended from the throne and advanced towards the altar, where the Emperor awaited her, followed by her retinue of Court ladies, and having her train borne by the Princesses Caroline, Julie, Eliza, and Louis. One of the chief beauties of the Empress Josephine was not merely her fine figure, but the elegant turn of her neck, and the way in which she carried her head ; indeed, her deportment, altogether, was conspicuous for dignity and grace. I have had the honour of being presented to many *real princesses*, to use the phrase of the Faubourg St.-Germain, but I never saw one who, to my eyes, presented so perfect a personification of elegance and majesty. In Napoleon's countenance, I could read the conviction of all I have just said. He looked with an air of complacency at the Empress as she advanced towards him; and when she knelt down—when the tears, which she could not repress, fell upon her clasped hands, as they were raised to Heaven, or rather to Napoleon—both then appeared to enjoy one of those fleeting moments of pure felicity, which are unique in a lifetime, and serve to fill up a lustrum of years. The Emperor performed, with peculiar grace, every action required of him during the ceremony; but his manner of crowning Josephine was most remarkable: after receiving the small crown, surmounted by the Cross, he had first to place it on his own head, and then to transfer it to that of the Empress. When the moment arrived for placing the crown on the head of the woman, whom popular superstition regarded as his good genius, his manner was almost playful. He took great pains to arrange this little crown, which was placed over Josephine's tiara of diamonds; he put it on, then took it off, and finally put it on again, as if to promise her she should wear it gracefully and lightly.'

It is almost painful, after reading this vivid and soul-stirring description, to have to descend to the level of the caricaturist descanting on the same subject; it is a kind of moral douche bath, giving all one's nerves a shock.

> Soon made they every preparation
> For a most brilliant coronation :
> 'Twas on, as must each bard remember,
> The nineteenth day of *dark* November [1]
> When all the streets were strew'd with sand,
> T' exhibit a procession grand ;
> And the Cathedral, lately scorn'd,
> With sumptuous frippery adorn'd.
> Brave Bonaparte and Josephine,
> Preceded by the Pope, walked in ;

---

[1] Coombe evidently did not think chronological accuracy of any importance, for Napoleon's coronation was on December 2, even if reckoning old style.

His Holiness the crown anointed,
And Boney Emperor appointed.

JOSEPHINE AT THE
CORONATION.   NAPOLEON CROWNING HIMSELF.

Then Corsica's impatient son,
Snatch'd up the Crown, and put it on.
The Crown was decked with French frippery,
And with the oil, was rendered slippery ;

JOSEPHINE AS EMPRESS.

Nap kept it on, tho', without dread,
To let them know *he had a head.*
And as to dally he was loth,
He rapidly pronounc'd the oath —

As soon as he the oath had swallow'd,
Another Coronation follow'd—
Fair Josephine advanced, and lo !
Nap put on her a crown also.
'Ah me !' thought she, 'there's something wrong,
I fear it will drop off 'ere long.'
Of holy oil, it seems, the fair
Had got too plentiful a share.
This pantomimic business o'er,
Now marched they grandly as before ;
For, tinsell'd pageantry united
With an equestrian troop, delighted
The new-made Emperor of Paris,
As much as Covent Garden Harris ;
And all the people, for this wise end,
Were in the finest garments dizen'd ;
They finish'd with illuminations,
Songs, music, dancing and orations.
The white wine, which in fountains flow'd,
Considerable mirth bestow'd.
The folks enjoy'd, free of expence,
The glare of lights, which was immense :
And the new Emperor, with glee,
Drank, till no longer he could see.

Authentic news of the coronation did not reach England for nearly a fortnight, and it was not till December 15 that the 'Times' was able to give its readers a full account of the ceremony. 'The Thunderer' waxed very wroth about it, as may be seen by the following extract from its leader of that date :—

'The " Moniteur " merely insinuates that the sun miraculously penetrated through a thick fog, to be present at it : a compliment which is a little diminished by a subsequent assertion, that the lamps were afterwards able to supply his place by giving a noon-day brilliancy to the night. Then follows a disgusting hypocritical panegyric upon the union of civil and religious acts and ceremonies, the sublime representation of all that human and divine affairs could assemble to strike the mind—the venerable Apostolic virtues of the poor Pope, and the most astonishing genius of Buonaparte crowned by the most astonishing destiny !

'The public will find these details, under their proper head, in this paper. To us, we confess, all that appears worthy of remark or memory in that opprobrious day is, that amongst all the Royalists and Republicans of France, it was able to produce neither a BRUTUS nor a CHŒREAS !

'The day subsequent to the coronation, the people of Paris were entertained upon the bridges, boulevards, and public places, with popular sports, dancing, and other pastimes and diversions.

' Upon the *Place de Concorde,* still stained with the blood of the lawful sovereign of France, were erected saloons and pavilions for dancing *waltzes.* Medals were given away to the populace ; illuminations, artificial fireworks, pantomimes, and buffoons, musicians, temporary theatres, everything was represented and administered that could intoxicate and divert this vain and wicked people from contemplating the crime they were committing. To the profanation of the preceding day, it seems that all the orgies of wantonness and corruption succeeded in the most curious and careful rotation, and that all the skill and science of the DAVIDS and CHENIERS has been exhausted to keep them for four and twenty hours from thinking upon what they had done.'

But not only in leaders did the ' Times ' pour forth its wrath ; it published little jokelets occasionally, which were meant to be very stinging, as, for instance : ' Monsieur NAPOLEON has distributed his Eagles by thousands. What his *talents* might be doubtful of accomplishing, he expects from his *talons.*'

The ' Daily Advertiser, too, of December 15 contains some pretty sentiments on the coronation, such as, ' If Modern Europe will, after such fair notice, and a notice so often repeated, by the French Government, still remain in sluggish inaction, in stupid astonishment, at the success of that Ruffian, who now wields the sceptre of CHARLEMAGNE, and has dragooned the POPE to his Coronation, it is evident that nations so besotted are only fit to be enslaved.'

CHAPTER XLI.

NAPOLEON'S LETTER TO GEORGE THE THIRD—NAVAL VICTORIES—
CROWNED KING OF ITALY—ALLIANCE OF EUROPE—WITHDRAWAL OF
THE 'ARMY OF ENGLAND.'

VERY shortly after his coronation, and with the commencement of the year 1805, Napoleon wrote a letter to George
the Third, intimating how beneficial peace would be to
both countries.

The text of this letter, and its answer, are as follow:—

Sire, my brother,—Called to the throne by Providence, and the
suffrages of the Senate, the people, and the army, my first feeling
was the desire for peace.   France and England abuse their prosperity : they may continue their strife for ages ; but will their
governments, in so doing, fulfil the most sacred of the duties
which they owe to their people?   And how will they answer to
their consciences for so much blood uselessly shed, and without
the prospect of any good whatever to their subjects ?   I am not
ashamed to make the first advances.   I have, I flatter myself,
sufficiently proved to the world that I fear none of the chances of
war.   It presents nothing which I have occasion to fear.   Peace
is the wish of my heart ; but war has never been adverse to my
glory.   I conjure your Majesty, therefore, not to refuse yourself
the satisfaction of giving peace to the world.   Never was an occasion more favourable for calming the passions, and giving ear only
to the sentiments of humanity and reason.   If that opportunity be
lost, what limit can be assigned to a war which all my efforts have
been unable to terminate ?   Your Majesty has gained more during
the last ten years than the whole extent of Europe in riches and
territory : your subjects are in the very highest state of prosperity :
what can you expect from a war ?   To form a Coalition of the
Continental powers ?   Be assured the Coalition will remain at
peace.   A coalition will only increase the strength and prepon-
derance of the French Empire.   To renew our intestine divisions?
The times are no longer the same.   To destroy our finances ?
Finances founded on a flourishing agriculture can never be destroyed.   To wrest from France her Colonies ?   They are to her
only a secondary consideration ; and your Majesty has already
enough and to spare of these possessions.   Upon reflection, you
must, I am persuaded, yourself arrive at the conclusion, that the
war is maintained without an object ; and what a melancholy prospect, for two great nations to combat merely for the sake of fighting !
The world is surely large enough for both to live in ; and reason

has still sufficient power to find the means of reconciliation, if the inclination only is not wanting. I have now, at least, discharged a duty dear to my heart. May your Majesty trust to the sincerity of the sentiments which I have now expressed, and the reality of my desire to give the most convincing proofs of it.

George the Third could not, constitutionally, personally reply to this letter, so Lord Mulgrave answered it, under date of January 14, and addressed it to Talleyrand. It ran thus :

His Britannic Majesty has received the letter addressed to him by the Chief of the French Government. There is nothing which his Majesty has more at heart, than to seize the first opportunity of restoring to his subjects the blessings of peace, provided it is founded upon a basis not incompatible with the permanent interests, and security, of his dominions. His Majesty is persuaded that that object cannot be attained but by arrangements, which may at the same time provide for the future peace, and security, of Europe, and prevent a renewal of the dangers, and misfortunes, by which it is now overwhelmed. In conformity with these sentiments, his Majesty feels that he cannot give a more specific answer to the overture which he has received until he has had time to communicate with the Continental powers to whom he is united in the most confidential manner, and particularly the Emperor of Russia, who has given the strongest proofs of the wisdom, and elevation, of the sentiments by which he is animated, and of the lively interest which he takes in the security and independence of Europe.

Apropos of this pacific overture, there is a very badly drawn picture by Woodward (February 1, 1805), 'A New Phantasmagoria for John Bull.' Napoleon is seated on the French coast, directing his magic lantern towards John Bull, exclaiming, ' Begar de brave Galanté shew for Jonny Bull.' The magic lantern slide shows Napoleon coming over on a visit, with a tricoloured flag in one hand, the other leading the Empress Josephine, whose dress is *semée* with bees. ' Here we come Johnny—A flag of Truce Johnny—something like a Piece ! all decked out in Bees, and stars, and a crown on her head ; not such a patched up piece as the last.' The Russian bear is on one rock, John Bull on another—the latter having his sword drawn. He says : ' You may be d—d, and your piece too ! I suppose you thought I was off the watch—I tell you, I'll say nothing to you till I have consulted Brother Bruin, and I hear him growling terribly in the offing.'

So we see that there was no hope of peace, as yet, and the war goes on. I can hardly localise the following caricature :—

Argus (January 24, 1805) drew 'The glorious Pursuit of Ten against Seventeen.

> God like his Courage seem'd, whom nor Delight
> Could soften, nor the Face of Death affright.'

The French and Spaniards are in full flight, calling out, 'By Gar dare be dat tam Nelson dat Salamander dat do love to live in de fire, by Gar we make haste out of his way, or he blow us all up.' Nelson leads on nine old sea dogs, encouraging them thus : 'The Enemy are flying before you my brave fellows, *Seventeen* against *Ten* of us. Crowd all the Sail you can, and then for George, Old England—*Death* or *Victory ! ! !* ' His followers utter such sentences as the following : ' My Noble Commander, we'll follow you the world over, and shiver my Timbers but we shall soon bring up our lee way, and then, as sure as my name is Tom Grog, we'll give them another touch of the Battle of the Nile '—' May I never hope to see Poll again, if I would not give a whole month's flip if these lubberly Parly vous would but just stop one half watch,' &c. &c.

The style in which our sailors worked is very aptly illustrated in a letter from an officer on board the *Fisgard*, off Cape St. Vincent, dated November 28, 1804.[1] We must remember that war was not officially declared against Spain until January 11, 1805 ; but this gentleman writes : ' We cannot desire a better station ; we heard of hostilities with Spain on October the 15th, and on that very day we captured two Ships. Lord Nelson received from us the first intelligence—we have already taken twelve ships and entertain hopes of as many more. Yesterday we fell in with the *Donegal*, Capt. Sir R. Strachan, who has taken a large Spanish Frigate, the *Amphitrite*, after a chase of 46 hours, and 15 minutes' action, in which the Spanish Captain was killed ; the prize was from Cadiz, with despatches

---

[1] *The Naval Chronicle*, 1805.

for *Teneriffe* and the *Havana*, laden with stores. The *Amphitrite* Frigate, of 42 Guns, was one of the finest Frigates in the Spanish Navy. The *Donegal* chased the *Amphitrite* for several hours, sometimes gaining upon her, and sometimes losing; at length the *Amphitrite* carried away her mizen top mast, which enabled the *Donegal* to come up with her. A Boat was then despatched by Sir Richard for the purpose of bringing the Spanish Captain on board. Some difficulty arose from neither party understanding the language of the other ; at length Sir Richard acquainted the Spanish Captain, that in compliance with the Orders he had received from his Admiral, he was under the necessity of conducting the *Amphitrite* back again to Cadiz, and he allowed the Spanish Captain three minutes to determine whether he would comply without compelling him to have recourse to force. After waiting six minutes in vain for a favourable answer, the *Donegal* fired into the *Amphitrite*, which was immediately answered with a broadside. An engagement then ensued, which lasted about eight minutes, when the *Amphitrite* struck her colours. During this short engagement the Spanish Captain was unfortunately killed by a musket ball. The *Donegal* has also captured another Spanish ship, supposed the richest that ever sailed from Cadiz, her cargo reported worth 200,000*l.*'

Another letter, dated November 29, adds, ' We have this day taken a large Ship from the River de la Plata.'

They had captured the following ships previous to December 3 :—

Nostra Signora del Rosario . value	£	10,000
Il Fortuna	„	8,000
St. Joseph	„	12,000
La Virgine Assumpto . .	„	6,000
Apollo	„	15,000
Signora del Purificatione .	„	40,000
Fawket	„	1,100
Gustavus Adolphus . .	„	1,000
A Settee	„	600
A Ship with Naval Stores .	„	40,000

On February 26, 1805, Gillray published ' The Plumb

Pudding in danger ; or State Epicures taking un Petit Souper—' the great globe itself, and all which it inherits,

THE PLUMB PUDDING IN DANGER.

' is too small to satisfy such insatiable appetites.'   Napoleon is taking all Europe, whilst Pitt is calmly appropriating all the ocean to himself.

There is now almost a total cessation of caricature until the autumn ; and it probably was in this wise.   Napoleon did not actively bother this country ; his thoughts were, for the time, elsewhere.   On March 17 a deputation from the Italian Republic waited upon him, stating that it was the desire of their countrymen that he should be their monarch, and accordingly on April 2 he and Josephine left Paris for Milan.

> Another project fill'd his head,
> For vanity must still be fed ;
> A second Charlemagne to prove,
> Our hero resolutely strove.
> Addresses manufactured he,
> All which were sent to Italy ;
> To get additional renown,
> He to restore the iron crown
> Of Italy resolved,—by which
> He hoped his pockets to enrich.
> T' obtain, was certainly his aim,
> O'er the Peninsula, a claim.
> Now, Nap, while filling out his wine,
> Told Josephine his bold design—

'My dear,' said he, and kiss'd her lip
To Italy, we'll take a trip.'
To bring about this great event,
The Emperor and Empress went.
When in Milan they both arrived,
To coax the people Nap contrived;
And being a great Saint believed,
With adulation was receiv'd;
He, by his condescension, proved
How dearly he *his children* loved.
And on the Twenty Sixth of May
Began our hero to display
Another Coronation splendid,
While on a throne he sat attended.
Now highly honor'd and rever'd,
The diadem of France appear'd
On his right hand, and *inter alia*
All its magnificent regalia.
Whilst on his left hand, to the sight
The crown of iron sparkled bright;
Tho' iron, this they used to call,
The cross was iron, that was all.[1]
The rest was diamonds and pure gold,
And very lovely to behold.
The Cardinal Archbishop then
Began the ceremony—when
Nap was Italian King protested,
And with th' insignia too invested;
The altar steps he hasten'd soon up,
And taking quick the precious boon up,
He placed the Crown upon his head,
And in a voice of thunder said
'Since heav'n has giv'n to me this Crown,
Who dares to touch it, I'll knock him down.'[2]

An amateur drew, and Gillray etched (August 2,
1805), 'St. George and the Dragon, a Design for an

[1] As a matter of fact, the crown is a broad circle of gold, set with large
rubies, emeralds, and sapphires, on a ground of blue and gold enamel. The
reason of its being called the ' Iron Crown ' is that, running round the centre
of the *interior* of the circle is a thin and narrow band of iron, which is supposed to be manufactured from one of the nails used in the Crucifixion of our
Saviour, and given by St. Helena to her son Constantine as a talisman to
protect him in battle.

[2] Free translation for ' God has given it me—let him beware who would
touch it,' the usual form of words when this crown was used.

S

Equestrian Statue from the Original in Windsor Castle.'
Napoleon (a most ferocious dragon) has seized upon poor
Britannia, who, dropping her spear and shield, her hair
dishevelled, and her dress disordered, with upraised arm,
attempts to avert her fate ; but St. George (George the
Third) on horseback, comes to the rescue, and, smiting that
dragon, cleaves his crown.

As a practical illustration of the servile adulation with
which he was treated, take the following etching by Woodward (September 15, 1805) : ' Napoleon's Apotheosis Anticipated, or the Wise Men of Leipsic sending Boney to
Heaven before his time ! !!   At the German University of
Leipsic, it was decreed that the Constellation called Orion's
Belt should hereafter be named Napoleon in Honor of that
Hero.—Query—Did the Wise men of Leipsic mean it as
an honor, or a reflection on the turbulent spirit of Boney,
as the rising of Orion is generally accompanied with
Storms and Tempests, for which reason he has the Sword
in his hand.'   Orion has his belt round Napoleon's neck,
and is hoisting him up to heaven thereby ; Napoleon is
kicking and struggling, and exclaims,'What are you about
—I tell you I would rather stay where I was.'   The German
savants are watching him through their telescopes, saying,
' He mounts finely '—' I think we have now made ourselves
immortal '—' It was a sublime idea '—' Orion seems to receive
him better than I expected.'   This is confirmed in ' Scot's
Magazine,' 1807 [1] : ' The University of Leipzig has resolved
henceforth to call by the name of Napoleon that group of
stars which lies between the girdle and the sword of Orion ;
and a numerous deputation of the University was appointed
to present the " Conqueror " with a map of the group so
named ! '

Napoleon hardly reckoned on Austria taking up arms
against him without a formal declaration of war, and was
rather put to it to find men to oppose the Allies, whose
forces were reckoned at 250,000 men ; whilst France,
though with 275,000 men at her disposal, had 180,000 of
them locked up in the so-called ' Army of England.'   We
can imagine his chagrin in having to forego his cherished

[1] Vol. xlix. p. 763.

plan of invasion, and being compelled to withdraw his troops from the French shores.

The 'Times' (how different a paper it was in those days to what it is now!) is jubilant thereupon.[1] 'The *Scene* that now opens upon the soldiers of France, by being obliged to leave the coast and march eastwards, is sadly different from that *Land of Promise*, which, for two years, has been held out to them, in all sorts of gay delusions. After all the efforts of the *Imperial Boat-Builder*, instead of sailing over the *Channel*, they will have to cross the *Rhine*. The bleak *forests* of Suabia will make but a sorry exchange for the promised spoils of our *Docks* and *Warehouses*. They will not find any equivalent for the *plunder* of the *Bank* in another bloody passage through "*the Valley of Hell*"; but they seem to have forgotten the magnificent promise of the *Milliard*.'

The French papers affected to make light of this death-blow to their hopes; one of them, quoted in the 'Times' of September 13, says: 'Whilst the German Papers, with much noise, make more troops march than all the Powers together possess, France, which needs not to augment her forces in order to display them in an imposing manner, detaches a few thousand troops from the Army of England to cover her frontiers, which are menaced by the imprudent conduct of Austria.'

The caricaturist, of course, made capital out of it, and Rowlandson (October 1, 1805) designed 'The departure from the Coast or the End of the Farce of Invasion.' Napoleon, seated on a sorry ass, is sadly returning, inland, homeward, to the intense delight of some French monkeys. His Iron Crown is tottering off his head, and his steed is loaded with the Boulogne Encampment, the Army of England, and Excuses for non-performance. The British Lion on the English cliffs lifts his leg and gives Boney a parting salute. The latter exclaims, ' Bless me, what a shower! I shall be wet through before I reach the Rhine.'

The action of the Allies is shown by the caricature, 'Tom Thumb at Bay, or the Sovereigns of the Forest roused at last,' by Ansell (October 1805), which shows the

---

[1] September 11, 1805.

Lilliputian Emperor, who has thrown away his crown and sceptre, being fiercely pursued by a double-headed eagle, a bear, and a boar, and is rushing into the open jaws of a ferocious lion. 'Which way shall I escape? If I fly from the Bear and the Eagle, I fall into the jaws of the Lion !!' Holland, Spain, and Italy, all have yokes round their necks—but, seeing Bonaparte's condition, Holland takes his off and lays it on the ground. The Spaniard, surprised, exclaims, 'Why! Mynheer, you have got your yoke off!' And the Italian, who is preparing to remove his, says, 'I think Mynheer's right, and now's the time, Don, to get ours off.' An army of rats is labelled, 'Co-Estates ready to assist.'

CHAPTER XLII.

SURRENDER OF ULM—BATTLE OF TRAFALGAR—PROPOSALS FOR PEACE—DANIEL LAMBERT.

MEANTIME the Austrians were in a very awkward position. General Mack was, from October 13, closely invested in Ulm, and Napoleon had almost need to restrain his troops, who were flushed with victory and eager for the assault. The carnage on both sides would, in such a case, have been awful ; but Napoleon clearly pointed out to Mack his position : how that, in eight days, he would be forced to capitulate for want of food : that the Russians were yet far off, having scarcely reached Bohemia ; that no other aid was nigh :—and on October 20, the gates of Ulm were opened, and 36,000 Austrian troops slowly defiled therefrom. Sixteen generals surrendered with Mack, and Napoleon treated them generously. All the officers were allowed to go home, their parole, not to fight against France until here had been a general exchange of prisoners, only being required ; and Napoleon sent 50,000 prisoners into France, distributing them throughout the agricultural districts.

Gillray drew (November 6, 1805) 'The Surrender of Ulm, or Buonaparte and Gen[l] Mack coming to a right understanding--Intended as a Specimen of French Victories --*i.e.* Conquering without Bloodshed ! ! ! ' It shows a little Napoleon, seated on a drum, whilst Mack and some other generals are grovelling on all fours, delivering up their swords, banners, and the keys of Ulm, to the conqueror. Napoleon, pointing to three large sacks of money, borne by as many soldiers, exclaims : ' There's your Price ! There's Ten Millions—Twenty !! It is not in my Army alone that my resources of Conquering consists !! I hate victory obtain'd by effusion of blood.' ' And so do I,' says the crawling Mack ; ' What signifies Fighting when we can settle it in a safer way.' On the ground is a scroll of ' Articles to be deliver'd up. 1 Field Marshal. 8 Generals in Chief. 7 Lieutenant Generals. 36 Thousand Soldiers. 80 pieces of Cannon. 50 Stand of Colours. 100,000 Pounds of Powder. 4,000 Cannon Balls.'

This subject also attracted the pencil of I. Cruikshank (November 19, 1805) : ' Boney beating Mack—and Nelson giving him a Whack !! or the British Tars giving Boney his Hearts desire, SHIPS, COLONIES and COMMERCE.' Mack is kneeling in a suppliant manner before Bonaparte, who stamps upon his captive's sword, addressing him : ' I want not your Forts, your Cities, nor your territories ! Sir, I only want Ships, Colonies and Commerce '—a very slight variation from the real text of his address to the vanquished Austrian officers : ' I desire nothing further upon the Continent. I want ships, colonies, and commerce ; and it is as much your interest, as mine, that I should have them.' During this peroration military messengers are arriving. One calls out, ' May it please your King's Majesty's Emperor. That Dam Nelson take all your ships. Twenty at a time. Begar, if you no come back directly they vill not leave you vone boat to go over in.' Another runs along crying, ' Run, ma foi, anoder Dam Nelson take ever so many more ships.' This is an allusion to the battle of Trafalgar (October 21, 1805),[1] where Nelson paid for his victory with his life. This is further illustrated in another portion of the engraving, by Nelson, who is towing the captured vessels, kneeling at Britannia's feet, saying : ' At thy feet, O Goddess of the seas, I resign my life in the service of my country.' Britannia replies : ' My Son, thy

---

[1] The news of the victory at Trafalgar was only published on November 6.

Name shall be recorded in the page of History on tablets of the brightest Gold.'

Rowlandson (November 13, 1805) further alludes to the surrender of Ulm and the battle of Trafalgar : ' Nap Buonaparte in a fever on receiving the Extraordinary Gazette of Nelson's Victory over the combined Fleets.' Boney is very sick and miserable, the combined effects of the news which he has read in the paper which falls from his trembling hands—the ' Extraordinary Gazette. 19 Sail of the line taken by Lord Nelson.' He appeals to four doctors, who are in consultation on his case : ' My dear Doctors ! those Sacrè Anglois have play'd the Devil vid my Constitution. Pray tell me what is the matter with me. I felt the first symptoms when I told Gen^1 Mack I wanted Ships, Colonies and Commerce. Oh dear ! oh dear ! I shall want more ships now—this is a cursed sensation— Oh I am very qualmish.' One doctor opines it is ' a desperate case,' another that he is ' Irrecoverable.' One recommends bleeding ; but one has thoroughly investigated the case, and found out the cause : ' Begar, me have found it out, *your heart be in your breeches!* '

> Now with such fury they push'd on,
> Memmengen the French Army won,
> And by the treachery of Mack,
> Ulm surrendered in a crack—
> Soon after the capitulation,
> The Austrians with consternation
> Laid down their arms, and to their shame,
> Napoleon's prisoners became——

There were no caricatures of the battle of Trafalgar— the victory was purchased at too great a cost ; but Gillray executed a serious etching in memory of Nelson, published on December 29, 1805, the funeral of the hero taking place on the subsequent 9th of January.

The following caricature shows the quality of news supplied to our forefathers :—

' John Bull exchanging News with the Continent ' is by Woodward, December 11, 1805, and represents Napoleon and a French newsboy on a rock called *Falsehood*, disseminating news the reverse of true. The ' Journal de

l'Empire' says that Archduke Charles is dead with
fatigue; the 'Journal de Spectacle' that England is invaded. The 'Gazette de France' informs us that the
English fleet is dispersed, and the 'Publicité' follows it
with the news that the combined fleets are sent in pursuit.
False bulletins are being scattered broadcast. These, however, have but little effect on John Bull, who, attired as a
newsboy, stands on the rock of Truth, flourishing a paper,
'Trafalgar London Gazette extraordinary,' and bellowing
through his horn, 'Total defeat of the Combin'd Fleets of
France and Spain,' which is vividly depicted in the background.

'Tiddy doll, the great French Gingerbread Baker,
drawing out a new Batch of Kings—his man Hopping

TIDDY DOLL, THE GREAT FRENCH GINGERBREAD BAKER, DRAWING
OUT A NEW BATCH OF KINGS.

Talley mixing up the Dough,' is a somewhat elaborate
etching by Gillray (January 23, 1806). The celebrated
gingerbread maker has, on a 'peel,' three kings, duly gilt
—Bavaria, Wurtemberg, and Baden—which he is just introducing into the 'New French Oven for Imperial Gingerbread.' On a chest of three drawers, relatively labelled
Kings and Queens, Crowns and Sceptres, and Suns and
Moons, are a quantity of 'Little Dough Viceroys, intended

for the next batch.'   Under the oven is an 'Ash hole for
broken Gingerbread,' and a broom—'the Corsican Besom
of Destruction '—has swept therein La République Française, Italy, Austria, Spain, Netherlands, Switzerland,
Holland, and Venice.   On the ground is a fool's cap and
bells, which acts as a cornucopia (labelled ' Hot Spiced
Gingerbread, all hot ; Come, who dips in my lucky bag '),
which disgorges stars and orders, principalities, dukedoms,
crowns, sceptres, cardinals' hats, and bishops' mitres ; and a
baker's basket is full of ' True Corsican Kinglings for Home
Consumption and Exportation.'

Talleyrand—with a mitre on his head, and beads and
cross round his waist, to show his ecclesiastical status ;
with a pen in his mouth, and ink-pot slung to his side, to
denote his diplomatic functions—is hard at work at the
' Political Kneading Trough,' mixing up Hungary, Poland,
Turkey, &c., whilst an eagle (Prussia) is pecking at a piece
of dough (Hanover).

To thoroughly understand this caricature, we must first
of all know something about *Tiddy Doll.*   He was a seller
of gingerbread, and was as famous in his time as was *Colly
Molly Puff* in the time of Steele and Addison.   He had a
refrain, all his own, like a man well known to dwellers in
Brighton and the West End of London—' *Brandy balls.*'
Hone[1] gives the best account of him that I know.   Dis-
coursing on *May fair,* he says : ' Here, too, was *Tiddy-doll* ;
this celebrated vendor of gingerbread, from his eccentricity
of character and extensive dealings in his way, was always
hailed as the king of itinerant tradesmen.[2]   In his person
he was tall, well made, and his features handsome.   He
affected to dress like a person of rank : white, gold-laced,
suit of clothes, laced ruffled shirt, laced hat and feather,
white silk stockings, with the addition of a fine white apron.
Among his harangues to gain customers, take this as a
specimen : " Mary, Mary, where are you *now*, Mary ?   I
live, when at home, at the second house in little Ball Street,
two steps under ground, with a wiscum, riscum, and a why
not.   Walk in ladies and gentlemen ; my shop is on the

---

[1] *Everyday Book,* vol. i. p. 575.
[2] He was a constant attendant in the crowd on Lord Mayor's show.

second floor backwards, with a brass knocker at the door. Here is your nice gingerbread, your spice gingerbread ; it will melt in your mouth like a redhot brickbat, and rumble in your inside like Punch and his wheelbarrow." He always finished his address by singing this fag end of some popular ballad.

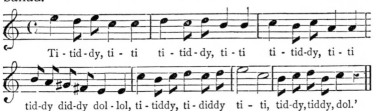

Ti - tid - dy, ti - ti   ti - tid - dy, ti - ti   ti - tid-dy, ti - ti

tid-dy did-dy dol - lol, ti - tiddy, ti - diddy ti - ti, tid-dy, tiddy, dol.'

Pitt died on January 23, 1806, and Fox succeeded him. It is probable that Napoleon reckoned somewhat on Fox's friendship, and hence the following caricature :—

'Boney and the Great Secretary' (Argus, February

BONEY AND THE GREAT STATE SECRETARY.

1806) gives a good portrait of Fox. Napoleon wishes to be friendly : 'How do you do, Master Charley, why you are so fine, I scarcely knew ye—don't you remember me, why I am little Boney the Corsican—him that you came to see at Paris, and very civil I was to you, I'm sure. If you come my way I shall be glad to see you, so will my wife and family. They are a little changed in their dress, as well as you. We shall be very happy to take a little *peace* soup with you, whenever you are inclined, Master Charley.' But Fox shakes his fist at him : ' Why, you little Corsican Reptile ! how dare you come so near the person of the Right Honble C—— J—— F—— one of his M—— principal Secretaries of State, Member of the P.C. &c., &c., &c., &c., &c., &c., &c., &c.—go to see You !!! Arrogant little Man, Mr. Boney—if you do not instantly vanish from my sight—I'le break every bone in your body—learn to behave yourself in a *peaceable* manner, nor dare to set your foot on this happy land without My leave.'

Of ' Pacific Overtures, or a Flight from St. Cloud, " over the Water to Charley," a new Dramatic Peace now re-

hearsing' (Gillray, April 5, 1806), only a portion is given in the accompanying illustration, but quite sufficient to explain the negotiations for peace then in progress.

This caricature is far too elaborate to reproduce the whole, and the allusions therein are extremely intricate and, nowadays, uninteresting. A theatrical stage is represented, with Napoleon descending in clouds, pointing to Terms of Peace, which are being displayed by Talleyrand, and saying, ' There's my terms.' These are as follow : ' Acknowledge me as Emperor ; dismantle your fleet ; reduce your army ; abandon Malta and Gibraltar ; renounce all Continental connexion ; your Colonies I will take at a valuation ; engage to pay to the Great Nation, for seven years annually, £1,000,000 ; and place in my hands as hostages, the Princess Charlotte of Wales, with ten of the late administration, whom I shall name.'

King George has stepped from his box on to the stage, and is surveying this vision through his glass, exclaiming : 'Very amusing terms indeed, and might do vastly well with some of the new made little gingerbread kings [1] ; but we are not in the habit of giving up either "ships, or commerce, or colonies" merely because little Boney is in a pet to have them ! ! !'

Ansell (April 1806) drew 'Roast Beef and French Soup. The English Lamb * * * and the French Tiger,' and it seems merely designed for the purpose of introducing Daniel Lambert, who was then on exhibition—'Daniel Lambert who at the age of 36 weighed above 50 Stone, 14 Pounds to the Stone, measured 3 yards 4 inches round the Body, and 1 yard 1 inch round the leg. 5 feet 11 inches high.' It shows the redoubtable fat man seated on a couch, carving a round of beef, which is accompanied by a large mustard-pot, a huge loaf, and a foaming pot of stout. Napoleon, seated on a similar couch, on the opposite side of the table, is taking soup—then an unaccustomed article of food with Englishmen—and looks with horror at the other's size and manner of feeding.

Daniel Lambert was like Mr. Dick in 'David Copperfield,' who would persist in putting King Charles the First's head into his Memorial ; he could hardly be kept out of the caricatures. Ansell produced one (May 1806)—'Two Wonders of the World, or a Specimen of a new troop of Leicestershire Light Horse.—Mr. Daniel Lambert, who at the age of 36 weighed above 50 Stone, 14 Pounds to the Stone, measured 3 yards 4 inches round the body and 1 yard 1 inch round the leg, 5 feet 11 inches high. The famous horse Monarch, the largest in the World is upwards

[1] On March 31 Joseph Bonaparte was made King of Naples, and Murat Grand Duke of Berg and Cleves. A few months subsequently, Louis Bonaparte was made King of Holland, and the following year Jerome King of Westphalia.

of 21 hands high, (above 7 foot)[1] and only 6 Years old.'
Lambert is mounted on this extraordinary quadruped, and,
sword in hand, is riding at poor little Boney, who exclaims
in horror, ' Parbleu ! if dis be de specimen of de English
light Horse, vat vill de Heavy Horse be ?   Oh, by Gar, I
vill put off de Invasion for anoder time.'

Yet once more are these two brought into juxtaposition,
in an engraving by Knight (April 15, 1806), ' Bone and
Flesh, or John Bull in moderate Condition.'   Napoleon is
looking at this prodigy, and saying, ' I contemplate this
Wonder of the World, and regret that all my Conquered
Domains cannot match this Man.   Pray, Sir, are you not
a descendant from the great Joss of China ? '   Lambert
replies, ' No Sir, I am a true born Englishman, from the
County of Leicester.   A quiet mind, and good Constitution,
nourished by the free Air of Great Britain, makes every
Englishman thrive.'

Another of Gillray's caricatures into which Napoleon is
introduced, but in which he plays a secondary part, is
called ' Comforts of a Bed of Roses ; v.de Charley's eluci-
dation of Lord C—stl — r—gh's speech !   Nightly Scene
near Cleveland row.'   This is founded on a speech of Lord
Castlereagh's, in which he congratulated the Ministry as
having ' a bed of roses.'   But Fox, in reply, recounted his
difficulties and miseries, and said : ' Really, it is insulting
to tell me I am on a bed of roses, when I feel myself torn,
and stung, by brambles, and nettles, whichever way I turn.'

Fox and Mrs. Fox are shown as sleeping on a bed of
roses, some of which peep out from underneath the rose-
coloured counterpane, but which display far more of thorns
than of roses.   There is the *India rose*, the Emancipation
rose, the French rose, the Coalition rose, and the Volunteer
rose.   Fox's slumbers are terribly disturbed ; his *bonnet
rouge*, which he wears as night-cap, has tumbled off ; his
night-shirt is seized at the neck, on one side by the ghost
of Pitt, who exclaims : ' Awake, arise, or be for ever
fall'n ! '   The other side is fiercely clutched by Napoleon,
who, drawn sword in hand, has just stepped on to the
bed from a cannon labelled ' Pour subjuguer le monde.'

---

[1] A ' hand,' as a measure in horse-flesh, is four inches.

Amidst a background of smoke appear spears, and a banner entitled ' Horrors of Invasion.' The Prussian eagle is preparing to swoop down upon him, and, from under the bed, crawls out a skeleton holding an hour-glass, whilst round its fleshless arm is entwined a serpent ' Intemperance, Dropsy, Dissolution.' John Bull, as a bull-dog, is trying to seize Napoleon.

' John Bull threatened by Insects from all Quarters' is by an unknown artist (April 1806). John Bull is on ' The tight little Island,' and seated on a cask of grog. With one hand he flourishes a cutlass, and the other grasps a pistol, of which weapon two more lie on the ground. With these he defies the insects, which come in swarms. There are Westphalian mites, American hornets, Dutch bluebottles, Italian butterflies, Turkish wasps, Danish gnats, and, worst of all, a French dragon-fly, in the shape of Napoleon. John Bull is saying : ' Come on my Lads—give me but good sea room, and I don't care for any of you—Why all your attacks is no more than a gnat stinging an Elephant, or a flea devouring Mr. Lambert of Leicester.'

A very clever caricature is by Knight (June 26, 1806) of ' Jupiter Bouney granting unto the Dutch Frogs a King. The Frogs sent their deputies to petition Jupiter again for a King. He sent them a Stork, who eat them up, vide Æsop's fables.' The discontented Dutch spurn their King Log, and pray, ' We present ourselves before the throne of your Majesty. We pray that you will grant us, as the supreme Chief of our Republic, Prince Louis.' Napoleon, as Jupiter, seated on an eagle (which is made to look as much like a devil as possible), says : ' I agree to the request. I proclaim Prince Louis, King of Holland. You Prince ! reign over this People.' And the stork is duly despatched on its mission. Talleyrand, as Ganymede, supplies Jupiter with *a cup of comfort for the discontented.*

CHAPTER XLIII.

NEGOTIATIONS FOR PEACE—DEATH OF FOX—NAPOLEON'S VICTORIOUS CAREER—HIS PROCLAMATION OF A BLOCKADE OF ENGLAND.

APROPOS of the negotiations for peace, there is a picture of Woodward's (July 1806), in which Fox is just closing the door behind a messenger laden with despatches. John Bull, whose pockets are stuffed with *Omnium* and *Speculation on Peace*, entreats him with clasped hands : 'Now do Charley, my dear good boy, open the door a little bit farther, just to enable me to take in a few of my friends at the Stock Exchange.' But Fox remonstrates : 'Really, Mr. Bull, you are too inquisitive—don't you see the door for Negotiation is opened ? don't you see the back of a Messenger ? don't you see he has got dispatches under his arm ? what would you desire more ? '

'Experiments at Dover, or Master Charley's Magic Lanthorn,' is by Rowlandson (July 21, 1806), and shows Fox seated on the seashore, projecting images on to the opposite coast. The slide he is passing through the lantern begins with a ' Messenger from Boulogne,' then a ' Messenger to Paris,' then ' More Dispatches ' ; and he is now showing Bonaparte as a newsboy, with his horn, calling out ' Preliminaries of Peace.' The next, and final, picture to come is a man waving his hat and shouting ' Huzza.' Fox is saying : ' There, Master Bull, what do you think of that—I told you I would surprize you. Preliminaries of Peace ! Huzza ! ' But John Bull is not quite satisfied with his conduct, and fancies there has been something kept from him. ' Why yes, it be all very foine, if it be true. But I can't forget that d—d Omnium last week—they be always one way or other in contradictions ! I tell thee what, Charley, since thee hast become a great man—I think in my heart thee beest always conjuring.'

' The Pleasing and Instructive Game of *Messengers*—or Summer Amusement for John Bull,' by Ansell (August 1806), shows us the Channel, on both sides of which a lively game is being kept up by means of racket bats, a constant supply of balls, in the shape of messengers, between the two countries, being kept in the air. Their messages are Peace, Hope, Despair, No peace, Passports, Peace to a Certainty, No peace, Credentials, Despatches, &c. On the French side, Napoleon and Talleyrand keep the game alive, 'Begar Talley, dis be ver amusant—Keep it up as long as you can, that we may have time for our project.' Sheridan, Fox, and others play on the English side ; John Bull being merely a spectator, not too much amused, as a paper, protruding from his pocket, shows : ' Very shy at the Stock Exchange.' Sheridan calls out : ' That's right my lads, bang 'em about. John Bull seems quite puzzled.' Fox asks : ' Is not it a pretty game Johnny ? ' Johnny, however, says : ' Pretty enough as to that, they do fly about monstrous quick to be sure : but you don't get any more money out of my pocket for all that !! '

Gillray gives us a veritable caricature in ' News from Calabria ! Capture of Buenos Ayres ! i.e. the Comforts of

NEWS FROM CALABRIA.

an Imperial Dejeune at St. Clouds ' (September 13, 1806), a portion only of which is given in illustration. Boney is here, terrific in his wrath ; poor Talleyrand, who has brought the news, is receiving grievous punishment from his Imperial master. Not only is his ear pulled (a favourite trick of Napoleon's), but he is being belaboured with the tea-urn, which is made in the form of the world : his master crying out : 'Out on ye Owl, noting but song of Death ! ! ' Napoleon has kicked over the breakfast-table, and the scalding contents of the tea-urn are being deposited in the lap of Josephine, who screams with agony and terror. The maids of honour and courtiers, though refrain-ing from open demonstration, look aghast at the imperial violence, which is not diminished by the presence of a number of messengers, whose news is particularly unwel-come : ' Spain in despair for the loss of her Colonies.' ' All Germany rising, and arming *en Masse*.' ' Holland starving, and ripe for a revolt.' ' St. Petersburg : refusal to ratify the French Treaty.' ' Prussia rousing from the Trance of Death.' ' Swedish defiance. Charles XII. redivivus.' ' Switzerland cursing the French yoke.' ' Italy shaking off her Chains.' ' La Vendée again in motion.' ' Portugal true to the last gasp.' ' Sicily firing like Etna.' ' Denmark waiting for an opportunity.' ' Turkey invoking Mahomet.' Naturally, all this bad news contributes towards making it a ' hard time ' for Talleyrand.

Argus gives us (September 1806) ' The Continental Shaving Shop. Boney beats Jemmy Wright, who shaved as well as any man, almost, not quite' (September 1806). As a barber, he is going to shave the Grand Turk, and, flourishing an enormous razor of Corsican steel, seizes his beard. This the Turk naturally objects to, saying : ' By the Holy Prophet, I must not part with my beard, why, my people will not acknowledge me for the grand Signor again at Constantinople.' Talleyrand, as assistant, is lathering the Turk's face, persuading him, ' Come, come, don't make such a fuss, my Master *will* cut away when he catches anybody in his shop.' Boney calls out : ' Lather away Talley. I'll soon ease him of his superfluities and make him look like my Christian customers.'

The sort of treatment they are likely to get is clearly set forth in an announcement on the wall. ' Nap Boney, shaver general to most of the Sovereigns on the Continent, shaves expeditiously, and clean, a few gashes excepted ; is ready to undertake any new Customer who is willing to submit to the above.' His treatment is exemplified by the appearance of Austria, whose gashed face and head is ornamented with strips of court-plaister. He is talking to John Bull, who looks in at a window: 'Come, Johnny, come in and be shaved, don't be frightened at the size of the razor, it cuts very clean, I assure you.' His reply is, ' By Goles so it seems, and leaves a dom'd sight of gashes behoind, as you and Mynheer can testify ! ! ' Poor Holland is in even a worse plight than Austria, and is talking to Prussia, who is sitting in a chair, ready lathered for shaving. Says he to the Dutchman: 'I hope he don't mean to shave me as he has you, and my neighbour Austria there ? I should not sit here so quietly with my face lathered.' Holland replies : ' Yaw Mynheer very close shaver, its nix my doll when you are used to it.'

' Political Quadrille ' is by Ansell (October 1806), and represents two sets playing that game of cards. One set is composed of George the Third, Russia, Spain, and Prussia. The other consists of Napoleon, Italy, Holland, and Austria. George the Third says : 'I never had luck when the Curse of Scotland[1] was in my hand—however I have now discarded it—Ay this will do—I have now a strong suit, without a *knave* among them.' Russia observes : ' I never had such luck since I have been a Russian, compleatly bested off the board—but that I must endeavour to forget, and try to play better in future.' Spain says: 'I was obliged to play, tho' it was *forced Spadille.* My Queen deceived me—but however I must not now give myself *Ayres,* as I have lost all my Dollars.' Prussia remarks : ' Shall I play or not ? If I play, I fear I shall be bested, and if not, they will call me *Prussian Cake.'*

In the other set of players, Napoleon says : ' I begin to fancy I can play alone—No, I can call a *King* when I please, I am strong in my suits—besides I know how to finesse my Cards.' Austria says : ' For the present I fear the game is up with me, so I *pass.'* Italy says : 'I fear it

[1] The nine of diamonds.

T

is nearly over with poor *Ponto*.' Holland reflects : ' I have got a *King* without calling one—but I have no *Trump* now, and I fear I shall lose all my fish.'

Fox died in September 1806, and was buried, October 10, in Westminster Abbey, close to the remains of his rival Pitt. With him were buried the last hopes of a peace with France, and, in October, finding all negotiations unsuccessful (Great Britain requiring Russia to be made a party to the Treaty, which France refused), Lord Lauderdale demanded his passports, and left for England.

Meanwhile, Napoleon marched on from victory to victory. The battle of Jena, the occupation of Erfurth, Greissen, Hall, Leipzig, Ascherleben, Bemburg, Spandau, Potsdam, and, lastly, of Berlin, were all in his triumphal march.

> A public entry having made,
> At Berlin he his airs display'd ;
> A Court day absolutely held,
> And due attendance there compell'd.
> Of Prussia's King he made a scoff,
> And all his little taunts play'd off.
> And here he issued a decree,
> The most invet'rate that could be,
> In hopes t' annoy Great Britain's trade,
> All Commerce with her he forbade.
> The Capture he ordain'd, 'tis true,
> Of British ships—the seizure, too,
> Of letters, if in English written,
> Or if directed to Great Britain ;
> And this he styled—a strange romance !
> The fundamental law of France.

The decree is dated from Berlin, November 21, 1806, and, after a preamble, states :—' 1. The British Islands are declared in a state of blockade. 2. All trade and intercourse with the British Islands is prohibited ; consequently letters or packets addressed to England, or written in the English language, will not be conveyed by post, and will be seized. 3. Every native of England, whatever his rank and condition, who may be found in the countries occupied by our troops, or by those of our allies, shall be made prisoners of war. 4. Every warehouse, and all merchandise and property of any description whatever, belonging to an English subject, or the produce of English manufactures or colonies, is declared good prize. 5. Trade in English merchandise is prohibited, and all merchandise belonging to England, or the produce of her manufactures, and colonies, is declared good prize. 6. One half of the produce of the confiscation of the merchandise, and property, declared good prize by the preceding articles, will be appropriated to the indemnification of the merchants, for losses they have sustained, through the capture of trading vessels, by English cruisers. 7. No vessel coming directly from England, or her colonies, or having been there since the publication of the present decree, will be received in any port. 8. Any vessel which, by means of a false declaration, shall contravene the above article, shall be seized, and the Ship and Cargo shall be confiscated as if they were English property,' &c.

The *Times*, of December 8, commenting on this proclamation, says :—' If our orders of Council, and our Navy are not competent to seal up the ports of France, we should be glad to know how Buonaparte, who can scarce venture to *steal* a ship to sea, is to retaliate with effect upon this country. We believe none of the nations, which are yet free to trade with us, will be deterred by a Decree emitted at Berlin, from sending their produce to the markets of Britain. Of all the follies that have ever escaped from Buonaparte, in the extravagance, and intoxication, of his ambition, and success, this we consider as one of the greatest. He, in fact, pledges himself to that which he has no adequate means whatever of carrying into effect. His Decree will have as little influence upon the trade of England, as his Navy has.'

Ansell designed (December 1806) ' Jack Tars conversing with Boney on the Blockade of Old England.' Napoleon is vapouring about behind his fortifications, flourishing his sword, ' The Terror of the Continent,' and saying : ' Begar by my Imperial decree, *England* is in a State of Blockade.' Two sailors are in a small boat called the *Nelson*, and one says : ' Why what do you mean by that, you whipper snapper—Heres Tom Pipes, and I, in this little cock boat, will Blockade you so that you dare not bring out a single vessel—Blockade, indeed ! you are a pretty fellow to talk of blockading !' His companion contemptuously adds : ' I wonder, Jack, you throw away your precious time in talking to such a lubber.' John Bull, pipe in hand, stands on the cliffs of Albion, roaring with laughter. ' I cannot help laughing at the whimsical conceit.'

Souley (December 1806) drew ' Bonaparte blockading John Bull.'

> Boney for want of proper Sail,
> By threats bombastic would prevail.

Boney and his army are crossing the Channel in their cocked hats ; he, presenting sword and pistol at John Bull, says : ' I'll Blockade ye, ye English Scoundrel. 'Tis you thwart all my designs—'Tis you and you only who dare oppose MY WILL. But I'll Blockade ye—and not one of your rascally Craft shall stir.' John Bull, convulsed with laughter, is dancing, and saying : ' Shiver my timbers, here's a go ! Ah ! Ah ! Ah ! Ah ! Why Master Boney you look like Neptune crossing the *Line.* I suppose next you will be blockading the moon.'

And so ends the year 1806.

CHAPTER XLIV.

NAPOLEON'S POLISH CAMPAIGN—BATTLE OF EYLAU—MEETING OF THE
EMPERORS AT TILSIT—CAPTURE OF THE DANISH FLEET.

1807 commences with ' JOHN BULL playing on the BASE Villain ' (artist unknown, January 1, 1807), in which we see that revered personage playing ' Britains Strike home ' on poor Boney, with a sword in lieu of a bow, and grasping him tightly round the neck.

In November 1806, Napoleon, with his army, had entered Poland, and, on December 18 of the same year, he entered Warsaw.

An unknown artist (January 1807) depicts ' The Entrance into Poland or another Bonne Bouche for Boney.' On their knees are the Polish magnates, who exclaim : ' What a happy day for Poland !' The foremost is kissing the toe of Napoleon, who says : 'Rise up *free* and *inde-pendent* Polanders, depend upon it you shall have a King, and I'll be Vice Roy *over him*.' Behind, a standard-bearer carries a flag, on which is shown a pair of shackles, a guillotine, and two crossed swords, with the legend, 'Comfort for the Poles.' Beside him, another French soldier is emptying a sack of fetters.

The Russians withdrew for a time, but only to return in force, and Napoleon had to change his tactics to meet them ; he therefore proposed to concentrate his forces, and compel the Russians to give battle, with the Vistula in their rear, and he himself between them and Russia. His despatches, however, were intercepted, and the battle was precipitated. Augereau's division lost its way, and was cut up by the Russians ; and Bernadotte did not come, as the despatches, bidding him do so, had been captured. The fight in the snow at Preuss Eylau was fearful, and the carnage, especially in the churchyard, was horrible. Four thousand men died there. The French put down their loss in this battle as 2,000 killed, 6,000 wounded ; while the loss of the Russians was 7,000 dead, 16,000 wounded, 12,000 prisoners, and 45 cannon taken.

That the blockade still galled us is evidenced by a caricature of Woodward's (January 27, 1807), who designed 'The Giant Commerce overwhelming the Pigmy Blockade.' Commerce is a strange figure : its cap is *Wedgwood ware*, its face *Staffordshire ware*, its eyes *Derby Porcelain*, and its mouth *Worcester porcelain*. Its body is *Wool*, arms of *printed calico*, and its hands are encased in *Woodstock gloves*. It wears a *Norwich shawl*, has *leather* breeches, *Fleecy hosiery* stockings, and *Staffordshire* shoes. It is actively employed in hurling various missiles at Napoleon, who is sheltered behind his fortifications. These implements of offence consist of such articles as *Birmingham steel, pig iron, scissors, combs, knives and forks, block tin, sugar, patent coffins, Birmingham buttons*, and a cask each of *London porter, Maidstone, Geneva*, and *British spirits*. Napoleon entreats : 'Pray Mr. Commerce don't overwhelm me, and I will take off de grande Blockade of old England.'

The two following caricatures were designed and published before the news had arrived in England of the
crushing defeat of the Russians at Eylau, which only
appeared publicly in the 'Times' of March 10.

Ansell (March 1807) gives 'Boney and his Army in
Winter Quarters.' In the background is a *State Prison for
Prisoners of War*; and, in the centre of the picture, the
Russian bear hugs poor Boney, and prepares to drop him
in the river Bug, in which is a board inscribed, ' Hic Jacet.
Snug in the Bug several thousands of the great nation.'
Bruin growls: ' Hush a bye! Hush a bye! take it all
quietly, you'll soon find yourself as snug as a bug in a rug.'
But Boney, writhing in the embrace, cries out: ' Oh D—n
the Bug, I wish I had never seen it. My dear Talley—
don't tell my faithful subjects the true state of my situation. Any thing but the truth, my dear Talley—Oh this
Cursed Russian bear, how close he hugs me.' Talleyrand, with one foot in the Vistula, and the other on land,
replies: ' Leave me alone for a Bulletin '—applies his lips
to a trumpet, from which issues a true and a false report.
The true one, ' 4000 prisoners, 3000 drowned, 12 Eagles
taken, 12000 killed,' is disappearing into thin air ; whilst
that ' For Paris' is as follows : ' Grand Bulletin. The
august Emperor of the great Nation informs his faithful,
and beloved, subjects, that, having performed wonders on
the banks of the Bug, he has now closed a glorious campaign for the season, and retired with ease, and comfort,
into Winter quarters.'

'The Political Cock horse' (Souley, March 10, 1807)
shows Napoleon's somewhat ragged white charger stumbling
over a stone, 'Insatiable Ambition.' Benningsen has
jumped up behind him, seized the reins, and hurled Boney
to the ground. In his fall he loses his sword ' Oppression,'
and cries out pitifully, ' Stop, stop, good Benningsen, don't
kill a poor fellow ! An Armistice ! an Armistice ! I have
very good proposals of peace for you.' But the relentless
Russian prepares to run him through with his sword,
saying: 'You Bombastic Scoundrel, Robber, Murderer,
Violator, Incendiary, &c., &c., &c. You thought of reigning with your Iron Crown (in) the North, as well as the

South. But know, Tyrant, that the Sons of the North are to be your Superior.' John Bull encourages him with 'Bravo, bravo, brave Russians : One home stroke more, and good bye to Master Boney.'

Of Gillray's caricature of 'The New Dynasty ; or the little Corsican Gardener Planting a Royal Pippin Tree,' only a portion is given —that relating to Napoleon. The Old Royal Oak is being hewn down by 'All the Talents,' and Talleyrand is busy digging a hole to receive Napoleon's royal pippin, which is to take its place. The topmost pippin, which is crowned, repre-

THE NEW DYNASTY, OR THE LITTLE CORSICAN
GARDENER PLANTING A ROYAL PIPPIN TREE.

sents Lord Moira, who claimed to be descended from the old kings of Ballynahinch. The others are, 'Countess of Salisbury beheaded 1505,' 'Duchess of Cleves put to death in 1453,' 'Henry de la Pole beheaded in 1538,' 'Plantagenet beheaded in 1415,' 'Crookback Richard killed at Bosworth,' 'Edmund, 4th son of Henry 2, beheaded.' The royal pippins behind, which have already been planted, and have taken root, are labelled respectively, 'Etruria, Wurtemburg, Saxon, Holland, and Italian ;' whilst on the ground, by a basket, are grafts, which respectively represent Sir Francis Burdett, Cobbett, and Horne Tooke.

Napoleon pursued his victories over the Russians. Dantzig was taken ; at Friedland the Russians lost 18,000 men and 25 generals, killed and wounded, and at last

Königsberg was taken by Soult, after having been evacuated by the Russians. It was time for them to beg for an armistice, and on June 21 one was concluded. Napoleon was asked to have an interview with the Emperor of Russia, to which he consented, and Tilsit was the place appointed ; and, in order that this meeting should be quite private, and free from interruption, Napoleon ordered a large raft to be moored in the middle of the Niemen, on which was erected a room with two antechambers, all elegantly furnished and decorated. Both the roof and the doors were ornamented with French and Russian eagles. On June 25 they met ; Napoleon reached the raft first, and stood on its edge to welcome Alexander. They met and parted in a most friendly manner. This incident, it is needless to say, afforded a fine subject to the caricaturist.

Ansell gives us, certainly, a more comic representation of the meeting of the Emperors than any other caricaturist

(July 1807). Bonaparte is hugging the Emperor of Russia in a most exaggerated style, saying : 'My dear Brother— receive this Fraternal Embrace out of pure affection.' But Russia, finding the raft tilting violently, and not liking such demonstrative affection, exclaims, ' Zounds, Brother, you'll squeeze me to death—besides, I find my side of the raft is sinking very fast.' Poor Prussia is floundering in the water, his crown floating away from him : ' What a Prussian cake

'I was to listen to him—I am afraid I shall never recover
it.'

> Nap, with the hopes of peace delighted,
> The Russian Emperor invited,
> And for this interview, with craft,
> Had been prepar'd a pretty raft,
> Which on the river Niemen floated,
> With two commodious tents, devoted
> To the sole use of the contractors,
> Who were indeed conspicuous actors;
> The signal given, as commanded,
> Each from his boat together landed,
> And on this raft, their ends to get,
> By Nap, was Alexander met—
> Exchanging the fraternal hug
> They took their seats in manner snug;
> When Nap began his wheedling jargon,
> And made, depend on 't, a good bargain.
> The peace of Tilsit, as recorded,
> A temporary rest afforded.
> And now three sovereigns, they say,
> Sat down together very gay:
> Meaning the Emperor of Russia,
> Our hero, and the King of Prussia :
> Their visits to each other, they
> Alternately were wont to pay.
> Napoleon talk'd of this and that,
> And entertain'd them with his chat.
> Their life guards, who were much delighted,
> To dinner, were by Nap invited,
> The brotherly embrace went round,
> There was not a discordant sound.
> In harmony the day they spent,
> Each countenance display'd content.
> Now matters were so well arrang'd,
> A while they uniforms exchang'd,
> And after they had dined, and talk'd,
> Together through the streets they walked.

Ansell drew (July 1807) 'An Imperial Bonne bouche,
or the dinner at Tilsit.' Napoleon, attended by his guards,
sits on one side of the table, and the Emperor of Russia
opposite to him ; the latter has but an empty plate, and a
castor of cayenne pepper before him, whilst Napoleon is

stuffing his mouth with ' Continental slices,' and has besides, immediately before him, ' Austerlitz biscuit,' ' Friedland Pye,' and ' Eylau Custard,' which he intends carving with his sword.   But he banters his brother Emperor with ' My dear Brother, you dont eat ; What is the matter with you ? see what a hearty meal our other beloved Cousin, and brother, is making,, from the Crumbs that fall from the table.'   And Prussia is seen on his knees, picking up some fragments of a ' Prussian Cake.'   Russia, with expectant knife and fork, looks very blankly at his *confrère*, and replies : ' How the deuce, brother, am I to eat when you keep everything to yourself ? '

'Mutual Honors at Tilsit, or the Monkey, the Bear and the Eagle ' (August 1807), by Ansell, represents Napoleon, as a monkey, seated on a drum, having a plaque upon his breast, inscribed ' Order of St. Andrew, to our Faithful &c. &c. &c. Fudge,' decorating a bear with 'The Legion of Honor.   To our trusty and beloved Cousin &c. &c. Fudge.' The poor bear wears a fool's cap and bells, and is muzzled, whilst its throat is galled by a spiked collar, called, in irony, ' Collar of Independence.'   Napoleon says, ' Really, Brother Bruin—you never look'd so fine in your life.   You cannot think how the medal, and cap and bells, become you.' But the bear ruefully ruminates, ' I shall really be ashamed to return to my own Fraternity.   I wonder what my old Friend, the Lion, will say.'   The Prussian eagle is also decorated with the collar of the Legion of Honour, but is in a wofully dilapidated condition, which is well explained by its own reflections : ' It is certainly very fine—but, what with having one of my heads chopped off—and the crown half cracked of the other ; besides having my wings cropp'd, I think, somehow, I was better off before.'

The English, perforce, had to keep up their courage, and one etching, by Ansell (August 1807), represents, in the background, Napoleon on his throne, and all the European sovereigns grovelling before him.   The foreground is occupied by Britannia and John Bull.   The former ask : ' Do give me your advice—what am I to do—All my foreign Allies have deserted me,—even Russia has joined them, they are bending at the feet of the usurper.'   John Bull, a truculent-looking sailor, with oaken cudgel, replies : ' What are you to do ? Why stick to me, your old and faithful ally John Bull, who will never desert you while he has a timber to support him.' The picture is called ' Britannia in tribulation for the loss of her Allies, or John Bull's advice.'

In ' The Polish Pie, or the Effects of the Peace at Tilsit ' (artist unknown, September 10, 1807), we see the Emperor of Russia, and Napoleon, carving a huge ' Polish pie,' the Russian's opinion of which is ' I think I never relished a Pie so well in all my life.' Whilst thus engaged, comes poor, wounded, tattered Prussia, humbly, with hat in hand : ' Pray give a part of the Pie to a poor broken-down Prussian—You know you promised me formerly you would not touch it ; but now you have reduced me to poverty, crutches, and a wooden leg—you'll not allow me a mouth-full, 'tis a very hard case indeed ! Pray remember a poor Prussian ! ' Napoleon turns to his brother Emperor, and opines, 'Suppose, Cousin, we give him a small piece of the *Crust*, just to keep him from grumbling.'

The Danes sought to curry favour with Napoleon, or perhaps they were obliged to act as they did ; but they closed their ports, such as Holstein, &c., to British ships, which John Bull could not stand. So Admiral Gambier, with a fleet, having on board 20,000 troops, sailed to set matters right. Negotiations failed, and the admiral used the *force majeure* at his disposal. Copenhagen was bombarded, and on September 8 the British took possession of the fortifications, &c., of Copenhagen, captured the whole Danish fleet, fully armed and equipped, consisting of 18 sail of the line, 15 frigates, 6 brigs, and 25 gun-boats, which were safely navigated to England, with the exception of one ship, which was stranded. Unfortunately, Copenhagen itself suffered severely, guns not being so scientifically constructed as at present, and accuracy as to range was impossible.

' Gulliver towing the Fleet into Lilliput ! ' (I. Cruikshank, October 16, 1807) shows Admiral Gambier swimming towards England, towing the captured vessels. George the Third, on a Martello tower, watching him through his spy-glass, and saying, with his accustomed iteration, 'What, What, Gulliver the 2nd—he—Gulliver the 2nd—More Nelsons—more Nelsons—brave fellows!' On the Continent Napoleon is seen furious, and the countries under his sway are in different attitudes of despair. Napoleon shouts out, 'Curse that fellow; here, Tally, stop him: what! will nobody stop him? Then begar, we never shall invade England, and all our schemes are frustrated.' On the coast of Zealand a Jack Tar is thus explaining to a native: 'Hold your jaw; You know as how you used to rob our forefathers, you lubber, and so you wanted to assist that French Monkey to do it again, but it would not do.'

Ansell published (October 21, 1807) 'Malignant Aspects looking with envy on John Bull and his Satellites, or, a New Planetary System.' In a centre medallion sits John Bull, happily smoking, and with a jug of good October by his side. He is surrounded by the British navy, and a halo of glory. Rushing towards him is 'A Corsican Comet Frenchified,' and chained to him is 'A Russian bear with two heads, an appendage to the Comet.' There is a 'Danish Mouse,' an 'Italian Greyhound,' an 'American Torpedo,' a 'Swiss Cheese,' a 'Spanish Puff,' a 'Dutch frog,' besides many 'minor Constellations with malignant aspects.'

CHAPTER XLV.

FRENCH ENTRY INTO PORTUGAL—BLOCKADE OF ENGLAND—FLIGHT OF THE PORTUGUESE ROYAL FAMILY—THE PENINSULAR WAR—FLIGHT OF KING JOSEPH.

On October 18 or 19 Junot entered Portugal, and then it was that John Bull began to fear for his stock of port wine. This is very amusingly put in a picture: 'In Port, and Out of Port, or news from Portugal,' which is the title of a caricature by Woodward (November 10, 1807), and it represents Bonaparte seated on a pipe of 'Genuine Old Port.' With folded arms he thus speaks: 'Now Master Jean Bull —more news for you. You'll soon be out of Port.' A miserable-looking 'Portugee' approaches John Bull, with cap in hand, saying: 'I be, d'ye see, de poor Portuguese. Vat he mean be de Port Wine; which he will be glad to change for your bag of guineas dere—begar—but dat is mine—between ourselves.' John Bull, who is sitting down, smoking, with a jug of ale and a huge bagful of guineas by his side, replies : 'D—n him, and his *Port* too—I am snug in *Port*, and while I have the port holes of my wooden walls, and a glass of home brew'd ale, his conquests shall never trouble me.'

Napoleon, in a decree dated from Hamburg, November 10, and also in another dated Milan, December 27, again declared England in a state of blockade, and he made all under his sway to cease all connection with that country, as far as commercial matters were concerned ; and this is how the caricaturist met it : —

'Blockade against Blockade, or John Bull a Match for Boney' (Ansell, November 1807), shows the different sides of a 'Wall of Blockade.' John Bull is well victualled, and has a fine surloin of beef, and a full tankard, &c. ; and he says : 'Now Master Boney, we shall see which will hold out the longest, my wall against yours. Aye, aye, I can see you. I have left a peep hole. I believe you will soon be glad to change your Soup Maigre for my Roast beef.' Boney, with only a basin of Soup Maigre before him, looks very disconsolate : 'Who could have thought that he would build a wall also—I really think I had better have left him alone—Some how I don't relish this Soup Maigre.'

'The Continental Dockyard,' by Woodward (November 27, 1807), shows a very tumbledown erection, called 'The Gallic Storehouse for English Shipping,' but it contains none. It only holds the 'Yaw Mynheer,' the 'Don Diego,' the 'Swede,' the 'Dane,' and the 'Napoleon,' on which a number of shipwrights are engaged, being driven to their task by Napoleon, with drawn sword. He thus addresses the master shipwright : 'Begar you must work like de Diable, ve must annihilate dis John Bull.' The unlucky foreman replies : 'Please you, my Grand Empereur, 'tis no use vatever. As fast as ve do build dem, he vas clap dem in his storehouse over de way.' Accordingly, we see in 'John Bull's Storehouse' a large collection of captured vessels from the Armada—'Portobello,' 'Camperdown,' 'St. Vincent,' 'Nile,' and 'Trafalgar.' John Bull and a number of sailors enjoy this cheering sight. Says he to them : 'I say my lads, if he goes on this way we shall be overstocked.' And a sailor remarks : 'What a deal of pains some people take for nothing.'

I. Cruikshank (December 20, 1807) gives us 'The Bear, the Monkey, the Turkey, and the Bull, or the true cause of the Russian war.' Bonaparte, as the French Monkey, is leading the Russian Bear by a collar and chain, and thus addresses him : ' The case is this, if you will make war against that overgrown Bull over the way, you shall have a slice of that fine Turkey ! and the Eastern Star.' The Turkey is represented as saying : 'I wish I was well out of their clutches, but I am afraid they will have me at last.' The *Eastern Star* appears on the horizon, and re-presents the Indies. A Bull, on the opposite coast, is in a menacing attitude, and bellows forth : 'You had better beware, for, remember the old adage—When you play with a Bull, take care of his horns.'

'John Bull refreshing the Bear's Memory' is by I. Cruikshank (December 20, 1807), and shows the former worthy opening an enormous volume, his journal, and thus addressing a crowned bear, who has a collar round his neck inscribed ' This bear belongs to Napoleon,' and who regards the book through an enormous pair of spectacles. ' So you say, Master Bruin, that my visit to Denmark has no parallel in History—do be so good as to turn your specta-cles to this page, and refresh your memory.' And he points to a page of his journal, in which is written : ' The Great, the Magnanimous, Catherine of Russia seized upon one third of the Kingdom of Poland, and kept it to herself. These peaceful Danes seized on the City of Hamburgh.'

On January 1, 1808, I. Cruikshank published ' Boney stark mad, or more Ships, Colonies, and Commerce.' It shows the fleet in the Tagus, and the British Admiral (Sir Sidney Smith) calling out through his speaking-trumpet, ' Bon jour, Monsieur, if you would like a trip to the Brazils, I'll conduct you there with a great deal of pleasure ; per-haps you would like a taste of Madeira by the way.' This is to Talleyrand, on whom Bonaparte is venting his rage, kicking him, and tearing off his wig, saying : ' Stop them,

stop them.   Murder, fire!   Why did you not make more
haste, you hopping rascal? now, all my hopes are blasted,
my revenge disappointed, and—I'll glut it on you—
Monster—Vagabond—Villain ! ! ! '

The explanation of this caricature is, that as the French
army was marching direct to Lisbon, the whole of the Portuguese Royal family embarked for the Brazils, on November
29, under convoy of a British squadron.

'Delicious Dreams ! Castles in the Air ! Glorious
Prospects ! vide an Afternoon Nap after the Fatigues of
an Official Dinner,' is by Gillray (April 10, 1808), and
shows the Cabinet asleep, a punch-bowl on the table, and
full and empty bottles all around.   They are so quiet that
the mice are licking the Treasury plates.   Behind Castlereagh's chair is a cat (Catalani).   Mr. Perceval sleeps with
his arms on the table ; the Duke of Portland in the chair-
man's seat ; Lord Liverpool with his back to the table ;
Canning, negligently lolling back in his chair, uses Lord
Melville, who is under the table, as a footstool.   The
delicious dream they see has for its background the Tower
of London, before which passes Britannia seated on a

triumphal car, fashioned somewhat like a ship, and drawn
by a bull ; and, behind the car, chained to it, come, first,
Bonaparte, the Russian Bear, Prussia, Austria, and Spain.

'The Corsican Tiger at Bay ' (Rowlandson, July 8,
1808) shows Napoleon as a Tiger (or rather, as the artist
has depicted him, a leopard), with his fore-feet on four
Royal Greyhounds, whilst a pack of *Patriotic Greyhounds*
are rushing to attack him.   John Bull, standing on the
white cliffs of Albion, presents his gun at him, singing the
nursery rhyme—

'There was a little man,
And he had a little gun,
And his bullets were made of lead——

D—me, but we'll manage him amongst us.' The *Russian Bear* and *Austrian Eagle* are chained together ; but Austria thus proposes : ' Now, Brother Bruin, is the time to break our chains.'   The Dutch frog, too, joins in the chorus : ' It will be my turn to have a slap at him next.'

'Boney Bothered, or an unexpected meeting' (Ansell, July 9, 1808).   This shows Boney having gone right

through the world, and, coming out on the other side, planting his foot on the East Indies, at Bengal ; but he is utterly astonished to find John Bull there also, armed with his redoubtable oaken cudgel.   ' Begar,' says he, ' Monsieur Jean Bull again ! Vat ! you know I was come here ? ' To which John Bull, from whose pocket peeps a bundle of *Secret Intelligence*, replies, ' To be sure I did—for all your humbug deceptions.   I smoked [1] your intentions, and have brought my Oak Twig with me, so now you may go back again.'

We now come to a period of our history which is in-teresting to all of us—the Peninsular War.   Napoleon had turned his attention to Spain, and the Spanish king had

[1] Suspected.

abdicated, and been sent to Fontainebleau, with ample allowances. Joseph Bonaparte had been chosen king of Spain, and Murat had his kingdom of Naples. But the Spanish nation did not acquiesce in these arrangements. They broke into open revolt, the English helping them with arms and money, and, on June 6, the Supreme Junta formally declared war against Napoleon. This much is necessary to explain the following caricature :—

Gillray (July 11, 1808) drew 'The Spanish Bull fight or the Corsican Matador in danger,' and kindly tells us that 'The Spanish Bull is so remarkable for Spirit, that unless the Matador strikes him dead at the first blow, the Bull is sure to destroy him.' In the *Theatre Royale de l'Europe* sits George the Third, a trident in one hand, his spy-glass in the other, keenly watching the exciting fight, as also are the delighted sovereigns of Europe, the Pope, the Sultan of Turkey, and the Dey of Algiers. The Spanish Bull has broken the Corsican chain and collar which bound him, and, trampling on his king, has gored and tossed the Matador, Napoleon, whose sword is broken in an ineffectual attempt to despatch the animal. On the ground are three wounded bulls—Prussian, Dutch, and Danish—bellowing for help.

U

Woodward gives us a capital caricature in ' The Corsican Spider in his web' (July 12, 1808). Napoleon is there represented as a bloated spider, 'Unbounded ambition,' and he is just swallowing a Spanish fly. There are plenty of flies in his web—Austrian, Dutch, Portuguese, Hanoverian, Etrurian, Prussian, Hamburg, Italian, Venetian, and small flies innumerable. The Pope fly is just being entangled, and says, ' I am afraid I shall be dragg'd in.' ' The Russian Fly' has touched the fatal web, and exclaims, ' I declare I was half in the web before I made the discovery.' In fact, the only two that are as yet free from the baneful mesh is the Turkish fly, who thinks, ' I am afraid it will be my turn next,' and the British fly, who, well and hearty, calls out, ' Ay, you may look, master Spider, but I am not to be caught in your web.'

To understand the next caricature, which, though dated July 27, must have been published somewhat later, we must note that Joseph Bonaparte entered Madrid, in state, on July 20, but, ominously, without any welcome from the *people*: although money was scattered broadcast, none but the French picked it up. He knew little of what was going on—how Moncey had been obliged to raise the siege of Valencia, and that Dupont had surrendered at Baylen. This latter piece of news he did not receive till the 26th or 27th of July ; when he learned also that Castaños, with constantly increasing forces, was marching towards Madrid, he left that city for Vittoria.

A broadside caricature (artist unknown, July 27, 1808) shows Joseph leaving Madrid, his crown falling off, heading his troops, who are carrying off heaps of treasure. It is headed ' Burglary and Robbery ! ! ! Whereas on the night of the 20th of July last, a numerous gang of French Banditti entered the City of Madrid, and burglariously broke into the Royal Palace, National Bank, and most of the Churches thereof, murdering all who opposed them in their infamous proceedings.

' The said banditti remained in Madrid until the 27th of the said month, and then suddenly departed, laden with immense booty, having stolen from thence several waggon-loads of plate, and every portable article of value, taking the road to France ; all patriotic Spaniards are hereby requested to be aiding, and assisting, in the apprehension of all, or any, of the said robbers ; and, whoever apprehends all, or any, of them, shall receive the thanks, and blessings, of every well-disposed person in Europe.

'The said Banditti were headed by *Joe Nap*, a ferocious ruffian of the following description :—He is about five feet seven inches high, of a meagre, squalid aspect, saffron-coloured complexion. He was, when he escaped, habited in a *royal robe*, which he is known to have stolen from the King's Wardrobe at Naples. He is a brother of the *noted thief* who has committed numberless robberies all over Europe, *murdered millions of the human race*, and who was latterly at Bayonne, where it is supposed he tarried, for the purpose of *receiving the stolen goods* which his brother was to bring from Spain.'

The war, in aid of Spain, against France, was now taken up in earnest, and Sir Arthur Wellesley was sent to Spain with a large body of troops, whilst reinforcements were to come from other quarters.

Almost one of the last of Gillray's political caricatures, and a very good one it is, is 'Apotheosis of the Corsican Phœnix' (August 2, 1808). It has an imaginary quotation from a supposed 'New Spanish Encyclopædia, edit. 1808. When the Phœnix is tired of Life, he builds a Nest upon the mountains, and setting it on Fire by the wafting of his own Wings, he perishes Himself in the Flames ! and from the smoke of his Ashes arises a new *Phœnix* to illumine the world ! ! !' This very graphic etching shows, on the summit of the Pyrenees, a globe, which is the nest of the phœnix—Napoleon, with orb and sceptre, but, his crown falling off, he has fanned all Europe into a blaze with his wings. Around his neck is a 'cordon d'honneur' of daggers, and, amid the smoke which rises from the pyre, is seen a dove with olive branch, having on its wings 'Peace on earth.'

I. Cruikshank still kept up the idea of *Tiddy-Doll* in 'The Oven on Fire — or Boney's last Batch entirely spoiled ! ! !' (August 24, 1808.) He is on his knees, with

arms outspread in consternation, for, in putting Dupont, on
a 'peel,' into the oven—'Spain and Portugal'—flames
burst out, labelled Asturian Legions, Army of Portugal,
Biscay, Catalonian Army, Army of Galicia, Andalusian
Army, Army of New and Old Castille, British Army and
Fleet, Estramadurean Army, Leon, Army of Valencia,
Murcia, and Army of Granada ; whilst in the centre of the
flames is the legend 'A people United can never be conquered.' Poor Dupont exclaims, 'Oh Nap, Nap ! what is
this ? Instead of a King, you've only made me a Dup(e)ont.'
Bonaparte himself cries out, 'Zounds, I shall be overwhelmed with this Patriotic Blaze. I did not think there
was a single spark left, but I find there is more than all
the Engines of France can extinguish.' Talleyrand, who
stands by his kneading-trough, which is labelled 'State
Prison,' rests quiet, and says, 'Aye Aye, I told you that you
would burn your fingers at that batch of Ginger-bread—
but I have nothing to do with it. I am only a *Jailor*, so
there is an end to all my glory.'

We have seen the European monarchs sitting down to a
game of quadrille. Ansell (August 1808) gives us its conclusion. Spain has suddenly arisen, and, upsetting the table,
seizes Napoleon by the throat, accusing him of foul play :
'I tell you, you are a Scoundrel, and if you do not restore
my King, whom you have stolen from the other table, and
reinstate *Ponto*—by the honor of a Spanish Patriot, I will
strangle you.' Trembling Bonaparte replies, 'Don't be so
boisterous, I only borrowed him, merely to make up the
pack.' The Pope is on the floor, and the stolid Dutchman,
with his hat in hand, says, 'Donder and Blixens, I be
quite tired of de game. Yaw ! Yaw ! now is de time for
me to rise.' At the other table all take a lively interest in
the squabble. George the Third rises from his seat and
grasps his 'heart of oak' stick, saying, 'What ! what ! a
dust, eh ? so much the better. Boney got the worst of the
game. I must lend a hand.' Russia, with hand on sword,
turns in his chair, remarking that 'Now is the time to rub
off the rust of Tilsit.' Prussia rises, exclaiming, 'If I don't
take advantage of the present opportunity, I shall indeed
be a Prussian Cake.' Austria reaches his hat and sword

from its peg on the wall, and says, 'Ah! Ah! the game has taken a different turn from what I expected, I must not be idle.'

The next caricature relates to the bad success of Napoleon's arms. The raising the siege of Saragossa, the defeat of Vimiera, and the Convention of Cintra, by which the French were to evacuate Portugal, were not facts likely to be relished in France.

'The Fox and the Grapes' is another of Woodward's (September 15, 1808), where the Corsican Fox interviews the Gallic Cock. The former says, 'Believe me, my dear Doodle doo, you would not like them—I found them so *sour* that I absolutely could not *touch* them,' in answer to the Cock's query—'But my good friend, you promised to bring me home some Spanish Grapes and Portugal plums : where are they ?'

'Prophecy explained' is by Rowlandson (September 17, 1808), and the text taken is from the Revelation of St. John (chap. xvii. verse 10): 'And there are seven kings, five are fallen, and *one* is, and the other is not yet come, and when he cometh he must continue but a short space.' The five that are fallen are the Kings of Würtemberg, Saxony, Holland, Bavaria, and Prussia, and these have fallen into a 'Slough of Disgrace and Ridicule.' The '*one* that is,' it is needless to say, is Napoleon ; and the 'one that continued but a short space,' is King Joseph, who, having been chased beyond the Pyrenees, has his crown snatched from him. There are many other caricatures on this subject of the flight of Joseph, but, although interesting, they hardly come within the scope of *personal* satire on Napoleon.

Rowlandson gives us (September 20, 1808) 'Napoleon the little in a Rage with his great French Eagle!!' Napoleon, with his sword drawn, and his hands clenched, is in a terrible rage with his brother Joseph, who, under the guise of a crowned eagle, is limping along with one leg in a sling. Napoleon thus addresses him : 'Confusion and Destruction—what is this I see ? Did I not command you not to return till you had spread your Wing of Victory over the whole Spanish Nation ?' And the poor bird

meekly replies : ' Aye, its fine alking Nap, but if you had
been there, you would not much have liked it—The Spanish Cormorants pursued me in such a manner, that they
not only disabled one of my legs, but set me a moulting
in such a terrible way that I wonder I had not lost every
feather ; besides, it got so hot, I could not bear it any longer.'

There is a caricature (September 24, 1808) of ' A hard
passage, or Boney playing Base on the Continent.'   He is
here represented as playing on the bass viol from the score
of the ' Conquest of Spain and Portugal.'   His task seems
hard, and he exclaims : ' Plague take it ! I never met with
so difficult a *passage* before.   But, if I can once get over
the *Flats*, we shall do pretty well, for you see the *Key* will
then change into *B* sharp.'   A muzzled Russian bear is
trying to play on the French horn, and says : ' Why that
is *Natural* enough, brother Boney, though this *French horn*
of yours seems rather out of order.'

CHAPTER XLVI.

PENINSULAR WAR, *continued*—MEETING AT ERFURT.

' THE Valley of the Shadow of Death ' is, as far as I know,
the last caricature of Gillray (September 24, 1808) in connection with Napoleon—if, indeed, it can be called a cari-

cature, for it is far too serious in its conception   Napo-
leon's situation at the moment is here firmly grasped.
He is surrounded by enemies.   With notched sword in
hand, he leads the Russian bear.   He is pursued by the
German eagle and the spirit of Charles XII.   Above is the
' Turkish New Moon Rising in blood,' the obscured portion

of which is represented by ' French Influence,' the bright crescent as ' English Influence,' and the whole is dropping blood. A fiery comet, with a tiara as a nucleus (the Pope), is darting thunderbolts of excommunication upon him ; whilst Junot and Dupont, shackled together at their necks, amidst clouds, seem to warn him of his fate. Immediately in front of him is a *Portuguese wolf,* which has broken its chain, a *Sicilian terrier,* and the *Leo Britannicus.* Death also appears, lance in one hand, hour-glass in the other, on a mule of ' True Royal Spanish breed.' In the Ditch of Styx is disappearing ' Rex Joseph,' whose hands and crown alone appear above water. Creeping upwards from the slime of the *Lethean Ditch,* is ' The Rhenish Confederation of starved Rats, crawling out of the Mud,' also ' Dutch Frogs spitting out their spite ' ; whilst the ' American Rattle Snake is shaking his tail,' and the ' Prussian scare-crow is attempting to fly.'

Certainly ' Nap and his Partner Joe ' is not one of Rowlandson's happiest efforts (September 29, 1808). Some Dons are kicking the brothers into the gaping jaws of a devil, singing meanwhile, ' So seeing we were finely nick'd, Plump to the Devil we boldly kick'd, Both *Nap* and his Partner *Joe.*'

' Nap and His friends in their glory ' (October 1, 1808) shews him, his brother Joseph, Death, and the Devil,

carousing.   Napoleon is rising and giving a toast.   'Come,
gentlemen, here is success to Plunder and Massacre.'
There is below a song to the tune of ' Drops of Brandy.

NAP.

These Spaniards are terrible rogues,
　　They will not submit to my fetters;
With patience so gracefully worn,
　　Nay, sought for, by Nations their betters.
But let us return to the Charge
　　And no longer with lenity treat them.
Once get them to lay down their arms,
　　And I warrant, brave boys, we shall beat them.
　　　　　　　　　Rum ti iddidy - iddidy
　　　　　　　　　Rum ti iddidy - ido.

DEATH.

Brother Boney, we'll never despair,
　　A trusty good friend I have found you.
Kill, plunder, and burn and destroy,
　　And deal desolation around you.
Then gaily let's push round the glass,
　　We'll sing and we'll riot and revel,
And I'm sure we shall have on our side
　　Our very good friend, here, the Devil.
　　　　　　　　　　　　Rum ti, &c.

THE DEVIL.

Believe me, friend Death, you are right.
　　Although I'm an ugly old fellow,
When mischief is getting afloat,
　　O ! then I am jolly and mellow.
As soon as these Spaniards are crush'd,
　　Again we'll be merry and sing Sirs,
And that we will quickly accomplish,
　　And *Joey* here, he shall be King, Sirs.
　　　　　　　　　　　　Rum ti, &c.

DON JOEY.

Excuse me from lending my aid,
　　You may jointly pursue them and spike them ;
But lately, I've seen them—and own,
　　I speak the plain truth,—I don't like them.
They *Liberty* cherish so dear,
　　That they constantly make her their guide, O,
Who pleases may make themselves King,
　　But may I be d—d if I do.　　Rum ti, &c.

'Apollyon, the Devil's Generalissimo, addressing his legions,' a portion of which is here reproduced, is by I. Cruikshank (October 7, 1808). His speech is as follows : ' Legions of Death. After having ravished, murdered, and plundered, on the banks of the Danube, and the Vistula, I shall order you to march through France, without allowing you a moment's rest ! ! I have occasion for you—the hideous presence of *Religion*, and *Loyalty*, contaminates the Continent of Spain, and Portugal. Let your *aspect*

APOLLYON, THE DEVIL'S GENERALISSIMO, ADDRESSING HIS LEGIONS.

drive them away from thence ; let us carry our conquering Eagles to the gates of Heaven : *there also we have an injury to avenge*—you have exceeded all modern murderers—you have placed yourselves on a level with the most *ferocious cannibals*—Eternal War, Robbery, and Plunder shall be the reward of your Exertions, for I never can enjoy rest till the Sea is covered with your Blood ! ! ' And the army rejoice, shouting : ' Ha, Ha, more Blood ! '

A rather clever broadside, artist unknown (October

1808), shows us 'General Nap turned Methodist Preacher.'
Napoleon, in a black gown, occupies the pulpit, having in
his hand a musket with fixed bayonet, on which is a windmill, and, in his wig, he has fixed a cross, tricoloured flag,
surmounted by a cap of liberty, and a crescent. In the
vestry hang a military uniform, an episcopal mitre, and
chasuble, or cope—a Turkish costume, a bottle of arsenic
for the poor sick of Jaffa, a musket labelled 'Scarecrow,'
and a bloody dagger, which does duty as the 'Imperial
Cross.' A general acts as clerk, the organ pipes are
cannon, and the audience, when not military, is seated
on drums. The letterpress is as follows: 'General Nap
turned Methodist Preacher, a new attempt to gull the
credulous ; dedicated to Mr. Whitbread. "*Dear Sam,
repeat my Words, but not my Actions.*" "Dearly beloved
brethren, Honour, Country, liberty ! this is the order of the
day ; far from us all idea of conquest, bloodshed, and war.
Religion and true Philosophy must ever be our maxim.
Liberty, a free Constitution, and no Taxes, that is our cry.
No Slave trade ; humanity shudders at the very thought
of it ! ! The brave, the excellent, English detest it. Yea,
we shall all be happy. Commerce, Plenty, and all sorts of
pretty things will be our lot. Good Jacobins, rise and
assert your rights. And you, brave soldiers, the honour of
France, Plunder and Blood shall once more be your cry.
Double pay and cities burnt will come down in showers
upon you. Yea ! ye shall all be Generals, all be members
of the Legion of Honour ! The Eagles will once more
cover the world. Now is the time to destroy Great Britain,
that treacherous country which always seeks our ruin.
Honour and Victory will lead us.

'"Dear Countrymen, without good faith there is no tie
in this world. Dear Jacobins, we all acknowledge no God,
and nothing else. Let the Altars be lighted up, and your
organs play the Marseillois, that sacred air, which fires
every Frenchman's breast. Yea, I swear by this holy
Cross I now hold in my hands, and in this sacred place,
that you are all free, and without restraint, that my intentions are pure; and that I wish for nothing else but Peace,
Plunder, and Liberty ! Amen ! ! "'

'Political Quacks, or the Erfurt Co-partnership commencing Business' (artist unknown, November 1808) shows
Napoleon, as a quack doctor, on a stage with a muzzled
bear (Russia), who is distributing handbills, and says :
'Ladies and Gentlemen, I am proud to say, as well as my
muzzle will permit me, that I have a large share in the
concern.' Seated behind Napoleon are his different
patients, whilst Death, grinning through a curtain, calls
out : 'Walk up, walk up, kill or cure.' Napoleon himself,
as the quack doctor, has in his hand one of his famous
cannon-ball pills, one of which 'is a dose,' and a trayful of
them is on the floor of the stage. They are named Naples,
Egypt, Lodi, Alps, Switzerland, &c. ; and he declaims :
'Ladies and Gentlemen, depend upon it here is no deception. Observe the patients ranged behind me. On my
right, a Prussian Gentleman, who was much afflicted with a
complication of disorders, till I cured him by administering
a few leaden Boluses—next to him is an Austrian patient,
entirely reliev'd by my Austerlitz draught, next to him is a
Spaniard, whose case is rather doubtful—I won't say much
about it. The next is a Dutchman—he was a little crack'd,
but I have made him as lame as a frog—beyond him is an
old gentleman of the Popish persuasion, whom I cured
with one bottle of my Italian drops—there are many more
in the background, whom I have cured of various disorders,
or have now in my care—but, Ladies and Gentlemen, let
me particularly draw your attention to the great Russian
bear, once a very fierce animal, but dumb like the rest of
his species, but after taking a dose of my Friedland Pills,
and an application of the Tilsit powder, he is able to converse like a rational being ! ! !' Talleyrand, who is on the
stage, calls out : 'Ah, Master Bull, what, are you among
the crowd ? come now, you and your Sweedish Friend
had better step up into the Booth, and take a dose or
two of my Master's pills.' But John Bull surlily declines
the invitation with, 'We'll see you and your Master d—d
first.'

This of course refers to the meeting of Napoleon and
Alexander at Erfurt, where, besides, were collected the
Kings of Prussia, Saxony, Bavaria, Würtemberg, and

Westphalia, the Prince Primate, the Princes of Anhalt,
Coburg, Saxe Weimar, Darmstadt, Baden, Nassau, and
Mecklenburg.   The two great potentates rivalled each
other in their courtesies.   But solid business was also to
be done ; they did not meet simply to waste their time in
fêtes.   Napoleon engaged not to meddle with Alexander's
designs on Sweden and Turkey, and not to help the Poles.
Alexander, on his side, promised not to interfere in Spain,
and to recognise the Kings of Spain and Naples.   And
they wrote a joint letter to George the Third, proposing a
general peace, on the basis that each should keep what he
had. The English Government, however, asked that Spain
and Sweden should be parties ; but this, not suiting the
designs of the Imperial thieves, the negotiations came to
an end.

> Nap, with the Russian Emp'ror, now,
> Became quite free, we must allow ;
> At Erfurth, the appointed spot,
> They met together, as I wot,
> And German kings and princes, too,
> Were present at this interview ;
> Save Emp'ror Francis,[1] who, they say,
> Sent an apology that day.
> How many compliments were paid,
> How great the pomp that was display'd.
> Oh, nothing—nothing could be grander
> Than Bonaparte and Alexander !
> Alternately they dined together,
> And often rode out in fine weather ;
> To be so jovial, gay, and free,
> Suited Napoleon to a T.
> Thro' Alexander's mediation
> With England, a negociation
> Was set a going, for the end
> Of leaving Spain without a friend.
> The British monarch, ever wise,
> Refus'd t' abandon his allies,
> Still Spain by England was protected,
> And Boney's terms with scorn rejected.

An unknown artist (November 19, 1808) gives ' The
Progress of the Emperor Napoleon.'   At first he is repre-

[1] Of Austria.

sented as 'A Ragged Headed Corsican Peasant'; next,
'Studying mischief at the Royal Academy at Paris'; then
'An Humble Ensign in a Republican Corps requesting a
situation in the British Army'; afterwards, 'A determined
Atheistical Republican General, ordering his men to fire on
the Parisians vollies of grape shot.' He then changes to 'A
Turk at Grand Cairo'; afterwards he became 'A runaway
from Egypt'; then 'A devout Catholic,' and, finally, 'An
Emperor on a throne of iniquities': on which throne is in-
scribed, 'Murders—Duke d'Enghien, Prisoners at Jaffa,
Palm, Capt. Williams, Pichegru, Cahon, Toussaint, &c., &c.
Robberies innumerable.'

CHAPTER XLVII.

RETREAT TO CORUNNA—THE BROKEN BRIDGE OVER THE DANUBE—
WAGRAM—JOSEPHINE'S DIVORCE.

IN the year 1809 there are very few caricatures of Napoleon.
After the taking of Madrid, Sir John Moore thought it
prudent to retreat, which he did, and, after many difficulties,
reached Corunna. The repulse of the French there, although
at the cost of Sir John Moore's life, enabled the troops to
be embarked.

Napoleon had but little rest, for in March the Austrians
again took up arms against him, to which he replied by
victoriously marching to Vienna, which was bombarded
before it capitulated. One incident in this campaign was
seized upon by the caricaturist. There had been much
fighting about Aspern and Essling, with pretty equal fortune, until the destruction of a bridge, caused by a sudden
rise of the Danube, which brought down timber rafts, barges,
&c., deprived Napoleon of all the advantage he had gained,
and compelled him to retreat to the island of Lobau.

There is a caricature by Rowlandson (June 12, 1809) of
'Boney's Broken Bridge.' An aged general, cocked-hat in
hand, is thus addressing Napoleon : 'With all due deference
to your little Majesty—It was the Austrian Fire-boats that
destroyed the Bridge.' Napoleon, however, turns on him
savagely, and, pointing to the broken bridge, says, 'Ah!
who is it that dares contradict me, I say it was some floating

timber, and the high swell of the river that caused the Shocking Accident.' The Austrian army, on the opposite bank, are singing a paraphrase of ' London bridge is broken down ' :—

> Boney's Bridge is broken down,
> Dance over the Lady Lea—
> Boney's Bridge is broken down,
> By an Arch Duke—ee.[1]

Ansell gives his version of this event, shewing the Austrian Archduke, pickaxe in hand, having destroyed the bridge, and, pointing to some ducks and geese, he sings :—

> The Ducks and the Geese with ease swim over,
>   Fal de rol de rido, Fal de rol de rido
> The Ducks and the Geese with ease swim over,
>   Fal de rol de rido, Fal de rol de rido

But Napoleon, dancing with rage, on the other side, yells out, ' You Rascal you ! How dare you break down my Bridge, If I knew how to get over, this invincible arm should make you repent your rashness.' In the background an officer calls out to the army, ' Invincible Army go back, the bridge is broke down and we should not be able to run away.'

It was in this retreat that Lannes was killed— but it was avenged at Wagram, a battle that so crippled the Austrians that they had to ask an armistice, which afterwards led to a peace between the rival nations.

> It seems he wanted satisfaction,
> So Wagram was the scene of action.
> By some, however, 'tis believ'd,
> The Emp'ror Francis was deceiv'd,
> That Boney had, in his caprice,
> Made secret overtures for peace,
> And a connubial match propos'd
> With which the Cabinet had clos'd ;
> They having been assured, that by it
> They should be peaceable and quiet.
> And that great Bonaparte might seem
> A victor worthy of esteem,
> Unknown to Francis they acceded,
> To such a battle as he needed ;

[1] ' The Broken Bridge, or Boney outwitted by General Danube,' June 1809.

So that the battle of Wagram,
They say was nothing but a sham—
In other words,—tho' low, but certain,
' 'Twas all my eye and Betty Martin.'
But if a sham, as it is said,
The farce was admirably played,
For twenty thousand men each lost.
So that they acted to their cost ;
But, be 't a real one, or a mock,
They fought both days till six o'clock ;
Nap to the vict'ry laid claim,
And saved the credit of his name.
Hostilities began to cease,
It seems both parties thought of peace.

Sauler (August 1809) shews us ' The rising Sun, or a view of the Continent.' This rising sun is inscribed ' Spain and Portugal,' and gives great uneasiness to Napoleon, who says, ' The rising sun has set me upon thorns.' He is employed in rocking a cradle, in which peacefully reposes a Russian bear, muzzled with ' Boney's Promises.' Behind is Sweden, who brandishes his sword, calling to Russia to ' Awake thou Sluggard, ere the fatal blow is struck, and thou and thy execrable ally sink into eternal oblivion.' Holland is fast asleep, and leans against Napoleon. Poland is represented by a shadow, and Denmark wears a huge extinguisher on his head. Turkey is virtually dead, on the ground ; but Austria is springing into activity, exclaiming, ' Tyrant, I defy thee and thy Cursed Crew.' Prussia is depicted as a lunatic, with straws in his hair, wearing a strait-waistcoat, and, with a very vacuous expression of countenance, is singing, ' Fiddle diddle dee, Fiddle diddle dee, The Mouse has married the humble bee —and I am Emperor of the Moon.' Underneath are the following lines :—

Just as the Rising Sun dispels
The gloom of night to bless us with new day,
So genuine Patriotism expels
Vindictive Tyrants from despotic Sway.
Thus Spain, the source of patriotic worth
(A Rising Sun of Freedom to the Earth),
Invites the Captive Nations to forego
The Yoke and crush their sanguinary foe.

Why then, ye Nations, will ye not embrace
The proffer'd Freedom smiling in your face?
Why dilly-dally when to sink or rise
Rests with yourselves—dare ye contemn the prize—
Is Freedom nothing worth, that for her sake
Ye dare not e'en *one* gen'rous effort make?
Alas! infatuated Monarchs see,
What is, and what your Fate must *ever* be.
    Spain is a Sun arising to illume
The threefold horrors of your future doom,
While she on Freedom's golden wings shall tow'r,
The Arbitress of Continental pow'r.
    Russia's a Bear amid impending woes,
Rock'd by th' insidious Tyrant to repose.
    Sweden's a Warrior of distinguished worth,
Sweden hath giv'n to many heroes birth.
    Austria's a Phœnix rising renovated,
Whose genial warmth with Spain, incorporated,
Longer disdains to crouch at the fell shrines
Of Usurpation, and the foulest crimes.
    Prussia, poor *Prussia*, with straightjacket on,
And Crown of Straw, proves what delays have done.
    Denmark too, half extinguish'd, shows,
The fruits of leaguing with old England's foes.
    And *Holland*, drowsy *Holland*, dreams
Of aggrandizement, potent Kings and Queens.
    While *Poland*, a mere shadow in the rear
(As proof of something *once* existent there),
Yields to the Yoke, nor dares its shackles break,
Lest by so doing, she her *Freedom* stake.
    Poor silly mortals, will ye ever bow
To the dread Shrine of Tyranny and Woe;
Or by co-operation overwhelm
The Scourge of Nations, and resume the Helm?

One of the great events of this year, as regards Napoleon, was his divorce from Josephine. That he loved her, as far as he could love any woman, there is no doubt; but there were State reasons why he should have another consort. His ambition could not be satisfied till he had an heir male of his own. The dynasty he fondly hoped to found ought not to descend to any of his brothers, and none but his own son could have any hold upon the affection of the French nation.

Nap oftentimes began to swear
That he must get a son and heir—
He, with affected sorrow, told
His present lady was too old,
He might as well have her grandmother,
And therefore he must seek another;
Yes, seek another,—so of course,
He intimated a divorce—
That with propriety, like Harry
The Eighth, another he might marry.
This was enforc'd by his mamma,
And recommended by Murat.
Yet at this very time, good lack!
He had a violent attack,
A kind of stupor he was in,
Attended by his Josephine;
And, as a certain author says,
It lasted very near two days;
On his recovery, he cried,
'A son and heir I must provide;'
Then giving Josephine a look,
His head repeatedly he shook,
He said—(he could refrain no longer)—
'I wish, my dear, that you were younger,
But you are old, and I despair
Of ever getting now an heir.'
While this he said, with doleful phiz,
She told him that the fault was his;
For several children she'd before,
And hoped to have as many more.
Now Josephine display'd her spirit,
Of patriotism she made a merit:
'If,' she observ'd, 'our separation
Will be of service to the nation,
Then I agree, with all my heart,
My dearest Emperor—to part—
That you may seek another fair,
And, if you can, provide an heir.'
When kindly her consent she gave
Nap scarcely knew how to behave;
At Josephine awhile he star'd,
He humm'd a bit, and then declar'd,
For fifteen years to him she'd been
All that was lovely and serene,

X

And that no better for himself e'er
Wou'd wish, but for his country's welfare—
Of course, for a successor's sake,
The sacrifice he needs must make.
He found no fault, as it appears,
But that she was advanc'd in years ;
To follies past he ne'er alluded,
For no such sentiment intruded ;
'Twas not for this he wish'd to sever,
Her virtue he suspected never ;
On this occasion, Nap, 'tis said,
A fine speech to the Senate made,
Assuring them it was with pain,
He a divorce strove to obtain ;
For still he Josephine regarded,
Tho' as a consort now discarded ;
But, notwithstanding, she should reign
And be considered as a queen.
Josephine, with an air divine,
Declar'd the throne she would resign,
And hop'd her Boney might, ere long,
Meet with a lady fair and young,
And in nine months procure a boy,
To be his comfort and his joy.
   'Twas on the 15th of December,[1]
As the Parisians well remember,
The parties in full court appear'd
And by a large assembly cheer'd ;
A kind of form took place, of course,
Which fully strengthened the divorce—
The Senate sent a deputation,
To ratify the separation,
Which, that it might be ne'er repeal'd,
Was, in their presence, sign'd and seal'd.
Nap was a long time ere he sign'd—
A proof of a perturbed mind ;
But some have thought, and so they might,
'Twas inability to write.
Soon as the pen the lady took,
Her hand for several minutes shook,
A proof of sorrow and regret,
Tho' she did not appear to fret.

---

[1] The divorce took place on December 16.

And 'twas the opinion of the sage
That it proceeded from old age.
When thus divorc'd—a parting kiss
Was confirmation of their bliss.'

How Josephine herself felt on this subject is pathetically told by Madame Junot, with an excessively womanly
grace :—

'I had an interview with the Empress at Malmaison :
I went thither to breakfast by invitation, accompanied by
my eldest daughter Josephine, to whom she was much attached. . . . "And Madame Mère, have you seen her since
your return ?" "Certainly, Madame, I have already been in
waiting." Upon this, the Empress drew closer to me—she
was already very near—and, taking both my hands, said, in
a tone of grief which is still present to my mind after an
interval of four-and-twenty years : "Madame Junot, I entreat you to tell me all you have heard relating to me. I
ask it as an especial favour—you know they all desire to
ruin me, my Hortense, and my Eugène. Madame Junot,
I again entreat, as a favour, that you will tell me all you
know !"

'She spoke with the greatest anxiety ; her lips trembled,
and her hands were damp and cold. In point of fact she
was right, for there could be no more direct means of
knowing what was passing, relative to her, than by learning
what was said in the house of Madame Mère. But it was
indiscreet, perhaps, to ask these questions of me. In the
first place, I should not have repeated the most insignificant
sentence which I had heard in Madame's drawing-room ;
in the second, I was quite at ease upon the subject ; for,
since my return, I had not heard the word *divorce* uttered
by Madame, or the princesses. The strength of mind of
the unfortunate wife failed totally on hearing the dreadful
word pronounced ; she leant upon my arm and wept
bitterly. "Madame Junot," she said, "remember what I say
to you this day, here, in this hothouse—this place which is
now a paradise, but which may soon become a desert to me
—remember that this separation will be my death, and it
is they who have killed me ?"

'She sobbed. My little Josephine, running to her, pulled

X 2

her by the shawl to shew her some flowers she had plucked, for the Empress was so fond of her, as even to permit her to gather flowers in her greenhouse. She took her in her arms, and pressed her to her bosom, with an almost convulsive emotion. The child appeared frightened ; but, presently, raising her head, and shaking the forest of light silken curls which clustered round her face, she fixed her large blue eyes upon the agitated countenance of her godmother, and said : " I do not like you to cry." The Empress again embraced her tenderly, and setting her down, said to me : " You can have little idea how much I have suffered when any of you has brought a child to me ! Heaven knows, I am not envious, but in this one case I have felt as if a deadly poison were creeping through my veins, when I have looked upon the fresh and rosy cheek of a beautiful child, the joy of its mother, but, above all, the hope of its father ! And I ! struck with barrenness, shall be driven in disgrace from the bed of him who has given me a crown ! Yet God is witness that I love him more than my life, and much more than that throne, that crown, which he has given me ! "

'The Empress may have appeared more beautiful, but never more attractive, than at that moment. If Napoleon had seen her then, surely he could never have divorced her.'

We have a most touching account in 'Memes's Memoirs of the Empress Josephine :' ' The divorce was, unquestionably, a melancholy reverse of fortune for Josephine, which she felt most severely, but she bore it with magnanimity. The particulars of the interview between her and the Emperor are very affecting. When Napoleon mentioned the necessity of a Divorce, he approached Josephine, gazed on her for a while, and then pronounced the following words : " Josephine, my excellent Josephine, thou knowest if I have loved thee ! To thee, to thee alone do I owe the only moments of happiness which I have enjoyed in this world. Josephine ! my destiny overmasters my will. My dearest affections must be silent before the interests of France." " Say no more," she replied, " I was prepared for this ; but the blow is not less mortal ! "

'Josephine, on hearing from his own lips the determination of the Emperor, fainted, and was carried to her chamber. At length the fatal day arrived.

'On December 15, 1809, the Imperial Council of State was convened, and, for the first time, officially informed of the intended separation. On the morrow, the whole of the family assembled in the grand salon at the Tuileries. All were in Court costume. Napoleon's was the only countenance which betrayed emotion, but ill concealed by the drooping plumes of his hat of ceremony. He stood motionless as a statue, his arms crossed upon his breast: the members of his family were seated around, showing in their expression less of sympathy with so painful a scene, than of satisfaction, that one was to be removed, who had so long held influence, gently exerted as it had been, over their brother. In the centre of the apartment was placed an armchair, and, before it, a small table with a writing apparatus of gold. All eyes were directed to that spot, when a door opened, and Josephine, pale but calm, appeared, leaning on the arm of her daughter, whose fast falling tears shewed that she had not attained the resignation of her mother. Both were dressed in the simplest manner. Josephine's dress of white muslin exhibited not a single ornament. She moved slowly, and with wonted grace, to the seat provided for her, and there listened to the reading of the act of separation. Behind her chair stood Hortense, whose sobs were audible, and a little farther on, towards Napoleon, Eugène, trembling as if incapable of supporting himself. Josephine heard in composure the words that placed an eternal barrier between her and greatness, between her and the object of her affection. This painful duty over, the Empress appeared to acquire a degree of resolution from the very effort to resign with dignity the realities of title for ever. Pressing, for an instant, the handkerchief to her eyes, she rose, and, with a voice which, but for a slight tremor, might have been called firm, pronounced the oath of acceptance; then, sitting down, she took the pen from the hand of the Comte Regnault St. Jean d'Angely, and signed it. The mother and daughter now left the salon, followed by Eugène, who appeared to suffer most severely of the three.

'The sad incidents of the day had not yet been exhausted. Josephine had remained unseen, sorrowing in
her chamber, till Napoleon's usual hour of retiring to rest.
He had just placed himself in bed, silent and melancholy,
when suddenly the private door opened, and the Empress
appeared, her hair in disorder, and her face swollen with
weeping. Advancing with a tottering step, she stood, as if
irresolute, near the bed, clasped her hands, and burst into
an agony of tears. Delicacy seemed at first to have
arrested her progress, but, forgetting everything in the fulness of her grief, she threw herself on the bed, clasped her
husband's neck, and sobbed as if her heart would break.
Napoleon also wept while he endeavoured to console her,
and they remained a few minutes locked in each other's
arms, silently mingling their tears, until the Emperor,
perceiving Constant[1] in the room, dismissed him to the
ante-chamber.

'After an interview of about an hour, Josephine parted,
for ever, from the man whom she so long and so tenderly
loved. On seeing the Empress retire, which she did in
tears, the attendant entered to remove the lights, and found
the chamber silent as death, and Napoleon sunk among
the bed-clothes, so as to be invisible. Next morning he
still showed the marks of suffering. At eleven, Josephine
was to bid adieu to the Tuileries, never to enter the palace
more. The whole household assembled on the stairs, in
order to obtain a last look of a mistress whom they loved,
and who carried with her into exile the hearts of all who
had enjoyed the happiness of access to her presence.
Josephine was veiled from head to foot, and, entering a
close carriage with six horses, drove rapidly away, without
casting one look backward on the scene of past greatness
and departed happiness.'

The only drawback to Memes's narrative is, that it does
not exactly tally with the 'Register of the Conservative
Senate,' of Saturday, December 6, 1809, extracts from which
are given in the 'Times' of December 27, 1809. In that
document Napoleon makes a speech, a portion of which is
as follows :—

[1] His second valet.

'The politics of my monarchy, the interest, and the wants, of my people, which have constantly guided all my actions, require that, after me, I should leave to children, inheritors of my love for my people, that throne on which Providence has placed me. Notwithstanding, for several years past, I have lost the hope of having children by my well-beloyed consort, the Empress Josephine. This it is which induces me to sacrifice the sweetest affections of my heart ; to attend to nothing but the good of the State, and to wish the dissolution of my marriage.

'Arrived at the age of forty years, I may indulge the hope of living long enough to educate, in my views and sentiments, the children which it may please Providence to give me : God knows how much such a resolution has cost my heart ; but there is no sacrifice beyond my courage, that I will not make, when it is proved to me to be necessary to the welfare of France. I should add, that far from ever having had reason to complain, I have only had to be satisfied with the attachment and affection of my well-beloved consort. She has adorned fifteen years of my life, the remembrance of which will ever remain engraven on my heart. She was crowned by my hand. I wish she should preserve the rank and title of Empress ; but, above all, that she should never doubt my sentiments, and that she should ever regard me as her best and dearest friend.'

English opinion on this act of Napoleon's may be gathered from the 'Times' of December 28, which thus comments upon it :—

'While the affair of the dissolution of Buonaparte's marriage was transacting in the Senate, he retired to Trianon. The repudiated Josephine withdrew, at the same time, to Malmaison, probably never to behold him again ; or, at most, only for a few minutes, during a visit of cold ceremony. Whatever errors there might have been in the early conduct of this woman, were in a great measure redeemed by her behaviour during her slippery, and precarious, exaltation. She has often stepped in between the rage of the tyrant to whom she was united, and the victim he had marked for destruction, and by her tears, and entreaties, softened him into pity and pardon. Such instances of

feeling, and humanity, had wrought a powerful impression
in her favour among the inhabitants of Paris, amongst
whom, her unmerited disgrace has probably occasioned no
less grief than astonishment. The temporary seclusion to
which Buonaparte appears to have condemned himself,
may possibly be for the purpose of preventing any opportunity of an explosion of public sentiment on this subject.
We think, on the whole, that Josephine has been hardly
treated. The reasons assigned for her repudiation have
existed in equal force for many years ; and the act itself
might have been carried into effect, with less outrage to her
feelings, at a former period.'

CHAPTER XLVIII.

FAILURE OF EXPEDITIONS TO SPAIN, PORTUGAL, AND HOLLAND—NAPO-
LEON'S WOOING OF, AND MARRIAGE WITH, MARIA LOUISA—BIRTH
OF THE KING OF ROME—NAPOLEON IN THE NURSERY.

IN closing the record of this year, I cannot omit to mention the fact of the failures of the expeditions to Spain,
Portugal, and Holland. The latter, or Walcheren expedition, as it was called, was just returning in a woful plight,
fever having thoroughly done its work among the troops ;
and, in December, the City of London, through the Lord
Mayor, memorialised the King on the subject of this latter
expedition, and prayed 'your Majesty will direct enquiry to
be forthwith instituted, in order to ascertain the causes
which have occasioned it.'

'To which Address and Petition his Majesty was
graciously pleased to return the following answer :—

'" I thank you for your expressions of duty and attachment to me and to my Family.

'" The recent Expedition to the Scheldt was directed to
several objects of great importance in the interest of my
Allies, and to the security of my dominions.

'" I regret that, of these objects, a part only has been
accomplished. I have not judged it necessary to direct
any Military Inquiry into the conduct of my Commanders
by sea or land, in this conjoint service.

' " It will be for my Parliament, in their wisdom, to ask for such information, or to take such measures upon this subject as they shall judge most conducive to the public good." '

This was the Royal, or Ministerial, snubbing to those men who were then giving of their blood, and treasure, without stint, and without grumble.

The ' Times ' of December 21, 1809, is very wroth about it, and the sturdy citizens answered it by having a Common Hall on January 9, 1810, at which it was resolved that instructions be given to the representatives of the City, to move or support an address to his Majesty, praying an inquiry into the cause of the failures of the late expeditions to Spain, Portugal, and Holland ; they also voted a similar address themselves ; and asserted a right to deliver their addresses or petitions to the King upon his throne. But they got no redress.

The year 1810 is mostly noteworthy to the caricaturist by Napoleon's second marriage. On February 1, 1810, a grand council was called together to help the Emperor in selecting another empress. But Napoleon had not been wasting his time since his divorce from Josephine. He had sent to the Emperor Alexander, proposing to marry his sister, the Grand Duchess Anna Paulovna ; but the Russian Emperor, although he professed great friendship for Napoleon, hardly cared about a closer alliance with him, and the proposal was declined.

The Council, in their wisdom, thought of an Austrian princess, and a proposal was made to the Austrian ambassador for the hand of the Arch-Duchess Maria Louisa, the result of which should have been, if there is any truth in the old rhyme,

Happy's the wooing
That's not long a-doing,

the perfection of bliss to the principal parties concerned. It was all settled in four-and-twenty hours, and Berthier, as Napoleon's proxy, married Maria Louisa at Vienna on March 11, and, two days afterwards, she started on her journey to France.

We are indebted to Madame Junot for an insight into

her innocent and childlike character : ' At length the day
of departure arrived. The young Empress bade farewell
to all the members of her family, and then retired to her
apartment, where etiquette required that she should wait
till Berthier came to conduct her to her carriage. When
Berthier entered the cabinet, he found her bathed in tears.
With a voice choked with sobs, she apologised for appearing so childish : " But," says she, " my grief is excusable.
See how I am surrounded here by a thousand things that
are dear to me. These are my sister's drawings ; that
tapestry was wrought by my mother ; those paintings are
by my uncle Charles." In this manner she went through
the inventory of 'her cabinet, and there was scarcely a
thing, down to the carpet on the floor, which was not the
work of some beloved hand.

'There were her singing birds, her parrot, and, above all,
the object which she seemed to value most,.and most to
regret—a little dog. It was of course known at the Court
of Vienna how greatly the Emperor used to be annoyed
by Josephine's favourite pet dogs, with *Fortuné* at their
head. Therefore, Francis II., like a prudent father, took
care that his daughter should leave her pet dog at Vienna.
Yet it was a cruel separation, and the princess and her
favourite parted with a tender *duo* of complaint.'

But the surprises in store for her on her journey soon
made her forget her dog and parrot. She was met at
Braunau by Caroline Bonaparte, Queen of Naples, and
sister of the Emperor. At this place, on the frontier of
Austria and Bavaria (the latter of which was then part of
the French empire), a wooden building had been erected
for the use of the French and Austrian suites. Napoleon
could play many parts, and he played the *rôle* of devoted
lover to perfection. At Munich an officer met the new
Empress with a letter from her husband. At Strasburg a
page was waiting for her with another letter, some choice
flowers, and some pheasants shot by the imperial gun ;
and every morning brought a page with a letter, which the
young bride immediately answered.

Every detail of her progress had been settled with
rigid ceremonial, and at one place (Compiègne) it was

appointed that he was to meet her, when 'the Empress should prepare to kneel, and the Emperor should raise her, embrace, and seat her beside him.' But the imperial bridegroom was far too impatient for that. Accompanied by the King of Naples (Murat), he left the palace privately, and pushed on to the village of Courcelles, where he anxiously awaited her arrival. When the carriage stopped, he ran towards it, opened the door himself, and jumped in without any announcement, the bride being only advised of his advent a moment before by the startled exclamation of the Queen of Spain : 'It is the Emperor ! '

Two days afterwards they made their state entry into Paris, where Napoleon, from a balcony at the Tuileries, presented his young bride to the assembled multitude.

Once more to quote Madame Junot : ' On returning from the balcony, he said to her, " Well, Louise, I must give you some little reward for the happiness you have conferred on me," and, leading her into one of the narrow corridors of the palace, lighted only by one lamp, he hurried on with his beloved Empress, who exclaimed, " Where are we going ? "—" Come, Louise, are you afraid to follow me ? " replied the Emperor, who now pressed to his bosom, with much affectionate tenderness, his young bride.

' Suddenly they stopped at a closed door, within which they heard a dog that was endeavouring to escape from the apparent prison. The Emperor opened this private door, and desired Louise to enter. She found herself in a room magnificently lighted ; the glare of the lamps prevented her for some moments from distinguishing any object. Imagine her surprise when she found her favourite dog from Vienna was there to greet her ; the apartment was furnished with the same chairs, carpet, the paintings of her sisters, her birds —in short, every object was there, and placed in the same manner as she had left them on quitting her paternal roof.

' The Empress, in joy and gratitude, threw herself in Napoleon's arms, and the moment of a great victory would not have been to the conqueror of the world so sweet as this instant of ecstasy was to the infatuated heart of the adoring bridegroom. After a few minutes had been spent in examining the apartment, the Emperor opened a small door; he beckoned to Berthier, who entered. Napoleon then said, "Louise, it is to him you are indebted for this unexpected joy: I desire you will embrace him, as a just recompense." Berthier took the hand of the Empress; but the Emperor added, "No, no, you must kiss my old and faithful friend."'

The civil marriage was celebrated on April 1 at St. Cloud, and the religious marriage on the 2nd in the Chapel of the Louvre; Napoleon's uncle, Cardinal Fesch, officiating.

We have just read the real story of the wooing and home-coming; I will not spoil it by repeating the caricaturist's version, quoting only a few lines:—

> Louisa off for Paris set,
> And by her anxious swain was met.
> To see the lady, what a throng!
> The road with flow'rs they strew'd along.
>
> No sooner Nap beheld her charms
> Than round the maid he threw his arms,

FIRST INTERVIEW WITH MARIA LOUISA.

> And gave her a true lover's kiss,
> As prelude to his greater bliss.
>
> .   .   .   .   .
>
> Oh what rejoicings and what fêtes!
> What hurly-burly in the streets!
> The marriage, as it was advised,
> Now publicly was solemnized;

The first of April, as they say,
Was chosen for the happy day,
When children, in and out of school,
Are trying to make each a fool.

This year is so unproductive of Napoleonic caricatures, that I can only find one worth mentioning, and this is apropos of the marriage : it is called 'Three Weeks after Marriage, or the Great little Emperor playing at Bo-peep,' and is by Rowlandson (May 15, 1810). It shows the conjugal relations of Napoleon and his Empress, as they were supposed to be. She is in a violent rage, and, having knocked down Talleyrand, she hits him over the head with a sceptre ; he, meanwhile, making moan : 'Begar she will give us all de finishing stroke. I shall never rise again.' She has plucked off her crown, and is about to throw it at the Emperor, who dodges behind an armchair, calling out, 'Oh Tally, Tally, rise and rally.' She fiercely declaims, 'By the head of Jove, I hate him worse than Famine or Disease. Perish his Family ; let inveterate Hate commence between our Houses from this Moment, and, meeting, never let them bloodless part.' Somebody, probably one of the marshals, has got behind the curtains for safety, calling out, 'Marblue. Vat a *Crown Cracker* she be.'

At the time of the marriage the English newspapers were much taken up with Sir Francis Burdett, and consequently Napoleon's marriage did not receive the attention it otherwise might have claimed. In a notice of the religious ceremony, however, the 'Times' breaks out with a little bit of spite, 'The Imperial Ruffian, and his spouse, again knelt at the "*Ite, missa est.*"'

The only other great event during this year, connected with Napoleon, was the abdication of the crown of Holland by his brother Louis, and the absorption of his kingdom into the French empire.

The birth of the King of Rome (on March 20, 1811) at last gave Napoleon the hope of founding a dynasty. He was very anxious about the welfare of Maria Louisa, hardly bestowing a thought upon his son, until assured of her safety.

'As [1] soon as the King of Rome was born, the event

[1] *Memoirs of Madame Junot.*

was announced by telegraph to all the principal towns of the empire. At four o'clock the same afternoon, the marks of rejoicing in the provinces equalled those in Paris. The Emperor's couriers, pages, and officers, were despatched to the different foreign Courts, with intelligence of the happy event. The Senate of Italy, and the municipal bodies of Rome and Milan, had immediate notice of it. The different fortresses received orders to fire salutes ; the sea-ports were enlivened by the display of colours from the vessels ; and everywhere the people voluntarily illuminated their houses. Those who regard these popular demonstrations as expressions of the secret sentiments of a people might have remarked that in all the faubourgs, as well as the lowest and poorest quarters of Paris, the houses were illuminated to the very uttermost stories. A fête was got up on the occasion by the watermen of the Seine, which was prolonged until a late hour of the night. Much of all this was not ordered : it came spontaneously from the hearts of the people. That same people, who, for thirty-five years previously, had experienced so many emotions, had wept over so many reverses, and had rejoiced for so many victories, still showed, by their enthusiasm on this occasion, that they retained affections as warm and vivid as in the morning of their greatness.

'The King of Rome was baptized on the very day of his birth (March 20, 1811). The ceremony was performed, at nine in the evening, in the chapel of the Tuileries. The whole of the imperial family attended, and the Emperor witnessed the ceremony with the deepest emotion. Napoleon proceeded to the chapel, followed by the members of the household, those of the Empress, of Madame Mère, the princesses, his sisters, and of the kings, his brothers. He took his station under a canopy in the centre of the chapel, having before him a stool to kneel on. A socle of granite had been placed on a carpet of white velvet embroidered with gold bees, and on the socle stood a gold vase destined for the baptismal font. When the Emperor approached the font bearing the King of Rome in his arms, the most profound silence pervaded. It was a religious silence, unaccompanied by the parade which might have been expected on such an occasion. This stillness formed a striking contrast with the joyous acclamations of the people outside.'

The news was announced to the British public in the ' Times ' of March 25 ; and in the ' Morning Herald ' of March 26 is an amusing

IMPROMPTU

On the French General Victor's *Defeat before* Cadiz.

> His VICTOR *vanquish'd*, and his Eagle taken,
> BONEY will stay at home to save his bacon ;
> Sip Caudle with his wife, and for young *Nap*,
> Make with parental daddle, sugar'd pap ;
> Content to see the Nurs'ry colours fly,
> By holding out his bantling's clouts to dry.

Rowlandson caricatures the birth of the King of Rome (April 9, 1811) in ' Boney the Second, or the little Babboon created to devour French Monkies.' The young Napoleon, naked, with the exception of a cocked hat, but with the cloven hoofs, and tail, of a devil, is being presented on a cushion to his father by a very buxom nurse. The cushion rests on a cradle, on which is inscribed ' Devil's Darling.' Napoleon is looking after the nursery arrangements, and is cooking a caudle of ' French blood,' which is to be drunk out of a ' Bitter Cup.' He turns his face towards his little son, and exclaims : ' Rejoice O ye Frenchmen, the Fruits of my Labour has produced a little image of myself. I shall, for the love I owe to your country, instill in my Noble Offspring the same principles of Lying, Thieving, Treachery, Letchery, Murder, and all other foul deeds for which I am now worshipped and adored.' The Pope is on his knees pronouncing a benediction, which, however, is of rather doubtful character.

[1] The Owl shrieked at thy Birth, an evil Sight,
The Night Crow cry'd foreboding luckless time,
Dogs howl'd, and hideous Tempests shook down Trees,
The Raven rook'd her on the Chimney Top,
And Chattering Pies in dismal discord sung.

[1] Third part of King Henry VI., act v. scene 6.

Napoleon was very fond of his little boy, and the caricaturist represents him in the nursery, thus—

But in his babe he found relief,
This was a cure for all his grief,
For his delightful dulcet squall
Wou'd not allow a tear to fall.
What wondrous splendor was devised
When the dear Infant was baptized ;
For Emperors, Kings, Queens, and Dukes
Assembled with their smiling looks,
Bestowing their congratulations,
And making curious observations.
With curiosity they eyed
The King of Rome—the father's pride,
And some old gossips cried ' Oh la !
How he resembles his papa.'

Madame Junot gives some interesting details of Napoleon as a father :—' On my return to France, I found the Emperor much altered in appearance. His features had acquired a paternal character. What a beautiful child was the young King of Rome ! How lovely he appeared as he rode through the gardens of the Tuileries in his shell-shaped *calèche*, drawn by two young deer, which had been trained by Franconi, and which were given him by his aunt, the Queen of Naples. He resembled one of those figures of Cupid which have been discovered in the ruins of Herculaneum. One day I had been visiting the young King, the Emperor was also there, and he was playing with the child—as he always played with those he loved—that is to say, he was tormenting him. The Emperor had been riding, and held in his hand a whip, which attracted the child's notice. He stretched out his little hand, and when he seized the whip, burst into a fit of laughter, at the same time embracing his father. " Is he not a fine boy, Madame Junot ? " said the Emperor ; " you must confess that he is." I could say so without flattery, for he certainly was a lovely boy. " You were not at Paris," continued the Emperor, " when my son was born. It was on that day I learned how much the Parisians love me. . . . What did the army say on the birth of the child?" I told him the soldiers were enthusiastic during many days ; he had already heard so, but was happy to receive a confirmation of their joy. He then pinched his son's cheek and his nose ; the child cried. " Come, come, sir," said the Emperor, " do you suppose you are never to be thwarted, and do kings cry ? " . . . He used to take the King of Rome in his arms, and toss him up in the air. The child would then laugh, until the tears stood in his eyes. Sometimes the Emperor would take him before a looking-glass, and work his face into all sorts of grimaces ; and, if the child was frightened and shed tears, Napoleon would say : " What, Sire, do you cry ? A King, and cry ? Shame, Shame ! "

' The hours at which the young King was taken to the Emperor were not precisely fixed, nor could they be, but his visits were most frequently at the time of *d'jeûner.* On these occasions the Emperor would give the child a little claret, by dipping his finger in the glass, and making him suck it. Sometimes he would daub the young Prince's face with gravy. The child would laugh heartily at seeing his father as much a child as he was himself, and only loved him the more for it. Children invariably love those who play with them. I recollect that once when Napoleon had daubed the young King's face, the child was highly amused, and asked the Emperor to do the same to *Maman Quiou,* for so he called his governess, Madame de Montes-quiou.'

Rowlandson's idea of the royal infant is given in a caricature (published April 14, 1811) called, ' Nursing the Spawn of a Tyrant, or Frenchmen Sick of the Brood.' [1]

[1] See next page.

Y

Maria Louisa is aghast at her offspring, who, screaming, threatens her with a dagger. She thus pours out her woes : ' There's no condition sure, so curst as mine! Day and night to dandle such a dragon—the little angry cur snarls

NURSING THE SPAWN OF A TYRANT, OR FRENCHMEN SICK OF THE BROOD.

while it feeds ; see how the blood is settled in its scarecrow face ; what brutal mischief sits upon his brow. Rage and vengeance sparkle in his cheeks ; the very spawn and spit of its tyrant father. Nay, now I look again, he is the very picture of his grandfather, *the Devil*!' This must have been pleasant for Napoleon to hear, which he evidently does, as he is but partially concealed behind a curtain.

Some one (name unknown, August 20, 1811) has given us, ' The Deputeys apointed by the Legislative Body, doing Homage to the King of Rome in the Nursery at St. Cloud.' His *gouvernante*, Madame de Montesquiou, presents him to the Deputies, who kneel and kiss him, saying : ' Madam Governess—not one of us can behold without a most lively interest, that August Infant—on whom rest so many Destinies, and whose Age and Charming Qualities inspire the most tender sentiments in the French and surrounding Nations.' The lady replies : ' Monsieurs—I thank you for the polite and flattering encomiums you are pleased to bestow on me—I thank you in the name of the young prince, whose Charms are inexpressible, and regret that he cannot add his personal sentiments to those which I entertain, to the Legislative Body.' In another portion of the picture the foul linen of the precious child is being washed and hung to dry.

CHAPTER XLIX.

A NAVAL ENGAGEMENT—NAPOLEON'S TOUR IN GERMANY—DECLARATION OF WAR WITH RUSSIA—ENTRY INTO WILNA—SMOLENSKO—BORODINO —ENTRY INTO MOSCOW—BURNING OF THE CITY—NAPOLEON'S RETREAT.

THE next caricature requires some little explanation. We find in the ' Courier ' of September 20, 1811, the following paragraph :—' Dover, September 19. Early this morning we heard a heavy firing on the opposite shore ; it continued at times all the morning, and was very hot about one o'clock ; the wind is to the southward, and eastward, which makes us hear very plain ; no news has arrived as to the cause ; by some it is conjectured that Buonaparte is at Boulogne, and by others, that the flotilla is out, and some of our cruisers firing at them. It still continues, though not so heavy as in the early part of the day.'

Details did not arrive till the 22nd, and then the ' Courier ' published an account of the naval engagement off Boulogne, on which the caricature is evidently grounded:

' The cause of the incessant firing on the French Coast, is now ascertained to be an engagement between the *Naiad*, 3 sloops, and a cutter, and 7 large French praams, each as large as a frigate, 11 gun brigs, and other small craft, 27 in all. The following letter gives an account of the engagement :—We took the Port Admiral in his praam, but afterwards ran off—However we took another, and brought her away—Buonaparte saw the engagement—he was in a boat with Marshall Ney.'

All accounts, though they do not agree in the number of French vessels engaged, are singularly unanimous as to the presence of Napoleon and Ney.

' The first glorious exploit of the Invincible Flotilla. Devils among the Flats, or Boney getting into Hot Water ' (unknown artist, September 20, 1811), represents one of the Flotilla returning much damaged, and full of corpses, only the captain and a steersman alive on board. Napoleon, who is in another boat, is in a fearful rage, tries to get at him, and is restrained by one of his marshals (Ney)—who remarks, ' Ma foi, take care, your Majesty will be in hot water up to the chin '—from throwing himself into the boiling water. ' You scoundrel,' says he, ' how dare you run away when you were 27 to 5. I'll order the guns of the batteries to sink every one of you.' But the captain excuses himself, ' Eh bien, mais, mon Empereur, you tell us de Jack Anglais be men, mais, by Gar, we find dem Devils.' To which a man in Napoleon's boat replies, ' Very true Monsieur Ney, de devils Jack Bulls make hot water all over de Vorld.' The spirit of Nelson appears, like a comet in the sky, darting lightning at the Flotilla.

The year 1812 was not fruitful in caricature of Napoleon. In May, accompanied by Maria Louisa, he visited the eastern part of France, met the King and Queen of Saxony at Freyburg, and entered Dresden in state. There he met the Emperor and Empress of Austria, the King of Prussia, and the Kings of Saxony, Naples, Würtemberg, Westphalia, and Bavaria, besides a heap of smaller potentates. The Emperor of Russia was not present ; he had concluded an alliance with Sweden against France, an alliance which was afterwards, during this year, joined by Great

Britain. In June, Napoleon visited Dantzig, and left it on the 11th. As a final measure, Count Lauriston was sent to Alexander, to see if the difference could be patched up, but the breach was made inevitable by the refusal of that monarch, or his ministers, to see him.

This decided Napoleon, and, from his head-quarters at Wilkowisky, he issued the following proclamation: 'Soldiers! the second war of Poland has commenced. The first was terminated at Friedland and Tilsit. At Tilsit, Russia swore eternal alliance with France, and war against England. She has openly violated her oath; and refuses to render any explanation of her strange conduct, till the French eagles shall have repassed the Rhine, and, consequently, left their Allies at her discretion. Russia is impelled onward by fatality. Her destiny is about to be accomplished. Does she believe that we have degenerated? that we are no longer the soldiers of Austerlitz? She has placed us between dishonour and war: the choice cannot for a moment be doubtful. Let us march forward then, and, crossing the Niemen, carry the war into her territories! The second war of Poland will be to the French arms as glorious as the first; but our next peace must carry with it its own guarantee, and put an end to that arrogant influence which, for the last fifty years, Russia has exercised over the affairs of Europe.'

In No. 1 of a series of caricatures on the Russian campaign, published in April 1813, and seemingly by G. Cruikshank, is represented, 'The Parting of Hector-Nap, and Andromache, or Russia threatened.' Napoleon's horse is waiting for him, the windows are crowded with ladies to see the departure. Napoleon is ecstatic at the sight of his little son, who is held aloft by Maria Louisa. The young King of Rome flourishes a sword, and says, ' I will kill the people, as my Papa does.' His mother wishes him to ' Kiss him, then, my dear! and he will bring you some of the naughty Russians to kill.' Napoleon bids ' Farewell! I go, I'll see, I'll conquer. On my return I'll greet our Son with a new Title.

> That's right, my boy, cause war to rage
> And rise the Tyrant of a future age.'

Napoleon started on this disastrous campaign, which was the prelude to his downfall, with an army of about four hundred and twenty thousand men, most of them doomed to perish in the snows of Russia. The river Niemen was crossed, and, on June 28, Napoleon made his public entry into Wilna, which had not long since, and very hurriedly, been evacuated by the Emperor Alexander.

But even the commencement of this campaign was marked by disaster. Napoleon had arranged all the details ; but the incompetence, or worse, of his subordinates failed to carry them out. After the Niemen had been crossed, not a third of the provisions necessary for the army had arrived, and at Wilna it was found that some hundreds of men had perished from want and fatigue. The mortality was worse among the horses, having lost about ten thousand. Before a battle was fought, and scarcely a month from the commencement of the campaign, there were twenty-five thousand sick men in the hospitals at Wilna.

Napoleon waited a fortnight at Wilna ; but the Russians were driven back from Ostrovno, by Murat, and more time was consumed at Witepsk. Then came the attack on Smolensko, on August 16 and 17, when the French lost 15,000, and the Russians 10,000 men, and the Russians still kept the city. But next day, when the French again advanced against it, they found it deserted. For this the Russian general, Barclay de Tolly, was deprived of his command, forasmuch as he had given up a holy city to the enemy without fighting a pitched battle for its preservation.

But, to proceed somewhat chronologically, we must remember that, on July 22, Wellington gained a great victory at Salamanca, where the French lost eleven pieces of cannon, two eagles, and six colours, one general, 136 other officers, and 7,000 prisoners. The general public did not know this news till the 4th of August, and the illuminations in its honour did not take place till the 17th, 18th, and 19th of August. It is to this event, doubtless, that the following refers.

In September 1812 was published a caricature of ' British Welcome or a Visit from the Bantam to the Lion.

> Though Bantam Boney claps his wings,
>   Yet this we may rely on :
> He'll turn his tail and run away
>   Whene'er he meets the Lion.'

And that is precisely as he is represented in the caricature. The pursuing lion says, 'So, my little Bantam, you
are come to pay me a visit—Well lets have a shake of
your claw.' But the bantam, with a very terrified expression of countenance, declines : 'Excusé moi, Mons' le
Lion, you gripe too hard.'

The battle of Borodino (or, as the French call it, Moskowa) was fought on September 7, and was, probably, the
bloodiest of all Napoleon's battles, but it laid Moscow
open to the conqueror.

> But soon the cloudless sun was gone,
> And a thick fog arose thereon—
> Nap prais'd the fog—indeed he did,
> Because his movements would be hid—
> And to the army, in array,
> This was the order of the day—
> 'Brave soldiers ! fight for endless glory,
> The wish'd-for field now lies before ye,
> You'll with abundance be supplied,
> Good winter quarters, too, beside—
> A quick return home—that is more ;
> Then fight, my lads, as heretofore ;
> Posterity will say—*There's one*
> *Who was at Moscow when 'twas won.*'
> The French and Russians now engaged,
> And furiously the battle raged ;
> In great confusion, and dismay,
> Poor Boney's scatter'd troops gave way ;
> Our hero his assaults repeated,
> And still the wounded French retreated.
> 'This battle,' Nap exclaim'd, 'has been,
> The greatest that was ever seen.'
> And true enough, our hero said,
> For eighty thousand men lay dead.

The French entered Moscow on September 14, a day
that Napoleon must have bitterly rued. I do not think
the burning of this city could be better told than by
Napoleon's own words [1] : 'Had it not been for that fire at

[1] *Napoleon in Exile*, by B. O'Meara.

Moscow, I should have succeeded. I would have wintered there. There were in that city about forty thousand citizens, who were, in a manner, slaves. For you must know that the Russian nobility keep their vassals in a sort of slavery. I would have proclaimed liberty to all the slaves in Russia, and abolished vassalage and nobility. This would have procured me the union of an immense and powerful party. I would either have made a peace at Moscow, or else I would have marched the next year to Petersburg.

' Alexander was assured of it, and sent his diamonds, valuables, and ships to England. Had it not been for that fire, I should have succeeded in everything. I beat them, two days before, in a great action at Moskowa ; I attacked the Russian army of two hundred and fifty thousand strong, entrenched up to their necks, with ninety thousand, and totally defeated them. Seventy thousand Russians lay upon the field. They had the impudence to say that they had gained the battle, though two days after, I marched into Moscow. I was in the midst of a fine city, provisioned for a year, for in Russia they always lay in provisions for several months before the frost sets in. Stores of all kinds were in plenty. The houses of the inhabitants were well provided, and many had left their servants to attend upon us. In most of them there was a note left by the proprietor, begging the French officers who took possession to take care of their furniture and other things : that they had left every article necessary for our wants, and hoped to return in a few days, when the Emperor Alexander had accommodated matters, at which time they would be happy to see us. Many ladies re-mained behind. They knew that I had been in Berlin and Vienna with my armies, and that no injury had been done to the inhabitants ; and, moreover, they expected a speedy peace. We were in hopes of enjoying ourselves in winter quarters, with every prospect of success in the spring. Two days after our arrival, a fire was dis-covered, which, at first, was not supposed to be alarming, but to have been caused by the soldiers kindling their fires too near the houses, which were chiefly of wood. I was angry at this, and issued very strict orders on the subject to the commandants of regiments and others.

'The next day it had advanced, but still not so as to give serious alarm. However, afraid that it might gain upon us, I went out on horseback, and gave every direction to extinguish it. The next morning a violent wind arose, and the fire spread with the greatest rapidity. Some hundred miscreants, hired for that purpose, dispersed themselves in different parts of the town, and, with matches, which they concealed under their cloaks, set fire to as many houses to windward as they could, which was easily done, in consequence of the combustible materials of which they were built. This, together with the violence of the wind, rendered every effort to extinguish the fire ineffectual. I, myself, narrowly escaped with life. In order to shew an example, I ventured into the midst of the flames, and had my hair and eyebrows singed, and my clothes burnt off my back; but it was in vain, as they had destroyed most of the pumps, of which there were above a thousand; out of all these, I believe that we could only find one that was serviceable. Besides, the wretches that had been hired by Rostopchin ran about in every quarter, disseminating fire with their matches, in which they were but too much assisted by the wind.

'This terrible conflagration ruined everything. I was prepared for everything but this. It was unforeseen, for who would have thought that a nation would have set its capital on fire? The inhabitants themselves did all they could to extinguish it, and several of them perished in their endeavours. They also brought before us numbers of the incendiaries, with their matches, as among such a *popolazzo* we never could have discovered them ourselves. I caused about two hundred of these wretches to be shot.

'Had it not been for this fatal fire, I had everything my army wanted: excellent winter quarters; stores of all kinds were in plenty; and the next year would have decided it. Alexander would have made peace, or I would have been in Petersburg.' I asked if he thought that he could entirely subdue Russia. 'No,' replied Napoleon;

'but I would have caused Russia to make such a peace as suited the interests of France. I was five days too late in quitting Moscow. Several of the generals were burnt out of their beds. I, myself, remained in the Kremlin until surrounded by flames. The fire advanced, seized the Chinese and India warehouses, and several stores of oil and spirits, which burst forth in flames, and overwhelmed everything.

'I then retired to a country-house of the Emperor Alexander's, distant about a league from Moscow, and you may figure to yourself the intensity of the fire, when I tell you that you could scarcely bear your hands upon the walls or windows on the side next to Moscow, in consequence of their heated state.

' It was the spectacle of a sea and billows of fire, a sky and clouds of flame ; mountains of red rolling flames, like immense waves of the sea, alternately bursting forth, and elevating themselves to skies of fire, and then sinking into the ocean of flame below. Oh ! it was the most grand, the most sublime, and the most terrific sight the world ever beheld.'

Napoleon, however, returned to the Kremlin on September 20, and, the main portion of the building being uninjured, a theatre was improvised therein. Early in October, he stated his determination to march on St. Petersburg, but never acted on it. Instead, he entered into negotiations for peace. Snow began to fall on October 13, a portent of an early winter, and winter quarters must be found. Events, however, did not march as he would have had them. On the 18th the Russians, under Beningsen, attacked and defeated Murat, and on the 19th Napoleon left Moscow, and the famous flight from thence began. Of the horrors of that flight, it is hardly the province of this work to dilate upon—mine is more to chronicle the feeling in England with regard to the events then passing. It may be said that it was bad taste to caricature such an appalling disaster—but when did a question of taste deter a satirist or caricaturist ? Take, as an instance, an event which many of us well remember, the death of the Emperor Nicholas of Russia in 1855. That solemn event

might well have been passed by, but it was food to the
caricaturist, and he made money out of it. See 'Punch'
of March 10, 1855, and note the ghastly cartoon of
'General Février turned Traitor. "*Russia has Two Generals in whom she can confide—Generals Janvier and
Février.*" Speech of the late Emperor of Russia.'

'Jack Frost attacking Boney in Russia' was published
in November 1812. A fearful-looking monster, mounted on
a northern bear, pursues Bonaparte (who flees), pelting him

all the way with
huge snowballs.
Napoleon is on
skates, and holds
his poor frost-
bitten nose, cry-
ing out, 'By gar,
Monsieur Frost
this is a much
colder Reception
than I expected.
I never experi-
enced such a
pelting before—
I find I must take
care of my nose,
as well as my
toes. Pray for-
give me this time,
and I swear by
St Dennis never
to enter your
dominion again.'
Jack Frost makes
answer, 'What,
Master Boney!
have I caught
you at last. I'll

GENERAL FROST SHAVEING LITTLE BONEY.

teach you Russian fare. Take that, and that, as a relish
and digest it.'

'General Frost shaveing Little Boney' (December 1,

1812) is very grim in its humour.   Bonaparte begs, but in
vain, for pity : ' Pray Brother General, have Mercy.   Don't
overwhelm me with your hoary element.   You have so
nipped me, that my very teeth chatter.   O dear—I am
quite chop fallen.'   But the unrelenting and unpitying
Frost replies, ' Invade my Country, indeed ! I'll shave,
freeze, and bury you in snow, you little Monkey.'

' Polish Diet with French Desert ' is the title of a caricature published December 8, 1812.   It represents Bonaparte spitted, and being roasted before an enormous fire,
on which is being cooked a frying-pan full of frogs, which,
however, jump out of it into the fire.   A Westphalian bear
is turning the spit and jeering at the poor victim.   ' How
do you like *Benningsen baisting*, Master Boney ? and your
Frogs?'   This ' Benningsen baisting' is being very liberally
supplied to Boney by a gigantic Russian, who holds a
huge ladleful of it in one hand, whilst with the other he
grasps a red-hot poker of Russian iron.   This ferocious
Cossack says, ' I'll Roast—Beast (baste)— Dish—& Devour
you !   He smoaks Brother Bruin—another turn and he is
done.'   Poor Napoleon, in his agony, calls out, ' Our situation may be fun to you, Mr. Bear—but Death to us.'

The following shows the estimation in which Bonaparte's bulletins were held by the English.

In December 1812 G. Cruikshank gave his idea of
' Boney hatching a Bulletin, or Snug Winter Quarters.'
With the exception of one Frenchman, who wears pieces

RETREAT FROM MOSCOW.

of board for snow-
shoes, and who
exclaims, ' By Gar,
he is almost lost !! '
Boney and all his
army are up to
their necks in
snow.   A general
asks him, ' Vat de
devil shall ve say in de Bulletin ? '   Boney replies, ' Say !!!!
why say we have got into comfortable Winter Quarters, and
that the weather is very fine, and will last 8 days longer.
Say we have got plenty of Soup Maigre, plenty of Minced

Meat—Grill'd Bears fine eating—driving *Cut-us-off* to the Devil. Say we shall be at home at Xmas to dinner—give my love to darling—dont let John Bull know that I have been Cow poxed—tell a good lie about the Cossacks. D—n it, tell anything but the truth.'

There was another version of 'The Valley of the Shadow of Death,' published December 18, 1812, but it is not so good as that by Gillray already given (September 24, 1808) :—

> By conflagrations always harass'd,
> No man was ever so embarrass'd ;
> He sought in vain a lurking place,
> Destruction star'd him in the face ;
> Hemm'd in—he sought for peace in vain—
> No peace could Bonaparte obtain ;
> He swore, when peace he could not get,
> The Russians were a barb'rous set.
> Intending now to change his rout,
> He sent Murat on the look out ;
> Murat, tho', met with a defeat,
> Which play'd the deuce with Nap's retreat.
> How great was Bonaparte's despair !
> He raved, he swore, he tore his hair—
> His troops were absolutely frozen,
> No man was sure he had his nose on.
> The Cossacks, too, made rude attacks,
> And laid some hundreds on their backs ;
> So, in the midst of an affray,
> Nap thought it best to run away.

According to the caricaturist, during the retreat Napoleon was nearly caught by Cossacks, and only saved by jumping out of window ; but as the same story is told of him during his retreat from Leipsic, they may as well be combined, and the reader will thus be enabled to apply it to whichever event he prefers :—

> He chang'd his dress—his horse bestrode,
> And in full speed to Wilna rode ;
> As soon as he began to fly,
> The Russians rais'd a *hue and cry*
> A great reward, as it is said,
> Was offer'd for our hero's head,

That some to take him might be bribed,
Thus Boney's person was described—
His figure rather short and thin—
Black hair—black beard—projecting chin—
Nose aquiline, with marks of snuff,
Arch'd eyebrows—manners very rough—
Stern countenance, dress'd rather mean,
And in a grey surtout oft seen.
But, notwithstanding his dismay,
Poor Bonaparte got safe away.
When he to Wilna's borders came,
He very wisely changed his name :
And in a sledge—'twas so contriv'd,
At Paris in the night arriv'd.

'Nap nearly nab'd or a retreating jump just in time.
Never did trusty squire with knight, Or knight with squire,
e'er jump more right—Vide Boney's Russian Campaign,'
was published in June 1813.   It shows the Cossacks

BONAPARTE'S ESCAPE FROM COSSACKS.

arriving, and Napoleon jumping out of window, to the
great detriment of the flower-pots, pigs, and poultry.   A
general inside the house calls out, 'Vite, Courez, mon
Empereur, ce Diable de Cossack dey spoil our dinner !!!'

He by the Cossacks was pursued,
But luckily a dwelling view'd—
And, while his legions bravely fought,
Protection in this house he sought ;

The guards, who had the place surrounded,
Were cut to pieces, kill'd and wounded.
Nap pricked his ears up at the rout,
He op'd the window and jump'd out—
Jump'd out ! how great, then, was his dread,
Fell he upon his feet—or head ?
No—not his feet—because he *sat*—
He could not fall like a Tom cat—
Nor would he break his pretty nose,
And so—another part he chose—
'Tis true—his bum was very sore,
His breeches, here and there, he tore ;
But such a trifle little matters,
A Man can run altho' in tatters—
So oft was Boney sore afraid
That he a pris'ner might be made ;
But, as the man would fain his cracks hide,
He tuck'd his skirts about his backside.

There is another caricature of Napoleon's escape from the Cossacks, by G. Cruikshank, published some time in 1813, entitled 'The Narrow escape, or Boney's Grand Leap *à la Grimaldi*!! No sooner had Napoleon alighted & entered a miserable house for refreshment, than a party of Cossacks rushed in after him. Never was Miss Platoff so near Matrimony!!! Had not the Emperor been very alert at Vaulting, and leapt through the Window, with the nimbleness of an Harlequin, while his faithful followers were fighting for his life, there would, probably, have been an end at once to that Grand Bubble, the French Empire.' There is nothing particular about this picture ; it is the same as the others—the same Cossacks, and the same episode of the leap.

CHAPTER L.

REJOICINGS IN ENGLAND OVER THE RESULT OF NAPOLEON'S RUSSIAN CAMPAIGN—THE EMPEROR'S RETURN TO FRANCE.

ONE of the last caricatures of this year is a very elaborate picture—'The Arms and Supporters of Napoleon Bonaparte the self created Emperor, alias the Corsican, and now the Curse of Europe.' It was published December

1812, but the artist is unknown, which is a pity, as the execution is very good. The animus that inspired it will be seen in the following Explanation, which accompanies it:—

The Crest represents the World, which, England and Sweden excepted, is set on fire everywhere by the incendiary Corsican ; his bloody actions and designs are expressed by the bloody hand and dagger reaching towards Spain. Tyranny, Hypocrisy, Barbarity and Villany are his standards, which are distinguishable through the smoke, and the fire, and have nearly enveloped the whole Globe.

His supporters are The French Devil, and the Corsican Devil.

The French Devil, or *le diable boiteux*, formerly a Nobleman and a priest : any body may easily guess that he, and Talleyrand, are one and the same creature : by the hour glass he indicates, however, that time is running away, and that Boney's downfall is fast approaching. The Gallic cock destroying religion is his emblem.

The Corsican Devil, who, being intoxicated with unbounded ambition, wears an Iron crown ornamented with thorns : he cuts down the cap of liberty, because tyranny is his idol. The Serpent and the hyena are very proper emblems of his infamous character and conduct.

Description of the Arms divided into Eight Quarters.

1. The Mushroom on a dunghill denotes his descent, or origin of family. The Crocodile expresses his treacherous transactions in Egypt, his apostacy, and his cowardly desertion from his army. The bloody hand, the guillotine, and the black heart, can only belong to such a monster.

2. Represents the shooting of 800 defenceless Turkish prisoners, near the town of Jaffa, ordered very coolly by the monster Boney.

3. Shews the poisoning his own sick soldiers in the hospital at Jaffa, by his express orders.

4. Exhibits a scene never known before in the Civilized World. The foul murder (for it cannot be called anything else, though Boney excuses it by his mock Court Martial) of the Duke d'Enghien.

5. Here the monster compels the Pope to come to Paris, and to assist at a blasphemous coronation, where Boney stands upon no ceremony with the Holy Father. Boney puts on the iron crown himself with one hand, whilst the other hand is employed in robbing the Catholic Church of its head.

6. Exhibits another shocking scene ; the truly English patriot, Captain Wright, is put to death, because he will not be a traitor to his king and country.

7. Here we behold the massacre of the defenceless citizens of Madrid, on the 2nd of May, 1808.

8. Represents the imprisonment of King Ferdinand the 7th because he will not renounce the Crown of Spain, nor marry Boney's niece.

The Motto is taken from Proverbs, chapter xxviii. verse 15—' As a roaring lion, and a ranging bear, so is a wicked ruler over the poor people.'

On December 16 of this year was published an 'Extra-ordinary Gazette' which perfectly electrified this country. It contained detailed reports of the successes over the French—news which filled every English heart with joy.

The 'Times' of December 17 says :—'We hardly know the terms in which we are to address the people of this and every other European country, on the subject of the *Extraordinary Gazette* contained in this day's paper. It does more than confirm our hopes—it does more than justify the ardent expressions of triumph, in which we indulged yesterday. And really, in speaking of the successes of the Russians, we are obliged to abate the excess of our joy. Not from any doubt of their magnitude, or reality, for upon these our countrymen may rely ; but from mere apprehension, lest the vicissitude of human affairs, which does not usually suffer mankind to exult beyond measure upon any occasion whatever, should, by we know not what unexpected reverse, abate somewhat of the transcendent felicity which is promised the world, by the overthrow, and disgrace, of its most detested and detestable tyrant. We shall only say, therefore, in so many words, that Buonaparte is wholly defeated in Russia ; he is conquered, and a fugitive. And what can we say more ? We have seen his army pass from victory to victory ; we have seen it overthrow kingdoms, and subjugate realms,—insult sovereigns, and oppress peasants—violate every human right, and diffuse every species of human misery. And now where is it ? Where shall we look for

z

it ? " A wide and capable destruction hath swallowed it up." In this awful event we rather admire in humility the dispensations of Providence, than exult with pride over the fall of a haughty foe ; it is hardly to be viewed as an occurrence between man and man, or between nation and nation ; but as a divine judgment upon the earth.'

To give an idea of the state of tension at which men's minds then were held, I may be pardoned if I give the following extract[1] : ' He [Professor Sedgwick] gave a curious account of Commemoration Day, on December 16, 1812. He was then a Fellow, and, on that day, not feeling well, had not been drinking his port wine so freely in the Combination Room, as it was, in those days, the custom of the Fellows to do. A man, he said, who did not then drink pretty hard, was considered a milksop. Leaving the other Fellows over their wine, he went to the gate, where the porter gave him a Newspaper, on opening which, he found the official announcement by Napoleon of the destruction of his grand army (*sic*). With this news he returned to the Combination Room, and there read the tidings, to the intense joy and excitement of all present. *Old and young,* he said, *wept like children.'* [2]

The Russians estimated the French losses by capture from their first invasion of Russia to December 26, 1812, at 41 generals, 1,298 inferior officers, 167,510 non-commissioned officers and privates, and 1,131 pieces of cannon.

Buturlin estimated the total loss sustained by the French in the Russian campaign at ' Slain in battle, one hundred and twenty-five thousand ; died from fatigue, hunger, and cold, one hundred and thirty-two thousand ; prisoners (comprehending forty-eight generals, three thousand officers, and upwards of one hundred and ninety thousand men), one hundred and ninety-three thousand ; total, four hundred and fifty thousand,' and this takes no count of the thousands of non-combatants who perished.

The destruction of his army, his crushing defeat, and

[1] *My Reminiscences,* by Lord Ronald Gower, vol. i. p. 209, ed. 1883.
[2] The italics are mine.—J. A.

Mallet's conspiracy, all determined Napoleon to return to France, and he reached Paris about half-past eleven at night on December 18. How different from his hitherto triumphal entries! Maria Louisa had retired to rest, and was woke by the cries of her attendants, who were frightened at the sight of a man muffled up in furs, not knowing he was their august master. And thus he slunk home!

In June 1813 was published 'Naps glorious return or the conclusion of the Russian Campaign.

> A few Usurpers to the Shades descend.
> By a dry death, or with a quiet end.'

In this plate we see Maria Louisa preparing to go to bed Madame Letitia, Napoleon's mother, pulling off her stockings. The old lady cries out, 'Ah, de Ghost!! de Ghost of mon Nap.' The Empress is frightened, and exclaims, 'Jesu Maria, what is this so woe begone? It cannot be my husband, he promised to return in triumph, it must be his Ghost.' Even his little boy, the King of Rome, doubts his identity. He is getting ready for bed, and already has his nightcap on, but he runs away in fright, crying, 'That ain't my Papa!! he said he would bring me some Russians to cut up. I think they have cut him up.' Whilst Bonaparte, who enters in a most dilapidated condition, with his toes coming through his boots, his sword and scabbard broken, and his face besmeared with dirt, calls out dolefully, 'Me voici! your poor Nap escape from de Cossack —by gar, I jump out of de window for my life, and I now jump into bed vid my wife.' The ladies-in-waiting have fainted, and one, having left the warming-pan in the bed, has set it on fire, and it is burning brightly.

On January 1, 1813, was published another caricature of the retreat from Moscow: 'Boney returning from Russia covered with Glory, leaving his Army in *Comfortable* Winter Quarters.

> Nap and Joe, from France would go
> To fill the world with slaughter,
> Joe fell down, and broke his crown,
> And Nap came tumbling after.'

Napoleon, with one of his generals, is in full retreat, in a sledge, leaving his army pursued by the Russians, and the ground strewn with dead men and horses. The general asks, 'Will your Majesty write the Bulletin?' 'No,' answers Napoleon, 'you write,it! tell them we have left the Army all well, quite gay, in excellent Quarters, plenty of provisions—that we travelled in great Style—received everywhere with congratulations, and that I have almost compleated the *repose of Europe.*'

George Cruikshank (February 22, 1813) produced, after a picture by David, a most laughable caricature, called 'The Hero's Return.

> Dishonest, with lopp'd arms, the man appears,
> Spoil'd of his nose, and shorten'd of his ears.
> She scarcely knew him, striving to disown
> His blotted form, and blushing to be known.'
>
> Dryden's *Virgil*, Book 6.

Poor Napoleon, in very evil case, *sans* nose, ears, fingers, and toes, is borne in, supported by two Mamelukes, and riding on the back of another, who is on all fours. The Empress is tearing her hair, and weeping violently, whilst a maid-of-honour is holding a smelling-bottle to her nose. Another lady-in-waiting has seized the King of Rome, who is yelling with fright at the sight his father presents. His very dog barks at him, and universal consternation prevails. The Oriental on the floor holds a glass bottle containing Napoleon's nose ; whilst three others in the rear bear respectively bottles which hold the Emperor's fingers, toes and ears.

After the return of Napoleon from Moscow, the following *jeu d'esprit* was published :—

> When Emperor Nap to France returned,
>   He much admired his boy ;
> The nurse, whose anxious bosom burned
>   T' increase the father's joy,
>
> 'How much he talks ! how much he's grown !'
>   Would every moment cry ;
> ' Besides he has learnt to run alone.'
>   Says Boney, 'So have I.'

Here is another :—

NAPOLEON A RUNAWAY FROM HIS ARMY.

'A new Achilles, I,' spake Gaul's stern chief,
Nor spake a lie—albeit he *were* a thief ;
For, like Achilles, to the untimely grave
Hosts he had hurled, the bravest of the brave ;
Insate of wrath, stiffnecked, implacable,
Wrecker of towns ; and fleet of foot as well ;
So like was he in much ; yet not in all ;—
The heel, that slew the Greek, has saved the Gaul.

Napoleon was not the man to sit still under defeat, and, very shortly after his return, he set himself to repair losses. These were heavy ; there was an entirely new artillery to be provided, remounts for his cavalry, and, what was of the greatest importance, a new army to be made. This he got by anticipating the conscription of 1814, and the patriotism of his people helped him largely with the remainder. The caricaturist has sharp eyes, and he produced ' Bonaparte reviewing his Conscripts,' which is an anonymous picture, dated February 23, 1813, and represents the Emperor, who is mounted on a jackass, and who has a very motley following, reviewing his Dutch light horse, who are mounted on frogs, every man with a keg of Hollands under his arm.

There is a very comical picture of ' Bonaparte addressing the Legislative Body ' after his return from Russia (designed December 1, 1812, published February 24, 1813). Here the discomfited Emperor is in very sorry plight : his coat is in tatters, his breeches cover only a very small portion of his legs, his toes are well out of his boots, and he in vain tries, with his handkerchief, to stop the tears which flow so copiously, as he says, ' I myself entered Russia. The Russian Armies could not stand before our armies. The French Arms were constantly victorious—A swarm of Tartars turned their parricidal hands against the finest provinces of that vast Empire which they had been called upon to defend—But the excessive and premature rigour of the winter brought down a heavy calamity upon my army—In a few nights I saw everything change.—The misfortunes produced by rigour of hoar frosts, have been made apparent in all their extent—I experienced great

losses—they would have broken my heart, if under such
circumstances, I could have been accessible to any other
sentiments than those of the interest—the glory—and the
future prosperity of my people—I have signed with the
Pope, a Concordat, which terminates all the differences
that unfortunately had arisen in the Church—The French
Dynasty reigns—and will reign in Spain—I am satisfied
with all my allies—I will abandon none of them—The
Russians shall return into their frightful climate.'

On March 6, 1813, appeared 'The Wags of Paris or
Downfall of Nap the Great. " But the circumstance said
to have annoyed the Emperor most, was, some Wags of
Paris taking of Dogs, and for sev'ral nights together tied
Tin Kettles to their tails, and labels round their necks,
with the words ' Run away from Moscow,' & giving them
liberty, they ran with velocity, and fury, in various directions, to the great Entertainment of the Parisians." *Courier*
1 *Mar.* 1813.' One of these dogs has got between Napoleon's legs, and is throwing him down, while he calls out,
'Sacré Dieu!! Plot Anglais!! Not a Dog in Paris but
shall feel my Vengeance!! Shoot! hang them all! Not
the Empress's Favorite shall escape. D—d John Bull—
d—d Russian bears, not content with hunting Me from the
frightful climate, but sends Mad Dogs to Hunt Me in my
own Capital!!!' The Governor of Paris replies, 'Sire, be
pacified. All the Dogs in Paris shall be tried by a Military
Commission for a Conspiracy against your Sacred Majesty.
All John Bull's bull dogs shall be destroyed! Pomeranian,
Danish Mastiffs & all but your Majesty's own breed of
Blood hounds.'

'Anticipation for *Boney*—or, a Court Martial on the
Cowardly Deserter from the Grand Army,' by G. Cruikshank (March 6, 1813), is an imaginary scene of what
might happen, did the Emperor meet with his deserts.
The Parisian mob have the upper hand, and a cobbler has
been proclaimed Emperor in his stead. Before this awful
being, Boney is dragged by a ferocious butcher, who, with
an enormous axe in one hand, holds in the other the halter
which encircles the neck of poor trembling Boney, who is
on his knees, with upraised, supplicating hands. The *sans-*

culotte Emperor Crispin is seated in a chair, on a *haut pas* ;
a cap of liberty, on a pole, behind him. In one hand he
holds a hammer, and one foot rests on a lapstone. Pointing to the wretched culprit, he says, ' Well ! you are found
guilty of cowardly deserting from the grand army, and, by
repairing here with your cobbling defence, you have done
a d—d bad job for yourself, and, as your time waxes near
its end, I would have you prepare your Sole for your Last.
So off with his head, Mr. Butcher.' The butcher looks
unutterable things at Boney, saying, ' Ah, D—n you we'll
cut off your head, and your Tail too !' The poor craven
wretch, with streaming eyes, and upstanding hair, pitifully
supplicates that at all events his head should be spared.
But the yelling mob cry out, ' Off with his head.' ' Aye,
Aye, he has butchered Millions.' And the women and
children scream, 'Where's my husband, wretch?' 'Where's
my Father ? ' ' Where's my Daddy ?' &c.

Drilling went on, a necessary step to the formation of
a new army, and the French temperament is well shown
in a caricature, published in April 1813, of ' Nap reviewing the Grand Army, or the Conquest of Russia anticipated,' in which, during the march past, he points to his
soldiers with his sword, and says to two of his generals,
' With this Army will I crush those Russian Scourges, and
make all Nations tremble at my wrath.' One general, in
his enthusiasm, exclaims, ' Parbleu ! vid dis Armée ve vil
conquer de Heaven ! ! !' The other, evidently an Anglo-
phobe, says, ' And de Hell too, dat we may send dere de
dam Anglais.'

In April Napoleon judged that his army was in a fit
state to take the field, and the caricaturist's idea of a
council of war is humorously told in the picture of ' Boney
and the Gay lads of Paris calculating for the next Triumphal entry into Moscow.' This broadside, which made
its appearance in April 1813, represents Bonaparte and his
generals in council. The latter are in different stages of
dilapidation, some having lost their noses, others with
their feet bound up, and all more or less suffering from
frost-bite. One, pointing to a map, says, ' By Gar, Sire,
we had better go to Petersburgh at once.' Napoleon

replies, 'Aye, and then we can march to Siberia, and
release the Exiles, who will gladly join us, and abjure their
tyrant.' Two generals, in conversation together, do not
seem to relish the plan. One remarks, 'Sacre Dieu, I no
like de Russia Campaign. I lose my nose, my fingers, and
toes, in de last.' And the other replies, 'Eh bien, den now we
lose all our odds and ends.' The letterpress is as follows :—

Master Boney was fain, after fighting with Spain,
  And loseing some thousands of men ;
To make an attack on the Russian Cossack,
  With Nations to assist him full Ten.

He began with a boast, that he'd scower their Coast,
  And drive them all into the Sea ;
He continued his blow, till he got to Moscow,
  His designed Winter quarters to be.

But when he got there, Lord how he did stare
  To see the whole place in a flame,
Not a house for his head, not a rug for his bed,
  Neither plunder, nor victuals, nor fame.

So he sent every Scout, who ran in and out,
  But brought neither forage, nor food ;
For that d—d Wittgenstein, so compleat hem'd him in,
  That they dared not to venture a rood.

Now the fire having ceas'd, and the frost much encreas'd,
  No cov'ring, no clothes to protect 'em ;
Boney thought to be packing, Kutusoff began hacking,
  And the Cossacks did fairly dissect 'em.

Says this Corsican wight, Why let my Friends fight,
  As for me, the old Proverb I'll follow,
He that fights and then runs, may, in spite of their guns,
  Live ! and some future day beat them hollow.

But take care, Master Nap, you meet with no trap,
  To poke either leg or your head in ;
Loss of legs stops your flight, lose your head, why the sight
  Will be welcome at Miss Platoff's [1] wedding.

In a sledge it is said, this King was convey'd,
  Like a criminal back into France ;
But his Army and Friends, to make them amends,
  He gave them a precious cold dance.

[1] The Hetman, Platoff, is said to have promised his daughter in marriage.
and a fortune for her dowry, to whoever would bring him Napoleon's head,

The frost kill'd one half, the rest Kutusoff
    Kill'd, or prisoners made in their flight ;
Thus the Russians did beat Nap and Friends so compleat,
    That no Armies e'er suffered such plight.
Now this madman, 'tis said, has ta'en in his head
    To attempt at another Campaign,
With but half of his friends, yet still he intends
    To venture to Moscow again.
But if Nap, and Ten more, were beaten before,
    By raw Russian troops single handed ;
With what chance can he hope against Russia to cope,
    When their force with Allies is extended ?
No, No, Master Nap, you'll not feather your cap
    Any more, for your race is near run ;
And your murderous heart, is destined, Bonaparte,
    To suffer for crimes it has done.
Then ye Nations whose voice through fear, not from choice,
    To this tyrant its homage has paid,
Join the brave Russian throng, that your miseries ere long
    May with Nap in Oblivion be laid.

CHAPTER LI.

THE ARMISTICE—BATTLE OF VITTORIA—DEFEAT AT LEIPSIC—THE BRIDGE BLOWN UP.

AN armistice was signed between the allies and Napoleon on June 4, 1813, to last till July 20 : six days' notice to be given of the recommencement of hostilities. But Wellington seems to have disregarded it ; for, on June 21, he defeated the French army commanded by Joseph Bonaparte, who had Marshal Jourdan under him, at Vittoria ; completely routing them, and taking 151 pieces of cannon, 415 ammunition waggons, all their baggage, besides many prisoners.

Needless to say, the caricaturist did not omit his opportunity. 'Mad Nap breaking the Armistice' (June 1813) is said to be taken 'from the original Picture at Dresden.'[1] Two messengers bring him their reports. One is 'English near Bayonne, Rising in South of France, 200,000 men

[1] Napoleon was at Dresden when he heard the news of the defeat at Vittoria.

joined the Bourbon Standard, Revolt at Toulon, Discontent at Paris, All Spain evacuated, and more losses.' The other messenger tells the furious Emperor : 'Diable ! Your Grand Army in Spain is totally routed, 180 Cannon, 400 Ammunition Waggons, All the Baggage ! 9000 head of Cattle, Military Chest full of money taken. Your brother, King Joey, gallop'd away on horseback, Devil knows where ! M. Jourdain has lost his wig and stick ! and the Enemy pursuing in all directions.' Bonaparte is in a towering rage, brandishing a poker, and kicking the last messenger, to whom he roars out : 'Away, base slaves. Fresh Torments ! Vile Cowards ! Poltroon Joe ! Traitor Jourdain ! Cursed Anglais ! I'll make Heaven and Earth tremble for this ! but 'tis lies ! base lies ! Give me my horse, I'll mount, and away to Spain ! England ! Wellington ! and Hell ! to drive Lucifer from his Infernal Throne for Treachery to ME !!' A frightened general standing by exclaims : 'My Poor Master ! is it come to this ? I must whip on this Strait Jacket, or he'll break all our bones, as well as the Armistice.'

As a corollary to this, although it does not belong to Napoleon proper, I cannot abstain from noticing a picture published July 9, 1813, of 'Jourdain and King Joe or Off they go—a Peep at the French Commanders at the battle of Vittoria.' The British troops have routed the French, who fly in all directions ; King Joseph and Marshal Jourdan, in the foreground, are doing the same. Says the king : 'Parbleu Monsr Marshal, we must run ! a pretty piece of business we have made of it. If my Brother Nap sends for me to the Congress, the Devil a clean shirt have they left me ! Could you not try your hand at a Convention again, my dear Jourdain ! as our friend Junot did in Portugal ? '

But Jourdain replies : 'Convention ! No, ma foi ! there is no tricking ce Lord Wellington, we have nothing to trust to but our heels, but I dont think they will save us, you need not be uneasy about a clean shirt for the Congress, Monsr Joe. Allons donc, run like de Devil ! run like your Brother Nap from Russia.'

George Cruikshank drew (July 8, 1813) a very humorous picture of 'Boney receiving an account of the

Battle of Vittoria—or—the Little Emperor in a great Passion !' A ragged postilion, mounted on the back of a kneeling soldier, holds up a long roll : 'King Joseph has been defeated by Wellington with the loss of 151 pieces of Cannon, 415 Ammunition Waggons, Bag and Baggage, Provisions, &c., &c., &c. The French have *one* very fine little Howitzer left. One Quarter of the Army is killed, the other wounded, the third Quarter taken prisoners, and the English are playing the Devil with the rest.'

Napoleon, before his throne, is stamping, tearing his hair, and flourishing his sword, to the undisguised terror of his Mameluke Rûstem ; he roars out : 'Oh !—!—!—!—! —!—!—! oh ! Hell and the Devil ! Death and D—na- —on !!! that cursed fiend John Bull will drive me mad ! Villains ! Villains ! 'tis all a lie, 'tis false as Hell, I say !! away with the —— scroll—it sears my very eyeballs !!! I'll cut it in Ten Thousand pieces—I'll kick ye to the Devil —away with it !!!' Russia, Prussia, and Austria are spec- tators. Russia suggests : 'Now is the time !' In this Prussia cordially agrees, and says to Austria : 'Now or never, will you not join us ?'

A SCENE AFTER THE BATTLE OF VITTORIA, OR, MORE
TROPHIES FOR WHITEHALL !!!

Only a portion is given of G. Cruikshank's ' A Scene after the Battle of Vittoria, or More Trophies for Whitehall !!!'

(July 10, 1813). The Duke of Wellington, on horseback, is receiving the captured colours, &c., which his officers lay at his feet. He is evidently satisfied with the result, for he exclaims : 'Why ! here's enough for three Nights Illumination !' A general replies : 'Three times three, my lord.' One presents him with a *bâton* : 'Here's Marshal Jourdan's Rolling pin ' ; and another, bringing in a captured standard, points to the group which forms our illustration, saying : 'And here comes their last Cannon !!'

The following caricature will do for any time during the year :—' John Bull teazed by an Earwig ' bears only the date of 1813, and is by an unknown artist. The old boy is at his frugal meal of bread, cheese, and beer, and has been reading the ' True Briton,' when he is interrupted by little Boney, who, perched on his shoulder, pricks his cheek with a Lilliputian sword. John Bull turns round half angrily, and says : 'I tell you what, you Vermin ! if you won't let me eat my bread and cheese in peace, and comfort, I'll blow you away, depend upon it.' To which the insect replies : 'I will have the cheese, you Brute you —I have a great mind to annihilate you, you great, over grown, Monster !!!'

In October 1813 came out an etching of 'Tom Thumb and the Giant, or a forced March to Franckfort. *Kings are his Centinels, vide Sheridan's speech.* A letter from Stralsund states that Buonaparte, on his journey to Paris, sent a Courier to the King of Wi——g[1] with orders for him to proceed to Franckfort on the Maine, and the latter would meet him there accordingly.' Tom Thumb, Napoleon, on horseback, prods on the King with his sword, telling him at the same time : 'On, Sir, to Franckfort, and there await my coming.' The poor fat King, with perspiring brows, piteously exclaims : 'Well, I am going as fast as I can—— Pretty work this for a Man of my Importance !! Was it for this you put a Crown upon my head !'

Napoleon's power was rapidly drawing to an end, and the crushing defeat he received at Leipsic on October 16, 17, 18, 19, gave it its death-blow. The news was promulgated throughout England by a ' London Gazette Ex-

[1] Würtemburg.

traordinary' of November 3. The 'Times' of the same date had hinted of reverses sustained by Napoleon, and on November 4 broke into jubilation thus: ' " Justice demands the sacrifice of the Tyrant," [1] such was the sentiment which concluded our last article,—a sentiment not dictated by any feeling of transient growth, but adopted after long and serious reflection on what is due to the moral interests, which are the best and surest interests of nations. The French people will now determine between the sacrifice of their Tyrant, and sacrifices of a very different description, sacrifices of their lives, their children, their treasure, their honour.

'We had already communicated to our readers the private information which we had received, stating that he had sustained " dreadful reverses " in a " series of actions," which had caused him " not only a great diminution in the numbers of his men, but also a serious loss of artillery " ; and that he had himself " escaped with the utmost difficulty to a place of comparative, and but comparative, safety." Such were the accounts which we believed "would be found to contain a very moderate statement of the Tyrant's losses " ; but we own our most sanguine hopes have been exceeded by the Official Statements received yesterday by Government, and made public ; first, in a brief form, by a letter from Lord CASTLEREAGH to the LORD MAYOR, and a Bulletin from the Foreign Office ; and, afterwards, in most gratifying detail, by an *Extraordinary Gazette.'*

The ' Morning Post ' of the same date heads the intelligence as ' The most Glorious and Important News ever received ; ' and the Prince Regent, who opened Parliament on November 4, alluded to it in his speech in these terms : ' The annals of Europe afford no examples of victories more splendid, and decisive, than those which have been recently achieved in Saxony.' London was brilliantly illuminated, and joy reigned throughout the kingdom.

One of the first caricatures on the subject is the ' Execution of two celebrated Enemies of Old England, and their Dying Speeches, 5 Nov. 1813,' which was by

---

[1] The real quotation is : ' Justice demands of her the sacrifice of her bloodguilty tyrant.

Rowlandson (published November 27, 1813), and is stated to be a representation of a 'Bonfire at Thorpe Hall near Louth, Lincolnshire, on 5 Nov. 1813, given by the Rev. W. C. to the boys belonging to the Seminary at Louth, in consequence of the arrival of news of the Decisive Defeat of Napoleon Buonaparte, by the Allies, at 11 o'clock on yᵉ 4th, & Louth Bells ringing all night.'

Guy Faux, who is got up like one of the old watchmen, is swinging on one gallows, and Napoleon, in traditional costume, on another, with a roaring bonfire under him. Men, women, and boys are rejoicing around. ' Guy Faux's Dying Speech. I, Guy Faux, meditating my Country's ruin, by the clandestine, and diabolical, means of the Gunpowder plot, was most fortunately discovered, and brought to condign punishment, by Old England, and here I bewail my fate.' 'Napoleon Buonaparte's Dying Speech. I, Napoleon Buonaparte, flattered by all the French Nation that I was invincible, have most cruelly, and most childishly, attempted the subjugation of the world. I have lost my fleets, I have lost the largest, and the finest, armies ever heard of, and I am now become the indignation of the world, and the scorn, and sport, of boys. Had I not spurned the firm wisdom of the Right Hon. Wᵐ Pitt, I might have secured an honourable Peace, I might have governed the greatest Nation ; but, alas, my ambition has deceived me, and Pitt's plans have ruined me.'

Rowlandson drew a 'Copy of the Transparency exhibited at Ackermann's Repository of Arts, During the Illuminations of the 5th and 6th of November 1813, in honour of the splendid victories obtained by the Allies over the Armies of France, at Leipsig and its Environs.

' The Two Kings of Terror.

' This Subject, representing the two Tyrants, viz. the Tyrant *Bonaparte*, and the Tyrant *Death*, sitting together on the Field of Battle, in a manner which promises a more perfect intimacy immediately to ensue, is very entertaining. It is also very instructing to observe, that the former is now placed in a situation, in which all Europe *may see through him*. The emblem, too, of the circle of light from mere *vapour*, which is so soon *extinguished*, has a good moral effect ; and as the Gas represents the dying flame, so does the Drum, on which he is seated, typify the *hollow*, and *noisy* nature of the falling Usurper.

'The above description of the subject, appeared in the *Sun* of Saturday, the 6th of November. These pointed comments arose from the picture being transparent, and from a circle, indicative of the strength, and brotherly union, of the Allies, which surmounted the same, composed of *gas* [1] of brilliant brightness.'

'Cossack Sports—or the Platoff Hunt in full cry after French Game' (November 9, 1813), shows Leipsic in the background, and the river Elster, into which the Cossac! : plunge, in full cry, after the 'Corsican Fox.' The Hetman, Platoff, cries, 'Hark forward ! my boys, get along ! he runs in view—Yoics, Yoics—There he goes—Tally ho !' His daughter, about whom the story is told (see footnote p. 344), is in mid stream, lashing her horse, and calling out, 'Hi ! ho ! Tally ho ! For a husband !' An army of French frogs in vain attempt to stop the Cossacks—they are routed, and fleeing.

A very cleverly drawn caricature is 'Caterers—Boney Dished—a Bonne Bouche for Europe' (November 10, 1813), and it gives us the sovereigns of Europe seated around a table, on which is a large dish, in the centre of which poses Napoleon, surrounded with a garnish of his marshals, seated, and with their hands tied behind them. The different sovereigns express their opinions upon the dish. Thus Russia says, 'I think Brother of Austria, this dish will be relish'd by all Europe.' 'And I think Brother of Russia they will admire th: *garnish*!' 'Pray let Wurtemburg join in that dish.' 'And Bavaria, if you please.' Holland thinks that 'Donder and Blikins, dat dish will please mein Vrow.' Poland says, 'It is rather too highly seasoned for my taste, but French.' The Switzer opines that 'William Tell never invented a better dish, I hope we shall have a taste of it !' Italy swears 'By the God of Love ! that is

---

[1] Gas was just then coming into notoriety as an illuminating power. Westminster Bridge was lit by gas December 31, 1813, but its use did not become general in London until 1816.

better dish den Maccaroni.' With tears streaming down
his face, a poor monarch prays, 'Oh dear! oh dear! I hope
they won't Dish the poor old King of Saxony.' Prussia
remarks to England, ' We must reduce the quantity of irri-
tating articles, before we can produce it as a finished dish
--What say you Steward of the Feast?' who replies, 'I
agree with your Highness, John Bull prefers moderation.'

On November 10, 1813, was published 'The Daw Script
of his Borrow'd Plumes, *vide Gay's Fables of the Daw
and the other Birds*,' which shows the different birds de-
spoiling the poor Daw, Napoleon. The double-headed
eagle, Russia, with one beak strips him of his Legion of

THE DAW STRIPT OF HIS BORROWED PLUMES.

Honour, the other head takes off his crown. Austria,
Prussia, and Sweden are rapidly denuding him of his borrowed plumes ; whilst Spain, Poland, and Bohemia are
hovering around. The background is taken up with a
Cossack spitting runaway Frenchmen on his lance.

Rowlandson gives us (November 25, 1813) 'A Long
pull, a Strong pull, and a pull altogether.' Here we see the
allies' ships riding freely on the ocean, the sun of tyranny
setting, and the allies giving all their strength in helping to
float the Texel fleet, which the Dutch are assisting them to
launch. Napoleon and his brother Joseph are in the background, the former dancing with rage, and crying out, 'Oh
Brother Joe—I'm all Fire. My Passion eats me up. Such

A LONG PULL, A STRONG PULL, AND A PULL ALTOGETHER.

unlooked for storms of ill fall on me. It beats down all my cunning, I cannot bear it. My ears are filled with noise, my eyes grow dim, and feeble shakings seize every Limb.' Joseph, whose crown has dropped off, says, 'Oh Brother Nap, brother Nap, we shan't be left with half a crown apiece!'

'The Corsican toad under a harrow' (Rowlandson, November 27, 1813) also alludes to the defection of Hol-

THE CORSICAN TOAD UNDER A HARROW.

land, the agonised Emperor calling out, 'Oh, this heavy Dutchman! O' had I enough to bear before !!!'

Rowlandson gives us (November 29, 1813) 'Dutch Nightmare, or the Fraternal Hug, returned with a Dutch Squeeze,' which represents Napoleon lying on a state bed, suffering the tortures of nightmare, his incubus being a very heavy Dutchman, who sits upon his breast calling out, 'Orange Boven,' and puffing his smoke right into the face of his victim.

Mr. Grego credits Rowlandson with the 'Head Runner of Runners from Leipsic Fair' (March 2, 1814), but both the design and drawing manifestly show that it is not by him. On the contrary, its internal evidence clearly shows it to be a German engraving, and much earlier in date, the town in the background being labelled Maynz. Napoleon is here represented as a running courier, and the speed at which he is going is shown by his being able to keep pace with a hare. The top of his staff is Charlemagne —or, as in the etching, Carolus Magnus. In his rapid

HEAD RUNNER OF RUNNERS, FROM LEIPSIC FAIR.

flight he is losing from his wallet all the things entrusted to him—Italy, Holland, Switzerland, the Rheinbund, &c.

His flight from Leipsic was well caricatured, and one episode, the premature blowing up of the bridge over the Elster, came in for severe comment. Colonel Montfort had orders to blow up the bridge, which was mined, as soon as the last of the troops had passed over. He, however, entrusted this duty to a corporal and four miners. The corporal, hearing shouting and cannonading, thought the allies were in possession of the city and pursuing the French forces. He therefore fired the bridge, which blew up, cutting off the retreat of four *corps d'armée*, and more than 200 cannon. Of course, the men so circumstanced had no option but to yield themselves as prisoners, after many had been driven into the river and drowned.

A A 2

At Dresden still our hero staid,
Because to budge he was afraid,

NAPOLEON'S FLIGHT FROM LEIPSIG.

And when he did, it was to meet
At Leipsic, a severe defeat :
The bridge here, as the story goes,
Nap wished to blow up with his foes ;
This to a col'nel he imparted,
Who was, perhaps, too tender hearted.
For to a captain, (so we've heard)
The Colonel the task transferred,
And he a corporal employ'd,
By whom the bridge should be destroy'd ;
But scarce had Nap the bridge passed thro',
When, helter skelter, up it flew !
It seems the truth cannot be traced ;
Either the corp'ral was in haste,
Or by some means, 'tis suspected,
'Twas just as Boney had directed ;
For the Explosion soon confounded
His waggon loads of sick and wounded :
And by these means, as oft he did,
He got of them immediate rid.

' Bonaparte's Bridge, to the Tune of This is the House
that Jack built' (December 1, 1813), supposed to be drawn
by *la Nourrice du Roi de Rome,* is in eight compartments,
which are thus described :—

This is the bridge that was blown into air.
These are the Miners who had the care
Of mining the Bridge that was blown into air.
This is the Corporal stout and strong,
Who fired the Mine with his match so long,
Which was made by the Miners, &c.

This is the Colonel of Infantry,
Who ordered the Corporal stout and strong
To fire the Mine, &c.

This is the Marshall of high degree
Who whispered the Colonel of Infantry
To order the Corporal, &c.

This is the Emperor who scampered away,
And left the Marshall of high degree
To whisper the Colonel, &c.

These be the thousands who cursed the day,
Which made him an Emperor, who scampered away, &c.

These are the Monarchs so gen'rous and brave,
Who conquer'd the Tyrant, and Liberty gave,
To thousands & thousands who cursed the day, &c.

CHAPTER LII.

NAPOLEON'S RETURN TO PARIS—HIS RECEPTION.

'GRASP all Lose all—*Atlas* enraged—or the punishment of unqualified ambition ' is the title of a picture (December 1, 1813) which represents Atlas, who is kneeling down, preparing to drop the whole world on Napoleon. The latter, who has been touching those parts of the earth which are in his possession, and boasting, 'France be mine! Holland be mine! Italy be mine! Spain and Poland be mine! Russ, Prussia, Turky, de whole world vil be mine!!!!' staggers back, exclaiming, 'Mons. Atlas, hold up, dont let it fall on me.' Atlas, whose look is fearful, says, 'When the Friends of Freedom, and Peace, have stopped your shaking it on my shoulders, and got their own again, I'll bear it. Till then you may carry it yourself, Master Boney.' Russia and Prussia are rushing away in fright. Says one, 'By Gar 'tis true, 'tis fall on you Head! votre Serviteur! we no stop to be crush vid you.'

This very clever caricature portrait of Napoleon was published by Ackermann, 101 Strand, on December 1, 1813. It is in the form of a broadside, and contains the following letterpress :—

NAPOLEON the FIRST and LAST, by the wrath of Heaven Emperor of the Jacobins, Protector of the Confederation of Rogues, Mediator of the Hellish League, Grand Cross of the Legion of Horror, Commander in Chief of the Legions of Skeletons left at Moscow, Smolensk, Leipzig, &c. Head Runner of Runaways, Mock High-Priest of the Sanhedrim, Mock Prophet of Mussulmen, Mock Pillar of the Christian Faith, Inventor of the Syrian Method of disposing of his own sick by sleeping Draughts, or of captured enemies by the Bayonet ; First Grave Digger for burying alive; Chief Gaoler of the Holy Father and of the King of Spain, Destroyer of Crowns, and Manufacturer of Counts, Dukes, Princes, and Kings ; Chief Douanier of the Continental System, Head Butcher of the Parisian, and Toulouese, Massacres, Murderer of Hofer, Palm, Wright, nay of his own Prince, the noble and virtuous Duke of Enghien, and of a thousand others ; Kidnapper of Ambassadors, High Admiral of the Invasion Praams, Cup Bearer of the Jaffa Poison, Arch Chancellor of Waste paper Treaties,

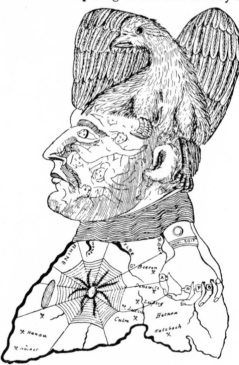

NAPOLEON THE FIRST AND LAST.

Arch Treasurer of the Plunder of the World, the sanguinary Coxcomb, Assassin, and Incendiary . . . . . to MAKE PEACE WITH ! ! !

This Hieroglyphic Portrait of the DESTROYER is faithfully copied from a German Print, with the Parody of his assumed Titles. The Hat of the Destroyer represents a discomfited French Eagle, maimed and crouching, after his Conflict with the Eagles of the North. His *visage* is composed of the Carcases of the Victims of his Folly and Ambition, who perished on the plains of Russia and Saxony. His throat is encircled with the *Red Sea*, in allusion to his Drowned Hosts. His Epaulette is a *Hand*, leading the Rhenish Confederation, under the flimsy Symbol of a *Cobweb*. The *Spider* is in Emblem of the Vigilance of the Allies, who have inflicted on that Hand a deadly Sting !

'The Corsican Munchausen humming[1] the Lads of Paris' (Rowlandson, December 4, 1813) shews Napoleon and his son on a stage, upon which is a throne, tottering, and an overthrown globe. The King of Rome is dressed in counterpart of his father, with long trailing sword, and using a stick as a *cockhorse*. Napoleon is vapouring to the assembled audience : ' Did I not swear I would destroy Austria ? Did I not swear I would destroy Prussia ? Did I not leave the Russians 1200 pieces of cannon to build a monument of the victory of Moscow ? Did I not lead 498,000 men to gather fresh laurels in Russia. Did I not burn Moscow and leave 400,000 brave soldiers to perish in the snow for the good of the French Nation ? Did I not swear I would destroy Sweden ? Did I not swear I would have Colonies and Commerce ? Did I not build more ships than you could find sailors for ? Did I not burn all the British Produce bought, and paid for, by my faithful merchants, before their faces, for the good of them, and my good people of Paris ? Have I not called my troops from Holland, that they might not winter in that foggy Climate? Have I not called my troops from Spain, and Portugal, to the ruin of the English ? Did I not change my religion, and turn Turk, for the good of the French Nation ? Have I not blown up the Corporal for blowing up the Bridge ? Have I not robbed the Churches of twenty flags to send to my Empress, for the loss of my own flags and Eagles ? And now, for the good of my Empire, Behold ! O ye Lads of Paris ! I have put the *King of Rome* in *breeches.*'

Rowlandson gives us 'Funcking[2] the Corsican' (December 6, 1813). A representation of all the crowned heads of Europe, each of whom is smoking a pipe very vigorously, uniting in tormenting Bonaparte with their tobacco smoke. The little Corsican, who is on the top of

---

[1] Deceiving.　　[2] 'Funking' is smoking, or causing a great smell.

a cask of 'Real Hollands Geneva,' is dancing with rage, and yells out: 'Oh you base Traitors and Deserters, Eleven Hundred Thousand Lads of Paris shall roast every one of you as soon as they can catch you!' In his excitement he has split the head of the cask, and there seems every probability of his disappearing. 'The fly that sips, is lost in the sweet.'

'The Mock Phœnix !!! or a vain attempt to rise again' is by Rowlandson (December 10, 1813). Napoleon is in a furnace, which is being diligently stoked and blown by Russia and Holland. Serpents come from the mouth of the furnace, and the soots, the products of combustion, take the form of fiends—Napoleon is partially consumed, and his crown is in a blaze.

'Friends or Foes—Up he goes—Sending the Corsican Munchausen to St. Clouds' is by Rowlandson (December 12, 1813), and shows the whole of the sovereigns of Europe combining to toss Napoleon in a blanket.

A most amusing caricature by Rowlandson (December 14, 1813) is 'Political Chemists and German Retorts, or dissolving the Rhenish confederacy.' John Bull naturally finds coal for a 'German Stove,' the fire in which a Dutchman blows with a pair of bellows. All the sovereigns of Europe stand round, enjoying Boney's discomfiture. The Emperor, who is vainly appealing to them, 'Oh spare me till the King of Rome is ripe for mischief yet to come,' is being put into a glass receiver, and is about to be covered up. Bernadotte is pouring in a bottle of sulphate of Swedish iron, and the Pope is hurrying forward with two bottles, one of fulminating powder, the other a vial of wrath. The products being distilled from him are Intrigue and Villainy, Ambition and Folly, Gasconade and Lies, Fire and Sword, Arrogance and Atrocity, Murder and Plunder. A Spaniard is pounding at a mortar inscribed 'Saragossa.'

In 'Town Talk' (December 1, 1813) is published 'Gasconading—alias the Runaway Emperor Humbugging the Senate.

Some are Short and some are Tall,
But it's very well known that he hums them all,
And then sings fal de ral tit.'

Napoleon crowned, and *en grande tenue*, stands before the throne, pointing to some trophies borne by soldiers, and thus addresses the Senate: 'Senators! the glorious success of our Arms has forced me to give way to the impulse of quitting the field of honour, that I might have the satisfaction of presenting to my faithful Senate the glorious trophies of our Victories. Senators! your restless, envious enemies shall be humbled to the dust; your Emperor wills it so; this Arrogant Confederacy shall be punished for their temerity, and our brave Soldiers shall repose in peace. Senators! for this purpose I shall require the small sum of 250,000,000, a sum the flourishing state of our finance will easily produce, and, to replace the vacancy made in my Army, 500,000 (men) from the conscription of 4 years to come will be all that I demand. Frenchmen, the Will of your Emperor, and the glory of the great Nation, requires it.' The Devil, peeping round from behind the throne, applauds: 'That's right my Boy. Humbug them out of another conscription to send me, before you come yourself.'

One Senator, as spokesman, thus addresses Napoleon: 'Great Emperor of the Great Nation, the Senate devotes the lives and property of the People to your service.' But this does not appear to be the universal consensus of opinion; for one grumbles, 'C'est dire un peu trop, cela!' Another asks: 'What has he done with the last Grand Army, that he wants so many again?' and one replies: 'They are gone to see how their friends in Russia do.' Another doubts the authenticity of the trophies: 'Why! these trophies belong to our Allies, c'est drôle cela!'

On December 12, 1813, George Cruikshank published 'Bleeding and Warm Water! or the Allied Doctors bringing Boney to his Senses.' Here poor Boney is in very evil case. With shaven head, and in an 'Allied strait waistcoat' (one sleeve of which is held by Russia, the other by Poland), he is seated on the stool of Repentance in a tub of hot water, consisting of a 'sea of troubles,' which is warmed by the flames of Moscow. He is surrounded by all the European sovereigns as doctors, each of whom prescribes his own remedy. Russia gives, as his opinion : ' I have found a constant application of this Russian *Knout* to work wonders !!' John Bull is giving him a fearful bolus, ' Invasion of France,' saying at the same time, ' Work away my Masters, I'll pay you your *fees. Ay, ay, rave and rant, Master Boney, but the Devil will Bone you at last.*' Holland is trying ' what *Dutch drops* will do,' by emptying out of a huge cannon a legion of armed Dutchmen on his shaven head. Poland bleeds him by stabbing his arm with a lance, and Prussia catches the blood in a ' Crown bowl,' congratulating himself, ' I think my *Crown* Razors have shaved his *Crown* pretty close.' Spain is applying a plaster to his back : ' Here is a Plaster of Spanish flies for him.' Poor Boney, one of whose legs is in the hot water, resists this treatment as far as possible, and yells out, ' Hence with your Medicines—they but drive me Mad. Curse on your *Dutch Drops*, your *Leipsig Blister*, and your *Spanish flies* ; they have fretted me to what I am. D—n your *Cossack Lancets*, they have drained my veins, and rendered me poor and vulnerable indeed—Oh ! how I am fallen—But I will still struggle—I will still be great—Myriads of Frenchmen still shall uphold the glory of my name, the grandeur of my Throne, and write my disgrace in the hearts of ye—ye wretched creatures of English gold.'

' The Head of the Great Nation in a Queer Situation,' by G. Cruikshank (December 1813), shows frightened Bonaparte, his magic wand broken, surrounded by his enemies. Wellington points a huge blunderbuss at him, telling the others to ' Take a good aim at the Head, gentlemen, and we shall soon settle the business.' Austria, Prussia, and Russia all point pistols at his head. Prussia thinks that ' by Gar, we shall make de Head look like de Plumb Pudding ; ' and Russia says, ' I'll rattle a few Snow balls at his Cranium.' Holland has a cannon which he is filling with bales of Orange Boven, saying, I'll deal out my oranges to him wholesale.' From the heavens, the hand of Justice is putting the ' Allied Extinguisher ' upon him. This picture is copied bodily from a French carica-ture, ' Le Chef de la Grande Nation dans une triste posi-tion.'

On December 25, 1813, was published one of Rowland-son's caricatures called the 'Mock Auction—or Boney selling Stolen Goods.' There is an announcement that ' speedily will be sold the 13 cantons of Switzerland,' and, among the property he has for sale, are the Papal Tiara, and several crowns, a lot of useless eagles, the kingdom of Bavaria, twenty flags the property of the Empress, the kingdom of Prussia, Saxony, kingdom of Westphalia, and the United Provinces. Some French officers are among the audience, which includes the crowned heads of Europe. The crown of Spain is on sale, and is lifted upon high for inspection. Spain jeeringly asks : ' That a Crown ? It's not worth half a crown.' Napoleon, seeing no chance of selling it, says : ' What ! no bidding for the Crown of Spain. Then take the other crowns and lump them into one lot.' Maria Louisa carries the King of Rome, who is like a little monkey, and who exclaims : ' I suppose daddy will put us up for sale.'

CHAPTER LIII.
L'HOMME ROUGE—NAPOLEON'S SUPERSTITION.

THIS ends the caricatures for the year 1813, at the close of which Napoleon was in Paris. Wellington and Soult were fighting their prolonged duel in Spain, to the great advantage of the former. One after another did the French garrisons surrender, until, at the close of the year, Santona alone remained to the French. His troops, shut up in garrison in Germany and Prussia, were in very evil case, from hardships and sickness. St. Cyr abandoned Dresden, and all the garrison were made prisoners of war. Stettin surrendered, and the Dutch revolted ; whilst at home the life-blood of the nation was being drained by a new con-scription of 300,000 men, and the taxes were increased by one half.

And here, as well as at any other place, I may intro-duce Napoleon's familiar spirit, ' *l'Homme Rouge.*' The be-lief in 'the red man,' in connection with the Emperor, was very widely spread ; but details of his personal appearance, and the times of his visits, are rarely to be met with, and are invariably contradictory. Napoleon's success had been so marvellous, that it is easily to be imagined it was popularly ascribed to supernatural agency.

In a small and very rare French book,[1] is an account of ' *The little red and green men, or the genius of Evil triumphing over the genius of Good.* Many persons, astonished at the success of Buonaparte in all which he undertook, asked by what tutelary divinity he was protected ?

'Some said, It is Europe which is being destroyed by itself, an effect natural to every country, over-populated, and too flourishing—Was it not thus with Egypt, Greece, Judea, and Rome ? Others, less philosophic, but easier given to conjecture, said, When he was in Egypt he several times absented himself from his staff.—Somebody generally came to him before he fought a battle, or undertook any enterprise.

'He frequently repeated, *God has given me the strength and the will to overcome all obstacles.* There was something supernatural . . . . and thenceforth endless questions were asked of those who were with him in the Egyptian expedition. At length, by dint of research, a part of the truth was discovered, which is as follows :—

'On the eve of the battle of the Pyramids, Buonaparte, at the council which was held in the morning, formally opposed the proposition to give battle. In the afternoon of that day, having gone, with some of the officers of his suite, to make a reconnaissance, and having approached one of the monuments of the pride of the Pharaohs,[2] he suddenly saw, coming out from it, a little man clothed in a long red robe, his head being adorned with a pointed cap of the same colour, after the manner of the priests of Isis, or the Chaldean sages, known under the name of Magi. He carried a little ring in his hand.

'This mysterious man only said these words to him : "Approach, young man, and learn the high destinies to which you are called, if you wish to be prudent and wise."

'Immediately, Buonaparte, as if he had been drawn by a

[1] *Buonapartiana, ou Choix d'Anecdotes curieuses.* Paris, 1814.
[2] One of the pyramids.

supernatural force, descended from his horse, and followed him into the interior of the pyramid, where he remained more than an hour.

'The officers of his suite, at first, paid little attention to this *rencontre*, taking the red man to be one of those charlatans, with which the world abounds, to the detriment of science and real knowledge ; they were even astonished that their general, to whom they accorded so much merit, lost precious time in interviewing a wretched cheat ; but, when they saw Buonaparte come out, all radiant with joy, saying to them, " Friends, let us give battle ; we shall conquer ! " and when they saw, that in spite of the inferiority of their forces, they should gain the most complete victory, they could only think of *the red man*. Is he a God ? Is he a Genius ? That was what they asked.

'Thenceforth the French, in Egypt, only marched from victory to victory, until the departure of Napoleon for France.

'We believe that all the deeds with which *the red man* has been credited are only fables which conjecturors have invented ; but, at least, in him they discover the emblem of a good Genius, who pointed out to Buonaparte what he ought to do to assure at least the love and gratitude of the people. But an evil Genius, whom they suppose to have been clothed in green, appeared to him at St. Cloud, at the time of the 18th Brumaire, and gave him counsels, which prevailed, for the misfortune of the world, over those of *the red man*, and led him to his ruin.'

Balzac, in a delicious booklet,[1] in which an old soldier gives the history of his beloved Emperor, makes him say, 'There is one thing which it would be unjust, if I did not tell you : In Egypt, in the Desert, near Syria, THE RED MAN appeared to him, in the mountain of Moses, to tell him, "All went well."

'Then at Marengo, on the evening of the Victory, he saw, standing before him, the Red Man, who said to him :

'" Thou shalt see the world at thy feet, and thou shalt be Emperor of the French, King of Italy, Master of Holland, Sovereign of Spain, Portugal, the Illyrian Provinces,

[1] *Histoire de l'Empereur, racontée dans une Grange par un vieux Soldat.*

Protector of Germany, Saviour of Poland, First Eagle of the Legion of Honour."

'This Red Man, do you see, was his idea, his own : a kind of lackey, who helped him, as many say, to communicate with his star.   I, myself, have never believed that but the Red Man is a veritable fact, and Napoleon has spoken of him himself, and has said that he visits him in troublous moments, and that he stays at the palace of the Tuileries, in the upper apartments.   Then at his Coronation, Napoleon saw him, in the evening, for the third time, and they were in deliberation about many things.   Then the Emperor went straight to Milan to crown himself King of Italy. . . .

'At length we found ourselves, one morning, encamped at Moskowa.[1]   It was there that I gained the Cross, and I take the liberty of saying that it was a cursed battle !   The Emperor was uneasy : he had seen the Red Man, who said to him :

' " My child, thou art going too fast, men will fail thee, and friends will betray thee." '

And the old soldier, almost at the end of his story, says, 'The remainder is sufficiently well known.   The Red Man passed over to the Bourbons, like a scoundrel, as he is. France is crushed,' &c.

It is needless to say that this legend was known in England, and was not lost sight of by the satirist.

> Poor Bonaparte, now, every day,
> Endeavoured to be wondrous gay ;
> To concerts, plays, and balls, he went,
> To hide, it seems, his discontent.
> Folks thought hostilities would cease,
> For gaiety 's a sign of peace.
> But soon, alas ! returned his gloom,
> And now our hero kept his room.
> One day he wish'd to be alone,
> And said he was at home to none,
> When suddenly there came a knock,
> Which dealt around a dreadful shock—
> His counsellor of State, 'tis said,
> Saw a tall man dressed all in red !

[1] Borodino.

'Your business, Sir?'—'A secret that—
I must see Bonaparte, that's flat'—
'He's not at home,' was the reply,
The red man answer'd—'that's a lie!'
The Counsellor to Boney ran,
Apprising Nap of this red man—
How very great the Emp'ror's dread—
'Art sure? and was he dress'd in red?'
Affecting then a kind of grin—
'No matter—shew the red man in.'
The red man, tho', as people say,
Ne'er waited to be shewn the way,
For in he bolted—and, what's more,
Immediately he clos'd the door—
The Counsellor of State, so shock'd
His ear, then, at the keyhole cock'd,
And tho' the red, tall, man he fear'd,
This conversation he o'erheard—
'Well, Emp'ror Boney—pray how do you?
This is my third appearance to you,
At Egypt once—next at Wagram—
You must remember who I am.'
'Yes, I remember, but what is it
Has now induced this sudden visit?'
'What is it! Nap, how can you ask?
Have you accomplish'd, pray, your task?
Four years, I for that purpose granted,
It was the very time you wanted;
And then I said—and say it now—
No longer time wou'd I allow;
'Twas quite sufficient, as you said,
And solemnly a vow you made,
That either Europe you'd subdue,
Or peace shou'd in that time ensue;
I told you, if I tricks foresaw,
That my protection I'd withdraw,
And therefore am I come again
To tell you but three months remain;
If Europe then, you have not got,
Or peace confirm'd—you'll go to *pot.*'
Our hero seem'd quite panic struck,
'Alas!' said he, 'I've had no luck—
I can't in three months undertake
An honourable peace to make—

A longer period, therefore, fix,
Let the three months, I pray, be six.'
' It cannot be—I'll grant no more '—
Nap followed him unto the door—

NAPOLEON AND THE RED MAN.

' Five months, I'm sure, you may allow '—
' I won't—mark well your sacred vow,
One or the other you must do—
Or else, depend on it you'll rue.'
' Then grant *four* months.'—' It cannot be—
Conquer, or be at peace, in *three*—
Such was the task you undertook '—
Then giving a contemptuous look,
' *Three months*—no longer—so good-bye '—
He said—nor waited a reply.
With indignation Boney burn'd,
While to his cab'net he return'd—
And there, as many people say,
He sullenly remain'd all day.

The English gave Napoleon the character of being very superstitious, and I believe, even now, ' Napoleon's Book of Fate,' and ' Napoleon's Dream Book,' are procurable.

In 1795 it is said that Napoleon paid a visit to a sorcerer named Pierre le Clerc, and expressed some doubt of his power. ' You are wrong,' said the magician, ' to doubt my art. I know more than you probably imagine. There was a prophecy of a certain Count Cagliostro, uttered ten years ago, on the French Revolution, which was not then thought of. This announced that a Corsican, voted or elected by the people, would finish it, probably by a Dictatorship.' Napoleon left the old man, and, it is said, did not visit him again until the eve of the fateful 18th Brumaire.

The seer gave him a number of cards, on each of which he was to write one letter of the question he wanted to ask, which was : 'What will become of the Corsican Napoleon Bonaparte, general, on account of the *Coup d'État* risked by him, at Paris, the 18th Brumaire, 1799?' These cards were well mixed and handed to the conjurer, who, after some manipulation, settled on thirteen cards, having the letters B, O, P, P, I, A, I, B, I, P, A, U, F, each of which letters he interpreted as the commencement of a Latin word ; and, on this basis, he constructed the following sentence : 'Bis Oriens, Populi Princeps, In Altum Incedit ; Bis Incidit ; Per Anglos Ultima Fata,'—or, He rises twice Prince of the People, and hovers over the heights ; twice he falls ; his last fatality will come from the English.

Napoleon then took fresh cards, and wrote : 'Josephine Marie Rose de Tascher de la Pagerie, wife of the General Napoleon Bonaparte.' Of these Pierre le Clerc selected three letters, H, E, A, which he interpreted as 'Herois Extinctus Amor,'—or, Love extinguishes itself in the heart of a hero.

There was a curious article in the 'Frankfurter Journal' of September 21, 1870, on the influence of the letter M on the life of Napoleon : 'Marbeuf was the first to recognise the genius of Napoleon at the Military College. Marengo was the first great battle won by General Bonaparte, and Melas made room for him in Italy. Mortier was one of his best generals, Moreau betrayed him, and Marat was the first martyr to his cause. Maria Louisa shared his highest fortunes ; Moscow was the abyss of ruin into which he fell. Metternich vanquished him in the field of diplomacy. Six marshals (Massena, Mortier, Marmont, Macdonald, Murat, Moncey) and twenty-six generals of division under Napoleon had the letter M for their initial. Marat, Duke of Bassano, was his most trusted counsellor. His first battle was that of Montenotte, his last Mont St. Jean, as the French term Waterloo. He won the battles of Millesimo,

B B

Mondovi, Montmirail, and Montereau ; then came the storming of Montmartre. Milan was the first enemy's capital, and Moscow the last, into which he entered victorious. He lost Egypt through Menou, and employed Miellis to take Pius VII. prisoner. Mallet conspired against him ; Murat was the first to desert him, then Marmont. Three of his ministers were Maret, Montalivet, and Mallieu ; his first chamberlain was Montesquieu. His last halting place in France was Malmaison. He surrendered to Captain Maitland of the *Bellerophon*, and his companions at St. Helena were Montholon and his valet Marchand.'

CHAPTER LIV.

NAPOLEON AGAIN TAKES THE FIELD—HIS DEFEATS—THE ALLIES AT PARIS—NAPOLEON ABDICATES—HIS ATTEMPT TO POISON HIMSELF.

ON January 1, 1814, Rowlandson published 'The double humbug, or the Devil's Imp praying for peace,' a picture in two parts. One represents Napoleon addressing the Senate from his throne, which stands on divers crowns : his friend, the Devil, being perched a-top. A soporific effect among his audience seems to be the outcome of his address, which is as follows : '*Extracts of Bonyparty's Speech, Sunday,* 19 *December,* 1813. Senators, Counsellors of State, Deputies from the Department to the Legislative Body. Splendid Victories have raised the Glory of the French Arms, during the Campaign. In these weighty circumstances, it was my first thought to call you around me. I have never been seduced by prosperity. I have conceived and executed great designs for the Prosperity and the happiness of the world, as a monarch and a father. I feel that Peace adds to the security of Thrones and that of Families. I have accepted proposals, and the preliminaries. It is necessary to recruit my armies by numerous Levies, and an increase of Taxes becomes indispensable —— I am satisfied with the sentiment of my people of Italy, Denmark, Naples, America, and the nineteen Swiss cantons ; and have acknowledged the laws which England has, in vain, sought, during four centuries, to impose on France—I have ordered discharges of Artillery on my coming and leaving you.'

The other portion of the picture shows the powers of Europe, before whom Napoleon kneels, surrendering colours and crowns ; all, save one of the latter (the French crown), and this he tucks under his arm. His deportment is abject, as is his speech : ' Gentlemen, Emperors, Kings, Rhenish Confederations, &c., &c., &c. Behold unto you a fallen Impostor, who has for many years been drunk, and intoxicated, with Ambition, Arrogance, and Insolence, who has foolishly and wickedly lost within a twelve Months, a Million of brave but deluded Frenchmen. Who has conceived the great and diabolical design of enslaving the world, and has lost all his friends except Yankee Maddison. Now, Gentlemen, to make amends for my sins, I solicit your pardon, and ask for Peace, on your own Terms, Gentlemen, and I will strictly adhere to all * * * * * * * * You may take all those Crowns back again, except the one belonging to the Bourbons. My Empress sends you also back the 20 flags I found in some of the Churches, in the course of my flight from Leipsig. As for the story, Gentlemen, of the Corporal and the blowing up the bridge, you must know 'twas a mere Humbug to gull the Lads of Paris.' Talleyrand also assures the crowned heads, that ' What my Master has said is true, so help me G—d. Amen.'

On January 21, 1814, Napoleon once more set out from Paris at the head of an army, and in this month he fought at Saint-Dizier, Brienne, Champ-Aubert, Montmirail, Chateau-Thierry-Nangis, and Montereau, but then the French arms were almost everywhere defeated. People could discern the beginning of the end. Meanwhile the caricaturist was busy.

' The Devil's Darling '[1] is another by Rowlandson (March 12, 1814) ; but it possesses no merit, except the very excellent likeness of Napoleon. He is in swaddling clothes, and being dandled by the arch-fiend.

Wm. Elmes (the 'W. E.' of occasional caricatures) drew (March 21, 1814) ' John Bull bringing Boney's nose to the Grindstone ' ; but it is not a new subject, as there is a contemporary caricature of the Scots bringing Charles the Second's nose to the grindstone. Russia is turning the stone

[1] See next page.

— the allied Powers looking on—and John Bull, who is performing the operation, says : 'Aye, Aye, Master Boney, I

THE DEVIL'S DARLING.

thought I should bring you to it one of these days. You have carried on the trade of grinding long enough, to the annoyance of your oppressed neighbours—One good turn deserves another—Give him a Turn brother Alexander—and let us see how he likes a taste.'

'The Allied Bakers, or the Corsican Toad in the hole' (April 1, 1814), is taken bodily from a French caricature, 'Le Tour des Alliés, ou le Corse près à être cuit,' although it bears on it '*G. H. inv^t Cruickshank fecit.*' The King of Prussia, Woronzow, and Blücher have a baker's peel, on which is a dish containing Boney, screaming, 'Murder, Murder,' as he is being put into the Allied Oven. Holland sits on the floor blowing the fire. A Frenchman, whose fickleness is shown by the weather-cock on his hat, is opening the oven door for his former master's destruction, saying : ' This door sticks ! I don't think I shall get it open !' Blücher shouts, ' Pull away Frank,[1] you keep us waiting.' Woronzow says, 'In with it, Blucher,' and the King of Prussia's opinion is, ' I tell you what, Woronzow, the Hinges want a little Russia Oil.' Wellington, who is bearing a tray on which is a Soult pie and a Bordeaux pie, shouts out, ' Shove altogether, Gentlemen ! D—n me, shove door and all in.'

Meanwhile, the allied Austrian, Russian, and Prussian troops had marched on to Paris, and, having defeated Marmont, March 30, 1814, the city was virtually at their mercy. Maria Louisa and the young King of Rome left Paris on March 29, and on the 31st the city capitulated, and the Emperor of Russia and the King of Prussia entered the city with the allied armies. The Emperor of Austria did not join them, probably out of deference to his paternal feelings. The ' Times ' of April 6, 1814, thus gives the news of the capitulation :—' Babylon the great is fallen ! Paris, the proud city, the city of philosophy, has bowed her neck to the Conqueror.'

' Boney forsaken by his Guardian Angel ' (April 3, 1814) shows the Emperor kneeling, one crown already having been taken from him by the arch-fiend, who now is taking another from off his head. The flames of hell are prominent in the distance. Bonaparte implores—' My Guardian Angel, my Protector, do not desert me in the hour of Danger.' But the Devil, exultant, says, ' Poh ! Poh ! you cannot expect to reign for ever ; besides I want you at home, to teach some of the young Imps wickedness.'

On April 3 the fickle French destroyed their idol, for the Provisional Government declared Napoleon deposed, and his dynasty abolished.

On April 5 Bonaparte formally abdicated the throne of France ; and, when we consider how long he had troubled the peace of this country, we can pardon the almost brutal exultation of the ' Times ' of April 11 :—

[1] In the French original it is ' *Tirez donc, Français, vous nous faites attendre !* '

'The most hateful of Tyrants has finished by proving himself the most infamous of cowards.

'Two *Extraordinary Gazettes* were published on Saturday; the latter of which contained BUONAPARTE'S renunciation of sovereignty, in the following terms:—

The Allied Powers having proclaimed that the Emperor NAPOLEON was the only obstacle to the re-establishment of the peace of Europe, the Emperor NAPOLEON, *faithful to his oath*, declares that he renounces for himself and his heirs, the Thrones of France and Italy; and that there is no *personal sacrifice*, even that of his life, which he is not ready to make in the interest of France.

Done at the Palace of Fontainebleau the — April, 1814.

'Thus has the last act of this wretch's public life been marked by the same loathsome hypocrisy which characterised him throughout his guilty career. When he has been solemnly deposed by his own confederates; when the execrations of all France, and of all Europe, are ringing in his ears; when his last army is deserting him by thousands, and an overwhelming force of the Allies is approaching, to drag him to a shameful death, if he refuses the proffer'd mercy—then, forsooth, his forced submission is a voluntary sacrifice, he is actuated by a principle of public spirit, he feels a religious regard for his oath ! ! !

'We did not think to have troubled our heads what should become of him, or his worthless carcase—whether he should crawl about upon the face of that earth, which he had so long desolated; or end a miserable existence by his own desperate hand; or be helped out of the world by the guillotine, the halter, or the *coup de grâce*. Certainly, if we had to choose the finest moral lesson for after ages, we could not have preferred any to that, which should at once expose the selfishness, the baseness, and the cowardice of a vainglorious mortal, whom adulation has raised almost to divine honours. And, as to any danger from his life— why, *Jerry Sneak* was a hero to him. Twice before, had he run away from the field of battle—but that, in the opinions of his besotted admirers, was profound imperial policy.

'When he first attempted to act CROMWELL, unlike the tough old Puritan, he had nearly fainted; but this was a transient qualm, that "overcame him like a summer's cloud;" and, besides,

Men may tremble, and look paler,
From too much, or too little valour.

'The abandonment of his throne was an act of undisguised, deliberate cowardice, not altogether unanticipated by us ; for it will be remembered that some months ago, in comparing the terms offered to him by the Allies, with *Fluellen's* offer of the leek to ancient *Pistol,* we said, that though he might vow "most horrible revenge," he would eat the leek. We had not then any reason to believe that he would be required to yield up crown and all ; but now that circumstances have led to such a point, his conduct in respect to it occasions us no surprise. That which displeases us, however, is, that in the very document which ought to have contained nothing more than his subscription to his own disgrace, he has been allowed to lay claim to something like honour—to shuffle in a lying pretence to virtue. This was not a time to indulge his vanity. The record of his punishment ought rather to have referred to real crimes than to fictitious merits.'

The illuminations on this occasion were very splendid—but perhaps the best of them all, as illustrating the popular feeling, was one which was simply 'Thank God.'

The following caricature must have been published before the news of the abdication reached England.

'Blücher the Brave extracting the groan of abdication from the Corsican Bloodhound' is by Rowlandson (April 9, 1814). The Prussian general having stripped Bonaparte of his crown and uniform, &c., is administering to him a sound shaking, whilst Louis the Eighteenth is being welcomed by Talleyrand and the whole French nation.

'The Corsican Shuttlecock, or a pretty Plaything for the Allies' (April 10, 1814), is by G. Cruikshank. Napoleon is the shuttlecock, which is kept

in the air by Schwartzenberg and Blücher.   The former
has just sent him to his comrade with—' There he goes !!
why Blücher ! this used to be rather a weighty plaything ;
but d—— me if it isn't as light as a feather now.'   Blücher
replies, ' Bravo Schwartzenberg, keep the game alive ! send
him this way, and d—— him, I'll drive him back again.'

'Europe,' by Timothy Lash 'em (April 11, 1814), gives
us a pyramid formed by all the States of that Continent.
It is surrounded by clouds, from whence issue the heads of
Napoleon's victims—' Wright, Georges, Pichegru, Moreau,
Palm, and Hofer '—and on the summit of the pyramid,
planting the Bourbon flag, is the ghost of the Duc d'En-
ghien, who hurls Napoleon into hell, where Robespierre and
Marat are awaiting him.

> His operations Nap pursued,
> And frequently the troops reviewed.
> One day, the first of April too,
> Boney attended the review.
> He thought the soldiers still his own,
> Tho' well the contrary was known.
> Some of the Generals, 'tis said,
> The Paris newspapers had read,
> And of the news, before the crowd,
> They talk'd together very loud.
> Our hero still retained his cheer,
> For he pretended not to hear.
> As soon as the review was done,
> Brave Marshal Ney (to have some fun,
> And let him know his fatal doom),
> Followed poor Boney to his room.—
> ' In Paris there's a revolution—
> You've heard of the new constitution.'
> Nap, seeming not to understand,
> Ney clapp'd the paper in his hand :
> He read, with evident attention,
> 'Twas gaining time tho' for invention.
> Alas, poor Nap ! 'tis as he feared—
> And like fall'n Wolsey he appear'd.
> Exactly the same scene indeed—
> *There is that paper for you—read :*
> *Then with what appetite you can—*
> *Go, eat your breakfast, my good man.*

Nap, spite of all, was very cool,
Tho' certainly an *April fool* :
But great indeed was his vexation,
When bade to sign his abdication ;
He looked aghast, he sigh'd, and trembled
Before the Generals all assembled—
Twas hard on Boney, we must own,
Thus to renounce his crown and throne.
How could he help it ? for—oh Lord !
There was a Cossack with a sword !
To add to *brave* Napoleon's dread,
There was a pistol at his head !

NAPOLEON SIGNING HIS ABDICATION.

So very furious look'd the men,
Poor Nap could scarcely hold the pen.
And when he did, so great his fright,
His name poor Nap could scarcely write;
At length, while he was sitting down,
He sign'd—'I ABDICATE MY CROWN.'

The scene, however, was not quite as the poet makes it
out, but it was bad enough, if we may credit Madame
Junot : 'We have read of the revolutions of the seraglio :
of those of the Lower Empire : of the assassinations of
Russia ; we have seen the blood-stained crowns of India
given to vile eunuchs ; but nothing in the pages of history presents any parallel to what passed at Fontainebleau during the days, and above all the nights, passed
there by the hero, abandoned by fortune, and surrounded
by those whom he supposed to be his friends. A thick

veil was drawn over the event, for the principal actors in it carefully concealed their baseness from the eye of the world.   Few persons are aware that Napoleon was doomed to death during the few days which preceded his abdication, by a band of conspirators composed of the most distinguished chiefs of the army.

' " But," said one of them in the council in which these demons discussed their atrocious project, " what are we to do with him ?   There are two or three among us, who, like Antony,[1] would exhibit their blood stained robes to the people, and make us play the part of Cassius and Brutus I have no wish to see my house burned, and to be sent into exile."   " Well," said another, " we must leave no trace of him.   He must be sent to heaven like Romulus." The others applauded, and then a most horrible discussion commenced.   It is not in my power to relate the details. Suffice it to say that the Emperor's death was proposed and discussed for the space of an hour, with a degree of coolness which might be expected among Indian savages armed with tomahawks.   " But," said he who had spoken first, " we must come to some determination.   The Emperor of Russia is impatient.   The month of April is advancing, and nothing has been done.   Now, for the last time, we will speak to him of his abdication.   He must sign it definitely—or——" A horrible gesture followed the last word.

' Yes, the life of Napoleon was threatened by those very men whom he had loaded with wealth, honours, and favours ; to whom he had given lustre from this reflection of his own glory.   Napoleon was warned of the conspiracy, and it must have been the most agonising event of his whole life.   The torments of St. Helena were nothing in comparison with what he must have suffered when a pen was presented to him by a man who presumed to say, " Sign—if you wish to live."   If these last words were not articulated, the look, the gesture, the inflection of the voice, expressed more than the tongue could have uttered.'

How these rats left the falling house !—Berthier, with a

[1] They alluded to the Duke of Bassano, Caulaincourt, Bertrand, and some others.

lie on his lips, promising to return, yet knowing full well he never meant to ; Constant, his valet, running away with 100,000 francs, and burying them in the forest of Fontainebleau ; and Rûstem, the *faithful* Mameluke, running away to Paris. Is it not a sickening sight to see these pitiful rogues deserting their master ?

On April 11 the treaty of abdication was signed by the allies, and by it Napoleon was to keep his title of Emperor, and have the sovereignty of the Island of Elba, where, however, he must permanently reside. He was guaranteed a revenue of 6,000,000 francs. Josephine and the other members of the Emperor's family were to have 2,000,000 francs divided amongst them ; and Maria Louisa and the King of Rome were to have the Duchies of Parma, Placentia, and Guastalla.

But, when all was finished, he felt his position too hard to bear. He would have recalled his abdication—but it was too late. Torn from his high estate, separated from his wife and child, deserted by the creatures of his bounty, life was not worth living for ; existence was wretched, and he tried to put an end to it by poison on the night of April 12. Baron Fain, in 'The Manuscript of 1814,' gives a good account of this occurrence, but not nearly as graphic as does Madame Junot :—

'Throughout the day his conversation turned on subjects of the most gloomy kind, and he dwelt much on suicide. He spoke so frequently on the subject, that Marchand,[1] his first *valet de chambre*, and Constant were struck with it. They consulted together, and both, with common consent, removed from the Emperor's chamber an Arabian poniard, and the balls from his pistol-case. The Duke of Bassano had also remarked this continued allusion to suicide, notwithstanding his efforts to divert Napoleon's thoughts from it. The Duke spoke to Marchand, after he had taken leave of the Emperor, previous to retiring to rest, and he expressed himself satisfied with the precautions which had been taken. The Duke had been in bed some time, when he was awoke by Constant,

[1] He accompanied the Emperor to Elba. Constant, as we have seen, left him.

who came to him pale and trembling : " Monsieur le Duc," he exclaimed, " come immediately to the Emperor. His Majesty has been taken very ill ! " The Duke of Bassano immediately hurried to the bedside of the Emperor, whom he found pale and cold as a marble statue. He had taken poison !

'When Napoleon departed for his second campaign in Russia, Corvisart gave him some poison of so subtle a nature, that in a few minutes, even in a few seconds, it would produce death. This poison was the same as that treated of by Cabanis, and consisted of the prussic acid which has subsequently been ascertained to be so fatal in its effects. It was with this same poison that Condorcet terminated his existence. Napoleon constantly carried it about him. It was enclosed in a little bag hermetically sealed, and suspended round his neck. As he always wore a flannel waistcoat next his skin, the little bag had for a long time escaped the observation of Marchand, and he had forgotten it. Napoleon was confident in the efficacy of this poison, and regarded it as the means of being master of himself. He swallowed it on the night above mentioned, after having put his affairs in order and written some letters. He had tacitly bade farewell to the Duke of Bassano and some of his other friends, but without giving them cause for the slightest suspicion.

' The poison was, as I have already observed, extremely violent in its nature ; but, by reason of its subtlety, it was the more liable to lose its power by being kept for any length of time. This happened in the present instance. It caused the Emperor dreadful pain, but it did not prove fatal. When the Duke of Bassano perceived him in a condition closely resembling death, he knelt down at his bedside and burst into tears : " Ah ! Sire ! " he exclaimed, " what have you done ? " The Emperor raised his eyes and looked at the Duke with an expression of kindness ; then, stretching to him his cold and humid hand, he said : " You see, God has decreed that I shall not die. He, too, condemns me to suffer ! " '

CHAPTER LV.

NAPOLEON LEAVES FOR ELBA—HIS RECEPTION THERE.

AFTER a sad parting with his old guard at Fontainebleau, on April 20, Napoleon left for Elba, embarking on board an English frigate on the 28th. We can now resume the caricatures.

Rowlandson produced (April 12, 1814) 'Bloody Boney, the Carcass Butcher ; left off Trade and retiring to Scare-crow Island.' Napoleon and the Empress, together with a bag of brown bread, are mounted on a donkey—he wears a fool's cap, and she belabours the ass with a 'Baton Marechale' ; the young King of Rome precedes them on a Corsican dog. The usual direction-post (a gallows) shows the road to Elba, and ravens are hankering after him, saying, 'We long to pick your bones.' A heavy-booted postilion is calling out, 'Be Gar, you Cocquin, now I shall drive my old Friends and bonne customers de English. Vive le Roi et le Poste Royale.'

Rowlandson plagiarised Gillray by almost slavishly copying 'Death of the Corsican Fox' (p. 158), only he substituted Blücher for George the Third, and changed the names on the dogs' collars to *Wellington, Swartzenberg,* Kutusoff, Duke of York, and Crown Prince. This etching is called 'Coming in at the death of the Corsican fox. Scene the Last' (April 12, 1814).

'A Grand Manœuvre ! or, the Rogues march to the Island of Elba,' G. Cruikshank (April 13, 1814). Here Napoleon is shewn weeping bitterly at his own disgrace His hands are bound behind him, his tattered uniform is put on wrong side in front, his boots have no soles nor toes, and his spurs are strapped in front ; some *gamins* are tugging at a halter which is round his neck, and are drag-ging him to a boat, in which sits the Devil, waiting for him ; Talleyrand is doing all in his power to expedite matters by pushing him behind with an 'Allied broom,' and he goes to his doom amidst universal execrations. The little King of Rome is in one of his coat-tail pockets, and calls out, 'By Gar, Papa, I have von *grand manœuvre* in your pocket.'

'The Rogue's March' is by Rowlandson (April 15, 1814),

From fickle Fortune's gamesome lap
What various titles flow ;
The Emperor of Conj'rors Nap,
The King of Beggars, Joe !

a portion of which is reproduced. Blücher is dragging
Napoleon and his brother, who are handcuffed, and on a
placard which he bears on his shoulder is inscribed ' Napoleon, late Emperor of the French, King of Italy, Pro-

THE ROGUE'S MARCH.

tector of the Confederation of the Rhine, Grand Arbiter
of the fate of Nations, &c. &c. &c., but now, by the permission of the Allied Sovereigns, Exile in the Isle of Elba,
an outcast from Society, a fugitive, a vagabond. Yet this
is the conceited mortal who said, I have never been seduced
by prosperity—Adversity will not be able to overcome
me.' In the background drummers are playing 'The
Rogue's March,' and all the European Powers dancing
round the old Bourbon flag, on which is written ' Rejoice
O ye Kings, Vive le Roi ! '

' The Sorrows of Boney, or Meditations in the Island

of Elba !!!' (April 15, 1814) shews the disconsolate Emperor, seated on the rocky isle, weeping copiously, and staring anxiously at the Continent of Europe which is so well guarded by ships. This engraving did former duty as 'Crocodile's tears' (p. 185).

On April 17, 1814, Rowlandson published 'The Affectionate farewell, or kick for kick,' which gives us Talleyrand kicking Napoleon and striking him with his crutch. 'Va t'en Coquin, I'll crack your Crown, you pitiful vagabond.' The fallen Emperor not only puts up with these insults, but, turning round, says, 'Votre très humble serviteur, Monsieur Tally.' His maimed soldiery call out, 'Bone him, my tight little Tally,' and one even goes so far as to shout out, 'What! let him sneak off without a mark or a scratch! No, no, I'll darken his daylights for him.'

'The Last March of the Conscripts, or Satan and his Satellites hurled to the land of oblivion' (April 17, 1814), represents Napoleon and his brothers all chained together in a gang, heavily fettered, in tatters, and being whipped by a most ferocious Cossack. To add to poor Boney's miseries, his little child is pulling at his coat-tails crying, 'Didn't you promise me I should be a King?' Talleyrand is rejoicing, and a large box of crowns and sceptres is labelled, 'To the right owners.'

'A delicate finish to a French Usurper' is by T. N. (April 20, 1814), although Mr. Grego places it as one of Rowlandson's—who possibly may have etched it.

> Boney, Canker of our joys,
>   Now thy tyrant reign is o'er ;
> Fill the Merry Bowl, my Boys,
>   Join in Bacchanalian roar.
> Seize the villain, plunge him in ;
>   See, the hated miscreant dies.
> Mirth and all thy train come in,
>   Banish sorrow, tears, and sighs.

This represents Bonaparte, seated on a throne of skulls and bones, very ill indeed. His crown of tyranny has fallen off and is broken, and he is in the act of disgorging 'The Throne of France,' having already done so with Holland, Rome, Portugal, &c.—in fact, all his previous

successes : nay, the very bees are flying away from off his
imperial mantle. Time is putting an extinguisher on his
head ; whilst the Duke of Wellington, the Emperor Alexander, he of Austria, and the Crown Prince, stand looking
at Blücher, who is administering his 'black draught' to
the patient. Three dancing females—two of them holding
a shield charged with the Bourbon lilies over the head of
the third—typify the joy of France at the Emperor's
downfall and Louis the Eighteenth's accession to the
throne.

'Boney at Elba—or, a Madman's Amusement' (April
20, 1814), is a very characteristic caricature.

> So high he's mounted on his airy Throne,
> That now the wind has got into his Head,
> And turns his brains to Frenzy.

Bonaparte, crowned with a straw crown, and wielding a
straw sceptre, is setting light to a straw cannon, with

BONEY AT ELBA—OR, A MADMAN'S AMUSEMENT.

which he is supposed to be aiming at straw dummies of
Russia, Prussia, Austria, and Sweden. The cannon naturally catches alight, and his army (one corporal) calls out,
'Ah ! Diable, mais you was burn Le Materiel, you burn
your playthings.' The mad monarch, however, persists, and
replies, 'Now these fellows shall know what the Conqueror
of the World can do —— Corporal ! D—— you Sir ! dont'
you blow up the Bridge till I order you.'

' " Cruce dignus," the Grand Menagerie, with an exact representation of NAPOLEON BONAPARTE,[1] the little Corsican monkey, as he may probably appear at the island of Elba,' is a reproduction of the engraving by Lee in 1803 of ' Pidcock's Grand Menagerie,' and, as the letterpress is almost identical, it is not worth giving again (published April 20, 1814).

The following broadside was published April 23, 1814, price 3*d.* :—

Cruce Dignus

EPITAPH

Underneath a GIBBET *over a* DUNGHILL
at ELBA.

Underneath this Dunghill
Is all that remains of a mighty Conqueror
NAPOLEON BUONAPARTE,[2]
Who, with inflexible Cruelty of Heart,
And unexampled Depravity of Mind,
Was permitted to scourge the Earth, for a Time,
With all the Horrors of War.
Too ignorant and incapable to do good to Mankind
The whole force of his mind was employed
In oppressing the weak, and plundering the industrious.
He was equally detested by all :
His enemies he butchered in cold blood :
And, fearing to leave incomplete the Catalogue of his Crimes,
His friends he rewarded with a poisoned Chalice.
He was an Epitome
Of all that was vicious in the worst of Tyrants ;
He possess'd their Cruelty, without their Talents ;
Their Madness without their Genius ;
The Baseness of one, and the Imbecility of another.
Providence at last,
Wearied out with his Crimes,
Returned him to the Dunghill from which he sprung,
BRITON !
Ere you pass by,
Kneel and thank thy God,
For all the Blessings of thy glorious Constitution ;

[1] Anagram upon Bonaparte's name, on his attempting to steal the Crown, &c. ' *Bona rapta pone, Leno!* Lay down the goods you have stolen, Rascal !'
[2] The first twenty-seven verses of the fourteenth chapter of Isaiah.

C C

Then return into the peaceful Bosom of thy Family, and continue
In the practice of those Virtues
By which thy Ancestors
Have obtained the Favor of the Almighty.

Tiddy doll, the gingerbread manufacturer, is once more introduced into caricature (April 21, 1814): 'Broken Gingerbread' (*G. H. inv*—*G. Cruikshank fec*). Napoleon

is at Elba, in an extremely dilapidated condition ; a wretched thatched hut has on it a board painted, 'Tiddy Doll, Gingerbread baker. N.B.— Removed from Paris.' On his head he carries a tray of broken gingerbread, and calls out, ' Buy my Images ! Here's my nice little gingerbread Emperors and Kings, retail and for exportation.' In the background can be seen the coast of France, on which the people are rejoicing and dancing round a flag, ' Vivent les Bourbons ! '

BROKEN GINGERBREAD.

El
' The Hellbaronian
Emperor going to take possession of his new Territory '
(April 23, 1814), by G. H., engraved by G. Cruikshank.
Here Napoleon, ragged and heavily fettered, is in an iron
cage, which is drawn by a mounted Cossack. Others surround and guard him, and we can well understand the
captive's ejaculatory ' Oh— d —n these Cossacks.'

' Nap dreading his doleful Doom or his grand entry
into the Isle of Elba ' (April 25, 1814), represents the

exiled Emperor at the moment of his landing. He has just been put ashore in a small boat, and his slender luggage, which is guarded by his solitary follower, a Mameluke, is deposited on the shore. With one hand in the breast of his coat, and the other thrust deep into his breeches pocket, suffering, too, from the impertinent inquisitiveness of the natives, it is no wonder that he appears downcast, and says, 'Ah, Woe is me, seeing what I have, and seeing what I see.' He is, however, tried to be comforted by a blowsy bumboat woman, who, offering him her long clay pipe, pats him on the back with ' Come cheer up my little Nicky, I'll be your Empress.'

George Cruikshank (May 1, 1814) gives us ' Snuffing out Boney,' an operation which is being performed by a gigantic Cossack.

Hardly a caricature, is a picture attributed to Rowlandson (May 1, 1814), in which is depicted Napoleon's throne overturned, together with his crown and sceptre. The Devil himself is clutching Napoleon, who is terrified at the heavenly apparition of a hand holding a flaming sword, and the legend, ' Thou 'rt doom'd to Pain, at which the Damn'd will tremble, and take their own for Joys.' This

etching is called 'The Tyrant of the Continent is fallen.
Europe is free. England Rejoices. *Empire and Victory
be all forsaken; To Plagues*, Poverty, Disgrace, and Shame.
Strip me of all my Dignities and Crowns. Take, O Take
your sceptres back, Spare me but life!'

CHAPTER LVI.

NAPOLEON AT ELBA—HIS OCCUPATIONS WHILST THERE—FAITH BROKEN
WITH HIM—THE VIOLET—GENERAL REJOICINGS AT HIS EXILE.

IN the 'Satirist' of May 1, 1814, is a picture by G.
Cruikshank, called '*Otium cum dignitate*, or a view of
Elba.' It is not a good one. Napoleon, ragged and
stockingless, smoking a short clay pipe, is blowing up the
fire with a pair of bellows. Bertrand is kissing a female,
probably Pauline, on the sly, and Jerome Bonaparte is
mending nets.   a

'Boney's Elbow Chair, a new Throne for a new Emperor ; or an old sinner brought to the stool of repentance.
A dialogue between one of his admirers & John Bull, on
his being laid up with a cutaneous or skin disorder' (G.
Cruikshank, May 5, 1814). Boney is in his rocky home
raggedly dressed, with a fool's cap on his head, and sitting
on a close stool. He is surrounded with medicine-bottles
and pots of brimstone and itch salve, and he is scratching
himself violently. John Bull says :—

'So ! your poor friend Nap Boney is kick'd from a throne,
And must sit on a stool close at Elba alone.'
'He is *not* poor,' said Nic, 'he has got fat and grown flabby.'
'He has also,' said John, 'got the Itch, or grown scabby.
For not even his wife will consent to go nigh him,
And all his old Mamelukes flout and defy him ;
Perhaps thou, in pity, will lift up his latch,
And rub him with Brimstone or help him to scratch.
Pray go, and take with thee the birds of thy feather,
And all catch the Itch, or grow scabby together.'

'Needs must when Wellington Drives, or Louis's
Return ! !' (May 1814) is a very badly drawn picture by
Marks. Louis the Eighteenth, unable to walk, by reason
of the gout, is being drawn along in a sort of Bath chair

What I was.

A CRUEL TYRANT.[1]

What I am.

A SNIVELLING WRETCH.

What I ought to be.

HUNG FOR A FOOL.

by Napoleon, and attended on either side by Blücher and Wellington. The latter is punishing poor Napoleon with a birch-rod, saying meanwhile, 'I desire, you will sing God save the King.' Boney, with his handkerchief to his eyes, says, 'I'll be d—d if I do.' Blücher is of opinion, 'You'l be d—d whether you do or not.'

A very commonplace caricature is 'The Tyrant, overtaken by Justice, is excluded from the world,' and it would not be noticed here did it not introduce us to a new artist, L. M. (? Lewis Marks). Napoleon, chained to his rock, disconsolately gazes at that world which he may not

[1] These three pictures are all on one plate, and are by Rowlandson, published May 1, 1814.

reach, the Devil meanwhile pointing the finger of scorn at
him (May 1814).

In 'the departure of Apollo and the Muses—or Farewell to Paris' (May 1814), by I. Sidebotham, we have the
restitution of the art treasures, taken by Napoleon, to their
different owners—a long string of waggons, filled with pictures, &c., are labelled Holland, Italy, Venice, Berlin, and
Vienna.   Louis the Eighteenth, at the Louvre, laments it,
and says, ' Dear Talley, persuade them to leave us a few of
these pretty things for my *chambers*, they will pacify the
Deputies, and amuse the people.'   Talleyrand replies, ' I
have tried every scheme to retain them, but it seems they
have *at last* found us out, and are not to be humbug'd any
longer.'   Apollo and the Muses have mounted a fine gold
car, which is drawn, not only by horses, but by the British
Lion as well—the former being postilioned by Blücher;
the latter by the Duke of Wellington, who calls out, ' Go
along, Blucher, let us haste to restore the stolen Goods.'

Of his entry into Elba the poet thus sings :—

> On board th' Undaunted he embark'd—
> ' A noble vessel,' he remark'd,
> And now the banish'd malefactor
> (So late a wild and busy actor),
> His entry into Elba made
> Upon the fourth of May.   'Tis said
> To see the wondrous little man
> Th' inhabitants all eager ran.

THE INHABITANTS OF ELBA.   NAPOLEON LANDING AT ELBA.

> A great blue coat our hero sported,
> And was most pompously escorted ;
> Three fiddles and two fifes preceded,
> For he some consolation needed ;

Pity my fall became the strain
Which they struck up to sooth his pain ;
'Oh change that doleful air,' he said,
And therefore the musicians played,
In hopes to comfort the poor elf,
Go to the De'il, and shake yourself.
'Give me a horse,' he cried ; of course
Nap was provided with a horse,
And round the island quick he rode,
Which his wild disposition shewed ;
The little children, at his view,
Cried out, 'Oh, there's a *bug-a-boo* !'
Without a wife—without a mother,[1]
Without a sister, or a brother,
And even of a friend bereft,
Poor Nap is to his conscience left.

On June 4, 1814, was published (artist unknown) 'An Imperial vomit,' in which Bonaparte is disgorging the kingdoms he has swallowed up. The Prince Regent, behind him, says, 'I think now my little fellow, you are pretty well clear'd out, and I hope you will never give us the trouble to Prescribe or Proscribe any more.'

'Drumming out of the French Army !!!' is the title of a picture published in June 1814. Blücher has Bonaparte in a drum, which he carries before him, beating him alternately with a birch-rod and a drum-stick, Russia, Prussia, and Austria looking on.

Lewis Marks produced, in June 1814, 'Boney and his new subjects at Elba.'[2] The poverty-stricken condition to which the Emperor is reduced is too graphically portrayed, and his ragged army of four is very vividly illustrated. He thus addresses them : 'Gentlemen, my friends despise and d—n England, Russia, Prussia, Germany, and Sweden, and obey me—and I will make kings of you all.'

Napoleon might well say that his 'territory was somewhat small ;' but, small as it was, his restless activity set to work to improve it. He made roads where none had existed, canals and aqueducts, a lazaretto, and stations for tunny-fishing. Vineyards were improved, and the little

---

[1] As a matter of fact, both his mother, Madame Letitia, and his sister, Pauline, went to Elba, soon after his arrival.   [2] See next page.

island was quite prosperous. Numerous visitors came to pay their respects to the Emperor, causing money to be

BONEY AND HIS NEW SUBJECTS AT ELBA (*see previous page*).

spent ; vessels brought provisions, and took away what the inhabitants had to export. Porto Ferrajo was gay and lively, its name being changed to Cosmopoli. A new flag was manufactured, having a red bend dexter, charged with three bees on a white field, and Moorish pirates were very chary of touching vessels bearing this flag. In May Cambrone brought out some volunteers of the old guard, and Napoleon exercised and inspected his little army.

But these things cost money, and that was one of the things wanting to Napoleon. The conditions of the treaty with him were shamefully broken. Hear what he says himself about it : [1] 'It was stipulated and agreed to, that all the members of my family should be allowed to follow me to Elba ; but, in violation of that, my wife and child were seized, detained, and never permitted to join a husband and a father. They were also to have had the Duchies of Parma, Placentia, and Guastalla, which they were deprived of. By the treaty, Prince Eugene was to have had a principality in Italy, which was never given. My mother

[1] *A Voice from St. Helena.* O'Meara.

and brothers were to receive pensions, which were also refused to them. My own private property, and the savings which I had made on the civil list, were to have been preserved for me. Instead of that, they were seized in the hands of Labouillerie the treasurer, contrary to the treaty, and all claims made by me rejected. The private property of my family was to be held sacred : it was confiscated. The dotations assigned to the army on the Mont Napoleon were to be preserved : they were suppressed ; nor were the hundred thousand francs which were to be given as pensions to persons pointed out by me, ever paid. Moreover, assassins were sent to Elba to murder me. Never,'continued Napoleon, ' have the terms of a treaty been more evidently violated, and indeed openly scoffed at, than those were by the allies.'

Louis the Eighteenth was very tame after Napoleon, who, in spite of his draining France of men and treasure, had implanted a deep personal love for him in sonal love for him in

THE PEDDIGREE OF CORPORAL VIOLET
(see next page).

the hearts of his people ; and, from some fancied saying

of his, that 'he would return in the spring,' the violet, the flower of spring, was taken as his emblem, and so worn. He was spoken of under the name of Caporal Violette, or Papa Violette, and the people comforted themselves with ' En printemps il reviendra.'

There were several coloured engravings of bunches of violets, bearing the portraits of Napoleon, Maria Louisa, and the King of Rome—or Prince of Parma, as he was then called—published in France ; notably one by Cann, ' Violettes du 20 Mars 1815,' from which, in all probability, Cruikshank took his caricature of ' The Peddigree of Corporal Violet (G. H. inv^t et del. etched by G. Cruikshank 9 June 1815)'; but, in the arrangement of the flowers, it is superior to any of the French pictures that I have seen.

For want of space, I have but partially reproduced it. It is described ' First as a Consular Toad Stool, rising from a Corsican Dunghill, then changing to an Imperial Sun Flower, from that to an Elba fungus' (where the illustration commences), ' and lastly to a bunch of Violets, which are so disposed as to represent a *whole length Profile of Buonaparte*, with a bust of *Maria Louisa*, and her Son, the *Prince of Parma*,' which portraits, undoubtedly existing in the picture, will be a pleasing exercise of patience on the part of my readers to discover.

Although not English caricature, I may be pardoned for giving, as a type of then French feeling, a song sung by the troops amongst themselves. It is full of slang of the period, which the notes will elucidate :—

> Pendant que Louis Dix-huit à gogo [1]
> Mangeait, buvait, faisait dodo,[2]
> Un beau jour, le Papa
> Quitte son île, et le voilà !
> *Chorus.*   Chantons le père de la violette
> Au bruit de sons,[3] et de canons '
> Quand à la cour on sait cela,
> Le Comte d'Artois monte son dada,[4]
> Mais pour barrer le Papa,
> Il faut un autre luron [5] que ça !
> Chantons, &c.

[1] Plentifully.   [2] Slept.   [3] Rolls of the drum.
[4] Horse, or, as we should say, 'gee-gee.'   [5] Stronger.

During Napoleon's exile Josephine had died, on May 29. She had lived quite long enough, and had experienced as many, and as great, vicissitudes as any woman.

In June the Emperor of Russia, the King of Prussia and his sons, with a numerous suite, visited London, and were made LL.D.'s at Oxford, great fun being made at the time about conferring the degree on Blücher, *Dr.* Blücher figuring in many caricatures.

'John Bull mad with Joy! or the First of August 1814,' shows the old fellow in ecstasies of delight. He has thrown away his hat, and is waving his wig, dancing all the time. The Prince Regent says, 'Ah, ha! Johnny, I knew you'd be delighted,' and shows him the 'Bill of Fare of the Grand National Jubilee for the Peace of 1814. Hyde Park—A grand fair—Messrs Gyngall, Richardson, and Punches shows—a grand sea fight upon the Serpentine—Fireworks in Kensington Gardens—plenty of gin and beer—St. James' Park—a Balloon—Chinese bridge and Pagoda—Boat race on the Canal—fireworks—plenty of port, sherry, claret, champagne, &c., &c., &c. Green Park—Castle and Temple—Fireworks and Royal Booths.' In his right hand the capering and joyous John swings a miniature gallows, on which hang the prince's enemies, and he cries out in his joy, 'Huzza for the Prince of Princes! Damn the lying London Papers! May Whitbread be drown'd in one of his own butts! and Tierney be choked with his long speeches. Here I have your enemies as they should be! I shall stick this in my Corn field to frighten the Crows! so Huzza, again and again, for the Prince of Princes.'

This was the outcome of the Grand Jubilee on August 1, which was celebrated in London—notably in the parks. 'Mad with joy' was the proper expression. See what this peace meant for the nation—a revival of trade, a remission of taxes, cheaper provisions, the reuniting to their families of beloved ones who had undergone so much for their country. No one can wonder that the people went 'mad with joy,' and were not ashamed to confess it. There was a pagoda on a Chinese[1] bridge thrown over the canal in

---

[1] We must recollect that George the Magnificent was then Regent, and his taste in architecture was decidedly Eastern.

St. James's Park, and at night fireworks were displayed thereon. Chinese lanterns all along the Mall and Bird-cage Walk. In the Green Park was a 'Temple of Concord,' near which was a fine booth for the accommodation of the foreign ambassadors and guests whom the Regent delighted to honour. Small men-of-war waged a mimic sea-fight on the Serpentine, and in Hyde Park was a regular fair. Sadler went up in his balloon, but nearly came to grief, and descended somewhat precipitately in Mucking Marshes, on the Essex coast, sixteen miles below Gravesend. Sad to say, about midnight the pagoda caught fire, and two people lost their lives. The fair in Hyde Park was kept going for several days afterwards.

So we leave the year 1814, with Napoleon seemingly safe, yet far from contented, and the English people revelling in the new and welcome blessings of peace.

CHAPTER LVII.

NAPOLEON'S ESCAPE FROM ELBA—UNIVERSAL CONSTERNATION—FLIGHT OF THE BRITISH FROM FRANCE—CARICATURES ON HIS RETURN.

A SOMEWHAT elaborate caricature is by George Cruikshank (January 1815), and is entitled 'Twelfth Night, or What you Will! now performing at the Theatre Royal Europe, with new Scenery, decorations, &c., &c., &c.' It represents a theatre, on the stage of which sit Wellington, Austria, Russia, and Prussia. The former has been dividing an enormous Twelfth Cake, with the help of a huge knife and Britannia's trident. Austria simply takes the whole of Germany, and remarks, 'I shall get my piece cut as large as I can. I don't think it is large enough.' Russia, who is not content with his huge piece of Russia in Europe, puts his hand on Poland, and, turning to a Pole, who is drawing his sword, says: 'Here brother, take possession of this piece, I think I can manage them both; besides, this has more plumbs on it, which will mix with mine.' Prussia, besides his own country, lays hands on Saxony, exclaiming: 'If I add this Saxon piece to my Prussian one, and put the figure of an Emperor on it, I think my share will look respectable.' Wellington, however, reflects, 'I have been assisting to divide the Cake, but I don't much like my office, the Gentlemen seem so dissatisfied.' Bernadotte comforts himself with 'Now I have got Norway, I can get a wind to blow which way I please.' Louis the Eighteenth and a Dutchman are in a private box ; and in one of the stage-boxes is John Bull and his dog, the former of whom shakes hands with and welcomes an American Indian, saying, 'I hope you won't disturb the peace.' In the opposite box are two Turks and a Hungarian; whilst in the box above is Spain, his crown stuck all over with gallows, and attended by a fearful-looking Jesuit, reading from a 'list of Prisoners to be hung for supporting a free Constitution.' The other Powers are on their knees on the stage, abjectly begging, 'Pray, Gentlemen, spare us a few of the small pieces, for we are almost starving.'

Napoleon was still at Elba, and Europe was enjoying a fool's paradise, as cannot be better shown than by a quotation from Rogers's 'Recollections' (if reliable): 'When Buonaparte left Elba for France, I (the Duke of Wellington) was at Vienna, and received the news from Lord Burghersh, our Minister at Florence. The instant it came, I communicated it to every member of the Congress, and all laughed ; the Emperor of Russia most of all.'

Doubtless they thought themselves secure, for they left Elba unguarded in the most singular manner. As Napoleon told O'Meara : 'I do not believe that Castlereagh thought I should have ventured to leave Elba, as otherwise some frigates would have been stationed about the island. If they had kept a frigate in the harbour, and another outside, it would have been impossible for me to have gone to France, except alone, which I would never have attempted. Even if the King of France had ordered a frigate, with a picked crew, to cruise off the island, it would have prevented me.'

Napoleon did not leave Elba till February 26, nor did he land at Cannes till March 1, when the news of his landing spread like wildfire. The 'Times' of March 11 says : 'Early yesterday morning we received by express from Dover, the important, but lamentable intelligence, of a civil

war having been again kindled in France, by that wretch
Buonaparte, whose life was so impoliticly spared by the
Allied Sovereigns. It now appears that the hypocritical
villain, who, at the time of his cowardly abdication, affected
an aversion to the shedding of blood in a civil warfare, has
been employed during the whole time of his residence at
Elba, in carrying on secret and treasonable intrigues with
the tools of his former crimes in France,' &c.

The caricaturists soon fastened on this event, which fell
upon Europe like a thunderbolt, and some time in March
was published ' The Devil to pay, or Boney's return from
~~Hell Bay~~, 25 Feb. 1815,' by I. L. Marks. Napoleon is
crossing the sea in a boat filled with soldiers, rowed by the
Devil, and steered by Death. He sees the dove of peace,
and immediately kills it with his pistol, saying, 'Away
from my sight, Peace, Thou art hateful to me.' The Devil
opines, ' We shall wade through seas of Blood after this ; '
and Death, waving a tricoloured flag on his dart, says, ' A
more expert hand at my Trade does not exist.' The populace are running to the shore to meet their returned Emperor with effusion, whilst poor gouty Louis is being carried
away on pickaback, lamenting, ' Oh Heartwell,[1] I sigh for
thy peacefull Shades.'

I. L. Marks drew ' 1 Mar. 1815. The European Pantomime.   Princeaple Caracters Harliquin Mr. Boney.
Pantaloon Louis XVIII. Columbine Maria Louiza. Clowns
&c. by Congress.'   Here Napoleon is making a terrific leap
from Elba to the French coast, where the poor pantaloon,
all gouty, shakes his crutch in impotent rage. The Empress and her little son welcome him, and Congress is
represented by the different sovereigns of Europe, who are
in a tent ; Russia pointing to a globe in the midst of
them.

Here is a somewhat homely, but contemporary, account
of how the news of Napoleon's escape was received in
London :—

> Twang went the horn ! ' confound that noise ! '
> I cried, in pet—' these plaguy boys

[1] Or Hartwell, in Buckinghamshire, where he resided whilst in England.

Are at some tricks to sell their papers,
Their *blasts* have given me the *vapours* !'
But all my senses soon were stranded,
At hearing ' Buonaparte's landed !'
' Landed in France !' so ran the strain,
And ' with eleven hundred men.'
' Ho, post !' ' Who calls ?' ' This way.' ' I'm coming !'
' The public surely he is humming,'
Said I. ' A paper—what's the price ?'
' A shilling.' ' Why, that's payment twice !'
' As *cheap as dirt*, your honour, quite ;
They've sold for half a crown to-night.'
' But is the News authentic, friend ?'
' *Ofishul*, sir, you may depend.—
The *Currier*, third edition.' ' So !
Well, take your money, boy, and go.'
Now for the news—by what strange blunder
Has he escaped his bounds, I wonder.

The flight of the British who were in France, upon
hearing the news of Napoleon's landing, is amusingly
shown in ' Hell broke loose or the John Bulls made Jack
Asses,' which is the euphonious title of a caricature by
G. Cruikshank, published March 20, 1815. In it we see depicted the flight of Louis the Eighteenth and all the English
then resident in Paris. They are departing in fearful haste,
and by all kinds of conveyances. One reflects, ' How
they will laugh at us at home for being so fond of spending
our Money in Foreign Countries.' Another complains, ' Oh !
dear, Oh ! dear, I have left all my valuables in Paris. I
wish I had never brought my prosperity into France.'
One man, gouty, is being dragged along in a go-cart.
Three men are mounted on a cow, whilst another holds on
by its tail ; whilst those on horseback, or in carriages, are
having their quadrupeds and vehicles requisitioned, ' Me
vant de horse to meet my old master Boney.' ' We want
de coach to join de grand Emperor ; we teach you now to
recover our lost honour and fight like devils.' Napoleon,
at the head of his army, says, ' Aye, Aye, I shall catch
some of the John Bulls, and I'll make them spend their
money, and their time, too, in France.'

' Boney's Return from Elba, or the Devil among the
Tailors (G. H. inv^t etched by G. Cruikshank, 21 March,

1815)' is indeed a scare. Before describing the picture, it would be as well to read the following lines which are at its foot :—

> Hush'd was the din of Arms and fierce debate,
> Janus once more had clos'd his Temple gate ;
> Assembled Congress fix'd the flattering Plan,
> For Europe's safety, and the Peace of Man.
> When, like a Tiger, stealing from his den,
> And gorg'd with blood, yet seeking blood again ;
> From Elba's Isle the Corsican came forth,
> Making his sword the measure of his worth.
> Hence plunder, force, & cunning blast his fame,
> And sink the Hero in the Robber's name ;
> Hence guiltless Louis from the throne is hurl'd,
> And discord reigns triumphant o'er the world.
> Swift as the vivid lightning's shock,
> The Exile darts from Elba's Rock !
> And like the Thunderbolt of fate
> Dethrones a King ! transforms a State !

Bonaparte, suddenly leaping from Elba, enters at an open window, knocking off the board, on which he had been sitting, the unlucky Louis the Eighteenth, who lies prone on the floor, crying, ' Help, help ! Oh ! I am knocked off my Perch.' John Bull goes to his assistance, comforting him with, ' Never fear old boy, I'll help you up again ; as for that rascal Boney, I'll sew him up presently.' Boney, meanwhile, is calmly seated on the tailor's bench, saying, ' Dont disturb yourselves, shopmates, I have only popped myself here as a cutter out. Where is my wife and son, Father Francis ?' Trembling Austria, goose in one hand, scissors in the other, says, ' I will send an answer shortly.' Terrified Holland exclaims, ' Donder and Blizen dat is de Devil !' Russia, pointing to a knout, says, ' I'll take a few Cossack *measures* to him.' Old Blücher, with a huge pair of shears, advances to Napoleon, exclaiming, ' Cutter out indeed !!! Yes, Yes, I'll cut you out, Master Boney.' Prussia, still seated, sewing, thinks, ' You have cut out a little work for us to be sure, but d—— me if you shall be foreman here.' Bernadotte opines that ' This looks like another subsidy.' Talleyrand is hiding himself under the bench ; and the poor Pope sprawling on the floor, forgets all Christian charity and language, and cries out, 'Oh! curse the fellow, I wish I had the power of a *Bull*, I'd kick him to *Hell*. D—n me if it isn't enough to make a saint swear.'

'A Review of the New Grand Army' (artist unnamed, March 1815) shows, in the background, a host of very tattered troops. In front is Napoleon, *the aghast Emperor*, and *his two friends and Pillars of the State*, Death and the Devil. On one side of him is a *Captain of Starved Banditti from the Alps*, whose aim and object is plunder, and he acts as aide-de-camp ; whilst a ferocious *Butcher from Elba*, reeking knife, and halter, in either hand, guards his other side, and acts as generalissimo. In a flood of light over Napoleon's head appears the *Dæmon of War presiding over the Tyrant*, bearing in one hand a flag, inscribed 'We come to redress Grievances,' and with the other pointing to '*Boundless Ambition.*'

G. Cruikshank etched (April 4, 1815) 'The Genius of France expounding her Laws to the Sublime People.' An enormous monkey, his tail ornamented with tricoloured bows, unfolds a tricoloured scroll, which a lot of much smaller monkeys are reading. It is 'The French Code of Laws.—Ye shall be vain, fickle, and foolish—Ye shall kill your King one day, and crown his relative the next.—You shall get tired of Him in a few weeks—and recal a Ty- rant, who has made suffering humanity bleed at every pore—because it will be truly *Nouvelle*—Lastly, ye shall abolish and destroy all virtuous Society and worship the Devil.—As for Europe, or that little dirty Nation, the English, let them be d—d. France, the Great Na- tion, against the whole World.'

'The Congress dissolved before the *Cake* was cut' is the title of an etching by G. Cruikshank (dated April 6, 1815), in which the sovereigns are seated round an enor- mous cake of Europe, which they were going to cut up and divide, but are startled by the sudden apparition of Napoleon, who, with drawn sword, strides into the room, trampling on the *decrees of the Congress, An account of the Deliverance of Europe*, and *a plan for the security of Europe.* The Dutchman falls off his stool, and spills his bottle of Hollands : 'Oh! Donder and Blizen, my Hollands is all

gone,' is his consolatory reflection. Russia starts up with
'Who the Devil expected you here,—this is *mal à propos*.'
Prussia 'Thought England had promised to guard him.'
Austria, in terror, yells out for somebody to 'hold him, seize
him.' The Pope pathetically laments, 'Oh dear, oh dear,
what will become of me?' Bernadotte shouts, 'Seize
him, Kill him'; but Poland, with folded arms, calmly asks,
'Who'll begin? there's the Rub!!!!' The only one of the
whole of them who has any presence of mind is Wellington, who jumps alertly to his feet and draws his sword.

THE FLIGHT OF BONAPARTE FROM HELL-BAY.

'The flight of Bonaparte from Hell-Bay' is by Rowlandson (April 7, 1815). It represents the arch-fiend, seated in his own peculiar dominions, engaged in blowing bubbles, on one of which he has mounted Napoleon, and sent him once more aloft, to the intense delight of admiring devils.

Rowlandson etched 'Hell Hounds rallying round the Idol of France' (April 8, 1815), which certainly is not a pleasant picture. A colossal bust of Napoleon, with a halter round his neck, is mounted on a pyramid of human heads, and around him, to testify their delight at his return, are dancing Savary, Fouché, Caulaincourt, Vandamme, Davoust, Ney, and Lefèbre. Devils, who say 'He deserves a crown of pitch,' are bringing one already alight. The foreground is strewn with corpses.

'Vive le Roi! vive l'Empereur! vive le Diable! French Constancy, French Integrity' (date uncertain, but some time in April 1815) is credited to Rowlandson. A French soldier, musket in one hand, snuff-box in the other, has three different knots of ribbon in his hat—a red one, 'Vive le Diable!' a white one, 'Vive le Roi!' and a tricoloured one, 'Vive l'Empereur!' A windmill typifies French stability, and a monkey and cat, embracing and fondling, show 'French union between the National Guard and troops of the Line.'

On April 12, 1815, was published an etching, not signed, but accredited to Rowlandson, 'Scene in a New Pantomime to be performed at the Theatre Royal, Paris. With entire new Music, Dances, Dresses, Scenery, Machinery, &c. The principal Characters to be supported by most of the great Potentates of Europe. Harlequin by Mr Napoleon. Clown by King Wirtemberg. Pantaloon, Emperor of Austria. To conclude with a comic song to be sung by the Pope, and a Grand Chorus by the crown'd heads.'

In this caricature we see Napoleon, habited as harlequin, a dagger in each hand, leaping into the unknown, through a 'practicable' portrait of 'Louis le bien aimé.' He is pursued by all the European Powers. Clown fires two pistols at him, but overthrows Spain, who has just drawn his sword. Russia pricks him in the rear with a

lance.   Holland and Prussia are firing at him ; whilst some
one is taking down from the wall the portrait of the Empress as Columbine.

In horrible taste is Rowlandson's picture of ' The Corsican and his Bloodhounds at the Window of the Thuilleries, looking over Paris' (April 16, 1815).   The scene
is a balcony, in which are Napoleon and some of his marshals.   The balcony is inscribed ' More horrors, Death and
Destruction.'   The Devil is hugging Ney and Napoleon,
and Death is pointing to the streets of Paris, where is a
surging mob, with heads on pikes, &c.

' The Corsican's last trip under the guidance of his
Good Angel' (April 16, 1815) has no artist's name attached.

THE CORSICAN'S LAST TRIP.

It represents Bonaparte, and the Devil, taking a prodigious
leap from Elba, to the throne, and sovereign power.

' The Phenix of Elba resuscitated by Treason' is by
G. Cruikshank (May 1, 1815), and is a very elaborate plate.
A witch, whose hands drop gore, presides over the resusci-
tation, saying, ' Rise, Spirit, that can never rest, sweet
Bloodthirsty Soul! Offspring of Treason! come forth.'
Obedient to her exorcisms, the Phœnix (Napoleon) rises
from a caldron, exclaiming, ' Veni, Vidi, Vici!' Around

the caldron gleefully dance the marshals of the Empire, singing, 'Ah ! ha ! by gar, now we shall begin our Bloody work again ;' and in the heavens is shown a genius, having a crown and sceptre in one hand, and a guillotine in the other, who says, 'Rise, rise, thou favor'd son of Fate ! Death or a Diadem shall reward thy labours.'

In one part of the picture is shown the Prince Regent indolently reclining on a divan, a huge decanter by his side, the prime minister presenting him with the news of the *Return of Boney to Paris* and the *Decision of Congress*: saying at the same time, 'May it please my Prince, but these are events we never calculated upon. I had no objection to the sacrifice of Saxony to the ambition of Prussia : I had no objection to the views of Alexander upon Poland : I had no objection to the transfer of Norway to Sweden : I had no objection to the union of Belgium with Holland : I had no objection to all these things; but I could not foresee that the people would be dissatisfied and wish for the return of Buonaparte—to which I have every objection.' The Regent, his eyes starting out of his head, exclaims, ' How ? shall I lose Hanover ? shall I lose all we have been fighting for ? '

In another part is Solomon's Temple, in which sit the Congress, wrangling over the division of a huge cake. Gouty Louis the Eighteenth, mounted on a donkey, is off, hard gallop, to Vienna, calling out, 'Gee up, Neddy—adieu to the Lily in the Violet season ! adieu to my good City of Paris ! ' whilst Wellington, on horseback, is going full speed to Belgium.

CHAPTER LVIII.

PREPARATIONS FOR WAR—THE SHORT CAMPAIGN—WATERLOO— NAPOLEON'S ABDICATION.

' THE Royal Allied Oak and self-created mushroom Kings ' is a curiosity on account of the many profiles contained therein. An account of them is given as under :—

> Behold the Oak whose firm fix'd stay
> Doth check Oppression's course,
> Whose slightest branch can ne'er decay,
> While strong with Virtue's force.

Our much lov'd Sovereign decks the branch,
    The highest of the Tree :
And peaceful Louis tho' driven from France,
    Among its boughs you'll see.

THE ROYAL ALLIED OAK AND SELF-CREATED MUSHROOM KINGS.

The Regent's Portrait next behold,
    Whose Councils Wisdom guides ;
And Russia's noble Monarch bold,
    Who check'd the Tyrant's strides.
Immortal Wellington next is seen,
    Whose fame can ne'er expire ;
And vet'ran Blucher's warlike mien
    That kindled Napoleon's ire.
The Mushroom race you have to seek
    In weeds about the root,

Who scarce dare at the Oak to peep,
Or at its princely fruit.

This clever picture is by I. Field, and was published May 29, 1815.

S. T. Taw, a new caricaturist, gives us 'The Crown Candidates, or a modest request politely refused' (May 1815). Louis the Eighteenth, Napoleon, and the young King of Rome are seated at a table. The former is saying, in the hopes of an amicable settlement being come to, 'Sire, when you have done with the Empire, I will thank you to let me have it.' Napoleon replies, 'I am sorry, Sire, it is engaged for that young Gentleman.' The King of Rome has a torn map, which he is trying to piece, and he says, 'I think I shall be able to unite them.'

G. Cruikshank drew (June 1, 1815) 'Preparing for War,' which is somewhat elaborate in detail. The centre is occupied by a funeral pyre, to which fire has already been applied, 'Sacred to the Bourbon cause, and dedicated to the Downfall of illegitimate Tyranny.' Atop of this is chained a bull, decked with flowers for the sacrifice, and draped with a cloth, on which is inscribed : 'Land Tax—Ditto Personal —Tax on Windows, Dogs, Houses, Servants, Clerks, Shopmen, Carts, Hair powder, Horses, Waiters, Travellers, Income, Armorial bearings,' &c. &c. Poor John Bull bellows, 'Alas, and must I come to this! have I bled for so many years in your service, and will you now take my life?' A typical representative of the House of Commons assures him that it is 'Better to die Johnny, than live, and see thrive the thing we hate—Let us arm—war—war —interminable war I say, down with the Regicide—no quarter to the Usurper—So I said at Congress, so I now repeat, and if it is your fate to expire at the Altar, Johnny, all I ask is that I may live to preach your funeral sermon.' A typical House of Lords is about to give him the *coup de grâce* with a pole-axe inscribed 'New War Taxes,' comforting him with 'No grumbling Johnny, you are a Noble *Sacrifice* and worthy of the Cause.' A number of empty bags are waiting to be filled—'Subsidies,' 'The Army,' 'The Navy,' 'Contractors,' &c.

The left-hand portion of the picture shows the Prince

Regent reclining idly on the throne undergoing his toilet. His idea of the gravity of the situation may be gathered from his speech : ' Why this looks like war ! Order me a brilliant Fête, send me a Myriad of Cooks and Scullions —say to me no more of Civil Lists and deserted wives, but of lascivious Mistresses and Bacchanalian Orgies—To it, Pell mell—my soul is eager for the fierce encounter—What, are my Whiskers [1] easier than they were ? ' One of his valets says, ' Your highness shall in all things be obey'd ' ; whilst one, who is measuring him round the waist, tells him, ' I think these will be the best stays your highness has had yet.'

In the background are seen soldiery, and Wellington and Blücher sharpening their swords. Poor gouty Louis is clad in armour, and is mounted on Talleyrand as a charger. He is accompanied by an army of two men, armed with bottles of *Eau Medicinal*, and his artillery is composed of rolls of flannel. He soliloquises : " Well—we've *Tally* for the Field to-morrow ! but don't forget the *Eau Medicinal* and the *Fleecy Hosiery* ; alas ! these gouty limbs are but ill adapted to Jack boots and spurs—I think I had better fight my battles over a cool bottle with my friend George.'

The extreme right of the engraving shews Napoleon giving orders to ' Let loose the Dogs of War ; ' which is obeyed by one of his marshals, who delightedly exclaims, ' Here is a glorious pack already sniffing human blood, and fresh for slaughter——On—comrades—on ! the word is Bonaparte, Beelzebub and Blood.'

[1] There is a very amusing skit about these 'R—l Whiskers,' which were assumed to be as false as the historical wigs, published early in 1816. It is too long to reproduce, although it is really laughable ; but, at all events, space can be found for the first few lines.

L'ADIEU.

From a puissant Prince to his Cast-off Whiskers, on his leaving London to make an Excursion.

Adieu, my dear Whiskers ! dear Whiskers, adieu !
I ne'er shall love Whiskers as I have lov'd you,
So becoming your form, and so brilliant your hue,
I, ne'er admir'd Whiskers as I've admired you.
Your curve was so lovely, so like a horse-shoe,
Not a Whisker at Court was so lovely as you.
The Baron Geramb's were immense, it is true,
But they didn't sweep round half so tasty as you.

It was time to prepare for war, with a vengeance. On March 25 a treaty had been concluded at Vienna between Great Britain, Russia, Austria, and Prussia, binding themselves to maintain the Treaty of Paris, to keep each 150,000 men in the field, and not to leave off until Napoleon had been rendered harmless.

British gold had to be lavishly employed : the King of Würtemberg receiving from our Government 11*l.* 2*s.* for each man, to the number of 29,000, which he bound himself to bring into the field.[1] But the campaign in Belgium was to be a short one. We all know it, and its glorious end, at Waterloo. The news of that victory flew as never news flew before, for on the 22nd inst. was published the following official bulletin :

'Downing Street, June 22, 1815.

' The Duke of Wellington's Dispatch, dated Waterloo, the 19th of June, states that on the preceding day Buonaparte attacked, with his whole force, the British line, supported by a corps of Prussians ; which attack, after a long and sanguinary conflict, terminated in the complete overthrow of the Enemy's Army, with the loss of ONE HUNDRED and FIFTY PIECES of CANNON, and TWO EAGLES. During the night, the Prussians under Marshall Blücher, who joined in the pursuit of the Enemy, captured SIXTY GUNS, and a large part of Buonaparte's BAGGAGE. The Allied Armies continued to pursue the enemy. Two French Generals were taken.'

Although jubilant exceedingly, the nation hardly yet comprehended the value of that victory ; in fact, in reading the immediate contemporary comments thereon, there seems to be a dread of Napoleon's powers of resource and recuperation, and the illuminations which followed were not so enthusiastically described as on some other occasions.

One caricaturist seems to have been gifted with prescience, for before the victory became known he had produced a caricature which was called ' A Lecture on Heads,'[2]

[1] *Times*, June 1, 1815.
[2] George Alexander Stevens gave the famous ' Lecture on Heads, *circa* 1763 or 1764, by which it is said that here and in America he cleared nearly 10,000*l.*

as Delivered by Marshalls Wellington and Blucher' (artist unknown, June 21, 1815), which shews these heroes dealing death and destruction on the French all round them, making the heads fly all over the place. Blücher shouts out, 'Blister 'em, Fire 'em, shoot 'em, Kick 'em, Lump 'em, Thump 'em, whack 'em, smack 'em.' Wellington sings—

Bold as Hector or Macbeth,
Ri tol, lol, la.
Where's the Fun like meeting Death,
Tol de ridy Tol de ray.

'Monkey's Allowance, more Kicks than Dumplings. A Farce Perform'd with Great Eclat at the National Theatre in the Netherlands,' is the title of a not particularly good picture by an unnamed artist in June 1815. It represents Napoleon, with his hands tied behind him, getting 'Monkey's Allowance' from the principal sovereigns of Europe.

WELLINGTON (*sings whilst kicking him*).
Master Boney with his fol der lol, le,
I buffet away on the *plain*, Sir ;

BLÜCHER.
And I'll assist your Worship's fist,
With all my might and main, Sir.

AUSTRIA.
And I'll have a Thump,
Although he's so plump,

PRUSSIA.
And we'll make such a woundy racket,

HOLLAND.
We'll ramp, we'll swear

RUSSIA AND SWEDEN.
We'll tear—oh rare,

LOUIS XVIII.
I warrant we'll pepper his jacket.

'R. Ackermann's Transparency on the Victory of Waterloo' is said to be by Rowlandson, and is without date. It, doubtless, was got up on the news of that great battle, but it is a very weak production. It simply represents Napoleon between Wellington and Blücher: the latter meets him with artillery, the former pursues him on horseback. Of course his crown has tumbled off. It is not an artistic picture by any means, but, doubtless, it evoked the enthusiasm of the masses, who were intoxicated with joy at the famous victory.

After the battle of Waterloo, Napoleon hastened to Paris, and, tired and covered with dust as he was, he immediately met his Ministers, and told them the extent of his disasters. They laid the intelligence before the Houses of Legislature, and on the morning of June 22 Napoleon received a deputation from the Chamber, who submitted to him that ' the state of war in which France was involved concerned much less the nation than himself, and that the Assembly had the means at command, if he would act so disinterested a part as to restore to it freedom of action according as circumstances might dictate.'

This was a pretty broad hint to Napoleon to abdicate, and he took it as such, and sent the following reply :—

' Frenchmen ! When I began the war to uphold national independence, I relied on the union of all efforts, all wills, and on the co-operation of all national authorities. I was justified in anticipating success, and I braved all the declarations of the Powers against my person. Circumstances seem to be changed. I offer myself as a sacrifice to the hatred against France. May your enemies prove sincere, and may it appear that they wage war against me alone ! My political life is terminated. I proclaim my son, under the title of Napoleon II., Emperor of the French. The present Ministers will form the Council of the Provisional Government. The interest which I take in my son induces me to invite the Chambers to organize a Regency without delay, by a special law. Unite for the general safety, and to secure national independence.

NAPOLEON.

At the Palace of the Elysée, the 22 June, 1815.

The ' Times,'[1] as usual, must speak bitter things of the fallen foe, and, anent his abdication, says, ' The wretch, with the blood of so many thousands on his head, seemed to carry about him all the coolness of that apathy which is part of his physical constitution ; and so degraded and demoralised are the Parisian populace, that they could see

---

[1] June 30, 1815.

the butcher of their race without the least emotion. He is, however, spoken of in the journals, and in the debates, without any share of that respect which but lately was attached to his name. After his former abdication, he was invariably termed the "Emperor"; but now he is called nothing but plain Napoleon.'

CHAPTER LIX.

NAPOLEON A PRISONER—SENT TO THE ISLE OF AIX—NEGOTIATIONS FOR SURRENDER—GOES ON BOARD THE 'BELLEROPHON.'

NAPOLEON retired to Malmaison, but was not long there before General Becker came to him and informed him that he was appointed by the Provisional Government to command the troops detailed for his protection. Napoleon knew the meaning of this message, but even being made a prisoner by his own soldiery did not quell his spirit.

But the presence of Napoleon at Malmaison embarrassed the Government, and Becker had orders to convey Napoleon with all speed to the Isle of Aix. Accordingly they set out, and reached Rochefort on July 3, where he remained until the 8th, when he embarked on board the 'Saale' frigate, but without any hope of getting to sea, because of the blockade of the port by the 'Bellerophon' and other English men-of-war. He occasionally landed on the Isle of Aix; but all hopes of reaching America seem to have been abandoned, as Las Cases and Savary were sent on board the 'Bellerophon' to inquire of Captain Maitland whether he knew anything of the passports Napoleon expected from the British Government, and whether any opposition would be offered to his sailing to the United States. Captain Maitland replied that he knew nothing of the intentions of his Government, but he certainly could not allow any ship-of-war to leave the port, and in the course of conversation asked, 'Why not seek an asylum in England?'

The hint thus dropped fructified; for, after another visit of Las Cases and General Lallemand on board the 'Bellerophon' on July 14, avowedly to repeat their previous questions, the matter was openly discussed, and on mentioning the result of their interview to the Emperor he agreed to this course, and desired Las Cases to tell Captain Maitland to prepare and receive him and his suite the next day. At the same time he entrusted General Gourgaud with an autograph letter to the Prince Regent, directing him to take it to England and deliver it into the Prince's own hands.

From the date of this letter, which was the 13th, it would seem that Napoleon had, on the previous day, made up his mind what course to pursue. The following is the text of the letter :—

Your Royal Highness,
Exposed to the factions which divide my Country, and to the enmity of the greatest Powers of Europe, I have terminated my political career ; and I come, like Themistocles, to throw myself upon the hospitality of the British People. I place myself under the protection of their laws, which I claim from your Royal Highness, as the most powerful, the most constant, and the most generous, of my enemies.

NAPOLEON.

Rochefort, 13th July, 1815.

On the 15th, then, Napoleon and suite went on board the ' Bellerophon,' where they were received by Captain Maitland and his officers ; the Emperor saying, ' I am come to throw myself on the Protection of your Prince and Laws.'

Caricature of such a scene seems to be in very bad taste, but as it was done, and is so truly comic, I cannot refrain from reproducing it.

' Compliments and Congées, or Little Boney's surrender to the Tars of Old England !!! ' is a highly humorous picture by G. Cruikshank (July 24, 1815). Napoleon surrenders himself, cringing and weeping, together with his suite, whom he describes, on board the ' Bellerophon,' and is received with due respect by Captain Maitland. The ex-Emperor says, ' O, Mr. Bull, I am so happy to see you, I always had a great regard for the British Sailors, they are such noble fellows, so brave, so generous ! ! You see I am in a great deal of trouble, but I hope you will take pity on me and my suite, namely my barber, my cook, and my washerwoman, together with a few of my *brave* generals who ran away with me from the Battle of Waterloo, and I do assure you we will have great *pleasure* in surrendering to the good English—I should feel extremely obliged if you would take us to America, but if you will not, I beg you will take us to England, for I hate those Bears, and cursed Cossacks, and as for the French Nation now—why they may be d—d.   Old England for ever I say.'   And his suite servilely follow their fallen master's lead with cries of ' Vivent les Anglais!'

COMPLIMENTS AND CONGÉES.

Captain Maitland receives him with doffed hat and his hand on his heart, saying, ' Indeed Mr. Boney I am greatly obliged to you for your compliments, and I assure you we are as happy to receive you, as you are to surrender.   I'm afraid they would not take that care of you in America, that they will in England.   Therefore I shall conduct you to the latter place, as quick as possible.'   The opinions of the sailors are more graphic than polite : ' My eyes, what a sneaking hound he is !!'   'I say Jack, do you think they'll clap him in Exeter Change amongst the wild beasts?' ' No, I suppose as how he'll be put in the Monkey's den in the Tower, or else they'll send him about with the dancing bear !'

Charles etched (July 15, 1815) ' The Bone-a-part in a fresh place.'   This represents Bonaparte caught in a spring man-trap, which has broken his leg.   He surrenders his sword to John Bull, who is dressed as a gardener : ' Here

take this Mr. Bull, you have me in your power—I must
trust to your usual generosity, and most humbly acknowledge that I am truly sorry I ever came here.' John Bull
makes no answer, but soliloquises thus instead : ' He has
plundered most of his neighbours' Gardens, but I thought
he would be sorry if ever he set his foot in mine. I suppose
this big sword is what he intended to cut my cabbages
with, and perhaps my head too ! but I'll have it for a
pruning knife, 'twill serve me to lop his Branches with, if
any should spring up after I have taken care of him.'

G. Cruikshank, in August 1815, published a contrast—
Buonaparte on the 17th of June—Buonaparte on the 17th
of July, 1815.' On the former date he is seen vapouring
on the French coast, flourishing his sword, and calling out,
' Ha, ha, you Bull beast, you Blackguard Islander, you see
I am come back again, and now you shall see what I shall
do with you, you wretch ! you thought I was done over,
did you ? you thought I was going to stay at Elba ? D—n
all Elbas, abdications, Englishmen and their Allies. I'll
play Hell with them all.' John Bull, seated securely on
his own shore, calmly enjoying his tankard of ale and his
long clay pipe, puffs out a huge mouthful of smoke at his
adversary, with a contemptuous ' You may be d—d. I'll
make a Tobacco stopper of you.'

But within one short month what a change had come
over the scene ! Napoleon, a weeping, kneeling suppliant,
on board the ' Bellerophon,' moans out :—

> O good Mr. Bull ! I wish you to know
> (Although you are my greatest foe,)
> That my career is at an end :
> And I wish you now to stand my friend.
> For, though at the Battle of Waterloo
> I was by you beat black & blue,
> Yet you see I wish to live with you,
> For I'm sure what is said of your goodness is true.
> And now if in England you'll let me remain
> I ne'er will be guilty of bad Tricks again.

John Bull, however, knowing the slippery customer he has
to deal with, reflects : ' Let me see ;—first of all you sprung
from the *Island* of *Corsica*, and when you was kick'd out of

France, and went to the *Island* of *Elba,* you made another spring into France again.—And now when you are kick'd out of France a second time, you want to come and live on my *Island*—But it won't do, Master Boney ; - you'll be making another spring into France again, I suppose—so I tell you what—I'll send you to the *Island* of *St. Helena,* and we'll see what sort of a spring you'll make then.'

George Cruikshank contributes a very badly drawn etching (September 1, 1815) of ' Boney's threatened Invasion brought to bear,—or, taking a View of the English coast from yᵉ Poop of the Bellerophon.' The English coast is represented by a ' Citadel,' in front of which is a gallows prepared. One of his suite points it out to him : ' By gar ! mon Emperor, dey have erect von prospect for you.' Napoleon, who is mounted on a breech of the gun, looks through his telescope and says, ' Me no like the d—n prospect.' A Jack Tar sitting on another gun gives as his opinion, ' I thinks as how, Master Boney, that instead of sending you to *Hell bay,* they should have sent you to Hell at once.'

CHAPTER LX.

NAPOLEON ON BOARD THE ' BELLEROPHON '—ARRIVAL AT TORBAY—
    CURIOSITY OF THE PEOPLE—THE ENGLISH GOVERNMENT DETERMINE
    TO SEND HIM TO ST. HELENA.

ON board the ' Bellerophon ' he was treated with every consideration by Captain Maitland. He was still looked upon as Emperor, and dined off his own gold plate, the dinner being ordered by his own *maître d'hôtel* ; and when he visited the ' Superb ' he was received with all the honours accorded to royalty, with the exception of a salute being fired. On the 16th July they set sail for England, and at daybreak on the 24th they were close to Dartmouth. Napoleon rose at six and went on the poop, surveying the coast, which he much admired : ' What a beautiful country ! it very much resembles Porto Ferrajo at Elba.'

About eight A.M. they anchored at Torbay, and no sooner was it known that Napoleon was on board the ' Bellerophon ' than the bay was covered with vessels and boats full of people. A neighbouring gentleman sent the

Emperor a present of fruit. What a different reception from the language of the ' Times ' [1] :—

' Our paper of this day will satisfy the sceptics, for such there were beginning to be, as to the capture of that bloody miscreant, who has so long tortured Europe, NAPOLEON BUONAPARTE. Savages are always found to unite the greatest degree of cunning to the ferocious part of their nature. The cruelty of this person is written in characters of blood in almost every country in Europe, and in the contiguous angles of Africa and Asia which he visited ; and nothing can more strongly evince the universal conviction of his low, perfidious craft, than the opinion which was beginning to get abroad, that even after his capture had been officially announced, in both France, and England, he might yet have found means to escape. However, all doubts upon this point are at an end, by his arrival off the British coast ; and, if he be not now placed beyond the possibility of again outraging the peace of Europe, England will certainly never again deserve to have heroes such as those who have fought, and bled, at Waterloo, for this, his present overthrow. The lives of the brave men who fell on that memorable day will have been absolutely thrown away by a thoughtless country ; the grand object attained by their valour will have been frustrated, and we shall do little less than insult over their remains, almost before they have ceased to bleed. But Fortune, seconding their undaunted efforts, has put it in our power to do far otherwise.

' Captain Sartorius of the *Slaney* frigate, arrived yesterday with dispatches from Captain Maitland of the *Bellerophon*, confirming all the antecedent accounts of Buonaparte's surrender, with various other details, and closing them by their natural catastrophe—his safe conveyance to England. He is, therefore, what we may call, here. Captain Sartorius delivered his dispatches to Lord Melville, at Wimbledon, by whom their contents were communicated to Lord Liverpool, at his seat at Combe Wood ; summonses were immediately issued for a Cabinet Council to meet at 12 o'clock ; what passed there was, of course, not

[1] July 25, 1815.

E E

suffered to transpire ; our narrative must therefore revert to the *Slaney* frigate, and the accounts brought by her. She had been sent forward by Captain Maitland to Plymouth, with the dispatches announcing that Buonaparte was on board the *Bellerophon*, with a numerous suite. But it was the intention of Captain Maitland himself, to proceed to Torbay, and not to land his prisoners until he had received orders from Government.

'Buonaparte's suite, as it is called, consists of upwards of 40 persons, among whom was Bertrand, Savary, Lallemand ! Grogan,[1] and several women. He has been allowed to take on board carriages and horses. but admission was denied to about 50 cavalry, for whom he had the impudence to require accommodation. This wretch has really lived in the commission of every crime, so long, that he has lost all sight and knowledge of the difference that exists between good and evil, and hardly knows when he is doing wrong, except he be taught by proper chastisement. A creature—who ought to be greeted with a gallows as soon as he lands—to think of an attendance of fifty horsemen ! He had at first wanted to make conditions with Captain Maitland as to his treatment, but the British officer very properly declared that he must refer him upon this subject to his Government.

'When he had been some time on board, he asked the Captain what chance two large frigates, well manned, would have with a seventy-four. The answer, we understand, which he received to this enquiry, did not give him any cause to regret that he had not tried his fortune in a naval combat with the relative forces in question. By the way, we should not have been surprised if he had come into an action with the two frigates, and then endeavoured to escape in his own, and leave the other to her fate. It has been the constant trick of this villain, whenever he has got his companions into a scrape, to leave them in it, and seek his own safety by flight. In Egypt, in the Moscow expedition, and at Waterloo, such was his conduct.

'He likewise had the assurance to address a letter to the Prince Regent, and M. Grogan, one of his party, was put

[1] General Gourgaud.

on board the *Slaney* as the bearer of it; but when this vessel reached Plymouth, the officer on duty there, with a decision that does him credit, refused Grogan permission to land : the letter is said to have been conveyed by Captain Sartorius, and its purport was understood, on board, to be a request for passports for America. We should have supposed that he had received too many checks before, for his presumption in addressing letters to the British Government, ever to have hazarded that experiment again ; but all reproofs are thrown away upon his callous heart ;—not that we should object to his humbly addressing the British throne for mercy, if he has anything to urge in extenuation of his crimes ; but the time has not yet come ; a momentary gleam of resolution on the part of his own Government, indicated by the imprisonment of Labédoyère, and others, led us to hope that his trial might have been safely entrusted to those to whom it primarily, and of natural right, belongs ; but, though this hope may have proved transitory, he is not, therefore, above the criminal justice of other countries, where established law, and a regular execution of it, prevails.

'The first procedure, we trust, will be a special commission, or the appointment of a court martial, to try him for the murder of Captain Wright. It is nonsense to say, as some have, that courts martial are instituted only to try offences committed by soldiers of the country to which they belong : it was an American court martial that tried and shot Major André as a spy ; and Buonaparte himself appointed commissions of all kinds, and in all countries, to try offences committed against himself.'

The same paper says : ' As soon as an august personage was informed of the capture of Buonaparte, he communicated this important intelligence to a prince of his family—" The ancient fable is at length realised : the *Chimera* is in the power of *Bellerophon*, and will not this time escape again."

'[Every reader knows that the Chimera was a terrible monster that vomited fire.]'

Rowlandson gives us (July 28, 1815) ' Boney's Trial, Sentence and Dying Speech, or Europe's injuries revenged.' Boney is in the felon's dock, backed up by his old friend the Devil. His indictment sets forth thus : 'Napolean Boneparte, The first and last, by the wrath of Heaven, Ex Emperor of Jacobins and Head Runner of Runaways, stands indicted 1st for the murder of Captain Wright, in the Temple at Paris. 2nd for the murder of the Duke d'Enghien, Pichegru and Georges. 3rd for the murder of Palm, Hofer, &c. &c. 4th for the murder of the 12 inhabitants of Moscow. 5th for innumerable Robberies committed on all Nations in Christendom, and elsewhere. 6th for bigamy, and lastly for returning from Transportation, and setting the World in an uproar.' Blücher presides, assisted by all the European sovereigns, and gives sentence thus : 'You, Nap Boneparte, being found guilty of all these crimes, it is fell to my lot to pronounce sentence of Death upon you. You are to be hung by the neck for one hour, till you are *Dead, dead, dead,* and your body to be chained to a mill stone, and sunk in the sea at Torbay.'

Napoleon, terrified at this sentence, weepingly implores, 'Oh Cruel Blucher ! Oh Cruel Wellington ! it is you that have brought me to this end. Oh, magnanimous Emperors, Kings and Princes ! intercede for me, and spare my life, and give me time to atone for all my sins. My Son, Napoleon the Second, will reward you for mercy shewn me.'

On July 26 orders came for the ' Bellerophon ' to go to Plymouth ; which being reached, two frigates, the ' Liffey ' and ' Eurotas,' were anchored, one on either side of her, and kept strict guard over her. No boat from the shore was allowed to come within a cable's length of her, and ships' boats continually rowing around kept that space clear.

The following description is by an eye-witness [1] :—

> There is nothing so dull as mere fact, you'll admit,
> While you read my detail, unenlivened by wit.
> My friends will believe, though they're told it in rhyme,
> That I thought to return in a far shorter time.
> When at once we're resolv'd, by half past on the move,
> And by two, but a trio, we reach Mutton Cove ;
> When approaching the quay, such a rabble and rout,
> That we ask ' My good friend, what is all this about ? '

[1] *A visit to Bonaparte in Plymouth Sound,* by a Lady. Plymouth, 1815.

'They are rowing a race, and some boats are come in,
While these people are waiting till t' others begin.'
Well aware of our folly, with risible lip,
The boatman we told to make haste to *the* ship :
On the colours of fish,[1] here by hampers full landing,
We gaze for amusement, while still we're kept standing ;
At length to the Admiral's stairs we have got,
See his party on board, and hear tunes from his yacht.
The day is delightful, the gale just enough
For the sea to look lively without being rough.
With those first at the ship, our sight costs the dearer,
As we've longer to wait, and not, in the end, nearer ;
For by land, and by water, so different the case is,
'Twas long before we were jam'd into our places ;
But on further advice we'll at present be dumb,
For half the spectators you know, are now come :
In one boat, a bevy, all sarcenet and veil,
In the next some good fellows while toping their ale.
'Avast ! here's the guard boat.' 'Aye here it comes smack.'
And the ladies cry 'Captain they'll drive us all back.'
Then some bully our men, with 'Skull out there, skull out,'
And others check these with ' Mind what you're about.'
Here's a crazy old boat, laded dry by a shoe,
There, a gay painted barge is forced on our view ;
In this, while Don Solus is jeered by the mob,
'See that empty boat, turn it out.' 'Here's a fine job.'
Cries one, of some dozens squeezed into the next,
'I've left the pork pie, Oh dear I'm so vex'd.'
In the long boat, that shews us profusion of oar,
From the Captain bursts forth, a most terrible roar
At his men, but the anger about who, or what,
Though they still remember, we soon had forgot.
Here infants were crying, mothers scolding downright,
While the next party laughs at some comical sight.
Now watches and spy-glasses make their appearance,
And Impatience, that vixen, begins interference ;
To beguile her, through portholes we eagerly stare,
For the nobles on deck are all taking the air.
' Hey dey what a bustle !' then ' All safe, all safe.'
The crowd is return'd to its chatter and laugh.
' Pray what was the matter?' ' From that boat, near the ship,
A woman fell over, and so got a dip.'
But a hum of applause, yes, his triumph is full,
Yet this hum of applause has betrayed our John Bull,

---

[1] Mackerel.

' What hum of applause ? come I prithee be brief : '
Why John was delighted to see them *ship beef.*
With a smile 'tis observed by the Briton polite,
How the glee of the crowd was improv'd, by the sight,
For the rough, honest tar, had declared from his heart,
That he thought this a sight that would beat Bonaparte.
Some, again, with composure, predict peace and war,
Others look at the great folks, and fancy a star ;
But we, much fatigued, six o'clock now approaching,
And on our good nature we thought them encroaching,
When boats are made bridges, nay, tempted to think,
That through some of these freedoms, not strange we should sink.
But here I must mention, when all was most merry,
As here is each size, from the long boat to wherry,
When the crowd should disperse, I was fearful, I own,
Lest your small boats, by barges, should then be run down.
But a truce with our hopes, our predictions and fears,
For now, yes at last, our grand object appears ;
And now every eye to the ship is directed,
Though to see Bonaparte, I no longer expected ;
For between us what number of men ! and aghast
We stood, as still thicker and thicker the mast. [? *mass*]
But now see Napoleon, who seems in his figure,
What we call mediocre, nor smaller, nor bigger ;
For in spite of our fears, how it was, I can't tell,
What our distance allowed of, we saw very well.
But in this we're full right, for now, hurry scurry,
Boat rows against boat, with the madness of fury ;
The show was all over, but time was outstaid
By some, and by others, attempts were still made
To get round the ship, in hopes Bonaparte might
At some place yet be seen, thus to perfect their sight.

This doggerel helps us to realise the intense desire of
the British public to get at least a glimpse at Boney, that
great bugbear who for so many years had been so great a
terror to them, and whose existence everyone, from the
highest to the lowest, had acutely felt in that tenderest
place of our social economy—the breeches pocket. They
all but carried out the threat, made twelve years previously,
of putting him in Pidcock's Menagerie, *vide* the following
extracts from a contemporary pamphlet [1] :—

[1] *Interesting Particulars of Napoleon's Deportation for Life to St. Helena,*
&c. London, 1816. Printed for W. Hone.

'The desire of all ranks to see him was excessive; the guardboats were unable to prevent them from closing the ship, and it was amusement on board to look at the boats contending for places. Napoleon generally walked the quarterdeck about eleven in the forenoon, and half past six in the afternoon. He ate but two meals in the day, both alike, meat of every description, different wines, coffee, fruit, &c. Immediately after each meal he rose first, and the others followed; he then either went on the quarter-deck or in the after-cabin to study. The comedy of *The Poor Gentleman* [1] was performed before him; he was much pleased at it; it went off very well; the scenery was good, but somewhat better dresses were wanted for the *female midshipmen*.[2]

'The immense number of persons who daily flock from all parts of the country to take a view of the person of Napoleon is incalculable. He generally gratified the public curiosity by making his appearance every afternoon for two hours.

'Upwards of one thousand boats were from morning to night round the *Bellerophon*. The seamen of the *Bellerophon* adopted a curious mode to give an account to the curious spectators in the boats of the movements of Napoleon. They wrote in chalk, on a board, which they exhibited, a short account of his different occupations—"At breakfast"—"In the cabin with Captain Maitland"—"Writing with his officers"—"Going to dinner"—"Coming upon deck," &c.'

Las Cases says: 'It was known that he always appeared on deck towards five o'clock. A short time before this hour, all the boats collected alongside of each other; there were thousands; and so closely were they connected, that the water could no longer be seen between them. They looked more like a multitude assembled in a public square than anything else. When the Emperor came out, the noise and gestures of so many people presented a most striking spectacle; it was, at the same time, very easy to perceive that nothing hostile was meant, and that, if

[1] By George Colman the younger.
[2] *i.e.* the midshipmen who took female parts.

curiosity had brought them, they felt interested on going away. We could even see that the latter sentiment continued to increase ; at first, people merely looked toward the ship, they ended by saluting ; some remained uncovered, and, occasionally, went so far as to cheer. Even our symbols began to appear amongst them. Several individuals of both sexes came decorated with red carnations.'

Napoleon knew that St. Helena had been fixed upon as the place of his future residence, and did not at all relish the idea ; but it was not officially announced to him until July 30 or 31, when Lord Keith went on board the 'Bellerophon' and presented him with the following despatch :—

' *Communication made by Lord Keith, in the name of the English Ministers.*

' As it may, perhaps, be convenient for General Buonaparte to learn, without further delay, the intentions of the British Government with regard to him, your Lordship will communicate the following information.

' It would be inconsistent with our duty towards our country and the Allies of his Majesty, if General Buonaparte possessed the means of again disturbing the repose of Europe. It is on this account, that it becomes absolutely necessary he should be restrained in his personal liberty, so far as this is required by the foregoing important object.

' The island of St. Helena has been chosen as his future residence ; its climate is healthy, and its local position will allow of his being treated with more indulgence than could be admitted in any other spot, owing to the indispensable precautions which it would be necessary to employ for the security of his person.

' General Buonaparte is allowed to select amongst those persons who accompanied him to England (with the exception of Generals Savary and Lallemand) three officers, who, together with his surgeon, will have permission to accompany him to St. Helena ; these individuals will not be allowed to quit the island without the sanction of the British Government.

' Rear Admiral Sir George Cockburn, who is named Commander in Chief at the Cape of Good Hope, and seas adjacent, will convey General Buonaparte and his suite to St. Helena ; and he will receive detailed instructions relative to the execution of this service.

' Sir G. Cockburn will, most probably, be ready to sail in a few days ; for which reason, it is desirable that General Buonaparte should make choice of the persons who are to accompany him, without delay.'

Of this interview Las Cases says : ' I was not called before the Emperor. The bearers of his sentence spoke and understood French ; they were admitted alone. I have since heard that he objected, and protested, with no less energy than logic, against the violence exercised on his person. " He was the guest of England," said Napoleon, " and not its prisoner ; he came of his own accord to place himself under the protection of its laws ; the most sacred rights of hospitality were violated in his person ; he would never submit voluntarily to the outrage they were preparing for him : violence alone should oblige him to do so," &c.'

CHAPTER LXI.

NAPOLEON IS SENT ON BOARD THE ' NORTHUMBERLAND '—HE PROTESTS AGAINST HIS EXILE—PUBLIC OPINION AS TO HIS TREATMENT.

THAT the Government was in earnest, as to his departure, was soon shown, for orders came on August 4 for the ' Bellerophon' to weigh, and join the ' Northumberland,' which was the ship in which Napoleon was to take his passage to St. Helena. He issued a formal protest :—

I hereby solemnly protest in the face of heaven and mankind against the violence that is done me ; and the violation of my most sacred rights, in forcibly disposing of my person and liberty. I voluntarily came on board the *Bellerophon*—I am not the prisoner, I am the guest of England. I came at the instigation of the Captain himself, who said he had orders from the Government to receive and convey me to England, together with my suite, if agreeable to me. I came forward with confidence to place myself under the protection of the laws of England. When once on board the *Bellerophon*, I was entitled to the hospitality of the British people. If the Government, in giving the Captain of the

Bellerophon orders to receive me and my followers, only wished to lay a snare, it has forfeited its honour, and disgraced its flag.

If this act be consummated, it will be in vain for the English, henceforth, to talk of their sincerity, their laws, and liberties. British faith will have been lost in the hospitality of the *Bellerophon*.

I appeal to History ; it will say, that an enemy, who made war for twenty years against the English people, came spontaneously, in the hour of misfortune, to seek an asylum under their laws. What more striking proof could he give of his esteem and confidence? But how did England reply to such an act of magnanimity? It pretended to hold out a hospitable hand to this enemy : and on giving himself up with confidence, he was immolated !   Napoleon.

Bellerophon, at Sea.   Friday, Aug. 4th, 1815.

On the 6th they anchored off Start Point, and were soon joined by the ' Northumberland ' and two frigates, full of soldiers, who were to form the garrison of St. Helena. By order, their arms were taken from them, with the exception of Napoleon, who was allowed to keep his sword ; all their money, diamonds, and saleable effects were put under seal ; but Napoleon might keep his plate, baggage, wines, and provisions. The search of his personal effects greatly exasperated him.

Between one and two o'clock P.M. of the 7th, the transfer from the ' Bellerophon ' to the ' Northumberland ' was made, and then, as there was nothing else to wait for, ' Cæsar and his fortunes ' sailed for St. Helena.

The ' Times ' (August 11, 1815) has the following short leader : ' We trust that we now, at last, take a long leave of Napoleon Buonaparte, except that we may, occasionally, have to instance him as an example of every crime, for the benefit of others : and, if the hand of man has dealt too leniently by his offences, it must not, on that occasion, be conceived that he is exempt from every other punishment. To what profession of faith he may now belong, we know not, as we believe he has been Atheist, Mahometan, and Roman Catholic, in succession, as best suited the particular purpose of the moment : indeed, such was the inherent baseness of the man, notwithstanding his eminent talents, and incessant activity, that he was in the habitual practice of the meanest arts of deception for the

promotion of his interest, never blushing at the subsequent
exposure of his falsehoods, or the discovery of his expedients, provided they had first promoted the object he had
in view.

'Yet if he is still a man, he must, now that he is reduced to solitude and leisure, have some religion or other
engraven in his soul, that will make him feel compunction
for the many horrible atrocities of which he has been
guilty. It is said that he needs incessant exercise for the
relief of his bilious complaint ; perhaps, also, he may now
first discover that he has need of incessant bustle also, in
order to abstract his attention from a certain mental
malady, called an evil conscience. In the midst of the
horror which his crimes always excited in well-constituted
minds, throughout Europe, there was a certain mixture of
contempt, or derision, excited by the little knaveries which
he practised, and the same feeling will not fail to mingle
itself in this the closing scene of his drama, on observing
the attendants of such a man, who had been used to sport
with oaths, to laugh at engagements, to make a mockery
of religion, to commit or direct murder in all its forms,
from the midnight assassination, up to the boundless
slaughter of the tented field, anxious to provide for the
amusement of his, and their, declining years, by a stock of
cards, domino and backgammon tables.'

Whilst they are on their journey, we will just glance at
the few remaining caricatures.

'The Ex-Emperor in a bottle' is a somewhat serious,
and well-executed, engraving (August 25, 1815). Napoleon
is enclosed in a glass bottle, which the Prince Regent, who
wears a superb hussar uniform, has just sealed with a seal
bearing the imprint of a cannon and the legend *Martial
Achievements* ; around are grouped the figures named in the
following verses—Louis the Eighteenth being on his knees,
his eyes being raised in pious thankfulness to Heaven.

> Ambition's dread career at length is o'er,
> And weeping Europe hopes for peace once more ;
> Sov'reigns in arms, at length the world have freed,
> And Britain's warlike sons no more shall bleed :
> The great Napoleon now resigns his sway,
> And in a bottle seal'd is borne away.

England's great Prince, whom Europe does confess
The potent friend of Freedom in distress,
With *Allies* brave, to the world impartial,
Seal'd up their foe with *Achievements martial*,
That he no more disturb the tranquil World,
Nor be again his bloody flag unfurl'd.

'Twas Alexander great, of generous mind,
With zealous Frederick, who to peace inclined,
Resolv'd with Francis, in propitious hour,
To free old Gallia from the Despot's power.
Her tyrannic Lord from rule is driven,
And grateful Louis offers thanks to Heaven.

The *Martial Heroes* next a tribute claim,
First Wellington, immortal is his fame :
And Blücher, who, for valour long renown'd,
Compell'd the Tyrant's legions to give ground :
The cautious Swartzenberg, of wise delays,
And the brave Platoff, ask their share of praise.

'The downfall of Tyranny and return of Peace ' is
by George Cruikshank, and, although not dated, is undoubtedly of the autumn of 1815. Justice, with a flaming
sword, has banished Napoleon to his rock of St. Helena,
where, chained, he is seized upon by the fiend as his own.
Peace with her olive branch, Plenty with her cornucopia,
Agriculture and Commerce, are welcomed by Britannia
with open arms.

Marks (August 1815) drew 'The Exile of St. Helena,
or Boney's Meditation,' in which there is a fairly accurate
delineation of the Rocky Island and its little town. Napoleon is standing with his feet astride, each planted on a
rock on either side the bay ; he weeps copiously, and the
expression of his countenance is very rueful.

'Napoleon's trip from Elba to Paris, and from Paris to
St. Helena' is the title of three engravings on one sheet,
by G. Cruikshank (September 1, 1815). In the first com-
partment is shown the battle of Waterloo, with the French
army in full flight. Napoleon is seated on the French
Eagle, which, however, has but one wing, for, as it mournfully observes, 'My *left* wing has entirely disappeared.'
The Emperor, whose crown and sceptre have fallen from
him, clutches the bird round the neck, exclaiming : ' Sauve

qui peut—the Devil take the hindmost—Run, my boys, your Emperor leads the way—My dear eagle, only con-

BONEY S MEDITATIONS ON THE ISLAND OF ST. HELENA. (AUGUST 1815.)
The Devil addressing the Sun.—*Paradise Lost,* Book IV.

duct me safe to Paris this time, as you did from Moscow and Leipsig, and I'll never trouble you again—Oh! d—n that Wellington!'

The middle picture shows Napoleon in the stern gallery of the 'Bellerophon,' talking to John Bull, who sits by his

fireside placidly smoking his pipe as usual.   Says the ex-
Emperor : 'My most powerful and generous enemy, how
do you do?   I come, like Themistocles, to seat myself
upon your hearth—I am very glad to see you.'   John Bull
replies : ' So am I glad to see you Mr. Boney, but I'll be
d—d if you sit upon my hearth, or any part of my house
—it has cost me a pretty round sum to catch you, Mr.
Themistocles, as you call yourself, but now I have got you,
I'll take care of you.'

The third is a sad one.   Napoleon is at St. Helena,
reduced to the sport of catching rats.   Across his breast he
wears a broad leather scarf, covered with brass rats, and sits
moodily before a baited trap, into which the rats decline
to enter.   He thus soliloquises :—

> Alas ! that I who caught Imperial flats,
> Should now sit here to watch these scurvy rats.
> I, who Madrid, Berlin, Vienna, Moscow, took,
> Am doom'd, with cheese, to bait a rusty hook !
> Was it for this I tried to save my bacon,
> To use it now for Rats, that won't be taken ?
> Curse their wise souls !   I had not half such trouble
> Their European brethren to bubble.
> When I, myself, was hail'd as Emperor Nap,
> Emperors and Kings I had within my trap :
> And to this moment might have kept them there,
> Had I not gone to hunt the Russian bear.

One of his suite sees a rat coming : ' Ah ! mon Dieu !
Dere, your Majesty, dere be de vilain rogues—Ah, monsieur rat, why you not pop your nose into de trap, and let
de august Emperor catch you ? '   A female attendant, with
a slice of bacon on a fork, says, ' Will your Majesty be
please to try dis bit of bacon ? Ah ! de cunning rascal !
Dere ! ma foi ! he sniff at de bacon.'

' General Sans Pareil ' (September 1, 1815) is an extremely elaborate picture, far too much so for reproduction ;
therefore it will be better to give the description at the
foot of the figure : ' The above Portrait of Buonaparte,
may be considered as an emblematical Index of his extraordinary Life.   The Design reflects the highest credit on
the Artist, who is a Frenchman : he has judiciously formed
the Hat of the different *Crowns* which Buonaparte placed

on other Men's *Heads.* The position of the forefinger and thumb are particularly deserving of notice, with the words *Moreau* and *Pichegru* on them, indicating that *Moreau* was his guide or *finger-post* to all his victories ; and the word *Pichegru* being on his thumb, is meant to imply that he always had him in view as being one great obstacle to his rising greatness ; while in the other hand he holds a nooze, or rope, as the means of ridding himself of so formidable an enemy. The words on his Breast are the names of the different kingdoms he has overrun or conquered. His Waistcoat is ornamented with the figures of the different Kings he had made ; the French call them "*La folie fabrique de sire*": indicative, that while the dark clouds of despotism hung over Buonaparte's empire, his Kings reflected their borrowed lustre ; but when once the Sun of universal restitution darted forth its rays, they melted " like wax before the sun." The artist has well contrived to put the little King of Rome, as a monkey, above the heads of the other Kings. The Bales and Casks of Goods, on his left thigh, denote the stoppage of Trade which his system of warfare had brought on the French People. The Beet root refers to the Decree issued for making Sugar of that plant, when he had lost all his West India Possessions. On his legs are represented Skulls, symbolic of Death, who accompanied him wherever he trod—His sword, which so often paralyzed the world, and conquered with a rapidity hitherto unknown, is placed in the form of a Comet or Meteor. Such is this brief and imperfect delineation of the above extremely curious and interesting Portrait.'

'Boxiana— or the Fancy' (artist unknown), October 1, 1815, shows the popular idea of the treatment Napoleon received. The gross, corpulent Prince Regent has thrown down his traditional three feathers, and is, like the ex-Emperor, stripped for the fight. Napoleon is on the ground, and the Regent is kicking him. A sweep has picked up one of the Prince's feathers, and shows it to Napoleon's backer, saying, 'Master, I found a white feather.' The backer calls out, 'Foul! foul! by all the rules of honor ! why even blackey cries shame.' A negro, who is acting as bottle-holder, cries out :—

What, Ben, my big hero, is this thy renown?
Is this the new go? Kick a man when he's down!
When the foe has knock'd under, to tread on him then,
By the fist of my father, I blush for thee, Ben!

The Regent's backer explains, 'He's only kicking, to try if there's any honor there, Blackey.' One of the spectators imagines that 'Themistocles will be well treated if we can find any honor in him!' Another says, 'Or we must send Themistocles to acquire honor at Botany.'

A French spectator turns to an Englishman, saying, 'Ah, je vois, you be de Jentelman! n'est ce pas bien Sauvage, Sare?' The reply is, 'Bien shove a—— e! No, d——e! mounseer, I think it more like kicking than shoving.' Another astonished looker-on exclaims, 'Vy, Charly, vot sort of a go d'you call this?' And a Frenchman advises his defeated champion, 'Vy you no go to de Russia, you only get little squeeze.'

CHAPTER LXII.

VOYAGE TO ST. HELENA—CESSATION OF CARICATURES.

THE 'Northumberland' crossed the Line on September 23, and the sailors had their then usual bit of fun. Neptune and Amphitrite came on board, and Napoleon's suite were introduced to them in a ceremonious and courtly manner, escaping the usual ordeal by some small presents to their Majesties. Napoleon, of course, was sacred, and, when he was told of the extreme, and unusual, tenderness with which his followers had been treated, he wanted to give the crew a hundred napoleons; but the admiral would not allow it. The caricaturist, however, gives a different version of the affair.

'Boney crossing the Line' is by Marks (September 1815), and illustrates the rough sports which then obtained on board ship. Napoleon, blindfolded, is thrown into a tub, where he is being subjected to the usual rough usage, at the command of Neptune, who, with his spouse, are drawn on a gun-carriage by sailors. Neptune says, 'I command you'l cleanse him from his iniquities.' Poor Boney little likes his treatment, 'I no like de English valet de Chambre, Have mercy.' Two French generals stand by, blindfolded, ready to undergo the same treatment. One says, ' I wish de Dirty Job was over ; ' the other, ' Be gar, me no like de shaving shop.' But a sailor remarks to them, ' Have Patience Gentlemen, and we'll shave you directly, and give you a good *lathering* as Old Blucher did ! ! ! '

The last caricature I shall reproduce is called ' Fast Colours, Patience on a monument smiling at grief, or the

FAST COLOURS.

Royal Laundress washing Boney's Court dresses (G. H inv^t, G. Cruikshank fec^t October 26, 1815).' It shows the poor fatuous Bourbon trying to wash out the tricolour, thus bemoaning the task : ' Bless me, how *fast* these *colours* are, I'm afraid I shall not get them *white*,[1] altho' I have got such a strong lather.' Napoleon, seated on his rocky home, says, ' Ha, ha ! such an old woman as you, may rub a long while before they'll be all *white*, for they are *tricoloured in grain.*' There is another print of the same date and subject, uncoloured, which has the addition of Wellington, Russia, Prussia, and Austria stirring linen in a copper of *Holy-Water.*

From this time the caricatures of Napoleon practically ceased ; and, in the collection of prints in the British Museum, I can find but two more, published in 1816— the ' Mat de Cocagne' and ' Royal Christmas boxes '—both of which are too silly to reproduce or describe. It is to the credit of the English, that, in this instance, they respected

[1] The Bourbon colour.

F F

the fallen. Napoleon had been captured, disarmed, and held in safe durance, and from that time, until his death, we hear but very little of him, and none of that news is either satirical or spiteful. Clearly, therefore, this book ends here. It has nothing to do with the voyage to St. Helena, or with the perpetual squabbles of Napoleon and his suite with Sir Hudson Lowe, which are fully recorded by O'Meara and Las Cases. To all intents and purposes, Napoleon was dead to the English when he left our shores ; and when he passed to his rest on May 5, 1821, all animosity died with him. Years had even tamed the bitter scribes of the ' Times,' as is evidenced by the leader in that paper (July 5, 1821) announcing and commenting on his decease :—

' Thus terminates in exile, and in prison, the most extraordinary life yet known to political history. The vicissitudes of such a life, indeed, are the most valuable lessons which history can furnish. Connected with, and founded on, the principles of his character, the varieties of fortune which Buonaparte experienced are of a nature to illustrate the most useful maxims of benevolence, patriotism, or discretion. They embrace both extremes of the condition of man in society, and therefore address themselves to all ranks of human beings. But Buonaparte was our enemy —our defeated enemy—and, as Englishmen, we must not tarnish our triumphs over the living warrior by unmanly injustice towards the dead.

' The details of his life are notorious, and we omit them. The community of which Buonaparte was in his early days a member, and the military education which he received, may, independently of any original bias of character, have laid the foundation of the greatness to which he attained, and of that mischievous application of unbridled power, through which he fell very nearly to the level whence he first had started. Nothing could be more corrupt than the morals of military society among the French before the Revolution—nothing more selfish, or contracted, than the views (at all times) of a thoroughbred military adventurer.

'Buonaparte came into active life with as much (but we have no reason to think a larger share of) lax morality and pure selfishness as others of his age and calling. The public crisis into which he was thrown, gave to profound selfishness the form of insatiable ambition. With talents and enterprise beyond all comparison greater than any against which he had to contend, he overthrew whatever opposed his progress. Thus, ambition in him was more conspicuous than others, only because it was more successful. He became a sovereign. How, then, was this pupil of a military school prepared to exercise the functions of sovereignty? An officer, as such, has no idea of divided power. His patriotism is simply love of his troops and his profession. He will obey commands—he will issue them —but, in both cases, those commands are absolute. Talk to him of deliberation, of debate, of freedom of action, of speech, nay, of opinion—his *feeling* is, that the body to which any of these privileges shall be accessible, must fall into confusion, and be speedily destroyed.

'Whatever pretexts may have been resorted to by Buonaparte—whatever Jacobin yells he may have joined in, to assist his own advance towards power—every subsequent act of his life assures us, that the military prepossessions in which he was educated, became those by which he was influenced as a statesman ; and we are well persuaded of his conviction, that it was impossible for any country, above all, for France, to be governed otherwise than by one sole authority—undivided and unlimited. It may, we confess, be no satisfaction to the French, nor any great consolation to the rest of Europe, to know through what means it was, or by what vicious training, that Buonaparte was fitted, nay, predestined almost, to be a scourge and destroyer of the rights of nations, instead of employing a power irresistible, and which, in such a cause, none would have felt disposed to resist, for the promotion of knowledge, peace, and liberty throughout the world.

' In hinting at what we conceive to be the fact, however, we are bound by regard for truth ; our business is not to apologize for Buonaparte ; but, so far as may be done within the brief limits of a newspaper, to analyze, and faithfully describe, him. The factions, also, which he was compelled to crush, and whose overthrow obtained for him

the gratitude of his country, still threatened a resurrec-
tion when the compressing force should be withdrawn.
Hence were pretexts furnished on behalf of despotism of
which men, more enlightened, and better constituted, than
Buonaparte, might not soon have discovered the fallacy.
Raised to empire at home, his ambition sought for itself
fresh aliment ; and foreign conquest was at once tempting
and easy.

' Here the natural reflection will obtrude itself—what
might not this extraordinary being have effected for the
happiness of mankind, and for his own everlasting fame
and grandeur, had he used but a moiety of the force, or
perseverance, in generous efforts to relieve the oppressed,
which he wasted in rendering himself the monopolist and
patron of oppression ! But he had left himself no resource.
He had extinguished liberty in France, and had no hold
upon his subjects, but their love of military glory. Conquest, therefore, succeeded to conquest, until nothing capable of subjugation was left to be subdued. Insolence, and
rapacity, in the victor, produced, among the enslaved
nations, impatience of their misery, and a thirst for vengeance. Injustice undermined itself, and Buonaparte,
with his unseasoned empire, fell together, the pageant of
a day.

' His military administration was marked by strict and
impartial justice. He had the art, in an eminent degree,
of inciting the emulation, and gaining the affections of his
troops. He was steady and faithful in his friendships, and
not vindictive, on occasions where it was in his power to be
so with impunity.

' Of the deceased Emperor's intellectual, and characteristic, ascendency over men, all the French, and some of
the other nations besides the French, who had an opportunity of approaching him, can bear witness. He seems to
have possessed the talent, not merely of command, but,
when he pleased, of conciliation and persuasion. With
regard to his religious sentiments, they were, perhaps, of
the same standard as those of other Frenchmen starting
into manhood at a time when Infidel writings had so
domineered over the popular mind, that revealed religion

was become a public laughing stock, and in a country where the pure Christian faith was perplexed with subtilties, overloaded with mummeries, and scandalized and discountenanced by a general looseness of morals. Upon the whole, Buonaparte will go down to posterity as a man, who, having more good at.his disposal than any other potentate of any former age, had actually applied his immense means to the production of a greater share of mischief and misery to his fellow creatures—one who, on the basis of French liberty, might have founded that of every other State in Europe—but who carried on a series of aggressions against foreign States to divert the minds of his own subjects from the sense of their domestic slavery ; thus imposing on foreign nations a necessity for arming to shake off his yoke, and affording to foreign despots a pretext for following his example.

'The sensation produced by the death of Buonaparte will be a good deal confined, in this country, to its effects as a partial relief to our finances, the expense of his custody at St. Helena being little short of 400,000*l.* per annum. In France, the sentiment will be more deep and complex, and, perhaps, not altogether easy to define. The practical consequence of such an event may be remotely guessed at by those who have had occasion to watch, in other Governments, the difference between a living and an extinct Pretender. A pretext for suspicion and severity in the administration of affairs may be taken away by a Pretender's death ; but then, a motive to moderation—a terror, now and then salutary, of popular feelings being excited in the Pretender's favour by misgovernment—is, at the same time, removed from the minds of reigning Princes. Buonaparte's son still lives, it is true ; but how far he may ever become an object of interest with any great party of the French nation, is a point on which we will not speculate.'

The last individual memorial I can find of Napoleon, in a popular form, was published by Hone in May 1821. It is a black-edged sheet, having, as heading, profile portraits of Napoleon, Maria Louisa, and the King of Rome, and down the sides four full-length portraits of Napoleon. It is called :—

Memorial

OF

NAPOLÉON

Born 15 Aug. 1769.   Died 5 May 1821.

He put his foot on the neck of Kings, who would have put their yokes upon the necks of the People : he scattered before him with fiery execution, millions of hired slaves, who came at the bidding of their Masters to deny the right of others to be free. The monument of greatness and of Glory he erected, was raised on ground forfeited again and again to humanity—it reared its majestic front on the ruins of the shattered hopes and broken faith of the common enemies of mankind.   If he could not secure the freedom, peace, and happiness of his country, he made her a terror to those who by sowing civil dissension, and exciting foreign wars, would not let her enjoy those blessings.   They who had trampled upon Liberty could not at least triumph in her shame and her despair, but themselves became objects of pity and deri- sion.   Their determination to persist in extremity of wrong, only brought on themselves repeated defeat, disaster, and dismay : the accumulated aggressions their infuriated pride and disappointed malice meditated against others, returned in just and aggravated punishment upon themselves : they heaped coals of fire upon their own heads : they drank deep and long, in gall and bitterness, of the poisoned chalice they had prepared for others : the de- struction with which they had threatened a people daring to call itself free, hung suspended over their heads, like a precipice, ready to fall upon and crush them.   'Awhile they stood abashed,' ab- stracted from their evil purposes, and felt how awful Freedom is, its power how dreadful.   Shrunk from the boasted pomp of royal state into their littleness as men, defeated of their revenge, baulked of their prey, their schemes stripped of their bloated pride, and with nothing left but the deformity of their malice, not daring to utter a syllable or move a finger, the lords of the earth, who had looked upon men as of an inferior species, born for their use, and devoted to be their slaves, turned an imploring eye to the People, and with coward hearts and hollow tongues invoked the Name of Liberty, thus to get the people once more within their unhallowed grip, and to stifle the name of Liberty for ever.

He withstood the inroads of *Legitimacy*, this new Juggernaut, this foul Blatant Beast, as it strode forward to its prey over the bodies and minds of a whole People, and put a ring in its nostrils, breathing flame and blood, and led it in triumph, and played with its crowns and sceptres, and wore them in its stead, and tamed its crested pride, and made it a laughing stock and a mockery to the nations. He, one man, did this, and as long as he did this (how or for what end, is nothing to the magnitude of this mighty question) he saved the human race from the last ignominy, and that foul stain that had been so long intended, and was at last, in an evil hour, and by evil hands, inflicted on it.

If NAPOLEON was a conqueror, he conquered the Grand Conspiracy of KINGS against the abstract right of the Human Race to be free. If he was ambitious, his greatness was not founded on the unconditional, avowed surrender of the rights of human nature. But, with him, the state of Man rose exalted too. If he was arbitrary and a tyrant, first, France as a country was in a state of military blockade, on garrison duty, and not to be defended by mere paper bullets of the brain ; secondly, but chief, he was not, nor could he become, a tyrant by 'right divine.' Tyranny in him was not 'sacred' : it was not eternal : it was not instinctively bound in league of amity with other tyrannies : it was not sanctioned by all 'the laws of religion and Morality.'

HAZLITT.

> Disgusting crew ! *who* would not gladly fly
> To open, downright, boldfac'd tyranny,
> To honest guilt that dares do all but lie,
> From the false juggling craft of men like these,
> Their canting crimes, and varnish'd villanies ;
> These HOLY LEAGUERS, who then loudest boast
> Of faith and honour when they've stain'd them most ;
> From whose affection men should shrink as loath
> As from their hate, for they'll be fleec'd by both ;
> Who, even while plund'ring, forge Religion's name
> To frank their spoil, and, without fear or shame,
> Call down the HOLY TRINITY to bless
> Partition leagues, and deeds of devilishness !

MOORE.

Even his old enemy, George Cruikshank, whose peculiarly impetuous temper had found a free vent in caricaturing Napoleon, left off doing so when he was in safe keeping, and only designed (in a publication called the 'Omnibus') a 'Monument to Napoleon' when he died. In a note to this design he says, ' As for me, who have skeletonised him prematurely, paring down the prodigy even to his hat and boots, I have but " carried out " a principle adopted almost in my boyhood, for I can scarcely remember the time when

I did not take some patriotic pleasure in persecuting the great enemy of England. Had he been less than that, I should have felt compunction for my cruelties; having tracked him through snow and through fire, by flood and by field, insulting, degrading, and deriding him everywhere, and putting him to several humiliating deaths. All that time, however, he went on "overing" the Pyramids and the Alps, as boys "over" posts, and playing at leapfrog with the sovereigns of Europe, so as to kick a crown off at every spring he made—together with many crowns, and sovereigns, into my coffers. Deep, most deep, in a personal view of matters, are my obligations to the agitator— but what a debt the country *owes to him*!'

INDEX.

NAP

fies the peace of Amiens, 117;
made Consul for life, 120; receives Fox, 121–23; behaves
rudely to Lord Whitworth, 128,
133–34; ultimatum, 135; tour
to Belgium, &c., 184; Cadoudal's conspiracy, 229; trial and
execution of the Duc d'Enghien,
229–30; proclaimed Emperor,
232–34; his coronation, 242–51;
sends a letter to George the Third,
252; visits Italy, 256; crowned
king of Italy, 257; his name
given to a constellation, 258;
war with Austria, 258; withdrawal of 'Army of England,'
259; surrender of Ulm, 260;
battle of Trafalgar, 261–62; negotiations for peace, 270; victories of
Jena, &c., 274; proclamation to
blockade England, 274; invasion
of Poland and entry into Warsaw, 276; battle of Eylau, 278;
capture of Dantzig, 279; meeting
with the Emperor of Russia at
Tilsit, 280–83; declaration of war
by England, 289; English troops
sent to Spain, 291; raising the
siege of Saragossa, 293; defeat at
Vimiera, 293; convention of
Cintra, 293; meeting of Emperors and Kings at Erfurt, 299;
the broken bridge across the
Danube, and the retreat to the
island of Lobau, 301; battle of
Wagram, 302; divorce from Josephine, 304–12; proposes to
marry the Grand Duchess Anna
Paulovna, 313; betrothal to
Maria Louisa, 313; his marriage,
316; birth of the King of Rome,
317; his christening, 318; Napoleon as a father, 320–21; said
to have been present at a naval
engagement off Boulogne, 324;
goes to Dresden, and meeting of
Sovereigns there, 324; visits
Dantzig, 325; war declared
against Russia, 325; entry into
Wilna, 326; battle of Smolensko,
326; battle of Salamanca, 326;
battle of Borodino, 327; entry
into Moscow, 327; burning of

NAP

Moscow, 328–30; flight from
thence, 330; nearly caught by
Cossacks, 333; rejoicings in
England, 337; his return to
Paris, 339–40; preparation for
war: anticipates the conscription
of 1814, 341; an armistice, 345;
battle of Vittoria, 345–47; defeat
at Leipsic, 348; losses and new
conscription, 363; campaign of
1814, 371; his deposition, 373;
his abdication, 373; conspiracy
to kill him, 378; treaty with regard to his abdication, 379; attempts to poison himself, 380;
sails for Elba, 381; his arrival
there, 390; his beneficent rule
and improvements, 391–92; faith
broken with him, 392; 'Caporal
Violette,' 393; leaves Elba,
397; lands at Cannes, 397; war
again declared, 409; campaign
in Belgium, 409; battle of Waterloo, 409; retires to Paris, 411;
he again abdicates, 411; a prisoner in French hands, 412;
negotiations for surrender to England, 412–13; goes on board the
'Bellerophon,' 413; letter to the
Regent, 413; arrival at Torbay,
416; is sent to Plymouth, 420;
anxiety of the English people to
see him, 420–24; sent to St.
Helena, 424; his protest against
it, 425; transferred to the
'Northumberland,' 426; sets
sail for St. Helena, 426; crosses
the line, 432; his death, 434
Napoleon and the letter M, 369
Napoleon's sisters, 168, 244, 247,
391
Napoleon's supposed credulity, 368
Napolione, Saint, 6
Navy, prizes, &c., 254–55
Nelson, 46, 52, 53–58, 59–62, 63,
111, 136, 254, 261–62
Nelson's receipt to make an Olla
Podrida, 40
'New Bellman's verses for Christ-
mas, 1803!' 225
Ney, Marshal, 105, 324
Nicholas as Napoleon's baptismal
name, 6